DIVINE PRINCIPLE

DIVINE PRINCIPLE

Published by
THE HOLY SPIRIT ASSOCIATION
FOR THE UNIFICATION OF WORLD CHRISTIANITY

REVEREND SUN MYUNG MOON

Editor's Note

The book you now hold in your hands is the first full translation of the *Divine Principle* from the original Korean. Translation of abstract thought from any one tongue to another poses severe difficulties to the translator. When a great work is rendered from Oriental to Western culture, some additional difficulties might be expected.

Preparation of the English version of the *Divine Principle* was no exception. Numerous difficulties were encountered in selecting the proper terminology and in making the complex thought clearly understandable to Western readers. When the problems appeared to be insurmountable, the literal translation was used so that the reader can see how the thought was expressed in the original text.

The *Divine Principle*, encompassing the profound thought of the Orient and based upon Christian beliefs and ideology, finds herein its first complete expression in English. As one ancient Oriental proverb says, "The beginning is halfway to the goal." A beginning has been made. Continued research and study will be devoted to the perfection of the English version.

With this explanation for any language difficulties or awkward phrases which you may encounter, the *Divine Principle* is commended to you.

Contents

DIVINE
PRINCIPLE

General Introduction

Everyone, without exception, is struggling to gain happiness. The first step in attaining this goal is to overcome present unhappiness. From small individual affairs to history-making global events, everything is an expression of human lives, which are constantly striving to become happier. How, then, can happiness be attained?

Every person feels happy when his desire is fulfilled. The word "desire," however, is apt to be misinterpreted. This is because everyone is now living in circumstances which can drive desire in the direction of evil rather than in the direction of goodness. The desire which results in unrighteousness does not

1

come from the "original mind of man"; that is, one's inmost self which delights in the law of God. The path to happiness is reached by overcoming the desire which leads to evil and by following the desire which pursues goodness. Man's original mind knows that evil desire will lead only to unhappiness and misery. This is the reality of human life: man gropes in the shadow of death as he searches for the light of life.

Has any man, by pursuing evil desire, been able to find the happiness in which his original mind could take delight? The answer is no. Whenever man attains the object of evil desire, he feels conscience-stricken. Would parents teach their children to do evil, or a teacher instruct his students to pursue unrighteousness? Again, the answer must be no. It is the nature of man's original mind to hate evil and to exalt goodness.

In the lives of religious men we can see an intense and relentless struggle to attain goodness by following the desire of the original mind only. Yet, since the beginning of time, no man has completely followed his original mind. For this reason the Bible says, "None is righteous, no, not one; no one understands, no one seeks for God." (Rom. 3:10-11)

The apostle Paul, who was faced with such wretchedness of heart, said in lamentation, "For I delight in the law of God, in my inmost self, but I see in my members another law at war with the law of my mind and making me captive to the law of sin which dwells in my members. Wretched man that I am!" (Rom. 7:22-24)

There is a great contradiction in man. Within the same individual, the power of the original mind, which desires goodness, is at violent war against the power of the wicked mind, which desires evil. All life, all matter is doomed to destruction as long as it contains such a contradiction. Every man who contains such a contradiction within himself lives on the brink of destruction.

Can it be that man was created with such a contradiction? The answer again is no. Nothing could ever have been created with such an inherent contradiction. The contradiction, therefore, must have developed in man after the creation. In Christianity, we call this development the "Fall of Man."

Due to his fall, man is always near the point of destruction. For this reason, he makes a desperate effort to remove the contradiction by following the good desire of his original mind and repelling the evil desire of his wicked mind.

To the grief of mankind, the ultimate solution to the problem of good and evil has not yet been reached. Regarding the doctrines of theism and atheism, if one of the two should be judged good, the other must be evil. Yet we have not reached a theory of an absolute nature concerning the problem of good and evil. Moreover, men and women remain entirely ignorant of the answers to many fundamental questions, such as: What is the original mind, the source of good desire? What was the origin of the wicked mind, which caused evil desire? What was the fundamental cause of the fall which permitted man to embody such a contradiction? Before being able to lead a good life by following the good desire of the original mind and repelling evil desire, it is necessary to overcome ignorance and be able to distinguish between good and evil.

Seen from the viewpoint of knowledge, the human fall signifies man's descent into the darkness of ignorance. Since man consists of two aspects, internal and external, or spiritual and physical, there are also two aspects of knowledge, internal and external, and two aspects of ignorance, internal and external.

Internal ignorance, in the religious sense, means spiritual ignorance; that is, ignorance of the answers to such questions as: What is man's origin? What is the purpose of his life? Do God and the next world exist? What are good and evil?

External ignorance is ignorance of physical reality; that is, ignorance concerning the natural world, which includes the human body; also, ignorance of such questions as: What is the basis of the material world? According to which natural laws do all physical phenomena occur?

From the earliest dawn of history to the present, men have constantly and earnestly searched for the truth with which to overcome this ignorance and restore the light of knowledge. Man has struggled to discover internal truth through the way of religion. Science has been the path taken toward the discovery of external truth.

Religion and science have been the methods of searching for the two aspects of truth, in order to overcome the two aspects of ignorance and restore the two aspects of knowledge. The day must come when religion and science advance in one united way, so that man may enjoy eternal happiness, completely liberated from ignorance and directed toward goodness, which is what the original mind desires. Then, mutual understanding will occur between the two aspects of truth, the internal and the external.

Man has been approaching a solution to the fundamental questions of life by following two different courses. The first course is to search for the solution within the material world. Those who take this route think it to be the sublime path. They yield to science, taking pride in its omnipotence, and seek material happiness. However, can man enjoy full happiness when he limits his search to external material conditions, centered upon the physical body? Science may create a pleasant social environment in which man can enjoy the utmost in wealth, but is such an environment able to satisfy the spiritual desire of the inner man?

The passing joys of the man who delights in the pleasures of the flesh are nothing when compared to the happiness experienced by a devout man of God. Gautama Buddha, who left the glory of the royal palace, was not the only one who has taken the long journey of life in pursuit of the Way. His goal was man's lost home—his status before the fall, his permanent domicile—though he did not know where it was. Just as a man becomes whole and sane when his mind is in harmony with his body, so it is with joy. The joy of the body becomes whole and sane when it is in harmony with the joy of the mind.

What is the destiny of science? Until now, scientific research has not embraced the internal world of cause, but only the external world of result; not the world of essence, but only the world of phenomena. Today science is entering a higher dimension; it is no longer concerned exclusively with the external world of result and phenomena, but has begun to examine the internal world of cause and essence as well. Those who have taken the path of science are concluding that, without the truth that relates to the spiritual world of cause; that is, the internal truth, man cannot attain the ultimate purpose of science; that is, the discovery of the external truth, which pertains to the external world of result.

A sailor making a voyage on the sea of the material world under the sail of science in search of the pleasures of the flesh may reach the coast of his ideal, but he will soon find it to be nothing more than a graveyard to hold his flesh. But when the sailor who has completed his voyage in search of external truth under the sail of science comes into contact with the sea-route to internal truth, under the sail of religion, he will be able to end his voyage in the ideal world, which is the goal of the original mind's desire.

The second course of human endeavor has been directed toward solving the fundamental questions of life in the essential world of "cause." Philosophy and religion, which have gone this way, have made substantial contributions. On the other hand, both philosophy and religion have been saddled with many spiritual burdens. In their own times, philosophers and saints have pioneered the way of life, but their deeds have often resulted in placing added burdens on the people of the present era.

Consider the matter objectively. Has there ever been a philosopher who was able to end human misery? Has there ever been a saint who has clearly shown us the way of life? The principles and ideologies presented to mankind so far have given rise to skepticism; they have created many themes which need to be untangled, and numerous problems to be solved. The lights of revival with which the great religions illuminated their respective ages have faded out with the ebb of the age, leaving only dim, sputtering wicks glimmering in the falling darkness.

Let us study the history of Christianity. For nearly 2,000 years Christianity grew, professed the salvation of mankind, and established worldwide dominion. But what has become of the Christian spirit which cast forth such a brilliant light of life that, even in the days of persecution under the Roman Empire, Romans were brought to their knees before the crucified Jesus? Medieval feudal society buried this Christianity alive. Yet, even in its grave, the torch of Christian religious reformation still shone out against the engulfing darkness of that age. It could not, however, turn back the tide of those dark days.

When ecclesiastic love expired, when the surging desire for material wealth swept the society of Europe and countless millions of starving masses shouted bitterly in the industrial slums, the promise of salvation came not from heaven but from earth. Its name was communism. Christianity, though it professed God's love, had turned out to be in reality a dead body of clergy trailing empty slogans. It was then only natural that a banner of revolt would be raised against a seemingly merciless

God. Christian society became the hotbed of materialism. Absorbing fertilizer from this soil, communism, the foremost materialist ideology, has grown rapidly and unchecked.

Christianity lost its capacity to surpass the practice of communism and has not been able to present a truth which overcomes communist theory. Christians watch communism grow within their own midst, expanding its dominion over the world. Although they teach and believe that all men are descendants of the same parents, many Christians do not like to sit with brothers and sisters of different skin color. This is a representative example of today's Christianity, which is deprived of the life force needed to practice the word of Christ.

There may come a day when such social tragedies will end, but there is one social vice which is beyond the control of many men and women today. That is adultery. Christian doctrine holds this sin to be the greatest of all sins. What a tragedy that today's Christian society cannot halt this degradation, into which so many people today are rushing blindly.

What these realities mean to us is that Christianity today is in a state of confusion. Split by the chaotic tide of the present generation, it is unable to do anything for the lives of the people who have been drawn into today's whirlpool of immorality. Is Christianity unable to achieve God's promise of salvation for the present era of mankind? Why have men of religion thus far been unable to fulfill their missions even though they have struggled desperately and devotedly in pursuit of internal truth?

The relationship between the essential world and the phenomenal world is similar to that between mind and body. It is the relationship between cause and result, internal and external, subjective and objective. Since man can attain perfect personality only when his mind and body become harmonized in perfect oneness, the ideal world can be realized only when the two worlds—one of essence, the other of phenomena—have been joined in perfect unity.

As it is with the relationship between mind and body, so there can also be no phenomenal world apart from the essential world, and no essential world apart from the phenomenal world. Neither can there be a spiritual world apart from a physical world, nor spiritual happiness apart from true physical happiness. Religion has until now de-emphasized the value of everyday reality; it has denied the value of physical happiness in order to stress the attainment of spiritual joy. However strenuously man may try, he cannot cut himself off from reality, nor can he annihilate the desire for physical happiness that follows him always like a shadow.

In reality, the desire for physical happiness persistently takes hold of men of religion, leading them into the depths of agony. Such a contradiction exists even in the lives of spiritual leaders. Many spiritual leaders, torn by such contradictions, have met a sad end. Herein is a principal cause for the weakness and inactivity of today's religions; the weakness lies in the contradiction which has not yet been overcome.

Another factor has fated religion to decline. Modern men, whose intelligence has developed to the utmost degree, demand scientific proof for all things. However, religious doctrine, which remains unchanged, does not interpret things scientifically. That is to say, man's interpretation of internal truth (religion) and his interpretation of external truth (science) do not agree.

The ultimate purpose of religion can be fulfilled only by first believing in and then by practicing the truth. But true belief cannot come about today without knowledge and understanding. We study the Bible to confirm our belief by knowing the truth. Jesus' performance of miracles and his revelation of signs were to let the people know that he was the Messiah and enable them to believe in him. Knowledge comes from cognition, and man today cannot cognize anything which lacks logic and scientific proof. To understand something, there must first be cognition. Thus, internal truth also requires logical proof. Religion has been moving through the long course of history toward an age in which it must be explained scientifically.

Religion and science began with the missions of dispelling, respectively, the two aspects of human ignorance. In their courses, these two areas of thought and exploration came into apparently uncompromising conflict with each other. In order for man to attain the good purpose of the original mind's desire, there must come a time when there is a new expression of truth, enabling mankind to bring these two matters together under one unified theme. These two matters are religion, which has been coming closer to science, and science, which has been approaching religion.

It may be displeasing to religious believers, especially to Christians, to learn that a new expression of truth must appear. They believe that the Bible, which they now have, is perfect and absolute in itself. Truth, of course, is unique, eternal, unchangeable, and absolute. The Bible, however, is not the truth itself, but a textbook teaching the truth. Naturally, the quality of teaching and the method and extent of giving the truth must vary according to each age, for the truth is given to people of different ages, who are at different spiritual and intellectual levels. Therefore, we must not regard the textbook as absolute in every detail (cf. Part I, Ch. III, Sec. V).

Religion came into existence as the means to accomplish the purpose of goodness in following the way of God according to the intention of the original mind. The need for different kinds of understanding compelled the appearance of various religions. Scriptures of different religions varied according to the mission of the religion, the people who received it, and the age in which it came. Scripture can be likened to a lamp which illuminates the truth. Its mission is to shed the light of truth. When a brighter light appears, the mission of the old one fades. Today's religions have failed to lead the present generation out of the dark valley of death into the radiance of life, so there must now come a new truth that can shed a new light.

Many passages in the Bible say that new words of truth will be given to mankind in the "Last Days." What will be the mission of the new truth? Its mission will be to present the internal truth that religion has pursued and the external truth searched for by science under one unified theme. It should also seek to overcome both the internal and external ignorance of man and offer him internal and external knowledge. It must eliminate the contradiction within man, who is receptive to both good and evil, by helping fallen man resist the way of evil and attain the purpose of goodness. For fallen man, knowledge is the light of life and holds the power of revival; ignorance is the shadow of death and the cause of ruin. No feeling or emotion can be derived from ignorance, no act of will can arise from ignorance. Thus, when knowledge, emotion and will do not function properly in man, life is no longer worth living.

If man is created to be unable to live apart from God, how miserable life must be when he is ignorant of God. Yet, can man know God clearly, even though he may diligently consult the Bible? Furthermore, how can man ever know God's heart? The new truth should enable us to know God as a reality. It should also be able to reveal His heart and feeling of joy at the time of creation, and His broken heart and feeling of grief as He struggles to save fallen man who rebels against Him.

Human history, woven of the lives of men who are inclined toward both goodness and evil, is filled with the story of struggle. These struggles have been external battles over property, land, and men. But today the external fighting is diminishing. People of different nations live together without racism. They strive to realize a world government. War victors seek to liberate their colonies, giving them rights equal to the rights of the great powers. Once hostile and disharmonious international relations are harmonized around similar economic problems as nations move toward the formation of common market systems all over the world. Meanwhile, culture is freely circulating, the isolation of nations is being overcome, and the cultural distance between East and West is being bridged.

One final war is thus left before us; that is, the war between the ideologies of democracy and communism. These internally conflicting ideologies are now in preparation for another external war, and both sides are equipped with dreadful weapons. The external preparations are, in reality, geared toward waging a final, decisive internal (spiritual) war. Which will triumph? Anyone who believes in the reality of God will answer "democracy." Yet, democracy today is not equipped with a theory or practice powerful enough to conquer communism. Therefore, in order that God's providence of salvation might be completely fulfilled, the new truth must bring all mankind into a new world of absolute goodness by elevating the spiritualism advocated in the democratic world to a new and higher dimension, finally assimilating even materialism. In this manner, the truth should be able to unite into one absolute way all the existing religions as well as all the "isms" and ideas which have existed since the beginning of human history.

Some people do, indeed, refuse to believe in religion. They disbelieve because they do not know the reality of God and of the next world. But, however strongly they deny spiritual reality, it is the nature of man to accept and to believe that which is proven in a scientific way. It is also the inherent nature of man to feel empty, void, and uneasy with himself if he has set his ultimate purpose of life in the external world of everyday things. When one comes to know God through the new truth, he learns about spiritual reality and comes to realize that the fundamental purpose of life is to be found not in the external world of matter, but in the internal world of spirit. Everyone treading this one way will meet one day as brothers and sisters.

If all men will thus meet as brothers and sisters at one destination through this one truth, what would the world founded on this basis be like? It would be a world in which all men form one big family under God. The purpose of truth is to pursue and to achieve goodness, and the origin of goodness is God Himself. Therefore, the world attained through this truth would be one in which all men would live together in wonderful brotherly love under God as our Parent. When man realizes that if he makes his neighbor a victim for his own benefit, he suffers more from the pangs of conscience than he profits from unrighteous gain, he will find it impossible to harm his neighbor. Therefore, when real brotherly love arises from the bottom of man's heart, he cannot do anything to cause his neighbor to suffer. How much more would this be true of men who live in a society in which they experience the actual feeling that God is their own Parent, transcendent of time and space, who watches their every action, and that this Parent wants us to love one another every moment? The new world, which will be established by the new truth, will usher in a new age when the sinful history of mankind has been liquidated. It must be a world in which no sin is possible. So far in human history, even those who have believed in God have committed sins. Their faith in God has taken the form of a concept rather than the form of living experience. If man could feel the presence of God and know the heavenly law that sinners are sent to hell, who then would dare to commit sin?

The world without sin could be called the "Kingdom of Heaven," the world which fallen man has long pursued. Since this world will be established as a reality on earth, it may well be called the "Kingdom of God on earth."

Thus, we can conclude that the ultimate purpose of God's providence of salvation is to establish the Kingdom of God on earth. It was already made plain in previous discussion that man fell from grace, and that the human fall came after the creation of man. From the standpoint of the reality of God, the answer to the question of which world God originally intended at the creation becomes evident (cf. Part I, Ch. III). We can say at this point, however, that this world is the Kingdom of God on earth, in which God's purpose of creation is realized.

Because of the fall, however, mankind has not been able to realize this world. Instead, man has brought about a world of sin and has fallen into ignorance. Therefore, fallen man has struggled unceasingly to restore the Kingdom of God on earth, which God originally intended. He has done this by seeking to overcome internal and external ignorance and pursuing ultimate goodness through all the periods of human history. The history of mankind, therefore, is the history of the providence of God through which God intends to restore the world in which His purpose of creation is fulfilled. To restore fallen man back to his originally intended state, the new truth should be able to reveal to him his ultimate destiny in the course of restoration by teaching him the original purpose for which God created man and the universe. Many questions must be answered by this truth.

Did man fall by eating the fruit of the Tree of the Knowledge of Good and Evil as the Bible literally says? If not, then what is the actual cause of the human fall? How could the God of perfection and beauty create man with a possibility of falling?

What was the reason for God's inability to prevent man from falling while He, being both omnipotent and omniscient, must have known the fall would take place? Why could God not save sinful man in an instant with His almighty power? These and many other questions have troubled the minds of deep thinkers and should be resolved by the new truth.

When the scientific nature of the world is observed, it can be concluded that God, the Creator, is the very origin of science. If human history is God's providence to restore the world to His original purpose of creation, it must be that God, Master of all laws, has manipulated providential history according to a plan and an order. Therefore, it is our most urgent task to discover how the sinful history of mankind began, what course it must follow, in what manner it will be concluded, and into what kind of world Providence will ultimately lead man. The new truth, then, should be able to resolve all the fundamental questions of life. With all these questions clarified, the reality of God as an absolute being who plans and guides history cannot be denied. When the truth is known, all will come to understand that the historical events which man has seen and experienced are the reflections of God's heart, struggling to save fallen man.

In addition, the new truth should be able to explain lucidly all the difficult problems of Christianity, since Christianity plays a major role in the formation of the world cultural sphere. Intellectual people cannot be satisfied by merely hearing that Jesus is God's son and the Savior of mankind. Many controversies have arisen in theological circles in an effort to understand the deeper significance of Christian doctrines. Thus, the new truth must be able to clarify the relationships among God, Jesus, and man in light of the principle of creation. Furthermore, the difficult questions of the Trinity should be elucidated. The question of why God's salvation for mankind has only been possible through the crucifixion of His son must be answered. When it is seen that no parent has been able to give birth to a sinless child entitled to the Heavenly Kingdom without redemption by a savior, is this not a sound proof that parents still pass on the original sin to their children even after their own rebirth in Christ? This inquiry leads to yet another question: What is the extent of redemption by the cross?

A vast number of Christians throughout the 2,000 years of Christian history have been confident that they have been completely saved by the blood of Jesus' crucifixion. Yet, in reality, not one individual, home or society has existed free from sin. The Christian spirit has actually been on the path of decline day after day. Therefore, there remain many difficult problems leading to a central contradiction between the present reality of Christianity and the belief in complete redemption by the ransom of the cross. The new truth which we are looking for should be able to explain all of these questions clearly and completely. There are more questions such as: Why will Christ come again? When, where and how will he come? In what manner will the resurrection of fallen men take place? What is the meaning of the Biblical prophecy that heaven and earth will be destroyed by fire and other natural calamities? The new truth should provide a key to all these difficult Biblical mysteries which are written in parables and symbols, and do so in plain language which everyone can understand, as Jesus promised in John 16:25.

Only through these answers and plain truths will all the denominations be united, as the divisions caused by differing interpretations of Biblical passages are broken down.

This new, ultimate, final truth, however, cannot come either from any man's synthetic research in the scriptures and in literature, or from any human brain. As the Bible says, "You must again prophesy about many peoples and nations and tongues and kings." (Rev. 10:11) This truth must appear as a revelation from God Himself. This new truth has already appeared!

With the fullness of time, God has sent His messenger to resolve the fundamental questions of life and the universe. His name is Sun Myung Moon. For many decades, he wandered in a vast spiritual world in search of the ultimate truth. On this path, he endured suffering unimagined by anyone in human history. God alone will remember it. Knowing that no one can find the ultimate truth to save mankind without going through the bitterest of trials, he fought alone against myriads of Satanic forces, both in the spiritual and physical worlds, and finally triumphed over them all. In this way, he came in contact with many saints in Paradise and with Jesus, and thus brought into light all the heavenly secrets through his communion with God.

The Divine Principle revealed in this book is only part of the new truth. We have recorded here what Sun Myung Moon's disciples have hitherto heard and witnessed. We believe with happy expectation that, as time goes on, deeper parts of the truth will be continually revealed. It is our earnest prayer that the light of truth will quickly fill the earth.

PART I

CHAPTER I

Principle of Creation

Throughout history, man has been struggling to solve the fundamental questions of life and the universe. Yet no one has been able to give satisfactory answers, for no one has known the original plan for the creation of man and the universe. Furthermore, there remains a fundamental question to be settled, a question not so much about the facts of existence as about the cause of existence. Questions about life and the universe, of course, cannot be solved without understanding the nature of God. The "Principle of Creation" deals with these fundamental questions.

SECTION I
The Dual Characteristics of God
and His World of Creation

1. DUAL CHARACTERISTICS OF GOD

How can we know the characteristics of God, who is an invisible being? We can know them by observing the world of His creation. For this reason, Paul said:

> Ever since the creation of the world his invisible nature, namely, his eternal power and deity, has been clearly perceived in the things that have been made. So they are without excuse. (Rom. 1:20)

Just as the work of an artist is a visible manifestation of its maker's invisible nature, every creation is a "substantial object" of the invisible deity of God, the Creator. His nature is displayed in each creation. Just as we can sense an author's character through his works, so we can perceive God's deity by observing His creation.

In order to know the nature of God's deity, let us examine the common factors which can be found throughout His creation. A creation, whatever it may be, cannot come into being unless a reciprocal relationship between positivity and negativity has been achieved, not only within itself but also in relation to other beings. For example, particles, which are the essential components of all matter, have either positivity or negativity, or a neutrality which is caused when the positive and negative elements neutralize each other. When the two characteristics enter into a reciprocal relationship, these particles form an atom.

Each atom assumes either positive or negative characteristics, and, as the dual characteristics within each atom enable that atom to have reciprocal relationships with other atoms, they proceed to form molecules of matter. Matter, which is formed in this way—according to the reciprocal relationship between these two characteristics—becomes nourishment for animals and plants when it is absorbed by them.

All plants exist and multiply through a relationship occurring between the stamen and pistil, while the same process occurs in the animal world through a relationship between male and female.

As for man, God created a man (male), Adam, in the beginning; then, seeing that it was not good that man should be alone (Gen. 2:18), He made a woman (female), Eve, as Adam's object, and for the first time God saw that His creation was "very good." (Gen. 1:31) Just as a positive or negative ion, even after dissociation, is found to be the combination of a proton (positive) and an electron (negative), the stamen or the pistil of the plant and a male or female member of the animal kingdom can also exist only through a reciprocal relationship between their dual essentialities of positivity and negativity. Also, there is a female characteristic dormant in every man, and a male essence in every woman. The aspects of each thing in the creation exist on a reciprocal basis, such as: inside and outside, internal and external, front and rear, right and left, up and down, high and low, strong and weak, long and short, wide and narrow, east and west, south and north. This is because all things are created to exist through a reciprocal relationship between their dual essentialities.

As we have seen, all things exist through a reciprocal relationship between the dual essentialities of positivity and negativity. We must also know the reciprocal relationship between another pair of dual essentialities, which is even more fundamental than that of positivity and negativity. Anything in existence has both an external form and an internal character. The external form is visible and reflects the internal character, which is invisible. Though the internal character cannot be seen, it assumes a certain form, so that the external form resembles the internal character as its visible form. "Internal character" and "external form" refer to the two characters which are the two relative aspects of the same existence. In this relationship, the external form may also be called a "second internal character," so together we call them "dual characteristics," or "dual essentialities."

We can take man as an example. Man consists of body, or external form, and mind, or internal character. The visible body resembles the invisible mind. The body assumes a form resembling the form projected by the mind. This is the reason one can perceive things about a man's invisible character and destiny by his outward appearance.

We call the mind "internal character" and the body "external form." Here again, since our mind and body are the two relative aspects of the same man, the body may be called the "second mind," or a duplication of the mind. We call these two together "the dual characteristics of man." Now we can understand the fact that everything exists through a reciprocal relationship between the dual characteristics of internal character and external form.

What then is the relationship between internal character and external form? The invisible internal character is the cause and is in the subjective position, while the visible external form is the result of the former and stands in an objective position to it. Accordingly, the reciprocal relationship which exists between the two is one of internal and external, cause and result, subject and object, or vertical and horizontal.

Let us again use man as an example. Since mind and body correspond to character and form, the body is a copy of the mind and should be completely under its command. Thus man can direct his life according to his will and purpose. The mind and body also assume a reciprocal relationship of internal and external, cause and result, subject and object, or vertical and horizontal.

Likewise, all the things of creation, though they may vary in dimension, have an invisible internal character which corresponds to the mind; since this is the cause and subject, it manipulates the external form, which corresponds to the human body. This relationship between mind and body enables the individual creation to maintain its existence as a being with a certain purpose. Animals have an aspect which corresponds to the human mind; since this is the subject and cause which directs toward a certain purpose, the animal body is able to live according to the purpose of its individual being. A plant also has an internal character which enables it to maintain its organic function.

Men can be united because the mind is a common factor in every person. Similarly, positive and negative ions are united to form a certain material because within each ion there are aspects of both internal character and external form which tend to unite, thus forming a molecule. Again, when an electron revolves around a proton to form an atom, it is because each contains an aspect of "character" that directs it toward the purpose of constructing an atom.

Modern science tells us that the particles forming the atom all consist of energy. We know that within energy itself there must also be an attribute of "character" which strives toward the goal of constructing a particle. Even beyond this, we must seek an absolute being as the ultimate cause of the entire world of reality. This cause, with its ultimate and unique character and form, brought all energy into existence. This ultimate being must be the First Cause of all beings, containing the absolute and subjective character and form. This First Cause of our existing world we call God. We call God's subjective character and form His "essential character" and "essential form." As Paul indicated, when we examine the factors which all creation have in common, we finally come to understand that God is the First Cause of the world of creation, and He exists as the absolute subject, having characteristics of both essential character and essential form.

We have already clarified the fact that everything in the creation exists only because of a reciprocal relationship between its dual characteristics of positivity and negativity. We naturally conclude that God, being the First Cause of all creation, also exists because of a reciprocal relationship between the dual characteristics of positivity and negativity. Genesis 1:27 says: "So God created man in his own image, in the image of God he created him; male and female he created them." This, too, explains to us that God is the absolute subject, who exists with His dual characteristics of positivity and negativity.

What is the relationship between the dual characteristics of character and form and the dual characteristics of positivity and negativity?

Fundamentally, God's essential character and His essential form assume a reciprocal relationship with His "essential positivity" and "essential negativity." Therefore, God's essential positivity and essential negativity are the attributes of His essential character and essential form. So, the relationship between positivity and negativity is similar to that which exists between character and form.

Accordingly, positivity and negativity also have a reciprocal relationship existing between internal and external, cause and result, subject and object, vertical and horizontal. This is the reason it is written in the Bible that God created the woman Eve as an object by taking the rib from the man Adam, who was the subject (Gen. 2:22). Here we call the positivity and negativity of God "masculinity" and "femininity," respectively.

The universe which was created with God as the center is similar to a man who has been created with his mind as the center. The universe is a perfect organic body created completely in accordance with God's purpose of creation. For this reason, the universe as an organic body has its own internal character and external form, with God as its internal character, while the physical universe is its external form. This is why God said that man, who is the center of the universe, was made in His own image (Gen. 1:27). Before creating the universe, God existed as the internal masculine subject, and He created the universe as His external feminine object. I Corinthians 11:7 says that man "is the image and glory of God," which testifies to this theory. Since God is the masculine subject of internal character we call Him "Our Father," emphasizing His masculine nature.

In brief, we know that God is the subject who consists of the dual characteristics of essential character and essential form. At the same time, He is a subject consisting of the dual characteristics of masculinity and femininity, the former representing His essential character and the latter representing His essential form. In relationship to the whole creation, God is the masculine subject representing its internal character.

2. RELATIONSHIP BETWEEN GOD AND THE UNIVERSE

We have learned so far that each and every creation is God's substantial object which is the manifested form of the invisible essentialities of God. Every substantial object is called an "individual truth incarnation." Man, being the substantial object of God who was created in His image, is called the "individual truth incarnation in image." Since all creation, other than man, is the symbolic object of God created in His indirect image, it is called the "symbolic individual truth incarnation."

Any individual truth incarnation, since it is a substance which manifests God's dual essentialities, can again be divided into a positive element and a negative one, the former resembling masculinity as the essential character of God and the latter resembling femininity as the essential form of God. Also, each individual truth incarnation is a substantial object of God; therefore, each not only reflects God's dual essentialities of character and form in the individual self, but each also has within itself the dual essentialities of positivity and negativity.

To sum up the relationship between God and the universe as seen from the viewpoint of its dual characteristics, the universe is God's substantial object consisting of individual truth incarnations. These are the manifestation of God's dual characteristics both in image and in symbol according to the principle of creation. That is, man is God's substantial object with His dual characteristics manifested as "direct image," while all things of the universe are the substantial objects of God with His dual characteristics manifested as "indirect image" (symbol). The relationship between God and the universe and the relationship between character and form is the same as the relationship between internal and external, cause and result, subject and object, and vertical and horizontal.

Let us examine the fundamental theory of the *Book of Changes (I Ching),* which is the center of Oriental philosophy, from the viewpoint of the principle of creation. This book emphasizes that the foundation of the universe is Taeguk (ultimacy) and from this comes Yang and Yin (positivity and negativity). From Yang and Yin come the "O-haeing" (five elements: metal, wood, water, fire and soil). All things were created from O-haeing. Positivity and negativity together are called the "Tao." The "Tao" is defined as the "Way," or "Word." That is, Taeguk produced the word (creative principle) and the Word produced all things. Therefore, Taeguk is the first and ultimate cause of all existence and is the unified nucleus of both positivity and negativity.

By comparing this with the Bible (John 1:1-3), "The Word was God . . . and all things were created through him," we can see that Taeguk, the subject which contains positivity and negativity, represents God, the subject who contains dual essentialities.

According to the principle of creation, the word (Logos) also consists of dual essentialities, and so the universe which was created by the Word contains dual essentialities. Consequently, the assertion in the *Book of Changes* that "positivity and negativity together is the Word," is valid.

However, the *Book of Changes* which observes the universe only from the viewpoint of positivity and negativity, does not explain the fact that all things have an internal character and external form within themselves. Accordingly, it has only verified the fact that Taeguk is the subject containing positivity and negativity and has not explained that Taeguk is originally the subject containing the dual characteristics of essential character and essential form. Therefore, the *Book of Changes* does not reveal that Taeguk is a God of personality.

Here we have learned that the foundation of Oriental philosophy contained in the *Book of Changes,* can ultimately be elucidated only according to the principle of creation.

SECTION II
Universal Prime Energy, Give and Take Action, and the Four Position Foundation

1. UNIVERSAL PRIME ENERGY

God is the Creator of all things. He is the absolute reality eternally self-existent, transcendent of time and space (Ex.

3:14). Therefore, the fundamental energy of His being must also be absolute and eternally self-existent. At the same time, He is the source of the energy which enables all things to maintain their existence. We call this energy "Universal Prime Energy."

2. GIVE AND TAKE ACTION

When a subject and an object are engaged in give and take action within a being, after having established a reciprocal relationship between themselves through the Universal Prime Energy, the energy necessary to maintain the existence of that being is produced. This energy provides power for existence, multiplication and action. The process which generates the necessary energy is called "give and take action." Therefore, Universal Prime Energy and the power of give and take action form a reciprocal relationship of cause and effect, internal and external, and subject and object. Consequently, Universal Prime Energy is a vertical power, while the power of give and take action is a horizontal power.

Let us further investigate God and His creation from the standpoint of Universal Prime Energy and give and take action.

God contains within Himself dual essentialities which exist forever. Through Universal Prime Energy, these two form a mutual or reciprocal relationship which develops into an eternal give and take action. The energy produced through this process is the force of give and take action. Through this force, God's dual essentialities establish a reciprocal base. This results in the "foundation of existence" upon which God, Himself, exists forever.

Each and every creation enters into give and take action between the dual essentialities that form an individual self by forming a reciprocal relationship through Universal Prime Energy. Through the force of give and take action, the dual essentialities produce a reciprocal base, which in turn produces a foundation of existence in an individual self; then upon this foundation, the individual self can stand as God's object and receive all the power necessary for its own existence.

For example: an atom comes to exist through the give and take action between a proton and an electron. This is the action of fusion. A molecule comes into being through the give and take action between a positive ion and a negative ion which causes a chemical reaction. Electricity is produced through the give and take action between positive electrical charges and negative electrical charges, which causes electrical action. All plants multiply through the give and take action between the stamen and pistil.

Animals maintain their existence and multiply through the give and take action between male and female. Between the animal kingdom and the plant kingdom, co-existence is made possible through give and take action. Plants give oxygen to animals and animals return carbon dioxide to plants. Flowers offer nectar to bees and bees pollinate flowers.

When we study the heavenly bodies, we find that the solar system exists through the give and take action between the sun and the planets. The earth and moon are also able to maintain their orbital movements through give and take action.

The human body maintains its life through the give and take action between arteries and veins, inhalation and exhalation, sympathetic and parasympathetic nervous sytems. An individual is able to achieve his purpose of existence through the give and take action between mind and body.

There is give and take action between husband and wife in a home, among individuals in a society, between government and people in a nation, and among nations in the world. Give and take action governs all relationships within man and all relationships among men.

However evil man may have been through all ages and in all places, he at least has the power of conscience remaining in his inmost self. This conscience is always at work, influencing him to live for righteousness. No one can prevent this power from operating within himself. It causes him to feel conscience-stricken at the moment of committing evil. If there were no conscience left in fallen men, God's providence of restoration would be impossible. Where does this power of conscience originate? Since all power comes from give and take action, the conscience must be no exception. The conscience is able to operate because it stands as an object to a certain subject, thus performing the action of give and take on a reciprocal base formed between the two. We know that the subject of the conscience is God.

The human fall signifies that through some act, man was cut off from having a give and take relationship with God, thus failing to unite into one body with Him. Instead, man entered into a give and take relationship with Satan, forming a reciprocal base with him. Jesus, having become one with God through the relationship of give and take, came to this world as His son. Therefore, if and when fallen man unites with Jesus in a perfect give and take relationship, he will be able to restore his original nature, thus entering again into a give and take relationship with God and becoming one with Him. Therefore, Jesus is called the "mediator" for fallen man, being the way, the truth and the life. He came to serve mankind with love and sacrifice, giving even his own life. If we turn to him with faith, we "should not perish but have eternal life." (John 3:16)

True Christianity is a religion of life, through which men can restore the vertical give and take circuit with God by establishing, through love and sacrifice, the horizontal give and take circuit between men centering on Jesus. The teachings and deeds of Jesus were solely for this purpose, as he indicated on numerous occasions:

Judge not, that you be not judged. For with the judgment you pronounce you will be judged, and the measure you give will be the measure you get. (Matt. 7:1-2)

So whatever you wish that men would do to you, do so to them; for this is the law and the prophets. (Matt. 7:12)

So everyone who acknowledges me before men, I also will acknowledge before my Father who is in heaven. (Matt. 10:32)

He who receives a prophet because he is a prophet shall receive a prophet's reward, and he who receives a righteous man because he is a righteous man shall receive a righteous man's reward. (Matt. 10:41)

And whoever gives to one of these little ones even a cup of cold water because he is a disciple, truly, I say to you, he shall not lose his reward. (Matt. 10:42)

3. THE FOUR POSITION FOUNDATION: THREE OBJECTIVE PURPOSES THROUGH ORIGIN-DIVISION-UNION ACTION

(1) Origin-Division-Union Action

When, through Universal Prime Energy, the dual essentialities of God enter into give and take action by forming a reciprocal relationship, the force of give and take action causes multiplication. This action causes the dual essentialities to separate into two substantial objects centered upon God. The substantial subject and object pair then enter into another give and take action by forming a reciprocal relationship, through Universal Prime Energy. By forming one unit they become an object to God. In this manner, God, as the origin, is divided into two separated substances, after which these two again unite to form one body. We call this process "origin-division-union action."

(2) Three Objective Purposes

When, according to origin-division-union action (O-D-U action), the origin has divided into two separated substances of subject and object which have again united into one body, four positions are formed. One takes a subjective position while the remaining three stand as objects, thus producing three objective bases. When they enter into give and take action among themselves, one of the four positions assumes the role of subject, while the other three fulfill their objective purposes respectively.

(3) The Four Position Foundation

When, according to O-D-U action, the origin is divided into two substantial objects, they assume the roles of subject and object respectively, and finally unite into one body. Thus three objective positions are fulfilled. Since these three objective positions are centered on the origin, four respective positions are formed altogether. This creates "the four position foundation."

The significance of the number "four" is derived from this four position foundation. And since this is the result of the fulfillment of the three objective purposes, the significance of the number "three" is also found here. The four position foundation is manifested as God, husband and wife, and their offspring. With God as the origin, husband and wife as the manifested subject and object, and their offspring as the result of their unity, one can see three distinct stages. Thus the four position foundation becomes the basis of the three stages because it is fulfilled in three stages according to O-D-U action. This is also the basis of the significance of the number "twelve," because each of the four positions will take three objects, thus bringing about a total of twelve objects. The four position foundation is the base for the fulfillment of God's goodness and is the ultimate goal of His creation. This is the base through which God's power is channeled to flow into all of His creation in order for the creation to exist. Therefore, the formation of the four position foundation is ultimately God's eternal purpose of creation.

(4) The Status of Existence of the Four Position Foundation

Whenever a creation has formed a four position foundation by fulfilling its three objective purposes through O-D-U action, it begins to perform global spherical movement in order to maintain its three-dimensional existence. Let us now investigate the reason for this.

When God's dual essentialities are divided and manifested into two substantial objects, one serving as subject and the other as object, they enter into a relationship and produce a reciprocal base. The object enters into give and take action by centering itself on the subject through centripetal force and centrifugal force. Consequently, the object begins to revolve around the subject, and thus they form one unit. According to this same principle, the subject, in turn, becomes an object to God, revolving around Him to form one unit with Him. When the object forms one unit with the subject, together they become a substantial object to God, since they reflect His dual essentialities. For this reason, any object must first unite with its subject before it is able to stand as an object to God.

This substantial object to God has within itself the dual essentialities of subject and object which perform continuous circular movement respectively, due to the give and take action between the two. Therefore, this circular movement forms a specific orbit on a horizontal level according to the particular motion of the subject and object. However, since this movement is generally performed with the angles of the orbit constantly varying, centering on the subject, this circular movement will eventually become spherical movement. Accordingly, all beings that have completed the four position foundation revolve in either circular or spherical movement, making the manner of existence three-dimensional.

Let us look at the example of the solar system. With the sun as the subject, all the planets act as its objects by forming a reciprocal relationship with the sun, through the action of give and take. Through the action of centripetal force and centrifugal force, each planet consequently revolves around the sun. During this process of revolution, the sun and the planets become one unit, thus creating the solar system. The earth, which in itself is a complex body of dual essentialities, is not the only body which rotates on its axis. The sun and the planets around it, which are complex bodies of dual essentialities in themselves, also rotate upon their own axes. The circular movement of the solar system which has been caused by the give and take action between the sun and the planets does not always occur on a single plane, but constantly changes its angle of orbit around the sun. Thus the solar system, by performing this spherical movement, becomes three-dimensional. In this manner, all the heavenly bodies exist in three dimensions, through either circular or spherical movement. The entire universe, which consists of numerous heavenly bodies, exists as one unit through give and take action, and moves spherically under the same principle, thus existing three-dimensionally.

When a proton and an electron, by forming a reciprocal base, enter into give and take action with the proton as the center, there occurs a circular movement which makes the two into one unit, and thus an atom is produced. The proton and the electron also have dual essentialities which are engaged in continuous individual movement. Therefore, the circular movement caused by the give and take action between the proton and electron does not occur on a horizontal level alone, but constantly changes its angle of movement so that it becomes spherical movement. Thus the atom, too, exists on a three-dimensional level.

The magnetic force occurring between the positive and negative poles of electricity also exists in spherical movement by the same principle.

Let us take man as an example. The body is the object to the mind, which is the subject. When the body forms a reciprocal relationship with the mind, it performs circular movement centered on the mind, thus forming one unit. If and when the mind becomes the object to God, and revolves around Him, becoming one unit with Him, and the body unites with the mind, the individual then becomes the substantial object to God, since he reflects God's dual essentialities. In this way he becomes a man in whom the purpose of creation is accomplished. The body and mind each contain a dual essentiality which continues to move individually; and so, the circular movement occurring through the give and take action between such a body and mind finally becomes a spherical movement by revolving around God, constantly changing its angles. Therefore, the man in whom the purpose of creation is accomplished is a three-dimensional being, always living in a spherical existence centered upon God. In this way he will be able to dominate even the invisible world of spirit (cf. Part I, Ch. I, Sec. VI).

Similarly, when the circular movement between a subject and an object occurring on a horizontal level becomes a spherical one through a three-dimensional orbit, the wonders of creation come into existence. That is, the beauty of the things of creation exists in infinite variety, and this is due to their varied orbit, form, state, direction, angle and speed of individual give and take action.

Every existence has its own internal character and external form, and naturally its spherical movement also contains that same aspect of character and form. Accordingly, there are both the center of character and center of form, even in the center of movement. What would the ultimate center of this spherical movement be? Man is the center of all creation, which was created to be the symbolic substantial object of God's dual essentialities. God is the center of all men, who have been created to be His substantial objects in His image. Therefore, the ultimate center of the spherical movement of the whole universe is God.

Let us further investigate this matter. Every substantial object of God contains a subject and an object within itself, and the subject is the center in their relationship. Therefore, the center of the unified body of subject and object also lies in the subject. The ultimate center of the subject is God, and the ultimate center of the unified body is also God. Therefore, when God's three objects form a respective basis of reciprocation, and their three centers (subjects) enter into give and take action, centering upon God in complete oneness with Him, fulfilling their three objective purposes, the four position foundation is completed for the first time.

Consequently, the ultimate center of the four position foundation is God. Every individual creation, having thus fulfilled the four position foundation, is an individual truth incarnation. As mentioned before, this exists in two forms: the truth incarnation in image (man) and the symbolic truth incarnation (all creation except man).

The universe consists of countless such individual truth incarnations, mutually related in good order, from the creature of the lowest grade to the highest, with man as the highest truth incarnation. Again, every individual truth incarnation moves spherically, with the lower individual truth incarnations in the objective position to the higher ones. The center of the spherical movement of this object is in the individual truth incarnation which is in the position of subject, on a higher level. Likewise, the centers of countless such symbolic individual truth incarnations are connected with one another from the lowest to the highest. Man, the individual truth incarnation in image, is the highest and central created being.

Let us illustrate this with an example. Today's science states that atoms are made of elementary particles which are composed of energy. Observing the purpose of existence of the individual truth incarnations at different stages, we can understand that energy exists in order to form elementary particles. The elementary particle, in turn, exists to form an atom, an atom to form a molecule, a molecule to form any type of matter, and all matter to form the whole universe.

For what purpose, then, does the universe exist; and what is its center? The answer is none other than man himself. That is why God, after creating man, told him to subdue the earth (Gen. 1:28). If there were no men to see and appreciate the universe, the universe could be compared to a museum without any visitors. The articles exhibited in the museum can display the value of their existence only when there is a man to appreciate, love, and take delight in them. Man is able to form a close relationship with them, and in this way they assume value. If there were no man to appreciate them, would they have any significance?

The same applies to the case of the whole universe with man as its center. Only through man are they mutually related in a united purpose. The relationship becomes apparent when man clarifies the source and the nature of all the materials which form the whole creation. Man alone studies and classifies the true characters of all the animals and plants, including everything on the earth and sea as well as the constellations which form the whole universe. As the center and subject of the creation, man enables the things of creation to have an organized mutual relationship with each other. Materials absorbed by the human body are changed into elements which maintain the physiological function of man, while the whole creation provides the material to make a pleasant living environment for him.

On the basis of external form, these are man's relationships to the universe, with man as the center. But there is still another relationship, with man as the center, on the basis of internal character. We may call the former a "physical relationship" while the latter we may call a "spiritual relationship."

The physiological elements of man, which consist of material substance, respond to the intellect, emotion, and will of his mind. This indicates that materials have certain elements through which they can respond to man's intellect, emotion, and will. Such elements form the internal character of matter, so that every creation is able to respond to human intellect, emotion, and will, though the degree of response may vary. It is because man is the center of the internal character of creation that he can become intoxicated with the beauty of nature, and experience the mystery of being one in harmony with it. Man was thus created to be the center of the whole creation, and so the point where God and man become one united body is where we find the center of the macrocosm.

Let us discuss man's being the center of the macrocosm from a different aspect. We call the two worlds, the visible and invisible, the "macrocosm," with man being the substantial center of this total macrocosm. Every creation forming the macrocosm is divided into a subject and an object element.

Here we may reach the conclusion that if Adam, who was the first human ancestor, had been perfected, he would have become the substantial embodiment of all the subject elements in the creation; and if Eve had been perfected, she would have become the substantial embodiment of all the object elements in the creation. If Adam and Eve together had grown wholesomely to the perfection stage—one becoming the lord of all the subjects in the creation, and the other becoming the lord of all the objects—and had they joined into one body as man and wife, they would have become a central body dominating the whole universe, since God created man to have dominion over the creation.

Man was created to be the center of harmony of the whole macrocosm. Thus, if Adam and Eve had become husband and wife after perfection, thus joining into one body as the substantial center of the dual essentialities contained in every creature, the macrocosm, which was created to have dual essentialities as an individual being, would also move in harmony with Adam and Eve as the nucleus. Likewise, the point at which Adam and Eve join into one body as a husband and wife is also the point at which God, the subject of love, and man, the object of beauty, become one unit, thus establishing the center of goodness. Here, for the first time, the purpose of creation is accomplished. God, our Parent, is able to abide with perfected men as His children, and peacefully rest for eternity. At that time, this center would become the object of God's eternal love, and through this, God would be stimulated with happiness for eternity. Here God's Word would be physically incarnated for the first time in human history. Therefore, this point would become the very center of the truth and also the center of man's original mind, which has been directing man to attain the purpose of creation. Consequently, the whole universe will perform a spherical movement of unified purpose, centered on the four position foundation, when a perfected man and woman become husband and wife, with God at their center. However, the universe lost this center when man fell; consequently, all of creation has been groaning in travail, waiting for the children of God—that is, men whose original nature of creation is restored—to appear and take their position as the macrocosm's center (Rom. 8:19-22).

4. THE OMNIPRESENCE OF GOD

Our understanding is thus increased, and we know that the four position foundation, having completed the three objective purposes through the O-D-U action, becomes one body with God through spherical movement centering on Him. This creates the basic foundation of both the power within every existing being, through which God may work, and the power which enables all beings in creation to maintain their existence. Likewise, God is omnipresent in the creation.

5. THE MULTIPLICATION OF PHYSIOLOGICAL BODIES

In order for a physical body to continue to exist, it must multiply, and this multiplication occurs through the O-D-U action caused by the action of give and take. For example, seeds of plants are produced through a give and take action between stamen and pistil. They will again multiply themselves, repeating the same course. In the animal world too, the male and female grow to have give and take action with each other, thus breeding and multiplying. The cell division of animals and plants also occurs through the give and take action.

If the body obeys the mind's desires, according to a certain purpose, it enters into the action of give and take with the mind, and they become companions. Whenever friends have give and take action wholesomely between them, their friendship will increase. Seen from this aspect, the universe is the substantial manifestation of the invisible God, occurring through the give and take action between His essential character and form, centered on the purpose of creation.

6. THE REASON EVERY BEING CONSISTS OF DUAL ESSENTIALITIES

Everything, in order to exist, needs energy—and this comes through give and take action. However, nothing can perform give and take action by itself. Therefore, in order to generate the energy to exist, there must be a subject and object who can perform give and take action.

Any movement that goes in a straight line will finally come to an end, and no being performing such movement can exist eternally. Consequently, in order to exist eternally, everything moves in circular motion. In order for revolution to occur, the action of give and take between a subject and an object must take place. Therefore, in order to exist eternally, God has dual essentialities. If His creation is to be an eternal object, it must reflect God's dual essentialities. In this way, "time" also maintains its perpetuity by going through periodic cycles.

SECTION III
The Purpose of Creation

1. THE PURPOSE OF THE CREATION OF THE UNIVERSE

Whenever God made a new species of creation, He saw that "it was good." (Gen. 1:4-31) This indicates that God wanted all of His creation to be good objects. This is because He wanted to feel happiness whenever He looked at His creation.

What, then, should His creation be like in order to make God happiest? After having created the universe, God finally created man in His image, after the pattern of His own character, with tremendous potential. Man was intended to enjoy and appreciate his position as an object to God. Therefore, when God created Adam and Eve, He gave them three great blessings: to be fruitful, to multiply and fill the earth, and to subdue it and have dominion (Gen. 1:28). Had man followed the words of this blessing and become happy in the Heavenly Kingdom of God, God also would have felt much happiness.

How should God's three great blessings have been fulfilled? This could have been possible only when the four position foundation, the basic foundation of creation, had been fulfilled. God's purpose in creating the universe was to feel happiness when He saw the purpose of goodness fulfilled in the Heavenly Kingdom, which the whole creation including man could have established after completing the four position foundation centered on God and fulfilling His three great blessings.

Consequently, the purpose of the universe's existence centered on man is to return joy to God, the Creator. Every being has a dual purpose. As already explained, every existence has both character and form; accordingly, its purpose is two-fold. One purpose pertains to internal character and the other to external form. The relationship between the two is exactly the same as that between character and form in any individual being. The purpose pertaining to the internal character is for the whole, while the purpose pertaining to the external form is for the individual. In other words, the former and the latter relate to each other as cause and effect, internal and external, and subject and object. Therefore, there cannot be any purpose of the individual apart from the purpose of the whole, nor any purpose of the whole that does not include the purpose of the individual. All the creatures in the entire universe form a vast complex linked together by these dual purposes.

2. OBJECT OF GOODNESS FOR THE JOY OF GOD

In order to understand more precisely the questions concerning God's purpose of creation, let us first examine how joy is produced. Joy is not created by the individual alone. Joy comes when we have an object, whether invisible or visible, in which our own character and form are reflected and developed, thus enabling us to feel our own character and form through the stimulation derived from the object.

For example, man feels joy as a creator only when he has an object; that is, when he sees the product of his work, whether it be a painting or sculpture, in which his plan is substantiated. In this way, he is able to feel his own character and form objectively through the stimulation derived from the product of his work. When the idea itself remains in the objective position, the stimulation derived from it is not substantial; therefore, the joy derived from it cannot be substantial either. God's joy is produced in the same manner as man's. Therefore, God feels joy when He feels His original character and form objectively through the stimulation derived from His substantial object.

We have explained that, when the Kingdom of Heaven is realized through the fulfillment of the three great blessings on the foundation of four positions, the perfect object through which God can feel joy is formed. Let us study how this perfect object for God's joy is formed.

God's first blessing to man was the perfection of his individuality. In order for man to perfect his individuality, his mind and body, which are the divided form of God's dual essentialities, must become united through the give and take action between them. Thus they form an individual four position foundation centered on God. The man whose mind and body have formed a four position foundation of the original God-centered nature becomes God's temple (I Cor. 3:16) and forms one body with Him (John 14:20). This means that man attains deity. Feeling exactly what God feels and knowing God's will, he would live as God would want. A man with his individuality thus perfected would have perfect give and take between his mind and body. In uniting together, his mind and body would form a substantial object to God. In that case, God becomes happy because He can feel His own character and form objectively through the stimulation coming from such a substantial object. Man's mind as subject feels the same way in relationship to his body. Therefore, when man has realized God's first blessing, he becomes a good object for the joy of God. A man with perfected individuality feels all that God feels, as if God's feelings were his own. Consequently, he cannot do anything which would cause God grief. This means that such a man could never fall.

In order for man to realize God's second blessing, originally, Adam and Eve, the divided substantial objects of God, after having perfected their respective individualities and thus fully reflecting God's dual essentialities, should have become husband and wife, forming one unit. They should have multiplied through having children, and established the four position foundation on a family level centered on God. Any family or society in which such a four position foundation centered on God is established would resemble a man of perfected individuality. Thus, a family or a society becomes the substantial object of man centered on God, and man and his object together become the substantial object of God. God and man would then be happy, for they would feel their own dual essentialities reflected in such a family or society. When man has actualized the second blessing, this also becomes a good object for God's joy.

Let us now learn why man becomes a good object for God's joy when he has actualized God's third blessing. First, we must discuss the relationship between man and the universe from the viewpoint of "character and form."

Before creating man, God made all things in the image and likeness of man's character and form. Therefore, man is the encapsulation of all things.

God began His creation with animals of a lower order, then created animals with a more complicated function; and finally He created man, who has the highest function. Therefore, man contains the structure, elements and essential qualities of animals. For example, man's vocal cords are so sophisticated that they are able to imitate the sounds of all the animals. The human shape and line are the most delicate and graceful, so that they often become a trying subject for student artists to draw.

Men and plants are of different structures and functions, but are similar in that they both consist of cells. Man contains the structure, elements, and essential qualities of plants, also. For example, a plant's leaf, seen from its function, corresponds to the human lung. Just as a leaf absorbs carbon dioxide from the air, the human lung absorbs oxygen. The trunk, stem, or branches of a plant correspond to the human heart in supplying nutriments to the whole body. The root of a plant corresponds to the stomach and intestines of a man, which absorb nutriments. Further, the shape and function of the xylem and the phloem of a plant correspond to that of the human artery and vein.

Man is also composed of earth, water, and air; consequently, he also contains mineral elements. The structure of the earth, too, is similar to that of the human body. The earth's crust is covered with plants, underground waterways exist in the substrata, and beneath all this lies molten lava surrounded by rocks. This closely corresponds to the structure of the human body: the skin is covered with hair, blood vessels exist in the musculature, and still deeper lies the marrow within the skeleton.

God's third blessing to man signifies man's qualification to dominate the whole creation. In order for man to actualize this blessing, he must first establish the four position foundation with the universe as his object, centering on God. Then, with man as the visible object in the image of God and the universe as the symbolic object in His indirect image, man's love and the beauty of creation perform give and take action to form one body in unity centering on God (cf. Part I, Ch. I, Sec. V, 2[3]).

The universe is the object in which man's character and form are manifested in substance. Therefore, man, whose center is fixed upon God, would feel immense joy when he objectively feels his own character and form through all things as his substantial objects. In like manner, God would enjoy utmost happiness by feeling His essential character and form through the world of His creation, which consists of man and all things in harmonious oneness. When man has thus actualized God's third blessing, this also becomes an object of goodness for God's joy. If God's purpose of creation had been actualized in this way, an ideal world, in which no trace of sin could be found, would have been established on this earth. We may call this world the

Kingdom of Heaven on earth. Man was created in the beginning to live in the Kingdom of Heaven on earth. At the moment of his physical death, he was to automatically transmigrate into the spirit world where he could enjoy an eternal life in the spiritual Kingdom of Heaven.

From all the facts explained thus far, we can understand that the Kingdom of Heaven is the world resembling a man with his individuality perfected in accordance with the essential character and form of God. Just as in man, where the mind's command is transmitted to the whole body through the central nervous system, thus causing the body to act toward one purpose, so in the Kingdom of Heaven, God's command is conveyed to all His children through the True Parents, causing all to work toward one purpose.

SECTION IV
Original Value of Creation

1. DETERMINATION OF THE ORIGINAL VALUE OF CREATION AND THE STANDARD OF VALUE

How can we determine the original value of things? The value of an object, according to the common standard, is determined by the reciprocal relationship between the purpose of the object and man's desire for it. The original value of an individual body is not latent in itself as an absolute. It is determined by the reciprocal relationship between the purpose of the individual body (as a particular kind of object centered on God's ideal of creation) and the desire of man (as the subject) to pursue the original value of the object. Accordingly, in order for an object to realize the original value of its creation, it must unite with man through give and take action, thus forming the original four position foundation by becoming the third object to God.

Then what is the standard of original value? Original value is determined when an object and a man, as subject, establish the four position foundation centered on God. The standard of value is God, the absolute being, because the center of the four position foundation is God. Therefore, the original value of an object, which is decided relative to the standard of God as the absolute reality, must be an absolute one.

For example, how is the beauty of a flower determined? Its original beauty is determined when God's purpose in creating the flower and man's spontaneous desire to pursue the flower's beauty are in accord with each other—when man's God-centered desire to find its beauty is fulfilled by the emotional stimulation he receives from the flower. This brings him perfect joy. In this way, the beauty of the flower will become absolute when the joy which man feels from the flower is perfectly centered upon the purpose of creation.

Man's desire to pursue the beauty of creation is the desire to feel his own character and form objectively. When God's purpose of creating the flower and man's desire to pursue its value are found to be in accord, the subject and object form a state of harmonious oneness. Therefore, in order for anything to possess original value, it must, with man as the subject, establish the four position foundation by becoming God's third object in a state of harmonious oneness centered on Him. Then, the original value of all things, determined by their relative relationship with God, is also absolute. Hitherto, the value of an object has never been absolute but only relative, because the give and take action between the object and fallen man has not been centered on God but on Satanic purpose and desire.

2. ORIGINAL INTELLECT, EMOTION AND WILL AND ORIGINAL TRUTH, BEAUTY AND GOODNESS

The human mind has three basic functions, constantly in action: intellect, emotion and will. Man's body acts in response to his mind's command. From this, we may conclude that man's body responds to his mind—and thus to his intellect, emotion and will. Therefore, man's every act should be a pursuit of truth, beauty and goodness. God, who is the subject of the human mind, is also the subject of human intellect, emotion and will. When man responds with his mind to God's original intellect, emotion and will, his body acts according to the will of God. Therefore, man's conduct would display the values of original truth, beauty and goodness.

3. LOVE AND BEAUTY, GOOD AND EVIL, RIGHTEOUSNESS AND UNRIGHTEOUSNESS

(1) Love and Beauty

When the two substantial bodies which result from the division of God's dual essentialities establish a four position foundation by performing give and take action on a reciprocal base, emotional forces work between the subject and object to unite them as the third object to God. Love is an emotional force given by the subject to the object; beauty is an emotional force returned to the subject by the object. The power of love is active and the stimulation of beauty is passive.

In the relationship between God and man, God gives love as the subject, while man returns beauty as the object. Between man and woman, man is the subject, giving love, while woman is the object, returning beauty. In the universe as a whole, man is the subject, who gives love to the rest of the creation, the object which responds in beauty. However, when the subject and object become united, there comes into being a love which is latent even in beauty and a beauty latent even in love. This is because when the subject and object unite in circular movement, the subject is able to stand in the position of the object, and the object in that of the subject. Between men, the beauty which a junior returns in response to the love of a senior is called "loyalty"; the beauty which children return in response to the love of their parents is called "filial piety"; the beauty which a wife returns in response to the love of her husband is called "virtue." The purpose of love and beauty is that the two separate substances divided from God's dual essentialities may become one through the action of give and take, thus establishing the four position foundation, and, as God's third object, fulfilling their purpose of creation.

Next, let us investigate the nature of God's love. The purpose of God's creation of man will be fulfilled only when Adam and Eve, after reaching perfection as the substantial objects of God's dual essentialities, unite and bear children. Thus they experience the three kinds of love which are given to their respective objects —parental love (the first type of love given to the object), conjugal love (the second type of love given to the object), and children's love (the third type of love given to the object)—in order to fulfill the three objective purposes and finally form the four position foundation. In relationship to each of the three objective loves in the four position foundation, God's love is subject. Therefore, God's love is manifested in the three objective loves and becomes the fundamental power for the establishment of the four position foundation. The four position foundation is a perfect object of beauty upon which we may receive and enjoy God's love perfectly; it is also the fundamental foundation of goodness in which God's purpose of creation may be fulfilled.

(2) Good and Evil

When a subject and an object fulfill the purpose of creation by becoming one through the action of give and take, the action or its result is called "good." When the subject and the object go against God's purpose of creation by establishing the four position foundation centered on Satan, such an action or its result is called "evil."

For example, when an individual fulfills God's first blessing to man by uniting his mind and body through the give and take action of love and beauty, and thus establishes the four position foundation on the individual level, this individual or the actions which produce such an individual are called "good." If Adam and Eve had become husband and wife through the give and take action of love and beauty in the respective positions of subject and object centered on God, and had established the four position foundation on the family level with their children, they would have created a family in which the purpose of creation was fulfilled, thus realizing God's second blessing to man. This family or the actions which establish such a family are called "good." Further, when a man, having perfected his individuality, places the creation in the objective position as his second self and becomes one with it, he produces God's third object. He then establishes the four position foundation under his control, thus realizing God's third blessing to man. This state or the actions to attain it are also called "good." On the other hand, when a man fulfills a purpose contrary to God's three great blessings by establishing the four position foundation centered on Satan, this act or the results of it are called "evil."

(3) Righteousness and Unrighteousness

In the course of fulfilling the purpose of goodness, the elements which bring about a life of goodness are called "righteousness." In the course of fulfilling the purpose of evil (Satan), the elements which cause a life of evil are called "unrighteousness." Thus, it is natural that we need to live a life of righteousness in order to attain the purpose of goodness. This is why righteousness always pursues the purpose of goodness.

SECTION V
The Process of the Creation of the Universe and the Period of Growth

1. THE PROCESS OF THE CREATION OF THE UNIVERSE

It is recorded in Chapter I of Genesis that the creation of the universe commenced with the creation of light out of the chaos, void, and darkness upon the face of the deep. God first created water and then separated the waters which were under the firmament from the waters which were above the firmament. Then He separated the waters from the land. After having created the plants, fish, birds, and mammals, He then created man. All this took a period of six days. Through this, we can see that there was a six-day period involved in the creation of the universe.

The process of creation as it is written in the Bible is in accord with the evolutionary sequence of creation known to modern scientists. In the beginning, the universe was in a gaseous state. Out of the chaos and void of the anhydrous age, the heavenly bodies were formed. After a spell of rainfall the world entered the aqueous age with a firmament of water. Then, due to volcanic eruption, land appeared out of the water, and was thus separated from the sea. Next, all the lower plants and animals came into existence. Then came fish, fowl, mammals, and finally man, in that order. Scientists calculate the age of the earth to be some thousand million years. When we consider the fact that the course of the creation of the universe described in the Bible, which was written thousands of years ago, coincides with the findings of scientific research, we are reassured that this record in the Bible is an actual revelation from God.

The universe did not suddenly come into being without a lapse of time, but it took considerable time for the generation of the universe to take place. Therefore, the six days until the completion of the creation of the universe are, in fact, not six days as calculated by the repetition of sunrise and sunset, but an indication that there were six periods in the course of creation.

2. THE PERIOD FOR THE GROWTH OF THE CREATION

The fact that it took six days—that is, six periods—to complete the creation of the universe indicates that a certain amount of time is necessary to complete the creation of any individual body in the universe.

We read in Chapter I of Genesis the story of the creation of the universe, in which each day's creation is described and each day is designated by a number. By this, also, we can understand that a period of time was necessary for the completion of each creation. The Bible states that, after the creation on the first day, "there was evening and there was morning, one day." (Gen. 1:5) Somewhere in the period from the evening, through the night, and until the next morning, the second day should begin; but the Bible states "one day" or the "first day," because any created being can realize the ideal of creation only in the new morning, after its perfection through the night, which is the period of growth.

Likewise, every phenomenon occurring in the universe brings about a result only after the lapse of a time interval. This is because everything made in the beginning was meant to be perfected through a certain period of time.

(1) The Three Orderly Stages of the Growth Period

The universe is the representation of God's essential character and form, substantially developed according to the principle of mathematics. We may infer that God is, in fact, mathematical. God is the absolute reality, the existing neutral center of the two essentialities; therefore, He is the reality of the number "three." Every created being, which is an image or symbolic likeness of God (Gen. 1:27), is created to go through the course of the number "three" in its existence, movement and growth.

Accordingly, the four position foundation, which was God's purpose of creation, was to be established through the course of three stages: God, Adam and Eve, and children. In order to establish the four position foundation and enter into circular movement, one must perform the three-stage origin-division-union action, accomplishing the three objective purposes, serving as object to three subjects, and subject to three objects. In order to stand in a stable position, a thing needs at least three points to support it. Therefore, in order for any creature to be perfected, it must grow to maturity through the three orderly stages of "formation," "growth" and "perfection." The number "three" appears throughout the natural world which consists of minerals, plants and animals. For example: matter exists in three forms—gaseous, liquid and solid; a plant consists basically of three parts—root, trunk or stem, and leaf; an animal consists of head, trunk and extremities.

Let us next draw examples from the Bible. Man, having fallen before completing the three stages of the growth period, could not fulfill the purpose of creation. Therefore, in order to attain this purpose, he must first go through those three stages. In the providence of restoration, God has worked to restore the number "three." As a consequence, there are many records in the Bible of the providence centered on the number "three": the Trinity (Father, Son and Holy Spirit), the three stages in Paradise, the three archangels (Lucifer, Gabriel and Michael), the three decks of Noah's ark, the three flights of the dove from the ark, Abraham's three offerings, the three days before the offering of Isaac, the three days of calamity during the period of Moses, the three-day period of separation from Satan in preparation for the Exodus, the three forty-year periods of restoration into Canaan, the three-day period of separation from Satan centering on Joshua before crossing the Jordan, Jesus' thirty years of private life and three years of public ministry, three wise men from the East with their three gifts, three major disciples of Jesus, three temptations of Jesus, the three prayers at Gethsemane, Peter's three denials of Jesus, the three hours of darkness during the crucifixion, and Jesus' resurrection after three days.

When did the first human ancestors fall? They fell during their growth period, while they were still immature. If man had fallen after he had achieved perfection, we could not believe in the omnipotence of God. If man could fall after he had become a perfect embodiment of goodness, the goodness itself would be imperfect. Accordingly, we would have to reach the conclusion that God, the absolute subject of goodness, is also imperfect.

In Genesis 2:17, God warned Adam and Eve that in the day that they ate the fruit of the Tree of the Knowledge of Good and Evil, they would surely die. From the fact that they had two choices, either to continue to live by obeying God's warning or accepting the way of death by going against it, we can imagine that they were still in an immature state. All things were created to reach perfection after they had grown through the three stages. Man could not have been created apart from this principle.

In which of the stages of growth did man fall? We can see that he fell at the final level of the growth stage. This can be logically proven by examining the various situations surrounding the fall of the first human ancestors, and by the details of the history of the providence of restoration. This will be further clarified by studying the first and second parts of this book thoroughly.

(2) Indirect Dominion

During the period of growth, each being in creation grows autonomously by the power of the Divine Principle. Therefore, God, as the author of the Principle, relates to the creation indirectly, dealing directly only with those results of its growth which are in accordance with the Principle. Therefore, we call this period God's "indirect dominion" or His "dominion over the result in the Principle."

All things reach their perfection through the dominion and autonomy of the Principle itself, by going through the period of growth (indirect dominion). However, man is created to attain his perfection not only through the dominion and autonomy of the Principle itself, but also by accomplishing his own portion of responsibility in passing through this period. That is, when we study God's Word, which says ". . . in the day you eat of it you shall die," (Gen. 2:17) we can understand that man's fall was his own fault and not God's. The first human ancestors were to become perfect by believing in the divine Word and not eating of the fruit. However, in their disbelief, they ate of it, thus causing the fall. In other words, the perfection or non-perfection of man depended not only on God's power of creation but also upon man's response. Therefore, man was created to reach his perfection by passing through the period of growth (indirect dominion), accomplishing his portion of responsibility, while God would fulfill His part as the Creator.

God created man so that man could reach his perfection only by accomplishing his portion of responsibility. God does not interfere with man in this regard. Man should inherit God's creatorship and participate in His work of creation. Thus, man may also enjoy the authority of a master, enabling him to rule all things from the position of the creator, just as God, man's Creator, has dominion over man (Gen. 1:28). This is the difference between man and the rest of creation. Thus, man reaches perfection only after having acquired the ability to rule the rest of creation, including the angels. He accomplishes this by going through the period of indirect dominion, fulfilling his own portion of responsibility, and inheriting God's creatorship. Therefore, man, who lost his qualification as the ruler because of the fall, can never fulfill the purpose of creation unless he goes through the indirect dominion. Thus, he may restore his dominion over all things, including Satan, by accomplishing his portion of responsibility in accordance with the principle of restoration. God's providence of salvation has been prolonged for so long because the central figures in His providence of restoration have repeatedly failed to accomplish their portions of responsibility, with which even God cannot interfere.

However great the grace of salvation through the cross of Christ may be, the providence of salvation calling at man's door will be nullified unless man himself has faith, which is his own portion of responsibility. God granted the benefit of resurrection through the crucifixion of Jesus, as His portion of responsibility, but it remains man's responsibility to believe (John 3:16, Eph. 2:8, Rom. 5:1).

(3) Direct Dominion

What is God's "direct dominion" and what is its purpose? Man enters the direct dominion of God when husband and wife fulfill the purpose of goodness through the perfect give and take action of love and beauty between them according to the will of the subject, in perfect oneness with God's heart, having established the four position foundation by becoming one united body. Therefore, direct dominion is the realm of perfection. We are destined to bring into being this direct dominion of God, because it must exist in order for the purpose of creation to be fulfilled. What significance does the direct dominion of God have for man?

If Adam and Eve had perfected themselves, centering on God, becoming one united body to form the four position foundation on the family level, and then had lived a life of goodness in perfect oneness with the divine heart, we would call this state the "direct dominion" of God. A man in such a state can put into practice the will of God by understanding it and by experiencing God's heart, which underlies it. Just as each section or nerve of the body is set into action by the command of the human mind, which is invisible, man would act out the will of God in obedience to His command, thus fulfilling the purpose of creation.

Next, let us discuss how man assumes direct dominion over all things. When perfected man as subject, and the physical world, as his object, become one united body centered on God and establish the four position foundation and when man thus fulfills the purpose of goodness through the perfect give and take action of love and beauty with the physical world according to his will, in perfect oneness with God's heart, man attains direct dominion over all things.

SECTION VI
The Invisible Substantial World and the Visible Substantial World Centering on Man

1. THE INVISIBLE SUBSTANTIAL WORLD AND THE VISIBLE SUBSTANTIAL WORLD

Since the universe was created after the model of man, who is in the image and likeness of God's dual essentialities, every existence, without exception, takes after man's basic form, which consists of mind and body (cf. Part I, Ch. I, Sec. I). Thus, in the universe there exists not only the visible substantial world, which resembles the human body, but also the invisible substantial world, which is modeled after the human mind. We call the latter the invisible substantial world, because we cannot perceive it with our five physical senses; however, we can perceive it with our five spiritual senses. The invisible world, like the visible world, is a world of reality. It is actually felt and perceived, through the five spiritual senses. The two substantial worlds together are called the "macrocosm."

Just as the body cannot act without a relationship with the mind, the original man of creation cannot act without a relationship with God. The visible world cannot enjoy its original value of creation without relating to the invisible world. In the same manner that we cannot understand a man's behavior without knowing his mind, we cannot really know the fundamental significance of human life without knowing God. Without understanding the invisible world, we cannot perfectly know the visible world. Thus, the invisible world is the subjective world; and the visible world is the objective world, the latter operating like a shadow of the former (Heb. 8:5). Man, upon his death, after his life in the visible world, goes to the invisible world in a spiritual body, having taken off his "clothes of flesh" (Job 10:11), and lives there forever.

2. POSITION OF MAN IN THE UNIVERSE

First, God created man to be the ruler of the universe (Gen. 1:28). The universe, except man, does not have internal sensibility to God. That is why God does not dominate the world directly; but by creating man to have complete sensibility to the universe, God lets him rule the universe directly. In creating man, God created his flesh with ingredients from the water, earth, and air, which are the main elements of the visible world. God did this to enable man to be sensible to and to have dominion over this world. He created the spirit man with spiritual elements to enable him to be sensible to and have dominion over the invisible world. On the Mount of Transfiguration, Moses, who had died nearly 1600 years before, and Elijah, who had died nearly 900 years before, appeared to Jesus (Matt. 17:3). These were actually the spirits of Moses and Elijah. Only man, who consists of both flesh and spirit, which enables him to dominate the visible and invisible worlds, can rule the two worlds.

Second, God created man to be the mediator and the center of harmony of the universe. When man's flesh and spirit, by becoming one through their give and take action, stand as the substantial object of God, the visible and invisible worlds also become the object of God by uniting through give and take action centered on man. Thus, man is the mediator and center of harmony between the two worlds. Therefore, man is like the air which enables a tuning fork to resound. Since man is created to communicate with the invisible world, he is meant to reflect everything happening in the world of spirit.

Third, God created man as the substantial microcosm of the whole. God first created the universe by developing, in substance, man's character and form. Thus, the spirit man is the substantial encapsulation of the invisible world, since God created the invisible world as the substantial development of the character and form of the spirit man. Likewise, the physical man is the substantial encapsulation of the visible world, since God created the visible world as the substantial development of the character and form of the physical man. Consequently, man is a microcosm, the encapsulation of the whole macrocosm.

Because of the fall of man, however, the whole creation lost its ruler. We read in Romans 8:19 that the creation waits in eager longing for the revealing of the sons of God (restored men of the original nature). Romans 8:22 continues with, "the whole creation has been groaning in travail together." This is because the give and take action between the visible and invisible worlds has been cut off due to the fall of man, rendering them unable to unite, since man was to be their mediator and center of harmony.

Jesus came as a perfected man in flesh and spirit. Therefore he was the substantial microcosm of the whole. That is why the Bible says that God has put all things in subjection under the feet of Christ (I Cor. 15:27). Jesus is our savior. He came to the world in order to perfect fallen men by striving to have them unite with him.

3. THE RECIPROCAL RELATIONSHIP BETWEEN THE PHYSICAL MAN AND THE SPIRIT MAN

(1) The Structure and Function of the Physical Man

The physical man consists of the dual essentialities, flesh mind (subject) and flesh body (object). The flesh mind enables the flesh body to multiply and provide protection. The instinct of an animal corresponds to the flesh mind. In order for the physical man to grow in good health, it must absorb air and light, which are invisible nourishment of a positive nature, while also taking in material elements, which are visible nourishment of a negative nature. All these must perform a perfect action of give and take though the circulation of blood.

The goodness or evil in the conduct of the physical man influences his spirit man to become either good or evil. This is because the physical man provides a certain element to the spirit man, which we call the "vitality element." In our everyday life, we know that our mind rejoices when our body performs a good deed, but feels anxiety after evil conduct. This is because the vitality element, which can be good or evil according to the deeds of man, is infused into our spirit man.

(2) The Structure and Function of the Spirit Man

The spirit man, which exists as an invisible substantial being, was created to be the subject to the physical man and to be felt and perceived through our spiritual senses. Through the spirit man we can communicate directly with God and have dominion over the invisible world, including the angels. Our spirit man is identical in appearance to our physical man, and it lives for eternity in the invisible world after leaving the physical body. Man desires to live forever because he has within himself a spirit man, which has an eternal nature.

This spirit man consists of the dual essentialities of spirit mind (subject) and spirit body (object). The spirit mind is the spirit man's central part, where God may abide. Our spirit man grows through the give and take action between the "life element" (positive) coming from God, and the "vitality element" (negative) coming from the physical man. The spirit man not only receives the vitality element from the physical man but also sends a certain element in return which we call the "living spirit element." We have seen that a man, influenced by another higher spirit, could feel infinite joy and new strength swelling up in him, even making it possible to heal a chronic disease. Such instances occur because the physical man receives the living spirit element from the spirit man. Further, the spirit man can grow only in the soil of the physical man. Therefore, the relationship between the spirit man and the physical man is like that between fruit and tree. When the physical mind responds to desires of the spirit mind, the physical man acts in accordance with the purpose of the spirit mind. Then the physical man receives the living spirit element from the spirit man. This brings good feelings and energy to the spirit man. Accordingly, the physical man, when it returns a wholesome vitality element to the spirit man, influences it to grow normally, in the direction of goodness.

The truth teaches us what it is that our spirit mind desires. When man comes to understand, through the truth, what our spirit mind desires, and when by putting it into practice he accomplishes his portion of responsibility, then the living spirit element and the vitality element enter into give and take action for the purpose of goodness. The relationship between the living spirit element and the vitality element corresponds to the relationship between character and form. Because the living spirit element is always at work in every individual, the original mind always inclines toward goodness, even in an evil person. However, unless a man leads a good life, the living spirit element cannot provide anything for the betterment of the physical man. Also, it cannot enjoy normal give and take action with the vitality element. Likewise, our spirit man can be perfected only through our physical life on earth.

Our spirit man should perfect itself by gradually growing through the three orderly stages in conjunction with our physical man, centering on the spirit mind, in accordance with the principle of creation. A spirit man which is in the formation stage is called a "form spirit," in the growth stage, a "life spirit," and in the perfection stage, a "divine spirit."

When our spirit man and our physical man establish the four position foundation by performing perfect give and take action centering on God, thus forming a united body, the spirit man becomes a divine spirit. At this level, the spirit man can feel and perceive everything in the invisible world. Since all the spiritual phenomena thus perceived by the spirit man are reflected and echoed in the physical man, presenting themselves as physical phenomena, man finally comes to feel spiritual phenomena even with his five physical senses. The Kingdom of God in heaven is the place where spirits go to live forever after leaving their physical bodies, when they have ended their physical life in the Kingdom of God on earth. The Kingdom of God in heaven can be realized only after the realization of the Kingdom of God on earth.

The sensibility of our spirit man is to be cultivated through its reciprocal relationship with our physical man during physical life on earth. Therefore, man should be perfected and experience God's perfect love on earth in order for his spirit man to experience God's perfect love in the invisible substantial world after his physical death. Thus, the character and qualities of the spirit man are formed during our earthly life. The aggravation of evil in the spirit of a fallen man is due to his sinful conduct during his earthly life. Likewise, the betterment of a fallen spirit man comes about only through the redemption of his sins during his physical life on earth. This was the reason Jesus came to earth in the flesh to save sinful mankind. Thus, we must lead a good life on earth. Jesus gave the keys of the Kingdom of Heaven to Peter (Matt. 16:19), and said that whatever is bound on earth shall be bound in heaven and whatever is loosed on earth shall be loosed in heaven (Matt. 18:18), because the primary purpose of the providence of salvation must first be realized on the earth.

The destination of the spirit man is decided by the spirit man himself, not by God. Originally, man was made so that after his perfection, he could breathe God's love perfectly. If a spirit man is unable to breathe this love perfectly, because of his sinful conduct, he feels pain when standing before God, who is the subject of perfect love. Consequently, such a spirit would automatically go to hell, which is the state farthest removed from the love of God. In addition, the multiplication of spirit men occurs at the same time as the multiplication of physical men through man's physical life, because the spirit man was created to grow only in the soil of the physical man.

(3) The Human Mind Seen from the Relationship between Spirit Mind and Physical Mind

The relationship between spirit mind and physical mind is like that between character and form. When these two become one through give and take action centered on God, the spirit man and the physical man naturally become one harmonious unit.

The give and take action between the spirit mind and the physical mind produces a united body, the human mind, which directs the individual toward the accomplishment of the purpose of creation. Man became ignorant of God because of the fall. Thus, he became ignorant of the absolute standard of goodness. But, according to the original nature of creation, the human mind always directs man toward what it thinks is good. This directing power is called human conscience. However, fallen man, being ignorant of the absolute standard of goodness, cannot set up the absolute standard of conscience. As the standard of goodness varies, so does the standard of conscience, and this causes frequent contention even among those who advocate a conscientious life. The part of the human mind which corresponds to character and always directs man toward the absolute standard of goodness is called the "original mind," and that which corresponds to form is called the "conscience."

Therefore, when man, due to ignorance, sets up a standard of goodness different from that of the original nature of creation, the human conscience directs toward that standard; however, the original mind rejects it and tries to turn the direction of conscience toward the standard of the original mind. When the spirit mind and the physical mind which are under the bondage of Satan become one unit through the action of give and take. man's development in the direction of evil is accelerated. We call this unit the "evil mind."

The original mind and conscience of man repel this evil mind and direct man toward goodness by helping him to separate himself from Satan and to face God.

CHAPTER II

Fall of Man

Men, without exception, are inclined to repel evil and to pursue goodness. But men, unconsciously driven by an evil force, repel the goodness desired by their original minds and perform evil acts which they do not really want to do. In Christianity, this evil force is known as "Satan." Because man does not know the real nature and origin of Satan, he has been unable to liquidate the force of Satan. In order to eradicate the source of evil, end the sinful history of mankind, and establish an era of goodness, we first must clarify the motivation of Satan and the nature of his being. In order to do this, we must study the "Fall of Man."

SECTION I
The Root of Sin

Until the present era, not a single man has known the root of sin. Christians have believed that Adam and Eve, the first man and the first woman, ate the fruit of the Tree of the Knowledge of Good and Evil, and that this act was the root of sin. There are a number of believers who assume that the fruit of the Tree of the Knowledge of Good and Evil is the fruit of an actual tree, while others believe that the fruit is a symbol. Such diverse opinions lead to differing interpretations and, hence, to confusion.

1. THE TREE OF LIFE AND THE TREE OF THE KNOWLEDGE OF GOOD AND EVIL

Many Christians to this day believe that the fruit which caused Adam and Eve to fall was literally the fruit of a tree. But, how could God—the Parent of man—make a fruit so tempting (Gen. 3:6) that His children would risk falling in order to eat it? How could He have placed such a harmful fruit where His children could reach it so easily?

Jesus said, "Not what goes into the mouth defiles a man, but what comes out of the mouth, this defiles a man." (Matt. 15:11) Then how could the food which man eats cause him to fall? The original sin of man has been inherited from the first man and the first woman. How could something edible be the source of that sin or the cause of transmitting that original sin to the children? That which is inherited is passed on through the blood lineage. What a man has eaten cannot be transmitted from one generation to the next.

There are many who believe that God created the fruit of the Tree of the Knowledge of Good and Evil and commanded man not to eat of it in order to test man's obedience to Him. We must ask: would a God of Love test man so mercilessly by a means that could cause his death? Adam and Eve knew they would die when they ate the fruit, for God had told them. Yet they ate it. We cannot understand why Adam and Eve, who were far from starvation, would disobey God's command at the risk of their lives. The fruit of the Tree of the Knowledge of Good and Evil must have been so extraordinarily stimulating and so ardently desired that fear of punishment—even death— could not deter them from eating it.

If the fruit of the Tree of the Knowledge of Good and Evil was not a material fruit, but a symbol, what does this symbol represent? To answer this question let us begin with an examination of the Tree of Life, which grew in the Garden of Eden along with the Tree of the Knowledge of Good and Evil (Gen. 2:9). When we grasp the true character of the Tree of Life, we will also know the nature of the Tree of the Knowledge of Good and Evil.

(1) The Tree of Life

According to the Bible, the hope of fallen man lies in the Tree of Life, that is, in becoming a Tree of Life. Israelites of the Old Testament looked toward the Tree of Life as their ultimate hope (Prov. 13:12). The hope of Christians from Jesus' day to the present time has been directed toward the Tree of Life (Rev. 22:14). Since the ultimate hope of fallen man is the Tree of Life, we can conclude that the hope of Adam before his fall was also the Tree of Life.

Why can we conclude that the hope of Adam was to attain the Tree of Life? Genesis 3:24 says that after Adam committed sin, God placed cherubim and a flaming sword to guard the Tree of Life. Due to his fall, Adam was driven from the Garden of Eden (Gen. 3:24) without having attained the Tree of Life. Ever since then, fallen man has set his hope upon attaining what Adam failed to attain—the Tree of Life.

What must Adam have hoped while he was in the process of growing to perfection? He hoped to reach perfect manhood without falling and thus fulfill God's ideal of creation. So we can now understand the importance of the Tree of Life as "manhood fulfilling the ideal of creation," as perfected Adam. The Tree of Life represents perfected Adam.

Had Adam attained the Tree of Life, all his descendants also could have attained the Tree of Life and thus they could have realized the Kingdom of Heaven on earth. But Adam fell and God placed the flaming sword at the entrance of the Garden to guard it. So the Tree of Life remains the hope of fallen man, who is trying to restore the ideal of creation.

Why is the quest to attain the Tree of Life so difficult that none have attained it? Fallen man, burdened with original sin, cannot achieve that goal by his own ability alone. A man who has fulfilled the ideal of creation on earth must come and draw all fallen men to himself in harmonious oneness (Rom. 11:17). Such a man must come to show fallen men the way. Jesus came as the Tree of Life to fulfill the hope of the Old Testament saints, who had waited for his advent (Prov. 13:12).

Acts 2:4 states that the saints, on the day of Pentecost, could receive the Holy Spirit, through whom all mankind might come to Jesus, the Tree of Life, and be joined with him. This would happen only after the distribution of the "tongues as of fire," that is, the sword of fire, which guards the way to the Tree of Life. In this way only are Christians spiritually joined with Jesus. Thus, no matter how devout their faith in Jesus, parents cannot but give birth to sinful children, who are required to undergo the redemption of sins. We know that even the most pious saints have not been able to remove the original sin; therefore, even they must transmit this sin to their children (cf. Part I, Ch. IV, Sec. I).

Therefore, Christ must come again on earth as the Tree of Life to carry out the providence of the redemption of mankind from original sin by grafting men into himself. This is the reason that the saints of the New Testament Age wait for the Tree of Life recorded in Revelation 22:14, which is, in fact, the Lord of the Second Advent.

We can understand that the purpose of God's providence of salvation is to restore the Tree of Life which was lost in the Garden of Eden (Gen. 2:9), to the Tree of Life mentioned in Revelation 22:14. Because of the fall, Adam could not attain the first Tree of Life. Therefore, Christ must come again as the last Adam (Rev. 22:13) in order to save fallen man. It is for this reason that Christ is called the "last Adam" (I Cor. 15:45).

(2) The Tree of the Knowledge of Good and Evil

God created Adam, and He also created Eve as Adam's spouse. Thus, when we find in the Garden of Eden a tree symbolizing manhood, we know there must be another tree symbolizing womanhood. The Tree of the Knowledge of Good and Evil, which was described as standing with the Tree of Life (Gen. 2:9), was thus the symbol of Eve.

The Bible refers to Jesus as the vine (John 15:5), or the olive tree (Rom. 11:17). Likewise, Adam and Eve are represented by two trees.

2. THE TRUE NATURE OF THE SERPENT

In the Bible we read that the serpent tempted Eve to sin (Gen. 3:4-5). What does this serpent signify? The answer is found by studying the true character of the serpent in the third chapter of Genesis.

The serpent described in the Bible could converse with man. Moreover, he caused the fall of man, who is a spiritual being. Therefore, the serpent also must have been a spiritual being. He knew God's intention to prohibit man from eating the fruit of the Tree of the Knowledge of Good and Evil. This tells us decisively that the serpent was spiritual.

In Revelation 12:9 we read further that the "great dragon was thrown down, that ancient serpent," who is called the devil by some, and Satan by others. This "ancient serpent" was the same one which tempted Adam and Eve in the Garden of Eden. This serpent is called the devil and Satan who, we know, has constantly directed the human mind toward evil. Therefore, Satan must be a spiritual being. If the devil is spiritual, the serpent symbolizing the devil also must be spiritual. So we are assured that the serpent which tempted the first man and the first woman was not an animal but was a spiritual being.

A question we must resolve, then, is whether the serpent existed before the time of the creation or was formed at the creation. If this serpent was a being in existence before creation with a purpose contrary to that of God, the struggle between good and evil in the world would be inevitable and eternal. God's providence of restoration, then, would come to naught; and monism, the belief that all things were created by one God, would be disproven. We cannot avoid the conclusion, therefore, that the spiritual being, likened to a serpent, was a being originally created for the purpose of goodness who later fell and was degraded to become Satan.

What kind of spiritual being could have conversed with man, known God's will, lived in heaven (the world of spirit), and could dominate the human soul, transcendent of time and space, even after this being's fall and degradation? There is no being endowed with such characteristics except an angel. The serpent, then, must have been a figurative term for an angel. We read in II Peter 2:4 that God did not spare the angels when they sinned but cast them into hell. So we must conclude that the true nature of the serpent, which tempted man to sin, was that of an angel.

The serpent's tongue is split in two. This symbolizes a man or being which utters two different things with one tongue, a being which lives a double life with one heart. The serpent is also the symbol of one who induces others to sacrifice themselves for his own benefit. The serpent twists its body around the prey, and then devours it. For these reasons, the Bible likened the angel which tempted man to a serpent.

3. THE FALL OF THE ANGEL AND THE FALL OF MAN

Now we know that the serpent which tempted man to fall was an angel, and that this angel, having fallen into sin, became Satan. Let us further investigate what kind of sin the angel and the man committed.

(1) The Crime of the Angel

Jude 1:6-7 reads:

And the angels that did not keep their own position but left their proper dwelling have been kept by him in eternal chains in the nether gloom until the judgment of the great day; just as Sodom and Gomorrah and the surrounding cities, which likewise acted immorally [committed fornication] and indulged in unnatural lust, serve as an example by undergoing a punishment of eternal fire.

From this we can reason that the angel fell as the result of an immoral act of unnatural lust, and that act was fornication.

Fornication is a crime which cannot be committed by one person alone. Therefore, we must know with whom the angel committed fornication in the Garden of Eden. In order to know that, let us first investigate what kind of crime was committed by man.

(2) The Crime of Man

In Genesis 2:25 we read that Adam and Eve were naked, and were not ashamed of their nakedness. But, after the fall, they became ashamed of their nakedness and sewed fig leaves together into aprons to cover their lower parts (Gen. 3:7). If they had committed sin by eating an actual fruit of a "tree of the knowledge of good and evil," they would have concealed their hands and mouths instead. It is the nature of man to conceal an area of transgression. They covered their sexual parts, clearly indicating that they were ashamed of the sexual areas of their bodies because they had sinned through them. From this we know that they committed sin through the sexual parts of their bodies.

In Job 31:33 it is written: "If I have concealed my transgressions from men, by hiding my iniquity in my bosom. . . ." Adam concealed his transgression by covering the sexual part of his body after the fall. This again indicates that the sexual part of Adam's body was the area of transgression. Thus we must conclude that Adam's sexual part became the place of transgression, because Adam committed sin through that part.

In the world before the fall of man, what act could man have performed at the risk of his life? It could be nothing else but an improper act of love. From the viewpoint of God's creation, love should be the most precious and holy act in the world. Nevertheless, men since the fall have often regarded the act of love as despicable, because love was the very cause of the human fall. This further demonstrates that man fell because of fornication.

(3) The Act of Adultery between the Angel and Man

Thus far, we have clarified the fact that man was tempted by an angel and fell. Both man and the angel fell because of fornication. In the world of creation, men and angels are the only spiritual beings capable of having a relationship of love. From the above, we can conclude that there must have been some act of adultery between man and the angel.

John 8:44 says, "You are of your father the devil, and your will is to do your father's desires." Again, Revelation 12:9 clarifies that the devil is Satan, and that Satan is the "ancient serpent" which tempted man. From these Biblical verses we can assert that man is the descendant of the devil and, naturally, the descendant of Satan; and thus, he is the descendant of the serpent. What were the circumstances surrounding the affair which made man the descendant of the fallen angel, Satan? These circumstances are related to the fact that adultery was committed between the first human ancestors and the angel. From this act, all men came to be born of Satanic lineage, apart from God's. In Romans 8:23, it says:

> ... we ourselves, who have the first fruits of the Spirit, groan inwardly as we wait for adoption as sons, the redemption of our bodies.

In Matthew 3:7, John the Baptist reproached the faithless people, calling them a "brood of vipers"—sons of Satan. Again, in Matthew 23:33 Jesus rebuked the Jews, saying, "You serpents, you brood of vipers, how are you to escape being sentenced to hell?"

From these Biblical references we can ascertain that there was an adulterous relationship between the angel and man, and this became the cause of the fall of man.

4. THE FRUIT OF THE TREE OF THE KNOWLEDGE OF GOOD AND EVIL

We have previously clarified the fact that the tree of the Knowledge of Good and Evil is Eve. What then does the fruit of the tree symbolize? It symbolizes Eve's love. Just as a fruit tree multiplies by the fruit which contains its seed, Eve should have multiplied children of goodness through her love centered on God. But instead, Eve multiplied children of evil through her love centered on Satan. Eve was created to become perfect through the period of growth; she could bear either good fruit or bad fruit through her love. Consequently, her love was called "the fruit of the Tree of the Knowledge of Good and Evil," while she herself was called "the Tree of the Knowledge of Good and Evil."

Then, what did the act of eating the fruit of the Tree of the Knowledge of Good and Evil signify? When we say we eat something, it means that we make it into our blood and flesh. Eve should have multiplied children of good lineage through her blood and flesh of goodness derived from the good "fruit" she ate in her love centered on God. Instead, she produced a sinful world by multiplying children of bad lineage through her blood and flesh of evil derived from the evil "fruit" she ate in her love centered on Satan. Accordingly, Eve's having eaten the fruit of the Tree of the Knowledge of Good and Evil signifies that she had a blood relationship with the angel (Satan) through her evil love centered on him.

Genesis 3:14 states that God cursed the fallen angel, saying he should go upon his belly and should eat dust all the days of his life. "Upon your belly you shall go" means that the angel becomes a miserable being, unable to function properly according to the original way of creation. To have to "eat dust" means that he has to live by receiving evil vitality elements from the sinful world, deprived of the right to have elements of life from

God, since he was thrown down from heaven (Is. 14:12, Rev. 12:9).

5. THE ROOT OF SIN

According to what has been elucidated by the Bible, we have come to understand that the root of sin is not that the first human ancestors ate a fruit, but that they had an illicit blood relationship with an angel symbolized by a serpent. Consequently, they could not multiply the good lineage of God, but rather multiplied the evil lineage of Satan.

Furthermore, there is another fact which demonstrates clearly that the root of man's sin stems from adultery. It is because the root of sin began by a blood relationship that the original sin is transmitted from generation to generation. Every religion which teaches how to eliminate sin has called adultery the greatest sin, and has emphasized an ascetic life in order to prevent it. This also demonstrates that the root of sin lies in adultery. The Israelites were circumcised as a condition of redemption to become God's elect, because the root of sin lay in having received evil blood because of adultery, and they wanted to sanctify themselves to make a condition that the evil blood be removed from their flesh as fallen men.

The principal cause of the downfall of numerous nations, national heroes and patriots, was adultery, because the urge to commit adultery, the root of sin, was always at work in the mind of man without his being conscious of it. We may be able to eradicate all other sins by elevating the ethics and the morality of man through religion, education, and improvement of the economic and social system. But in present conditions no one can prevent the crime of adultery, which has become increasingly prevalent as the development of civilization makes human life easier and more indolent. Therefore, we can never expect the ideal world to be established unless we can eradicate the source of this crime. Accordingly, the Lord of the Second Advent must be able to solve this problem completely. All these facts prove that the root of sin lies in adultery.

SECTION II
The Motivation and Process of the Fall

We have already clarified in Section I the fact that the serpent was an angel who caused Eve to fall. Since the motivation of the human fall lay within the angel, we must know something about the angel before we can really know the motivation and process of the fall.

1. THE CREATION OF THE ANGEL, HIS MISSION, AND HIS RELATIONSHIP TO MAN

All beings were created by God. The angels were no exception. God created the angelic world before anything else. Genesis 1:26 records the story of creation: "Let us make man in our image, after our likeness," putting the first person in the plural. This is not because He was speaking as a trinity, as many theologians have interpreted, but because He was speaking to the angels, who had been created before man (Gen. 1:26).

God created the angels as servants who were to assist in the creation of the universe, and in His dispensation for it (Heb. 1:14). The angels conveyed to Abraham the important words of blessing from God (Gen. 18:10), heralded Mary's conception of Christ (Matt. 1:20, Luke 1:31), and unchained Peter and led him out of prison (Acts 12:7-11). We can find numerous examples in the Bible of the angels working for God. In Revelation 22:9 the angel calls himself a "servant," while in Hebrews 1:14, angels are said to be "ministering spirits." Again, we may find in many Biblical verses solid proof of the angels having been created to honor and praise God (Rev. 5:11-12, 7:11-12).

Let us now investigate the relationship between man and angels, according to the principle of creation. Since God created men as His children, giving them dominion over all creation (Gen. 1:28), man was supposed to dominate the angels, too. I Corinthians 6:3 says that man has the authority to judge the angels. Many who communicate with the spirit world frequently see angels ministering to the saints in Paradise. This, too, is a good example illustrating that angels minister to men.

2. THE SPIRITUAL FALL AND THE PHYSICAL FALL

Since God created man in spirit and flesh, the fall also took place in spirit and flesh. The fall through the blood relationship between the angel and Eve was the spiritual fall, while that through the blood relationship between Eve and Adam was the physical fall.

How could there be a sexual relationship between the angel and man? Feelings and sensations are felt and responded to in the invisible, or spirit world. Contact between a spirit and an earthly man (who has a spirit) is not very different from contact between two earthly human beings. Therefore, sexual union between a human being and an angel is actually possible.

We can understand what has been said here even more clearly through the following stories. There are recorded instances in human society of an earthly man leading a married life with a spirit. There is the story of the angel who, in wrestling with Jacob, touched the hollow of his thigh and put it out of joint (Gen. 32:25). Still another story is about the angels who appeared in Abraham's home and ate the meat and other food he had prepared for them (Gen. 18:7-8), and the two angels visiting Lot who ate the unleavened bread he baked for them.

The men of the city, excited in sexual desire upon seeing them, surrounded the house and called to Lot, "Where are the men who came to you tonight? Bring them out to us, that we may know them." (Gen. 19:5) These incidents illustrate the possibility of contact between men and angels.

(1) Spiritual Fall

God created the angelic world (Gen. 1:26) and put Lucifer (signified by "Day Star, son of Dawn," Is. 14:12) in the position of archangel. Lucifer was in a position to monopolize God's love as the mediator between God and the angelic world, just as Abraham was the channel for God's blessing to the Israelites. However, God, after creating men as His children, loved them much more than He loved Lucifer, who had been created as His servant. In fact, Lucifer received the same amount of God's love as he had before the creation of man, but when he saw that God loved Adam and Eve more, he felt that God loved him less than before. This situation is similar to the Biblical story of the laborers who had begun working early in the morning; seeing that those who were hired late and worked little received the same wage as they, they felt underpaid, though they received the promised amount (Matt. 20:1-15). Lucifer, who felt a decrease of love, tried to tempt Eve to submit to him, in order that he might enjoy the same position in human society that he did in the angelic world. This was the motivation of the spiritual fall.

All things were created to receive God's dominion through love. Therefore, love is the source of life and the essence of happiness; love is the ideal of all creation. Accordingly, the more one receives God's love, the more beautiful he or she becomes. So it was very natural that Eve looked most beautiful in Lucifer's eyes. Moreover, when Eve was susceptible to his temptation, Lucifer was strongly stimulated by an impulse of love toward Eve. At this point, Lucifer dared to seduce Eve at the risk of his life. Lucifer, who left his position due to excessive desire, and Eve, who desired to have her eyes opened like God's through a sexual relationship before she was ready for it, thus formed a reciprocal base, and had sexual intercourse with each other through their give and take action (Gen. 3:5-6). Since the power of love derived from their give and take action was not based on the Principle, they fell into an illicit relationship of spiritual love.

According to the principle that men were created to exchange elements with the objective being with whom they have become one body through love, Eve received certain elements from Lucifer when she joined into one body with him through love. First, she received from Lucifer the sense of fear, which came from his guilty conscience because of their violation of the purpose of creation. Second, she received wisdom enabling her to perceive that her intended spouse in the original nature of creation was not Lucifer but Adam. At that time Eve was still in the period of immaturity. Therefore, she was immature in her wisdom compared to the archangel, who had already reached a certain level of maturity. Thus she received the wisdom of the archangel.

(2) Physical Fall

Adam and Eve should have become husband and wife, eternally centered on God, after their perfection. However, Eve joined with Adam after she had the illicit relationship with the archangel in her period of growth. Adam, too, fell in his growth period. The premature conjugal relationship thus established between Adam and Eve was centered on Satan and caused the physical fall.

As mentioned above, Eve obtained, from the spiritual fall with the archangel, the sense of fear arising from the pangs of her guilty conscience, and the wisdom to understand that her intended spouse was not the archangel but Adam. Eve then seduced Adam in the hope that she might rid herself of the fear derived from the fall and stand before God by becoming, even then, one body with Adam, who was meant to be her spouse. This was the motivation behind the physical fall.

Eve, having become one body with the archangel through their illicit sexual relationship, was in the position of the archangel to Adam. Therefore, Adam, whom God loved, looked very beautiful to her. Adam was Eve's only hope for returning to God. Feeling this, Eve tempted Adam, just as the archangel had tempted her. Adam and Eve formed a reciprocal base, and through their give and take action, the power of love drew them closer. This powerful love made Adam leave his original position and finally caused Eve and him to have an illicit sexual relationship.

Adam, by becoming one body with Eve, inherited all the elements Eve had received from Lucifer, in the same manner she did. These elements were then transmitted to their descendants. Despite Eve's fall, if Adam had reached perfection without forming a reciprocal base with the fallen Eve, he as the perfected subject would have remained intact, and the providence to restore Eve alone would have been much easier. However, Adam also fell, and mankind has multiplied in sin to the present day, thus perpetuating the lineage of Satan.

SECTION III
The Power of Love, the Power of the Principle, and God's Commandment

1. THE HUMAN FALL SEEN FROM THE VIEWPOINT OF THE POWER OF LOVE AND THE POWER OF THE PRINCIPLE

Man was created to live in accordance with the Principle. Therefore, it cannot be that the power of the Principle would cause the fall, and throw man off the track. We can compare this to a train which cannot run off the track by itself. For a train to run off the track, there must be a breakdown in the engine or the rail, or an external force stronger than its own running force must collide with it, coming from a different direction. Likewise, man can fall when a certain power, stronger than that of the Principle which makes him grow, and with a different purpose, collides with him. The power which is stronger than that of the Principle is nothing else but the power of love. Therefore, man, in an immature state, could fall because of the power of love, if it was not centered on the Principle.

Why, then, was the power of love stronger than the power of the Principle, such that man fell when he met with love headed for a different purpose?

According to the principle of creation, God's love is the subjective love, manifested through the four position foundation, which is established by having perfected the three objective purposes through the three objective loves. Therefore, love is the source of man's life and happiness, because without God's love the four position foundation, which is the purpose of man's creation, could never be established. God, through love, should have dominion over man, who is created through the Principle. Therefore, in order that love may have the greater value, the power of love must be stronger than that of the Principle. If the power of love were weaker than that of the Principle, God's love would not be able to dominate man, who was created through the Principle. Rather, man would be concerned with the Principle more than with God's love. This was the reason that Jesus wanted to raise his disciples with the truth and save them with love.

2. THE PURPOSE OF GOD'S GIVING MAN THE COMMANDMENT

What could have been the purpose of God's giving Adam and Eve the commandment not to eat the fruit? If Adam and Eve, who were not in God's direct dominion of love due to their immaturity, should enter into a reciprocal relationship with the archangel based on unprincipled love, they could fall, since the power of love was stronger than that of the Principle. But, however strong the power of the archangel's love was, if they had followed God's commandment without responding to the angel, performing the action of give and take with God alone, they could not have fallen. In that case, the power of unprincipled love could not have any effect. Since they formed a reciprocal base with the archangel and performed give and take action with him, against God's commandment, the power of illicit love made them deviate from the Principle.

It was not simply because He wanted to prevent him from falling that God gave such a commandment to man while he was yet immature. God also wanted man to enjoy dominion over all creation by having him inherit His creative nature. Thus, Adam and Eve should have perfected themselves through their faith in the Word, as their own portion of responsibility (cf. Part I, Ch. 1, Sec. V, 2[2]).

God gave this commandment not to the archangel but to man; He sought to exalt man's dignity and qualification in the principle of creation so that man might dominate even the archangel from the position of God's son.

3. THE PERIOD NECESSITATING THE COMMANDMENT

Would God's commandment not to eat of the fruit have been necessary forever? Seen from the viewpoint of love, the fulfillment of God's second blessing is that Adam and Eve enter into God's direct dominion through His love by becoming husband and wife, centering on God's love, and multiplying their children (Gen. 1:28). Therefore, man was created to be allowed, by the Principle, to eat the fruit after his perfection.

Since the power of love is stronger than that of the Principle, Adam and Eve could not have fallen if they had become husband and wife after their perfection, and entered into God's direct dominion through their absolute love. In this case, no man nor any other power could break the power of this absolute conjugal love. Moreover, the power of the archangel's love, which is supposed to be lesser and weaker than man's, could by no means have severed their reciprocal love centered on God. Therefore, God's commandment not to eat of the fruit would have been necessary for Adam and Eve only in the period of their immaturity.

SECTION IV
The Result of the Human Fall

What was the result brought about in the world of creation, including man and the archangel, by the spiritual and physical fall of Adam and Eve? Let us examine this important question.

1. SATAN AND FALLEN MAN

We have previously mentioned that Lucifer, the fallen archangel, was called Satan. Man fell, becoming Satan's child, because he formed the four position foundation centered on Satan, thus becoming one body with him through their blood relationship. Therefore, Jesus said that fallen men are of their father the devil (John 8:44), and on many occasions called them the brood of vipers, that is, sons of Satan (Matt. 3:7, 12:34, 23:33). Romans 8:23 says, ". . . not only the creation, but we ourselves, who have the first fruits of the Spirit, groan inwardly as we wait for adoption as sons . . ." This is because man could not inherit God's lineage, but inherited Satan's instead, due to the fall of the first human ancestors.

If Adam and Eve had established the four position foundation centered on God after having perfected themselves, the world under the sovereignty of God could have been established at that time. However, they fell in the period of immaturity, thus forming the four position foundation centered on Satan. Therefore, the world came under Satanic sovereignty. John 12:31 says that Satan is the "ruler of this world", while in II Corinthians 4:4 Satan is called the "god of this world." This is the manner in which Satan came to dominate man, who had been created to be the dominator of the whole creation, and thus came to dominate the creation as well. Therefore, Romans 8:19 says that the creation waits with eager longing for the revealing of the sons of God. This signifies that all creation, being now under the dominion of Satan while it should be dominated by perfected men, is anxious to repel Satan and to see the revealing of the men of the original nature of creation, who are entitled to dominate all creation in love.

2. SATAN'S ACTIVITIES IN HUMAN SOCIETY

Satan is constantly accusing men before God, just as he did with Job (Job 1:9-11), in order to put them into hell. However, even Satan cannot perform this kind of evil action without having an object with whom to form a reciprocal base for give and take action. The objects of Satan are the evil spirits in the spirit world. The objects of these evil spirits are the spirit men of evil men on earth. The objects of the spirits of evil men on earth are their own physical bodies. Therefore, Satanic power, conveyed by evil spirits, results in the evil physical activities of earthly men. Therefore, we read in Luke 22:3 that Satan entered into Judas Iscariot. Again in Matthew 16:23, Jesus called Peter

"Satan." In the Bible, evil spirit men are called "angels" of the devil (Matt. 25:41).

To restore the earthly Kingdom of Heaven (Part I, Ch. III, Sec. II) means to realize the world in which Satan can never act, by man's severing completely his reciprocal base with Satan and restoring his reciprocal base with God, thus entering into give and take action with Him. That God keeps Satan in a bottomless pit in the Latter Days signifies that Satan will be unable to act since he will have lost his object with which to work. In order for man to be able to cut off his reciprocal base with Satan and be rightfully able to judge him (I Cor. 6:3), he must know the true character of Satan's crime and accuse him before God. However, God, in creating angels and men, gave them freedom; and so He cannot restore them by force. Therefore, man should be able to make Satan come to a natural surrender by exalting the Word, through the accomplishment of his own portion of responsibility by his own volition, before he can be restored to the status of a man of the original nature of creation. The history of the providence of restoration has been prolonged for such a long time because God is developing His providence according to such principles.

3. GOOD AND EVIL SEEN FROM THE NATURE OF PURPOSE

We have already defined good and evil in the "Original Value of Creation" (Part I, Ch. 1, Sec. IV). Let us now investigate good and evil, seen from the nature of purpose. If Adam and Eve had established the four position foundation centered on God through the love with which they were originally endowed, they would have realized the world of goodness. But they realized a world of evil because they had established the four position foundation centered on Satan through their love which had a purpose contrary to goodness. Therefore, good and evil can result from the same action, but have a different direction and purpose. There are many examples illustrating that human nature, considered evil, would be good if it pursued the purpose of God's will. For instance, human desire or ambition, usually considered evil, is part of the original nature of creation endowed by God in the beginning. This is true because the purpose of creation was to obtain joy, and joy can be attained only when desire is fulfilled. If man had no desire or ambition, he could have no joy. If man had no desire or ambition, he would have no ambition to receive God's love, to want to live, to perform good deeds, nor to develop. In this way, neither God's purpose of creation nor the providence of restoration could be fulfilled. The maintenance and development of human society, too, would be impeded.

The original desire of man, being the original nature of creation, comes to realize goodness if it is fruitful for the purpose of God's will. On the contrary, if it is fruitful for the purpose of Satan's will, it results in evil. From this principle, it is self-evident that even the world of evil, when turned toward the purpose of goodness centered on Christ, will be restored to perfect goodness, thus realizing the Kingdom of God on earth (cf. Part I, Ch. III, Sec. II, 2). Accordingly, the providence of salvation is to change the direction of the fallen world, heading toward the purpose of Satan, to the direction of the Kingdom of Heaven on earth, in order to realize God's purpose of creation.

The standard of goodness upheld in the course of this providence is not absolute but relative. This is because, during a specific age, it may be considered good to follow the purpose of the sovereign's ideology, while it is considered evil to go against his purpose. But once the age and the sovereign change, bringing a different ideology, the purpose will also change, and with it the standard of good and evil. In any religion or ideology, it is "good" for the adherents to follow the purpose defined by the doctrine, while to go against it is "evil." But for those of a different religion or ideology, or those who change their beliefs, the standard of good and evil would naturally differ according to the difference in purpose.

The principal cause behind the conflicts and revolutions which constantly take place in human society is the change in the standard of good and evil which occurs, as the purpose sought by men varies. The standard of goodness in the course of restoration is thus not an absolute one but a relative one. However, when the sovereignty of Satan is expelled from the earth, and God, the eternal absolute Being transcendent of time and space, restores His sovereignty with His absolute ideology, the purpose determined by the ideology, and the resultant standard of goodness, will also be absolute. This will be the world of macrocosmic ideology which will be established by the Lord of the Second Advent. In fact, human history has been the struggle in pursuit of the absolute goodness of our original mind's desire, constantly undergoing conflicts and revolutions. Accordingly, the conflicts and revolutions which take place in human society will continue until the world of absolute goodness is established.

4. THE WORKS OF GOOD SPIRITS AND EVIL SPIRITS

"Good spirits" is the collective name for God, good spirit men on His side, and angels. What we call "evil spirits" are Satan and all the evil spirit men on his side. The works of good spirits and evil spirits, as in the case of good and evil, start at the same point in the same manner but are directed toward different purposes.

Those who are involved in the works of good spirits enjoy an increasing sense of peace and righteousness; even the physical health of the individuals will improve. The works of evil spirits make individuals feel an increasing sense of insecurity, fear and egoism, even hindering the physical health of the obsessed. Those who are ignorant of the Principle find it very hard to discern the good or evil of the spiritual works. With the lapse of time, the results will reveal the nature of the spirit. However, fallen men, situated halfway between good (God) and evil (Satan), may sometimes cooperate with the work of both good and evil spirits. In many cases, even the works of evil spirits may combine with the works of good spirits after a certain period. So it is very difficult for people who are ignorant of the Principle to discern between them. It is a pity that in this age, many ministers and other religious workers condemn, from ignorance, the works of good spirits as those of evil spirits, thus going against God's will without being aware of it. No one in the present day of such increasing spiritual phenomena can guide men in spiritual communication unless he can discern between the works of good spirits and evil spirits.

5. SIN

Sin is the act of violating the heavenly law by establishing a condition in which one forms a reciprocal base with Satan, and enters into the action of give and take with him. We can classify human sin into four kinds. First is man's "original sin," which is the sin derived from the spiritual and physical fall of the first human ancestors. Original sin is the root of all sins.

Second is man's "hereditary sin," which is the sin of the ancestors transmitted to the descendants through blood lineage. The Ten Commandments state that the sin of the parents will be conveyed through several generations (Ex. 20:5).

Third is the "collective sin." This is the sin for which everybody is collectively responsible, even though it is neither his own sin nor a hereditary sin. An example of this kind of sin is the crucifixion of Jesus. The chief priests and scribes of the people had Jesus crucified; therefore, all the Jews have undergone God's punishment, taking the responsibility as a whole. Likewise, all mankind has had to suffer and will bear common responsibility until the Second Advent of the Lord.

Fourth is the "individual sin," which everyone commits himself. As mentioned above, we call original sin the root of all sins. Hereditary sin corresponds to the trunk, while collective sin and individual sin correspond respectively to the branches and leaves of a tree. All sins come from original sin, which is the root of all sins. Therefore, man cannot fundamentally liquidate all sins without getting rid of original sin. However, no one has been able to uncover this root of sin. Only Christ, the True Parent who comes as the root of life, can uncover the root of sins and liquidate it.

6. THE ORIGINAL NATURE OF THE FALL

Eve inherited from the archangel all the characteristics that came about when the archangel committed a sexual act with Eve against God's will. Then Adam, who entered into a blood relationship with Eve—who in turn was in the position of the archangel to him—came to inherit the same characteristics. In this manner, these characteristics gave rise to the fallen nature of man. We call these the "original nature of the fall."

The basic motivation that thus caused the original nature of the fall lay in the jealousy the archangel felt toward Adam. How could there be any such thing as jealousy in the archangel, who had been created for the purpose of goodness? Originally, the archangel was endowed with wisdom and desire, as the original nature of creation. He could compare and discern that God's love toward men was greater than that toward himself. It was quite natural for him to entertain the hope of receiving greater love than anyone else because he possessed a spontaneous desire for the greatest love. Such a desire was automatically conducive to jealousy. Therefore, jealousy was a by-product of the original nature of creation, like the shadow of a thing produced by the light.

However, after perfection, man could never fall due to such incidental desire. He would not dare commit such a crime, because he would know that the torment he would experience in fear of self-destruction, after fulfilling such a desire, would be far greater than the momentary satisfaction he would enjoy by fulfilling it.

The world after the accomplishment of the purpose of creation should be a systematic society, resembling a man in its form, in which all men have an integrated relationship with one another. So, the harm which comes to an individual is felt by the whole. Therefore, the whole body would keep the individual members from destruction. Similarly, in the world in which the purpose of creation is fulfilled, any incidental desire occurring from the original nature of creation would be used for the development of human society; it could never cause man to fall.

We may roughly divide the original nature of the fall into four aspects. The first is the failure to take the standpoint of God in loving others. The motivation of the archangel's fall lay in his jealousy of Adam; he did not love him from the same standpoint as God. This led him to defile Eve. The nature by which a courtier feels jealous of a king's favorite, instead of loving him from the standpoint of the king, is another example of the original nature of the fall.

The second is to leave one's own position. Lucifer fell by leaving his position because of an unrighteous desire to enjoy the same position of love in human society as he did in the angelic world, and due to his attempt to receive more love from

God. Any act that is performed apart from one's own position and limit, out of an unrighteous desire, is without exception a manifestation of this original nature of the fall.

The third is to reverse the dominion. The angel who was supposed to be under the dominion of man, dominated Eve, reversing the principled order. And Eve, who was supposed to be under the dominion of Adam, dominated him instead. This resulted in the fall. Human society was thrown out of order by those who left their positions and reversed their dominions. This resulted because of the third original nature of the fall.

The fourth is to multiply the criminal act. If Eve had not multiplied her crime in Adam after her fall, Adam would have remained intact. To restore Eve alone would have been easy. However, Eve caused Adam to fall, multiplying her crime in him. The desire of evil men to induce their colleagues to commit crimes with them also comes from this original nature of the fall.

SECTION V
Freedom and the Fall

1. THE SIGNIFICANCE OF FREEDOM SEEN FROM THE VIEWPOINT OF THE PRINCIPLE

In discussing the nature of freedom in light of the Principle, we must first understand that there is no freedom apart from the Principle.

The word "freedom" expresses collectively both free will and free action which accompanies it. Because the former and the latter are in the relation of character and form, perfect freedom is only possible when these two are combined. Naturally, where there is no free will, there is no free action.

Free will not followed by free action cannot be perfected. Free action comes from free will, and free will is the manifestation of one's original mind. The minds of men of the original nature of creation cannot operate apart from the Principle, which is the Word of God. Therefore, there can be no free will apart from the Principle, and naturally no true free action can follow. We can conclude that, for men of the original nature of creation, there is no freedom whatsoever apart from the Principle.

Secondly, there is no freedom unaccompanied by responsibility. Man, created according to the Principle, is to perfect himself by accomplishing his portion of responsibility through his own free will (cf. Part I, Ch. 1, Sec. V, 2[2]). Accordingly, man, in pursuit of the purpose of creation, always tries to accomplish his responsibility according to his free will; therefore, there can be no freedom unaccompanied by responsibility.

Thirdly, there is no freedom without actual results. The purpose of man's attempt to accomplish his own portion of responsibility is to attain the purpose of creation, and thus bring about actual results by which he can make God happy. Accordingly, freedom always seeks actual results in the accomplishment of God's purpose of creation. There is no freedom whatsoever without actual results.

2. FREEDOM AND THE HUMAN FALL

As previously explained, freedom cannot exist apart from the Principle. Therefore, in accordance with the principle of creation, freedom is always accompanied by responsibility and it is always in pursuit of actual results to make God happy. Consequently, free acts according to free will should always result in goodness. Therefore, it cannot be that man would fall because of freedom. This is why in II Corinthians 3:17 it is stated, "The Lord is the Spirit, and where the Spirit of the Lord is, there is freedom." We call this kind of freedom "the freedom of the original mind."

Since Adam and Eve had been advised by God not to eat the fruit of the Tree of the Knowledge of Good and Evil, they should have kept the commandment in accordance with the freedom of their original mind, without God's intervention. When Eve was about to deviate from the Principle, the freedom of her original mind, seeking the actual results of goodness and responsibility in the Principle, apparently worked to keep her from going off the track by arousing a sense of insecurity and fear within her. Even after the fall, this freedom of the original mind surely worked to have man return to God. Therefore, man could not have fallen due to the freedom of the original mind. On the contrary, the human fall had its fundamental cause in the fact that the power of the non-principled love was stronger than the directive power of the freedom of the original mind. After all, man lost his freedom because of the fall. However, God can work His providence of restoring man's freedom because man, though fallen, still has a remainder of his original nature which seeks freedom in God. It is sound proof of man's progress toward restoring this freedom, long lost due to Satan, that, as time goes by, man's zeal for the pursuit of freedom grows, and he seeks it even at the risk of his life. Therefore, the purpose of man's search for freedom is to accomplish the purpose of creation by bringing about actual results, and to accomplish his responsibility in the Principle through his free action in accordance with his free will.

3. FREEDOM, THE FALL, AND RESTORATION

Angels were created to minister to men. Thus, men were free to deal with the angels. However, Eve, at the time of her temptation, was still immature both in wisdom and in heart. Thus, when Eve was blinded in wisdom (knowledge) and confused in heart (feeling) by the temptation of the angel, she was forced to go beyond the line of fall even though she felt anxiety due to the freedom of her original mind, which was in pursuit of actual results and responsibility. This is because the power of love with the angel was stronger than the freedom of her original mind. However free Eve may have been to deal with the angel, she should have believed in God's commandment not to eat the fruit, thus restraining herself from responding to the temptation of the angel. Had Eve restrained herself, she would not have fallen. In that case, the power of the non-principled love with the angel could not have been generated. Despite the fact that freedom allowed Eve to respond to the angel, leading her to the line of fall, it was by no means freedom but the power of non-principled love that made her overstep the line of fall.

Since man was created to deal with the angels in freedom, Eve came to deal with Lucifer. By Eve's performing give and take action with him on a reciprocal base, they fell into non-principled love, and the power of this love caused them to fall. On the contrary, fallen man can also stand in the objective position to God in freedom. Therefore, if man performs the action of give and take with God on a reciprocal base according to the truth, he can restore the original nature of creation by the power of principled love. Man came to cry for freedom because of the directional nature of the freedom of his original mind, which seeks to restore the original nature of creation.

Man, due to the fall, became ignorant of God and of His heart. Therefore, human will, due to this ignorance, could not take a direction with which God could be pleased. However, in fallen man the "heart-and-zeal" for the freedom of the original mind directed toward the purpose of creation has been renewed, as spirit (internal knowledge) and truth (external knowledge) have developed according to the age in the providence of restoration. Subsequently, man's heart-and-zeal toward God has also been restored, heightening his desire to live in accordance with God's will.

As man's volition for the restoration of freedom is cultivated, he naturally seeks to create the social circumstances in which he can realize freedom. Social revolution is unavoidable when the circumstances of the age cannot satisfy the desires of the men belonging to the age. The French Revolution in the 18th century is a representative example. Revolution will continue until the freedom of the original nature of creation is restored completely.

SECTION VI
The Reason God Did Not Interfere with the First Human Ancestors' Fallen Act

God, being omniscient and omnipotent, foresaw the possibility of the fallen act of the first human ancestors. He did not lack the power to prevent Adam and Eve from committing the act. Why, then, did God not intervene to prevent the act of the fall when He foresaw it? This is one of the most important questions, but has been left unsolved throughout human history. We can give the following three points as the reasons God did not interfere with man's fallen act.

1. FOR THE SAKE OF THE ABSOLUTENESS AND PERFECTION OF THE PRINCIPLE OF CREATION

According to the principle of creation, God created man so that, by inheriting His creative nature, man might dominate all things even as God dominates mankind. However, man must perfect himself by accomplishing his portion of responsibility in order to inherit God's creative nature. We call this period of growth the "sphere of indirect dominion," or the "sphere of dominion over the result of the Principle." While men are in this sphere, God does not dominate them; instead, He seeks to have them fulfill their portion of responsibility. God is to dominate men directly only after their perfection. If God should interfere with their acts during the growth period, it would amount to God's ignoring man's portion of responsibility. In that case, God Himself would be ignoring the principle of creation, in which He exalts man as the dominator of all things by giving him a creative nature. If the Principle should be ignored, the absoluteness and perfection of the Principle would be lost. Since God is the Creator, both absolute and perfect, the principle of creation which He set forth should also be absolute and perfect. Therefore, God could not interfere with the act of the fall while men were in the period of growth, for the sake of the absoluteness and perfection of the principle of creation.

2. IN ORDER THAT GOD ALONE BE THE CREATOR

God intervenes with beings or acts only within the Principle, but He does not interfere with beings or acts outside the Principle and thus not of His creation. Therefore, if God interferes with any such being or act, that being or act becomes recognized as part of the Principle.

When viewed from this standpoint, if God had intervened in the fallen act of the first human ancestors, it would have meant that even the act of the fall would have been given the value of creation, and that this sinful act would have been recognized as part of the Principle. If so, it would have caused God to set up a new principle which would have called for His recognizing the sinful act as an act of the Principle. Since Satan initiated this process, this means that Satan would have created a new principle, making himself a creator along with God. In order that God alone be the Creator, He could not interfere with the act of the fall.

3. IN ORDER TO SET UP MAN AS THE DOMINATOR OF ALL THINGS

God created man and blessed him, and set him up to be the dominator of all things (Gen. 1:28). In order for man to dominate all things as God desired, he should have possessed certain qualifications as a lord because he could only dominate others from a position superior to theirs.

Just as God was qualified to dominate all men because He was the Creator, man had to have the creativity of God in order to be qualified as the dominator of all things. Therefore, God made man to perfect himself by accomplishing his own portion of responsibility through the period of his growth, in order to qualify him as the dominator of all things. Therefore, man should possess the qualities of dominion that can be obtained only by perfecting himself through such a course in the Principle, before he can dominate all things. If God directly dominated and interfered with man in the period of his immaturity, it would result in making him the dominator of all things when he was not yet qualified to be a dominator, for he did not have the creativity of God, and had not accomplished his portion of responsibility. It would be a contradiction to deal with an immature man and a perfect man on an equal basis. More than that, this would ignore the principle of creation, which He set up in order to make man dominator of all things by giving him even His power of creativity. Therefore, God, who made the world according to the Principle, could not interfere with the act of the fall of the immature man, who was still in the sphere of indirect dominion, in order that He could later set man up in the position of dominator over all things.

CHAPTER III

Consummation of Human History

Man has lived through all the centuries without knowing in what manner human history started and where its goal lies. We remain ignorant of the problems concerning the consummation of human history.

Many Christians believe literally what is written in the Bible, in which it is stated that in the Last Days the heavens will be kindled and dissolved and the elements will melt with fire (II Peter 3:12); that the sun will be darkened and the moon will not give its light and the stars will fall from heaven (Matt. 24:29); and that with the archangel's call and with the sound of the trumpet of God, the dead in Christ will rise first, and those who are alive and remain shall be caught up together with them in the clouds to meet the Lord in the air (I Thess. 4:16-17).

It is one of the most important problems for Christians to decide whether everything will be realized literally, as the Bible says, or whether it has been stated in symbolic terms, as has proven to be the case in many parts of the Bible. In order to solve this problem, we should first answer certain questions about God's purpose for creating all things, the significance of the human fall, and the purpose of the providence of salvation.

SECTION I
The Fulfillment of God's Purpose of Creation and the Fall of Man

1. THE FULFILLMENT OF GOD'S PURPOSE OF CREATION

As has been discussed in the "Principle of Creation," God's purpose in creating man was to feel joy upon seeing His goal realized. Therefore, the purpose of man's life is to return joy to God. In what manner, then, can man return joy to God and manifest perfectly the original value of his existence?

All creation was created to be the object of God's joy. However, man, as has been clarified in the "Principle of Creation," was created to be the substantial object to God, returning joy to Him through the action of his own free will. Therefore, man cannot become the object of God's joy unless he knows God's will and lives according to it by his own effort. Consequently, man was created in such a way that he could know God's will and live by it forever, experiencing God's heart-and-zeal as his own. We may call this status of man the "perfection of individuality." Adam, Eve, and many prophets and saints have been able to communicate with God directly because man was created to enjoy such capabilities.

The relationship between God and a man of perfected individuality can be compared to that between our mind and body. Our body, as the temple of our mind, obeys the command of our mind and acts upon it. Since God abides in the mind of a man of perfected individuality, such a man will become God's temple and live according to God's will. A man of perfected individuality becomes one body in unity with God, just as our mind does with our body. Therefore, I Corinthians 3:16 says, "Do you not know that you are God's temple and that God's spirit dwells in you?" and John 14:20 says, "In that day you will know that I am in my Father and you in me, and I in you." The man who has attained one body with God, having His spirit dwell in him by perfecting his individuality and thus forming a temple of God, comes to have deity and can by no means commit sin; naturally, he cannot fall. A man of perfected individuality is a man of perfect goodness.

If a man of perfect goodness should fall, this would mean that goodness itself has the potentiality of ruin; this is impossible. Moreover, if a man created by the omnipotent God should fall after his perfection, we would have to deny God's omnipotence. Therefore, a man of perfected individuality could never fall, because, being the object of joy to God, who is the eternal subject of absoluteness, man should likewise possess absoluteness and perpetuity.

If Adam and Eve of perfected individuality, incapable of sin, had established a home and society without sin by multiplying children of goodness according to God's blessing, (Gen. 1:28), this would have been the Kingdom of Heaven, which would have been realized as a huge family centered on the same parents. The Kingdom of Heaven is in the form of a man of perfected individuality. Just as the members of man's body work in a horizontal relationship with one another according to the vertical command of the brain, so society should be organized so that men may live in a horizontal relationship with one another according to the vertical command of God. In such a society people could not perform any act which would hurt their neighbors, because the whole society would experience the same feeling toward those in trouble as God would feel in His grief over them.

Regardless of how pure and sinless the men of this society might be, if they had to live in an undeveloped civilization similar to that of primitive people, this would not be the kind of Kingdom of Heaven both God and man have long awaited. Since God blessed man to be the dominator of all things (Gen. 1:28), men of perfected individuality should have subdued the natural world through highly developed science, and established an extremely pleasant social environment on earth. This would be the place where the ideal of creation would be realized. It would be nothing other than the Kingdom of Heaven on earth.

When perfected man, after having lived in the Kingdom of Heaven on earth, goes to the spirit world, the Kingdom of Heaven will be realized in the spirit world. Therefore, God's purpose of creation is to establish the Kingdom of Heaven on earth.

2. THE FALL OF MAN

As stated in the "Principle of Creation," man fell while he was in his immaturity and still in the period of growth. Questions as to why the growth period was necessary for man and why the first human ancestors fell during their immaturity were answered in that chapter.

Man, due to his fall, could not become the temple of God; instead, he became the dwelling place of Satan and became one body with him. Naturally, man came to have an evil nature in place of deity. So it has come about that men of evil nature have established evil homes, societies, and an evil world, by multiplying children of evil. This is the Hell on earth in which fallen men have been living. Men in Hell have not been able to establish good horizontal relationships with each other because their vertical relationship with God was cut off. Accordingly, they came to indulge themselves in acts which injure their neighbors, because they could not experience the pains and troubles of their neighbors as their own.

Men who live in Hell on earth transmigrate into Hell in the spirit world after they leave their physical bodies. In this manner, man established the world of Satan's sovereignty instead of the world of God's sovereignty. Thus we call Satan the "ruler of this world" (John 12:31) or the "god of this world." (II Cor. 4:4)

SECTION II
The Providence of Salvation

1. THE PROVIDENCE OF SALVATION IS THE PROVIDENCE OF RESTORATION

This sinful world brings man sorrow and causes God to grieve (Gen. 6:6). Would God, then, leave this world of grief as it is? If the world of goodness, which God created for the utmost joy, is to continue forever as a world of sin full of grief due to the human fall, God should be called a God of failure and inability. Therefore, God will save this world of sin by all means.

To what extent should God save this world? First, God must save it to such an extent that man can be restored to the position he had reached before the fall of the first human ancestors. God must do this by completely driving out the evil power of Satan from this world of sin (Acts 26:18). Then, God must develop His providence to such an extent that He can dominate the world directly through the fulfillment of the good purpose of creation (Acts 3:21).

To save a sick man is to restore him to the status he had before the sickness occurred. To save a drowning man is to restore him to the state he was in before he began to drown. Likewise, to save a man fallen in sin means to restore him to the original sinless position which he enjoyed in the beginning. Therefore, God's "providence of salvation" is the "providence of restoration." (Acts 1:6, Matt. 17:11)

The human fall is, of course, the result of man's own error. However, God, too, is responsible for the result, as the Creator. If God had not created man, the fall would not have occurred. Therefore, God has felt compelled to restore the result of man's error to its original status before the fall. God is the everlasting subject. Therefore, the life of man, who was created as His eternal object of joy, should also have eternity. According to the principle of creation, God created man for eternity. Even though man fell, God cannot annihilate him, because this would nullify the principle of creation. Therefore, God must save man and restore him to his original position in creation.

God promised to realize His three great blessings after the creation of man (Gen. 1:28). He says in Isaiah 46:11, "I have spoken, and I will bring it to pass; I have purposed, and I will do it." According to His own words, God has been working to fulfill His promise by developing the providence of restoring these blessings, long lost due to Satan. When Jesus said to his disciples in Matthew 5:48, "You, therefore, must be perfect, as your heavenly Father is perfect," he meant that they should be restored to the position of the original man of creation. Seen from the principle of creation, the original man of creation should be as perfect as God, having eternal deity because of his oneness with God.

2. THE PURPOSE OF THE PROVIDENCE OF RESTORATION

What is the purpose of the providence of restoration? It is to realize the Heavenly Kingdom, God's eternal object of goodness, which was His original purpose of creation. In the beginning, God created men on earth and intended to realize the Kingdom of Heaven on earth centering on them. However, He could not fulfill His will because of the human fall. Therefore, the primary purpose of the providence of restoration can only be to restore the Kingdom of Heaven on earth. Jesus, who came in order to fulfill the purpose of the providence of restoration, told his disciples to pray that God's will be done on earth as it is in Heaven (Matt. 6:10), and warned his people to repent, for the Kingdom of Heaven was at hand (Matt. 4:17), because the purpose of the providence of restoration is to restore the Kingdom of Heaven on earth.

3. HUMAN HISTORY IS THE HISTORY OF THE PROVIDENCE OF RESTORATION

We have previously clarified that God's providence of salvation is the providence of restoration. Therefore, human history is the period of the providence through which God intends to save fallen men and have them restore the original world of goodness. Let us now study, from various standpoints, the fact that human history is the history of the providence of restoration.

Firstly, we will consider human history from the standpoint of the history of the development of cultural spheres. In all ages and countries, even evil men have had in common the original mind's desire to follow goodness, by repelling evil. Therefore, all entertain the identical fundamental purpose of pursuing and realizing goodness, though it is true that they have created a history of struggle through constant conflicts which arise from differences, according to time and place, in their respective standards of goodness and its attainment.

Why, then, does the original mind of man direct itself irresistibly toward goodness? This is because God, the subject of goodness, created man as His substantial object in order to realize the purpose of goodness. Therefore, man's original mind seeks goodness, even though fallen men have been unable to lead good lives, due to Satan's work. The goal of the history which is woven by such men should be to attain the world of goodness.

However hard the original mind of man may struggle to attain goodness, man fails to find real goodness in this world under the rule of Satan. Therefore, man has come to find his subject of goodness in the world transcendent of time and space. What has been born out of this inevitable demand of man is religion. Man, who fell into ignorance of God due to the fall, has always tried to meet God by constantly pursuing goodness through religion. Even though individuals, races or nations of a certain religion may have perished, religion itself has survived up to the present. Let us now study these historical facts, centering on the history of the rise and fall of nations.

When we examine the history of China, we find that each age of Ch'un Ch'iu was followed by a unified age of Ch'in; while the age of Ch'ien Han, Shin, Hou Han, San Kuo, Si Tsin, Tung Tsin and Nan Pei Ch'ao were followed by the unified age of Sui and T'ang; and the ages of the Five Dynasties (Pei Sung, Nan Sung, Yuan, Ming and Ch'ing) were followed by today's Republic of China. Through all these ages China has seen the rise and fall of many nations and with this many changes in political power, but the three Far Eastern religions of Confucianism, Buddhism, and Sun-Kyo are still in full force.

When we study the history of India, we see that the Mauryas empire was followed by that of Andhra, which was followed in turn by those of Gupta, Barudanah, Sahman, Razuni, Maghal, and today's India. Though the nation suffered many changes through all these ages, Hinduism survived. Again, when we observe the history of the Middle East, we see that the Empire of Saracen was followed by East and West Karif, which in turn was followed by Seljuk Turkey and Osman Turkey, with their political powers ever changing. Nevertheless, the religion of Islam has continued to exist.

Further, let us examine the main current of Western history. The leadership of the Western world was held in turn by Greece, Rome, Gaul, Spain and Portugal. Then, temporarily held by France and The Netherlands, it was taken by Britain, and is currently divided between the United States and the Soviet Union. Nevertheless, Christianity has continued to flourish. Even in the Soviet Union, under the tyranny established on the foundation of materialism, Christianity has survived.

By examining the rise and fall of nations from this standpoint, we can also see that those powers which persecuted religion all perished while those that protected and fostered religion prospered. We have witnessed in history that the central role has moved from one nation to another, in each case shifting to a country that elevated religion more than did the previous one. Thus, the history of religion teaches us that the day will come, without fail, when the world of communism, which persecutes religion, will perish.

Many religions have existed in human history. Among them, the religions with the greatest influence inevitably formed cultural spheres, 21 to 26 in number. However, with the flow of history, the inferior has either been absorbed into the superior, or has united with it by degrees. In recent years, there have emerged from the rise and fall of nations four great cultural spheres—East Asia (Confucianism, Buddhism), Hinduism, Islam, (Mohammedanism), and Christianity. They are now being formed into a worldwide cultural sphere, centering on Christianity. Therefore, we may perceive from this historical trend that Christianity has, as its ultimate mission, the accomplishment of the purpose of all religions that have directed their course toward the goal of goodness. The history of the development of cultural spheres shows us a trend toward forming a worldwide cultural sphere, centering on one religion, through the unification of numerous religions. This is proof that human history is leading toward the restoration of one unified world.

The second way we can understand that human history is the history of the providence of restoration is by examining the common trend of religion and science. It was already stated in the "General Introduction" that religion and science, working respectively to overcome the two aspects of human ignorance since the fall, should be unified today. Religion and science, which have developed individually without mutual connection, are now forced to meet at one place after having progressed respectively toward the same goal. This tells us clearly that human history has followed the providential course of restoring the original world of creation. Had it not been for the fall, the intellectual capacity of man would have developed to the utmost degree in spirit (internal truth), thus naturally encouraging a corresponding degree of external development through science. Science then would have advanced very quickly, bringing about today's level of scientific development in the days of our early human ancestors.

However, due to the fall, man fell into ignorance without being able to attain a highly developed society. Since then, he has striven to restore the ideal world of scientific development which was purposed in the beginning, by overcoming his ignorance by means of science. Today's highly developed scientific world is being restored externally to the stage directly prior to the transition into the ideal world.

The third way we can perceive that human history is the history of the providence of restoration is from the trend of the history of struggles. Battles over wealth, land and people have accompanied the development of human society throughout history, up to the present moment. This struggle has widened its scope, expanding from the family to the tribe, and on to the societal, national, and finally to the worldwide level. The two worlds of democracy and communism are now confronted with a final ideological war. At the close of the sinful history of mankind, nations will have passed through the historical stage in which people thought they could derive happiness from the wealth, land and people they had plundered. After World War I we saw the defeated nations forced to release their colonies, but after World War II the victorious nations voluntarily released their colonies and set them free. The great powers of today have allowed minor powers, often even smaller and weaker than a city within the great powers, to become member states of the United Nations. The great powers have made them brother nations not only by supplying them with food, but also by giving them rights and duties equal to those of the great powers.

What, then, will the final struggle be like? It will be a struggle between ideologies. However, the struggle between the two worlds of democracy and communism will never cease unless the ultimate truth appears, which can overcome completely the materialistic view of history that threatens the world today. When this ultimate truth that can solve the problems of religion and science as one unified theme appears, the communist ideology, which has hitherto attempted to develop by science alone, denying religion, will be overcome. Thus, the two worlds will finally be unified completely under one ideology. Thus, seen from the trend of the history of human struggles, we cannot deny the fact that human history is the providential history of restoring the original world of creation.

The fourth way we can look into this question centers on the Bible. The purpose of human history is to restore the Garden of Eden with the Tree of Life in the center (Gen. 2:9; cf. Part I, Ch. II, Sec. I, 1). The "Garden of Eden" does not mean the limited area in which Adam and Eve were created, but the whole earth. If the Garden of Eden were the limited region where the first human ancestors were created, how would it be possible for the countless numbers of mankind to live in such a small place? An extremely large number of people would be necessary in order to fill the earth according to God's blessing to man (Gen. 1:28).

Due to the fall of the first human ancestors, this earthly Garden of Eden, which God intended to establish with the Tree of Life in the center, fell into the hands of Satan (Gen. 3:24). Therefore, when the sinful history of mankind that began in Alpha concludes in Omega, the hope and glory of fallen men will be for them to wash their robes and enter the restored Garden of Eden, and thus restore their right to the Tree of Life (Rev. 22:13-14). What, then, do these Bible verses signify?

As was clarified in the "Fall of Man," the Tree of Life signifies the perfected Adam, who was intended to be the True Father of mankind. Due to the fall of the first human parents, their descendants were born with original sin; therefore, in order that these children of sin may be restored as original men of creation, all men must be reborn, as Jesus said (cf. Part I, Ch. VII, Sec. IV, 1). Therefore, history is man's search for the True Father who is to give new life to mankind; namely, Christ. The Tree of Life mentioned in Revelation as the one which the saints of the Last Days are to find means none other than Christ, the Savior. From these Biblical records, we know that the purpose of human history is to restore the Garden of Eden in its original form, centered on Christ, who is to come as the Tree of Life.

In Revelation 21:1 we also read that at the close of the age a new heaven and a new earth will appear, signifying that the old heaven and earth which have been under Satanic dominion are to be restored as the new heaven and earth under the dominion of Christ, centered on God. Also, Romans 8:19-22 says that the whole creation groaning under Satanic dominion waits in travail for the revealing of the sons of God with the original nature of creation. They will be well qualified to dominate all creation, in order that it be made new (Rev. 21:5) by being restored to the original position of creation, rather than perishing by fire in the Last Days.

Considered from these standpoints, we can perceive quite clearly that human history is the history of God's providence to restore the original world of creation.

SECTION III
The Last Days

1. MEANING OF THE LAST DAYS

We have already stated that the three great blessings God granted our human ancestors were not realized centering on God, due to the fall of man. Instead they were realized centering on Satan in the non-principled realm. Human history, though it started in evil, is in fact the providential history of restoration through which God has been working. So the sinful world under Satanic dominion will be transformed into the world of good sovereignty, once the three great blessings centered on God are fulfilled.

The age in which the sinful world under Satanic sovereignty is transformed into the ideal world of creation under God's sovereignty is called the "Last Days." In other words, the "Last

Days" means the age in which Hell on earth is transformed into the Kingdom of Heaven on earth. Therefore, this will not be a day of fear in which many natural calamities will take place, as Christians up to the present have believed, but a day of joy when the unique hope of mankind, held firmly throughout the long course of history since the creation of the world, will be realized. Since the human fall, God has continued His providence to liquidate the world of sin and restore the world of goodness having the original nature of creation. (Details will be discussed in Part II, Ch. I.) Nevertheless, in each case, man failed to carry out his portion of responsibility, thus frustrating the realization of God's will. As a consequence, the Bible apparently indicates that there have been many Last Days.

(1) Noah's Day Was the Last Days

Genesis 6:13 states, "I have determined to make an end of all flesh; for the earth is filled with violence through them; behold, I will destroy them with the earth," thus indicating that Noah's day was the Last Days.

Why can Noah's day be called the Last Days? God was going to destroy the corrupt world centered on Satan with the flood judgment after the sinful history of 1,600 years, leaving only Noah's family, who believed in God. On the basis of Noah's faith, God intended to restore the ideal world of His sovereignty. Therefore, Noah's day can be called the Last Days (cf. Part II, Ch. I, Sec. II). Due to the corrupt act of Ham (Gen. 9:22), Noah's second son, God's will was nullified, because Noah's family failed to carry out its portion of responsibility on behalf of all mankind.

(2) Jesus' Day Was the Last Days

God's predestination for His will to attain the purpose of the providence of restoration is an absolute one, which cannot be changed (cf. Part I, Ch. VI). Therefore, even though His providence of restoration centering on Noah was not accomplished, God called other prophets to lay the foundation of faith. He sent Jesus to destroy the sinful world centered on Satan and restore the ideal world centered on God. So, Jesus' day was also the Last Days. That is why Jesus said that he came as the master of judgment (John 5:22). This is also why Malachi prophesied:

> Behold, the day comes, burning like an oven, when all the arrogant and all evildoers will be stubble; the day that comes shall burn them up . . . so that it will leave them neither root nor branch. (Mal. 4:1)

Jesus came to restore the ideal world in the form intended at the creation. However, due to the disbelief of the faithless people, man's portion of responsibility was left unaccomplished, prolonging the fulfillment of God's will until the time of the Lord's Second Advent.

(3) The Day of the Lord's Second Advent Is also the Last Days

Jesus was ultimately crucified, thus accomplishing only spiritual salvation. He is to attain the purpose of the providence of salvation both in spirit and body after the Second Advent (cf. Part I, Ch. IV, Sec. I, 4), fulfilling the restoration of the Kingdom of God on earth. Naturally, the day of the Lord's Second Advent would also be the Last Days. This is why Jesus said that, "As it was in the days of Noah, so will it be in the days of the Son of man" (Luke 17:26), and also that there would be many natural calamities at the time of the Second Advent (Matt. 24:29).

2. BIBLICAL VERSES CONCERNING THE SIGNS OF THE LAST DAYS

Many Christians believe that in the Last Days various natural calamities and radical changes beyond the imagination of modern men will occur in human society, as the Biblical verses literally say. However, if we understand that human history is the providential history to restore the world to the original form intended by God at the creation, then we know that the signs of the Last Days will not literally take place. Let us examine what is symbolized by the Biblical records which concern the Last Days.

(1) Heaven and Earth Destroyed (II Peter 3:12, Gen. 6:13) and a New Heaven and a New Earth Created (Rev. 21:1, II Peter 3:13, Is. 66:22)

Genesis 6:13 says that God wanted to destroy the earth because it was filled with violence and corruption in the Last Days. However, He did not actually destroy the world. We know that the earth is eternal from Biblical verses such as Ecclesiastes 1:4, which says, "A generation goes, and a generation comes, but the earth remains forever," and Psalms 78:69, which says, "He built His sanctuary like the high heavens, like the earth, which He has founded forever." God, the subject, is eternal; therefore, His objects should also be eternal. Naturally, the earth, which was created as the object of God, should be eternal.

God, omnipotent and omniscient, could not have felt joy over His creation if He had made it with the possibility of its being destroyed by Satan. To what can we compare this? To destroy a nation means to overthrow the sovereignty, while to erect a new nation (Rev. 21:1) is to establish a nation of new sovereignty. Consequently, to destroy heaven and earth means to overthrow the sovereignty of Satan, who is dominating them; and to found a new heaven and a new earth means to restore the new heaven and earth under the sovereignty of God (Rev. 21:1).

(2) Heaven and Earth Judged by Fire (II Peter 3:12)

II Peter 3:12 says that in the Last Days "the heavens will be kindled and dissolved and the elements will melt with fire!" In

Malachi 4:1 it is prophesied that, in Jesus' day, he will come as the master of judgment (John 5:22, 9:39) and will judge with fire. In Luke 12:49, Jesus said he came to cast fire upon the earth. Nevertheless, we cannot find any signs of his judgment with literal fire at that time. This, then, must be figurative speech. James 3:6 says, "the tongue is a fire." Accordingly, we understand that judgment by fire is judgment by the tongue, which naturally means judgment by the Word. Thus judgment by fire is judgment by the Word.

Let us then look up the Biblical verses concerning judgment by the Word. John 12:48 says that he who rejects Jesus and does not receive his sayings has a judge, and the Word that Jesus has spoken will be his judge on the Last Day. II Thessalonians 2:8 says that the lawless one will be revealed, and the Lord Jesus will slay him with the "breath of his mouth"; that is, his Word. Further, Isaiah 11:4 reads, ". . . and he shall smite the earth with the rod of his mouth [tongue], and with the breath of his lips [words] he shall slay the wicked"; while John 5:24 says, "he who hears my word and believes Him who sent me, has eternal life; he does not come into judgment, but has passed from death to life." Thus, judgment by fire signifies judgment by the Word.

What must be the reason, then, for judgment by the Word? John 1:3 states that man was created by the Word. Consequently, God's purpose of creation was that the first man should have accomplished the purpose of the Word by becoming the incarnation of the Word; but he fell without keeping the Word of God, thus leaving the purpose of the Word unaccomplished.

Therefore, God attempted again to fulfill the purpose of the Word by re-creating fallen men according to the Word; this is the providence of restoration by the Word of truth (Bible). John 1:14 says, "The Word became flesh and dwelt among us, full of grace and truth; we have beheld his glory, glory as of the only Son from the Father." Thus, Christ will come again as the incarnation of the Word. By becoming the standard of judgment by the Word, he will judge to what extent mankind has fulfilled the purpose of the Word. The purpose of the providence of restoration will be accomplished with the fulfillment of the purpose of the Word, so judgment should be done with the Word as the standard and measure. In Luke 12:49 Jesus said, "I came to cast fire upon the earth; and would that it were already kindled!" He had come as the incarnation of the Word (John 1:14), proclaiming the Word of life.

(3) The Dead Rise from Their Tombs (Matt. 27:52, I Thess. 4:16)

In Matthew 27:52-53, it says that when Jesus died:

> The tombs also were opened, and many bodies of the saints who had fallen asleep were raised, and coming out of the tombs after his resurrection they went into the holy city and appeared to many.

This does not mean that their flesh literally rose from corruption (cf. Part I, Ch. V, Sec. II, 3). If the saints of the Old Testament Age living in the spirit world had literally risen and, coming out of the tombs, had gone into the city and appeared to many people, they would surely have testified to the Jewish people about Jesus, because they knew that Jesus was the Messiah. If this had happened, even though Jesus had already been crucified, then no one, upon hearing these testimonies, could have failed to believe in Jesus. If the saints of the Old Testament Age had thus been raised from the tombs, again assuming their flesh, their deeds should have been recorded in the Bible. However, there are no such records in the Bible.

Then, what is the meaning of "rising from the tombs"? This is a record of spirit men of the Old Testament Age being resurrected and appearing on earth in spirit (cf. Part I, Ch. V, Sec. II, 3), just as the spirits of Moses and Elijah appeared to Jesus on the Mount of Transfiguration (Matt. 17:3).

Then what does "tomb" signify? The realm of form spirits, which was the dwelling of the Old Testament Age saints, was a darker place than Paradise, which was opened by Jesus. This form-spirit realm was called a "tomb." The spirit men of the Old Testament Age staying in this region of the spirit world appeared to the earthly saints.

(4) Earthly Men Caught Up to Meet the Lord in the Air (I Thess. 4:17)

The "air" mentioned here does not mean the sky. In the Bible, "earth" generally means the fallen world of evil sovereignty, while "heaven" means the sinless world of good sovereignty. Our understanding is increased when we read the Biblical verse which says, "Our Father who art in heaven" (Matt. 6:9), though God is omnipresent. Also, we find, ". . . but he who descended from heaven, the Son of man" (John 3:13), even though Jesus was born on earth.

Thus, "to meet the Lord in the air" signifies that the saints will receive the Lord in the world of good sovereignty when Christ comes again and restores the Kingdom of Heaven on earth by overthrowing the Satanic sovereignty.

(5) Sun and Moon Darkened, Stars Fall from Heaven (Matt. 24:29)

Genesis 37:9 describes the dream of Joseph, the eleventh of the twelve sons of Jacob:

> Then he dreamed another dream, and told it to his brothers, and said, 'Behold, I have dreamed another dream; and behold, the sun, the moon, and eleven stars were bowing down to me.' But when he told it to his father and to his brothers, his father rebuked him, and said to him, 'What is this dream that you have dreamed? Shall I and your mother and your brothers indeed come to bow ourselves to the ground before you?'

Joseph grew to be a man and became the prime minister of Egypt. Then it actually happened, as in the dream, that his parents and brothers indeed came to bow before him. According to these Biblical verses, the sun and the moon symbolize parents, and the stars symbolize children. As stated in "Christology" (cf. Part I, Ch. VII), Jesus and the Holy Spirit came as the True Parents in place of Adam and Eve to give rebirth to mankind. Therefore, the sun and the moon symbolize Jesus and the Holy Spirit, and the stars symbolize the saints as their children.

In the Bible, Jesus is likened to the "true light" (John 1:9) because he came as the Word made into flesh (John 1:14), as the light of truth. Naturally, the sunlight here means the light of the words of Jesus, and the moonlight means the light of the Holy Spirit, who came as the Spirit of truth (John 16:13). Therefore, for the sun and the moon to lose their light means that the New Testament Words of Jesus and the Holy Spirit will lose their light.

How could the New Testament Words come to lose their light? Just as the Old Testament Words lost their light when Jesus and the Holy Spirit came with new Words in order to fulfill the Old Testament Words, so the New Testament Words Jesus gave to the people at the First Advent also will lose their light when Christ comes again with the new Word, in order to fulfill the New Testament Words, thus making a new heaven and a new earth (Rev. 21:1; cf. Part I, Ch. III, Sec. V, 1). Here, for the Words to lose their light means that the period of their mission has elapsed with the coming of the new age.

Stars falling from heaven signifies that the saints in the Last Days will offend the Lord and fail. Just as the leaders of the Jewish religion who had an eager longing for the coming of the Messiah all fell by offending Jesus, the Messiah, it was prophesied that, in their ignorance, many Christians who anxiously await the Second Advent of the Lord will likewise offend and fail him in that day, thus falling in the same manner (cf. Part II, Ch. VI, Sec. II, 2).

In Luke 18:8 Jesus asked, ". . . when the Son of man comes, will he find faith on earth?" On another occasion (Matt. 7:23) he said that he would declare to the devout Christians, "I never knew you; depart from me, you evildoers." All this he said to warn the Christians of the Last Days against their possible offense, because he foresaw their disbelief.

SECTION IV
The Last Days and the Present Days

When Jesus talked about the coming death of Peter, Peter asked him what would become of John. Jesus answered him saying, "If it is my will that he remain until I come, what is that to you?" (John 21:18-22) The disciples, hearing this, thought that Jesus might return within John's lifetime. Besides, Jesus said to his disciples, ". . . you will not have gone through all the towns of Israel before the Son of man comes" (Matt. 10:23), and again he said, "Truly I say to you, there are some standing here who will not taste death before they see the Son of man coming in his kingdom." (Matt. 16:28) Because of such words, not only the disciples of Jesus, but also numerous Christians have since believed that the Lord might come in their lifetime, and always were haunted by a feeling of tension about their days being the Last Days. This is because they did not know the fundamental meaning of the Last Days.

By examining the present fulfillment of the three great blessings to man, which God set up as the purpose of His providence of restoration, we can prove that today is the Last Days. This is the reason Jesus said:

From the fig tree learn its lesson: as soon as its branch becomes tender and puts forth its leaves, you know that summer is near. So also, when you see all these things, you know that he is near, at the very gates. (Matt. 24:32-33)

1. THE PHENOMENON OF THE RESTORATION OF THE FIRST BLESSING

As already discussed in the "Principle of Creation," God's first blessing to Adam and Eve was for them to perfect their individuality. We can tell from the following phenomena that God's providence of restoring fallen men to their original state of creation with perfected individuality has reached its final stage.

The first way we can see this is from the fact that the spiritual standard of fallen men is being restored. As stated above, a man of perfection becomes one body with God in heart-and-zeal, so that man and God become able to communicate with each other fully and freely. Adam and Eve, though not quite perfect, were in the stage of communicating directly with God when they fell and caused their offspring to fall into ignorance of God.

As fallen men come to receive the benefit of the age in the providence of restoration, their spiritual standard is restored by degrees. Therefore, in the Last Days many saints reach the point where they can communicate with God, as Acts 2:17 says:

In the last days . . . I will pour out my Spirit upon all flesh, and your sons and your daughters shall prophesy, and your young men shall see visions, and your old men shall dream dreams.

In these days, there are many believers coming forth with abilities of spiritual communication. From this we can tell that we are entering a new age in which we may restore God's first blessing after having perfected our individuality, because this is the Last Days.

Second, the historical trend of fallen men's restoration of the freedom of the original mind is further proof. Man was deprived of the freedom of coming before God because, due to the fall, he came under the dominion of Satan, and has ever since had restricted freedom. But today man's heart-and-zeal has reached the highest level, where people are in search of the original mind's freedom even at the risk of their lives. This is evidence that with the coming of the Last Days, fallen men are now entering the new age, in which they can come freely before God. They will enter the new age by perfecting their individuality, thus restoring God's first blessing to them, which has been long deprived by Satan.

Third, the original value of fallen men, which was endowed at the creation, is being restored. This is another clear proof. The original value of men, horizontally observed, is that of equality between people, and this may not appear so precious. But when vertically observed, centered on God, each and every individual bears the most august, macrocosmic value (cf. Part I, Ch. VII, Sec. I). Men lost their original value because of the fall. In the present age, however, the democratic ideology has reached its culmination, and men have come to pursue the original value of individuality endowed at the creation. This may be seen in the liberation of slaves, liberation of minority groups and liberation of the minor powers, together with the demand for human dignity, equality between the sexes and equality among all people. This is proof that the Last Days have come and that fallen men are now entering the new age, in which they will restore God's first blessing to men.

Fourth, the original love endowed at the creation is being restored. The world in which God's ideal of creation is fulfilled will have the form of a perfected man. People of this world, all having formed one body vertically with God, will naturally form one body horizontally with one another. Consequently, people of this world cannot but become like one body, interrelated vertically and horizontally by God's absolute love. Due to the fall, man's vertical love with God was cut off, thus causing the severance of the horizontal love among people; and so human history has been woven with struggles. Today, however, since humanitarianism is reaching its culmination, men are increasingly in pursuit of the original love.

Thus, we recognize that the present day is the veritable Last Days, in which men can perfect their individualities centered on God by restoring God's first blessing to men.

2. THE PHENOMENON OF THE RESTORATION OF THE SECOND BLESSING

God's second blessing was for Adam and Eve to attain their true parenthood by multiplying children of goodness, and then to establish homes, societies and a world of good sovereignty. But due to the fall, Adam and Eve became evil parents multiplying evil children and thus formed a world under the bondage of the evil sovereignty. God has conducted the providence of restoring men's spiritual standard by separating men from Satan on an internal basis through religion, while on the other hand He has separated men from Satan on an external basis through various struggles and wars. Thus He has conducted His providence of restoring the sovereignty of goodness on both an internal and an external basis.

Human history, then, has been the restoration of God's second blessing to men, accomplished by the separation of men from Satan on both an internal and an external basis and by finding those children of God who will be able to attend the returning Lord, our True Parent. Therefore, we perceive from the phenomenon of the restoration of God's sovereignty on both an internal and an external basis that today is the veritable Last Days. (This restoration has appeared through the history of the development of cultural spheres centering on religion, and through the history of the rise and fall of nations).

Let us now study how the history of the development of cultural spheres has progressed, causing the present age to be the Last Days. As repeatedly discussed in the history of the development of cultural spheres, God established cultural spheres centered on religion by sending prophets and saints to fallen men. These saints established various religions in accordance with man's original mind, which was directed toward ultimate goodness. Consequently, there have emerged many kinds of cultural spheres in the history of mankind. As time has gone by, these have either united, or been absorbed by one another. In the present day there is a clear trend of one worldwide cultural sphere being established centered on Christianity. This kind of historical trend shows us that God's second blessing to men is being restored, with all the races standing side by side as brothers centered on Christ, who is the nucleus of Christianity.

What makes Christianity different from other religions is that its purpose is to restore the one great world family which God had intended at the creation. This is to be accomplished by finding the True Parents of mankind through whom all men can become children of goodness through rebirth. This signifies that Christianity is the central religion that will accomplish the purpose of God's providence of restoration.

Thus, the restoration of God's second blessing to men can be seen in the formation of one final worldwide cultural sphere centered on Christianity, in which all men will be elevated to the position of children of goodness centered on Christ and the Holy Spirit, who are the True Parents of mankind (cf. Part I, Ch. VII). Thus we cannot deny that we are entering the Last Days today.

Next, we shall investigate how the history of the rise and fall of nations, having progressed toward the purpose of restoring the sovereignty of goodness, is leading the present age into the Last Days. It is an error, brought about by ignorance of the fundamental providence of God, to regard the cause of struggles and wars as merely the conflict of interests among different ideologies.

Mankind has had a sinful history that began with the evil sovereignty centered on Satan, which was caused by the fall of the first human ancestors. Since God's purpose of creation is unchanging, the final goal of human history is the restoration of God's sovereignty of goodness, which is to be achieved through the separation of men from Satan. If the world of evil sovereignty were to go on without struggles and wars, this evil world would continue forever, leaving the sovereignty of goodness eternally unrestored. Therefore, God has worked His providence of restoring the heavenly sovereignty by degrees, sending His prophets and saints. Evil sovereignties have been destroyed by better ones, through the religions of goodness which God founded.

Thus, struggles and wars have become the inevitable course through which man has had to go in order to fulfill the providence of restoration. A more detailed discussion of this question will be made in Part II. Since human history is following the providential course of restoration through indemnity, evil may sometimes seem to prevail when seen within a limited time span; but in the end it will surely be destroyed, or absorbed and assimilated into the realm of a better standard. The rise and fall of nations by wars is thus the inevitable result brought about by the providential course for the restoration of the sovereignty of goodness.

This is why God ordered the Israelites to destroy the seven tribes of Canaan. When Saul disobeyed Him, leaving some of the

Amalekites alive with their cattle, God severely punished him (I Sam. 15:18-23). Thus, God not only directly ordered the Israelites to destroy the Gentiles, but even destroyed the Israelites of the northern dynasty when they turned to evil, by delivering them into the hands of the Assyrians (II Kings 17:23). We must understand that God did so in order to destroy the sovereignty of evil and restore the sovereignty of goodness. Therefore, struggles and fights between individuals of God's side are evil, because they result in the destruction of the good sovereignty itself; but for the good sovereignty to destroy the evil sovereignty is an act of goodness because it is to fulfill the purpose of God's providence of restoration.

In this manner the history of the struggle for separating sovereignty from Satan by gradually gaining lands and wealth all over the world has practically come to restore the Heavenly sovereignty. As for men, they are being restored to the Heavenly side on a worldwide basis, by going through the individual level, family level, societal level and national level. Thus the providence for the separation of men from Satan, starting from the age of clan society and going through the ages of feudalism and monarchism, has now come into the age of democracy. In present human society, we see the division into the two worlds of democracy and communism, the former being the ideology to establish the Heavenly sovereignty and the latter being that to establish the Satanic one.

In this way, human history, which started under the evil sovereignty centered on Satan, has now come to form two opposing sovereignties on a worldwide basis. As the original human nature, heading for ultimate goodness, is awakened through religion, philosophy and ethics, it produces the separation of the power of the good sovereignty from that of the evil one. These two sovereignties, with opposing purposes, can never coexist. Upon the consummation of human history, they will surely arrive at the point of intersection, causing a conflict of an internal nature centering on ideology, which may very possibly cause an external war centered on military power. Then, finally, the sovereignty of Satan will perish forever, leaving the sovereignty of God restored as the everlasting single sovereignty of Heaven.

Today is the Last Days because it is the time of intersection, when the world of good sovereignty under God and the world of evil sovereignty under Satan are confronting each other in the final battle.

In human history, which has hitherto separated the good sovereignty from the evil one, the evil sovereignty sinks down to destruction while the good sovereignty rises toward prosperity, just as in muddy water the mud sinks down, while the clear water rises upward. Thus, in the Last Days, these two sovereignties of good and evil will for a period meet at the point of intersection, the former will remain forever as God's, while the latter will perish in eternal darkness.

Thus, when these two sovereignties of good and evil are at the point of intersection, it is called the Last Days. Since this is the time when the perfection of the growth stage, from which Adam and Eve fell, should be restored by indemnity, all mankind wanders about in ideological chaos, just as the first human ancestors in the Garden of Eden were confused without knowing what to do after the fall.

During the long course of the providence of restoration, there have been several occurrences of the Last Days in which the two sovereignties of good and evil came to the point of intersection. Both the time of Noah and that of Jesus were called Last Days, with the two sovereignties at the point of intersection. But each time men failed to accomplish their portion of responsibility and were unable to destroy the sovereignty of evil; and God again had to start His providence for the separation of the good from the evil sovereignty. Consequently, we will see another intersection of the two sovereignties at the time of the Second Advent of the Lord. The course of the providence of restoration has thus repeated periodically the spiral movement of affairs going through the circular course toward the purpose of creation. This is why there have been many periods of similar nature in human history (cf. Part II, Ch. III, Sec. I).

3. THE PHENOMENON OF THE RESTORATION OF THE THIRD BLESSING

God's third blessing to men signifies Adam and Eve's dominion over the world of creation after they attained perfection. Man's dominion over the world of creation has two aspects—internal and external. We can see that in the present age the two aspects of man's dominion, lost with the human fall, are being restored.

Internal dominion means the dominion of heart-and-zeal. When a man has perfected his individuality he becomes one in heart-and-zeal with God; thus he is able to experience God's own heart-and-zeal. On the day when man, after having perfected himself, comes to love the world of creation with heart-and-zeal identical to God's, and when he receives the beauty returned by the creation, he becomes the dominator in heart-and-zeal over the world of creation. However, due to the fall, man failed to experience God's heart-and-zeal and has not been able to regard the creation with God's heart-and-zeal. Nonetheless, God has been working His providence of restoration by means of religion, philosophy and ethics, constantly elevating by degrees the spiritual standard of fallen men toward God. Thus, man in the present age is restoring his qualification as the dominator in heart-and-zeal over the world of creation.

External dominion means domination through science. If man, having perfected himself, had been able to dominate the world of creation internally with heart-and-zeal identical to that which God had over the world of creation at the time of its creation, man's scientific achievement could have reached its culmination in an extremely short time, because man's spiritual sensibility would have been developed to the highest dimension. Thus, men could have dominated externally all the things of creation. In consequence, man not only could have subdued the world of nature, including the heavenly bodies, at the earliest possible date, but he also could have brought about an extremely comfortable living environment due to the economic development that would have accompanied scientific achievement.

However, man, by losing his spiritual light due to the fall and by thus being deprived of his internal domination over the things of creation, fell to the status of a barbarian with a spiritual sensibility as dull as that of the animals. Thus, he lost the external domination over creation. Man, according to God's providence of restoration, now has restored his spiritual light. Consequently, both his internal and external dominations have, by degrees, been restored. Therefore, scientific development in the present day has also reached its highest degree. So it has come about that modern men have created an extremely comfortable living environment, due to economic developments which followed brilliant scientific achievements.

We see then that God's third blessing to men is being restored, and from this we cannot deny that today we have reached the Last Days.

As we have observed repeatedly, the development of the cultural spheres also shows that a worldwide cultural sphere is now being formed centered on one religion. Nations, too, are moving toward one worldwide structure of sovereignty, starting from the League of Nations, through the United Nations and reaching today for world government. Regarding economic development, the world is now on the threshold of forming one common market. Extremely well-developed transportation and communication facilities have reduced the limitations of time and space. Men are able to communicate with one another on the earth as easily as if the earth were the garden of a house in which people of all the different races of the East and the West lived as one family. All mankind is crying out for brotherly love.

However, a home is formed around the parents; there alone can true brotherly love occur. Therefore, upon the Second Advent of the Lord as the True Parent of mankind, all men will come to live harmoniously in the garden as one family.

From this too we may know that today is surely the Last Days. There must be one final gift which history, having thus progressed, is about to present to mankind. This must be the ideology of the macrocosmic nature that can bind all the strangers who now live in turmoil within one world without any true purpose, into one family centered on the same parents.

SECTION V
The Last Days, the New Truth,
and Our Attitude

1. THE LAST DAYS AND THE NEW TRUTH

Fallen men overcome their internal ignorance by raising their spiritual and intellectual standard through "spirit and truth" (John 4:23), according to their religion. Regarding truth, there are two kinds: internal truth (religion), which will overcome internal ignorance, and external truth (science), which will overcome external ignorance.

Accordingly, man has two kinds of intellect: internal intellect, which is awakened by internal truth, and external intellect, which is awakened by external truth. Therefore, internal intellect in its pursuit of internal truth has set up religion, while external intellect in its pursuit of external truth has set up science. Spiritual matters pertaining to the invisible world first come into spiritual cognition through our spirit men by means of the five spiritual senses; then they are physiologically recognized through the resonance of the five physical senses. The truth from the visible world, however, comes directly into our cognition by means of the five physical senses. Thus, the process of cognition takes place through both the spiritual and physical courses.

Since man was made so that he could be perfect only when his spirit man and physical man are united, spirit and truth must be in perfect harmony, awakening man's spiritual and intellectual standard, before the two-sided cognition through both the spiritual and physical courses can completely coincide. Then, for the first time, man will come to have perfect cognition of the world of creation.

In this manner, God is conducting His providence of restoring men to the original nature intended at the creation by raising, through both spirit and truth, the spiritual and intellectual standard of men, who fell into utter ignorance due to the fall. Man, sharing the benefit of the age in God's providence of restoration, is gradually being elevated in his spiritual and intellectual standard as history progresses. Therefore, both spirit and truth, which are the means for raising the spiritual and intellectual standard, must also be elevated to higher levels by degrees. Although spirit and truth must be unique, eternal and unchanging, the extent, degree and method of teaching and expressing them to men, who are in the process of restoration from the status of ignorance, should vary according to the age.

For example, in the age before the Old Testament (from Adam to Moses), God did not provide the people with words of truth, but merely commanded them to offer sacrifices. Men in that age, being ignorant, could not receive the truth directly from Him. When the spiritual and intellectual standard of the people was elevated, He gave the Law to the people of Moses' day, and the Gospel to those of Jesus' day. Jesus did not say that his word was the truth, but that he himself was the way, the truth and the life (John 14:6). This is because his words were only a means of expressing himself as the truth; and the extent, degree and method of expressing the truth should vary according to those who receive the words.

From this, we must realize that Biblical words are a means of expressing the truth and are not the truth itself. Seeing matters from this point of view, we can understand that the New Testament was given as a textbook for the teaching of truth to the people of 2,000 years ago, people whose spiritual and intellectual standard was very low, compared to that of today. It is thus impossible to satisfy completely man's desire for truth, in this modern scientific civilization, by using the same method of expressing the truth, in parables and symbols, which was used to awaken the people of an earlier age. In consequence, today the truth must appear with a higher standard and with a scientific method of expression in order to enable intelligent modern man to understand it.

We call this the new truth. This new truth, as discussed in the "General Introduction," should be able to resolve completely the problems of religion and science according to one unified theme and thus overcome man's internal and external ignorance.

Let us investigate other reasons that the new truth must appear.

As noted, the Bible is not the truth itself but a textbook teaching us the truth. In this textbook, most of the important parts of the truth are revealed in parables and symbols. Consequently, the method of interpretation can differ according to the reader. Differences in interpretation have produced many denominations. Since the source of denominational divisions is not in man but in the expressions used in the Bible, the divisions and quarrels cannot but increase. Therefore, we cannot expect the divisions and quarrels between denominations to come to an end. This will hinder the fulfillment of the providence of restoration under the unification of Christianity, unless there appears a new truth that can elucidate the fundamental contents of the Bible so clearly that everyone can recognize and agree with it. Therefore, Jesus promised to give us new words of truth in the Last Days, saying:

> I have said this to you in figures; the hour is coming when I shall no longer speak to you in figures but tell you plainly of the Father. (John 16:25)

Jesus died on the cross without being able to say all that he wanted to say because of the disbelief of the people. As he said, "If I have told you earthly things and you do not believe, how can you believe if I tell you heavenly things?" (John 3:12) Jesus also said to his disciples, "I have yet many things to say to you, but you cannot bear them now." (John 16:12) This disclosed how sorrowful he was, because he could not tell even his own disciples what he had deep in his heart.

The words Jesus left unuttered will not forever remain a secret, but are to be revealed some day as a new truth through the Holy Spirit, as Jesus told us:

> When the Spirit of truth comes, he will guide you into all the truth; for he will not speak on his own authority, but whatever he hears he will speak, and he will declare to you the things that are to come. (John 16:13)

Again we read:

> I saw in the right hand of him who was seated on the throne a scroll
> written within and on the back, sealed with seven seals. (Rev. 5:1)

On this very scroll were the words the Lord is to give us in the
Last Days. When John wept because no one was found worthy to
open the scroll or to look into it, since there was no such person
in heaven, on earth, or under the earth, one of the elders said:

> ... the Lion of the tribe of Judah, the Root of David, has con-
> quered, so that he can open the scroll and its seven seals. (Rev.
> 5:3-5)

The Lion born of the Root of David signifies Christ. Thus, the
day must come when Christ will open the sealed scroll, which
has long remained a secret to mankind, and reveal the new
truth to all the saints. Therefore, it is said, "You must again
prophesy about many peoples and nations and tongues and
kings." (Rev. 10:11) Again, it is said:

> And in the last days it shall be, God declares, that I will pour out my
> Spirit upon all flesh, and your sons and your daughters shall
> prophesy, and your young men shall see visions, and your old men
> shall dream dreams; yea, and on my menservants and my maid-
> servants in those days I will pour out my Spirit; and they shall
> prophesy. (Acts 2:17-18)

Thus, from many standpoints the new truth must come in
the Last Days.

2. THE ATTITUDE WE SHOULD TAKE IN THE LAST DAYS

If we observe the progression of the history of the providence
of restoration, we see that the new always begins when the old
is about to expire. Consequently, the period when the old ends
is the very period when the new begins. The close of the old
history is the starting period for the new history.

Mankind is now at the point of intersection where the two sovereignties of good and evil are confronting each other. These two sovereignties, which started at the same point, have headed in opposite directions ever since, and have borne their own worldwide fruits respectively. People of this age fall into internal insecurity, terror and chaos due to the shallowness of their ideals and ideologies. Externally, they are afraid, as they face the threat of conflicts and struggles with terrifying weapons. In the Last Days many devastating phenomena will occur. As the Bible says:

> For nation will rise against nation, and kingdom against kingdom, and there will be famines and earthquakes in various places. (Matt. 24:7)

It is inevitable that such misery should take place, in order that the dominion of evil be annihilated, and that of good be exalted. God, without fail, will set up the center of the sovereignty of goodness in order to establish a new age out of this misery. Noah, Abraham, Moses and Jesus were the central figures of their respective new ages. Therefore, we must find the central figure of the new history, whom God has designated, in order that we might be participants in the new age as God wants us to be.

The providence of the new age does not start after the complete liquidation of the old age, but is born and grows in the circumstances of the period of consummation of the old age, always appearing to be in conflict with that age. Accordingly, this providence is not easily understood by those who are accustomed to the conventions of the old age. This is why the sages of history who came in charge of the providence of a new age all became victims of the old age. We can give the example of Jesus, who, coming at the close of the Old Testament Age as the center of the new providence of the New Testament Age, appeared to the believers of the Mosaic Law to be a heretic whom they could not understand. Finally, he was rejected because of their disbelief of him, and was crucified. This is why Jesus said, "New wine must be put into fresh wine skins." (Luke 5:38)

Christ will come again at the close of the New Testament Age as the center of the new providence to establish the new heaven and earth, and will give us new words for the building of the new age (Rev. 21:1-7). Therefore, he is apt to be rejected and persecuted by Christians at the time of the Second Advent just as Jesus was persecuted and derided at his coming by the Jews, who said he was possessed by Beelzebub, the Prince of Demons (Matt. 12:24). Therefore, Jesus predicted that first the Lord must suffer many things and be rejected by the generation at the time of the Second Advent (Luke 17:25). Therefore those who, in the transitional period of history, are tenaciously attached to the environment of the old age and comfortably entrenched in it will be judged along with the old age.

Fallen men, being very dull in their sensitivity toward spiritual things, will generally emphasize the old truth in following the course of the providence of restoration. In other words, these people will not respond to and follow the providence of the new age even though the providence of restoration is bringing about the new age, because in most cases they are still attached to the view of truth of the old age. Those who can perceive spiritual things, however, will understand the providence of the new age spiritually, and come to respond to it, even though they may face discrepancies between the new view of truth and that of the old age.

The disciples of Jesus, therefore, were not overly attached to the Old Testament. Rather, they followed what they felt spiritually in their hearts. The reason men of prayer and conscience feel a sense of extreme spiritual anxiety and urgency in the Last Days is that, while they vaguely feel spiritual things and are willing to follow the providence of the new age in their hearts, they have not met the new truth that can lead their external selves in the right direction. Therefore, if these men would only listen to the new truth leading them to the providence of the new age, they would be awakened in heart and intellect by spirit and truth simultaneously. They would be able to recognize perfectly the demand of God's providence for the new age. Naturally, then, they will come to respond to it with untold happiness. Thus, modern men of the Last Days must try to perceive spiritual things through humble prayer.

Thus, we should not be attached to conventional ideas but should at all costs find the new truth leading them to the providence of the new age. We can do this by directing our external self toward a spiritual purpose. Then we must ascertain whether the truth thus found becomes one with our spirit, producing a true heavenly joy deep within our heart. By doing this, the saints of the Last Days can find the way to true salvation.

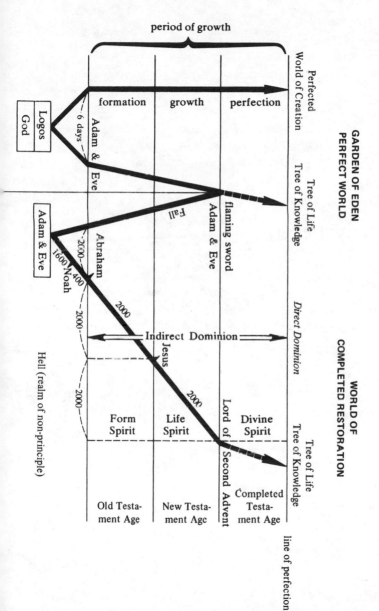

The World of Creation and the Providence of Restoration Through the Substantial Development of the Word.

CHAPTER IV

Advent of the Messiah

The word "messiah" in Hebrew means the "anointed one," especially signifying the king. The Israelites believed the Word of God that He would send a king or Messiah to save them; this was the Messianic expectation of the Israelites. In this sense, Jesus Christ came as the Messiah, "Christ" meaning "Messiah" in the Hellenic language.

The Messiah must come in order that the purpose of God's providence of salvation be fulfilled. Man needs salvation because of the human fall. Therefore, we must understand the questions concerning the human fall in order to solve the problems of salvation. "Fall" implies that God's purpose of creation was left unfulfilled, so we must first elucidate the purpose of creation before we discuss the questions concerning the human fall.

God's purpose of creation was to be fulfilled with the establishment of the Kingdom of Heaven on earth. Due to the fall of man, an earthly hell was brought about instead of the Kingdom of Heaven on earth. Ever since, God has continued His providence to restore the Kingdom of Heaven on earth. Consequently, the purpose of human endeavor is to restore the Kingdom of Heaven on earth. These questions have already been discussed in detail (cf. Part I, Ch. III, Sec. I-II).

SECTION I
The Providence of Salvation through the Cross

1. THE PURPOSE OF JESUS' COMING AS THE MESSIAH

The purpose of Jesus' coming as the Messiah was to fulfill the providence of restoration; his coming was primarily to save fallen men. Consequently, the Kingdom of Heaven on earth should have been established by Jesus. We may see this even from what Jesus said to his disciples, "You, therefore, must be perfect, as your heavenly Father is perfect." (Matt. 5:48) According to the principle of creation, a man who has fulfilled the purpose of creation becomes one body with God, possesses deity, and cannot commit sins. This kind of man, seen from the purpose of creation, is one who is perfect as the heavenly Father is perfect. Therefore, Jesus' words to his disciples meant that they should become citizens of the Heavenly Kingdom, after having been restored as men who have fulfilled the purpose of creation.

Thus, Jesus came in order to establish the Kingdom of Heaven on earth, having restored fallen men as citizens of the Heavenly Kingdom. For this reason he told his disciples to pray that God's will be done on earth as it is in Heaven (Matt. 6:10). He also urged the people to repent, for the Kingdom of Heaven was at hand (Matt. 4:17). For the same reason, John the Baptist, who had come to prepare the way of the Lord, also announced the nearness of the Kingdom of Heaven (Matt. 3:2).

What would the man be like, then, who became perfect as the heavenly Father is perfect, having restored himself as the man in whom the purpose of creation is fulfilled? Such a man would become one body with God, inseparable from Him, living in accordance with God's will. Feeling exactly what God feels, he would possess deity. This man is not in need of redemption or of a savior, nor does he need the life of prayer and faith required by fallen men, because he is without original sin. Such a man, being himself without original sin, comes to multiply children of goodness without original sin; in consequence, his children are not in need of a savior for the redemption of their sins.

2. WAS THE PROVIDENCE OF SALVATION FULFILLED THROUGH REDEMPTION BY THE CROSS?

Since human history began, there has not been a single man, however devout a saint he may have been, who has lived a life in complete oneness with God. Not a single man has experienced God's own heart and feeling, or possessed the same deity. Consequently, there has not yet been a saint who did not need redemption from sin and a life of prayer and faith. Even a man as devout as Paul was compelled to lead a life of faith and tearful prayers (Rom. 7:18-25). All parents, however devout, cannot give birth to a child without sin who may go to the Kingdom of Heaven without redemption by the savior. From this, we perceive that parents are still transmitting original sin to their children.

What does the reality of the life in faith of the Christian teach us? It tells us straightforwardly that redemption through the cross cannot completely liquidate our original sin, and that it leaves man's original nature not yet perfectly restored. Jesus promised the Lord would come, because Jesus knew he could not fulfill the purpose of his advent as the Messiah through redemption by the cross. Christ had to come again to fulfill perfectly the will of God, because God's predestination to restore the Kingdom of Heaven on earth was absolute and unchangeable.

Did his sacrifice on the cross then come to naught? Not at all (John 3:16). If it had, Christian history could not have existed. We can never deny the magnitude of the grace of redemption by the cross. Therefore, it is true that our faith in the cross can bring about redemption. It is equally true that redemption by the cross has been unable to remove our original sin and restore us as men of the original nature who cannot sin; thus, it has been unable to establish the Kingdom of Heaven on earth.

Then, the question arises as to the extent of redemption by the cross. The faith of modern men of intellect cannot be directed unless we can solve this problem.

3. THE CRUCIFIXION OF JESUS

Let us first examine Jesus' crucifixion from the viewpoint of the words and actions of the disciples that were recorded in the Bible. There was one evident feeling common among the disciples concerning Jesus' death. They were grieved and mortified by Jesus' death. They were indignant at the ignorance and disbelief of the people who caused the crucifixion of Jesus (Acts 7:51-53). Christians since have commonly entertained the same feeling as did the disciples of Jesus' days. If Jesus' death had been a natural result of God's predestination, there would have been no reason for the disciples to decry it, though it may have been inevitable for them to grieve over his death. From this, we can ascertain that Jesus' having to take the path of death was unjust and undue.

Next, let us further investigate from the viewpoint of God's providence whether Jesus' crucifixion was a natural result of God's predestination. God called the chosen people of Israel, the descendants of Abraham; He raised and protected them, and at times led them through the discipline of trials and hardships. He comforted them by sending prophets who promised that in the future He would send them a Messiah. He had the people erect tabernacles and temples in preparation for the Messiah. He sent the wise men from the East as well as Simon, Anna, John the Baptist and others to testify widely to the birth and the appearance of the Messiah.

Especially concerning the birth of John the Baptist, all the Jews knew that the angel appeared to testify to his conception (Luke 1:13); and the signs which occurred at the time of his birth stirred all Judea in expectation (Luke 1:63-66). Besides, his ascetic practices in the wilderness were so impressive that the Jewish people questioned in their hearts whether perhaps he were the Christ (Luke 3:15). Needless to say, God sent such a great man as John the Baptist to bear witness to Jesus as the Messiah so that the Jewish people would believe in Jesus. Since God's will was thus to have the Israelites believe that Jesus was the Messiah, the Israelites, who were supposed to live according to God's will, should have believed in him as the Messiah. If they had believed in Jesus as the Messiah according to God's will, how could they have crucified him, after having waited for him for such a long time? It was because, against God's will, they did not believe that Jesus was the Messiah, that the Israelites crucified him. We, therefore, must realize that Jesus did not come to die on the cross.

Next, let us further investigate, according to Jesus' own words and deeds, whether his crucifixion was truly the means to fulfill the whole purpose of his coming as the Messiah. As the Bible clearly states, Jesus expressed in both word and deed his wish to have the people believe he was the Messiah. When the people asked him what they must do to be doing the works of God, Jesus answered them, "This is the work of God, that you believe in him whom He has sent." (John 6:29)

Jesus grieved over the treachery of the Jewish people; and finding none to appeal to, he wept over the city of Jerusalem and even cursed the city to be destroyed so utterly that not one stone would be left upon another, not to mention the Israelites, the chosen people, whom God had led in love and care for 2000 years. Jesus clearly pointed out their ignorance, saying, "... you did not know the time of your visitation." (Luke 19:44)

Jesus lamented over the disbelief and stubbornness of the people, saying:

> O Jerusalem, Jerusalem, killing the prophets and stoning those who are sent to you! How often would I have gathered your children together as a hen gathers her brood under her wings, and you would not! (Matt. 23:37)

Jesus reproached them for their ignorance which kept them from believing in him even though they read the Scriptures, which testified to him, and he said in great sorrow:

> You search the scriptures, because you think that in them you have eternal life; and it is they that bear witness to me; yet you refuse to come to me that you may have life. (John 5:39-40)

Again, he said sorrowfully, "I have come in my Father's name, and you do not receive me," and he went on to say, "If you believed Moses, you would believe me, for he wrote of me." (John 5:43-46)

Jesus performed many miracles and signs in the hope that he might restore the people's belief. However, they condemned him as being possessed by Beelzebub when they saw the amazing works which Jesus did. Seeing the painful situation, Jesus said, ". . . even though you do not believe me, believe the works, that you may know and understand that the Father is in me and I am in the Father." (John 10:38) On another occasion, he even cursed them in great indignation, prophesying that they would suffer (Matt. 23:13-36). Jesus himself, through his words and deeds, tried to make them believe in him, because it was God's will for them to do so. If the Jewish people believed that he was the Messiah, as both God and Jesus wanted, could they have crucified him?

From the above, we can see that Jesus' crucifixion was the result of the ignorance and disbelief of the Jewish people and was not God's predestination to fulfill the whole purpose of Jesus' coming as the Messiah. I Corinthians 2:8 says, "None of the rulers of this age understood this; for if they had, they would not have crucified the Lord of glory." This should be sufficient proof.

If Jesus' crucifixion had originally been God's predestination, how could he have prayed even three times that the cup of death might pass from him? (Matt. 26:39) In fact, he thus prayed desperately because he knew too well that the history of affliction would be prolonged until the time of the Second Advent if the disbelief of the people should forbid the realization of the Kingdom of Heaven on earth, which God had endeavored to establish.

In John 3:14 we read, "As Moses lifted up the serpent in the wilderness, so must the Son of man be lifted up." When the Israelites were on their way from Egypt into the land of Canaan, they failed to believe in Moses, and at that time fiery serpents appeared and began to kill the people; then God had a bronze serpent lifted up on a pole, and those who looked at it survived. Similarly, due to the Jewish people's disbelief in Jesus, all were destined to hell; and Jesus, foreseeing that after his crucifixion as the "bronze serpent" only those who looked at him and believed in him would be saved, said this with a deeply sorrowful heart.

Another way we may know that Jesus was crucified due to the disbelief of the people is from the fact, as Jesus foretold, that the chosen nation of Israel declined after his death (Luke 19:44).

Isaiah 9:6-7 says:

> For to us a child is born, to us a son is given; and the government will be upon his shoulder, and his name will be called 'Wonderful Counsellor, Mighty God, Everlasting Father, Prince of Peace.' Of the increase of his government and of peace there will be no end, upon the throne of David, and over his kingdom, to establish it, and to uphold it with justice and with righteousness from this time forth and for evermore. The zeal of the Lord of hosts will do this.

This is the prediction that Jesus would come upon the throne of David and establish a kingdom that would never perish throughout eternity. Therefore, an angel appeared to Mary at the time she conceived Jesus and said:

> And behold, you will conceive in your womb and bear a son, and you shall call his name Jesus. He will be great, and will be called the Son of the Most high; and the Lord God will give to him the throne of his father David, and he will reign over the house of Jacob for ever; and of his kingdom there will be no end. (Luke 1:31-33)

From these passages, we can see plainly that God had called the Israelites, the chosen people, and had led them through afflictions and hardships for 2,000 years, in order to establish an everlasting Kingdom of God on earth by sending Jesus as the

Messiah. Jesus came as the Messiah; but, due to the disbelief of and persecution by the people, he was crucified. Since then, the Jews have lost their qualification as the chosen people and have been scattered, suffering persecution through the present day.

4. THE LIMIT OF SALVATION THROUGH REDEMPTION BY THE CROSS, AND THE PURPOSE OF THE LORD'S SECOND ADVENT

If Jesus had not been crucified, what would have happened? He would have accomplished the providence of salvation both spiritually and physically. He would have established the Kingdom of Heaven on earth which would last forever, as expressed in the prophecy of Isaiah (Is. 9:6 7), in the instruction of the angel appearing to Mary (Luke 1:31-33), and in Jesus' own words announcing the imminence of the Kingdom of Heaven (Matt. 4:17).

God first created man's flesh with the earth, and then He breathed into his nostrils the breath of life and made him into a living soul (Gen. 2:7). Man was created to have both spirit and body; his fall also came about both spiritually and physically. Naturally, salvation must include both spirit and body.

Since the purpose of Jesus' advent as the Messiah was to accomplish the providence of restoration, he should have fulfilled the salvation of both spirit and body. To believe in Jesus means to become one body with him; therefore, Jesus likened himself to the true vine, and his followers to its branches (John 15:5). He said, ". . . you will know that I am in my Father, and you in me, and I in you." (John 14:20) Jesus said this because coming in the flesh, he wanted to save fallen men both spiritually and physically. If they had become one with him in both spirit and body by believing in him, fallen men could have been saved both spiritually and physically. Because the Jewish people disbelieved Jesus and delivered him up for crucifixion, his body was invaded by Satan, and he was killed. Therefore, even when Christians believe in and become one body with Jesus, whose body was invaded by Satan, their bodies still remain subject to Satan's invasion.

In this manner, however devout a man of faith may be, he cannot fulfill physical salvation by redemption through Jesus' crucifixion alone. Since the original sin lineally transmitted from Adam has not been liquidated, any saint, however devout he may be, still has original sin and cannot help giving birth to the children of original sin. To prevent the condition of Satanic invasion which constantly comes through the flesh due to the original sin, we have to torment and deny our flesh, in order to live a religious life. We must pray constantly (I Thess. 5:17) in order to prevent the condition of Satanic invasion that comes because of original sin, which has not been annihilated, even through redemption by the cross.

Jesus could not accomplish the purpose of the providence of physical salvation because his body was invaded by Satan. However, he could establish the basis for spiritual salvation by forming a triumphant foundation for resurrection through the redemption by the blood of the cross. Therefore, all the saints since the resurrection of Jesus through the present day have enjoyed the benefit of the providence of spiritual salvation only. Salvation through redemption by the cross is spiritual only. Even in devout men of faith, the original sin remains in the flesh and is transmitted continuously from generation to generation. The more devout a saint becomes in his faith, therefore, the more severe becomes his fight against sin. Thus, Christ must come again on the earth to accomplish the purpose of the providence of the physical, as well as the spiritual salvation, by redeeming the original sin which has not been liquidated even through the cross.

As mentioned before, even the saints redeemed by the cross have had to continue to fight against original sin. That is why even Paul, who was the center of faith among the disciples, lamented over his inability to prevent sin from invading his flesh, saying, ". . . So then, I of myself serve the law of God with my mind, but with my flesh I serve the law of sin." (Rom. 7:22-25) He said this to express the joy of the fulfillment of spiritual salvation as well as to deplore the failure to accomplish physical salvation. Again, in I John 1:8-10 John confessed, saying:

> If we say we have no sin, we deceive ourselves, and the truth is not in us. . . . If we say we have not sinned, we make him a liar, and his word is not in us.

Thus, we who can gain salvation through the crucifixon of Jesus cannot escape from being sinners because the original sin still works in us.

5. TWO KINDS OF PROPHECY CONCERNING THE CROSS

What must be the reason, then, that in Isaiah 53 Jesus' suffering on the cross is prophesied, if his crucifixion was not the result of God's predestination? Until now, many people have thought that the prophecies in the Bible about Jesus foretold only his suffering. When we read the Bible anew with a knowledge of the Principle, we can understand that, just as the prophet Isaiah foretold in the Old Testament Age (Is. 9, 11, 60), and as the angel of God prophesied to Mary, Jesus was expected to become king of the Jews in his lifetime and establish on earth an everlasting kingdom of which "there will be no end." (Luke 1:31-33) Let us then investigate why there were two kinds of prophecies.

God created man to be perfected only by accomplishing his portion of responsibility (cf. Part I, Ch. I, Sec. V, 2[2]). However, in actuality, the first human ancestors fell without having accomplished their portion of responsibility. Thus, man could either accomplish his portion of responsibility in accordance with God's will, or, on the contrary, not accomplish it against God's will.

To give an example from the Bible, it was man's portion of responsibility not to eat the fruit of the Tree of the Knowledge of Good and Evil. Adam could perfect himself by obeying God's commandment not to eat of the fruit; on the other hand, he could die by eating the fruit, as actually happened. God gave the Ten Commandments to the people of the Old Testament Age as a condition of man's responsibility in the providence of salvation. Thus, man could be saved by keeping the Commandments, or be ruined by not keeping them. It was the Israelites' portion of responsibility to obey Moses' command on their way from Egypt to the blessed land of Canaan. They could enter the blessed land of Canaan by obeying Moses' command, or not enter it by disobeying his command. In fact, God willed that Moses lead the Israelites into the blessed land of Canaan (Ex. 3:8) and commanded him to do so; but due to their disbelief, the people perished in the wilderness, leaving only their posterity to reach the destination.

Man thus has his own responsibility to accomplish, and he may fulfill it according to God's will or not fulfill it against His will, thus resulting in only one of the two possibilities being realized. Therefore, it was inevitable for God to give two kinds of prophecy regarding the fulfillment of His will.

It was God's portion of responsibility to send the Messiah, but to believe in him was man's responsibility. Therefore, the Jewish people could either believe in the Messiah according to

God's will or not believe in him, against His will. Therefore, God had to give two kinds of prophecy, thus providing for two possible results, according to man's success or failure to accomplish his responsibility. God prophesied both about what might happen if the Jewish people failed to believe in the Messiah, as was written in Isaiah 53, and about what would happen if they fulfilled His will in glory by believing in and serving the Messiah, as was recorded in Isaiah 9, 11 and 60, and Luke 1:30. However, due to the disbelief of the people, Jesus died on the cross, and the prophecy of Isaiah 53 was realized, thus leaving the others to be accomplished after the Lord's Second Advent.

6. BIBLICAL VERSES WRITTEN AS IF JESUS' CRUCIFIXION WERE INEVITABLE

In the Bible we find many verses written as if Jesus' suffering through crucifixion were inevitable. One of the representative examples of this is that Jesus reproached Peter, who tried to dissuade him when he prophesied about his suffering on the cross, and said, "Get behind me, Satan!" (Matt. 16:23) Otherwise, how could Jesus reproach Peter so bitterly? In fact, Jesus was then resolved to take the cross as the condition of indemnity to pay for the accomplishment of even the spiritual salvation of man when he found that he was unable to accomplish the providence of both spiritual and physical salvation (Luke 9:31). In that situation, Peter's dissuading him from taking the way of the cross was a hindrance to the providence of spiritual salvation through the cross; so, he reproached Peter.

In the next place, when Jesus uttered his last words on the cross, saying, "It is finished" (John 19:30), he did not mean that the whole purpose of the providence of salvation was attained through the cross. Knowing that the disbelief of the people was at that point inalterable, Jesus chose the way of the cross in order to establish the foundation of the providence of spiritual salvation, leaving the providence of physical salvation to the time of the Second Advent. Therefore, Jesus meant by the words "it is finished" that he finished establishing the basis for the providence of spiritual salvation through the cross, which was the secondary providence of salvation.

In order for us to have a right faith, we must first establish direct rapport with God in spirit through ardent prayer and next, we must understand the truth through correct reading of the Bible. This is the reason that Jesus told us to worship God in spirit and truth (John 4:24).

From the time of Jesus through the present, all Christians have thought that Jesus came to the world to die. This is because they did not know the fundamental purpose of Jesus' coming as the Messiah, and entertained the wrong idea that spiritual salvation was the only mission for which Jesus came to the world. Jesus came to accomplish the will of God in his lifetime, but had to die a reluctant death due to the disbelief of the people. There must first appear on the earth the bride who can relieve the humiliated and grieving heart of Jesus before Christ as the bridegroom can come again—this time to complete his mission with his bride. Jesus said, "Nevertheless, when the Son of man comes, will he find faith on earth?" (Luke 18:8) in lamentation over the possible ignorance of the people, which he could foresee.

We have clarified the fact that Jesus did not come to die, but if we ask Jesus directly through spiritual communication, we can see the fact even more clearly. When direct rapport is impossible, we should seek the testimony of someone with such a gift in order to have the kind of faith that will entitle us to be the "bride," in order to receive the Messiah.

Section II
The Second Advent of Elijah and John the Baptist

It was foretold by the prophet Malachi that Elijah would come again (Mal. 4:5), and it was Jesus' testimony that John the Baptist was none other than the second advent of Elijah (Matt. 11:14, 17:13). However, John the Baptist himself, as well as the Jewish people in general, did not know the fact that John was the second advent of Elijah (John 1:21). John's doubt of Jesus (Matt. 11:3), followed by the disbelief of the people, finally compelled Jesus to take the way of the cross.

1. THE TREND OF JEWISH THOUGHT CONCERNING THE SECOND ADVENT OF ELIJAH

During the period of the United Kingdom, the "ideal of the temple" was invaded by Satan, due to the corruption of King Solomon.

God set up the ideal of the temple the second time. In order to prepare the people to receive the Messiah as the substantial temple, He worked for the separation of Satan by sending them four major prophets and twelve minor prophets. It was to stop Satan from preventing the realization of this ideal that God had his people destroy the god Baal by sending his special prophet Elijah and having him fight against the prophets of Baal on Mt. Carmel. However, Elijah ascended into heaven without having fully accomplished his divine mission (II Kings 2:11), and Satan's power was again rampant.

Therefore, in order that the ideal of the substantial temple, Jesus, might be realized, there should first be the providence of having another prophet succeed Elijah and accomplish the mission of separating Satan, which he had left undone on the earth. Because of this providential necessity, the prophet Malachi foretold the second advent of Elijah (Mal. 4:5).

The fervent hope of the Jewish people who believed in these prophecies was, of course, the advent of the Messiah. But we must know that they nonetheless longed for the second coming of Elijah. This is because God clearly promised the people, through the prophet Malachi, that He would send the prophet Elijah prior to the advent of the Messiah in order to have him prepare the way of the Lord (Mal. 4:5). Meanwhile, the prophet Elijah had ascended into heaven nearly 900 years before the birth of Jesus (II Kings 2:11), and we are familiar with the occasion when he appeared to Jesus' disciples in spirit (Luke 9:31). The Jewish people believed that Elijah, being in heaven, would come from heaven in the same manner as he had ascended into heaven. Therefore, the Jewish people of that time were waiting for Elijah to come again, looking up into heaven in the expectation that Elijah would come on the clouds.

However, there had been as yet no rumor of Elijah's coming as Malachi had prophesied, when Jesus appeared, claiming to be the Messiah; thus, great confusion was caused in Jerusalem. So, the disciples were faced with an argument against Jesus' being the Messiah (Matt. 17:10): if Jesus were he, then where was Elijah who was to come before him? (Mal. 4:5) The disciples, at a loss as to how to reply, asked Jesus directly; and he answered that John the Baptist was none other than Elijah himself, for whom they had waited (Matt. 11:14, 17:13). Jesus' disciples, who believed him to be the Messiah, could believe without question Jesus' testimony that John the Baptist was Elijah. But how could the Jewish people accept it, when they did not know who Jesus was? Jesus himself, knowing that they would not easily believe his testimony, said, "If you are willing to accept it, he is Elijah who is to come." (Matt. 11:14) The Jewish people could not believe Jesus' testimony that John the Baptist was Elijah because it came after John himself clearly denied the fact (John 1:21).

2. THE WAY OF THE JEWISH PEOPLE

Jesus said that John the Baptist was none other than Elijah, for whom the Jewish people had waited so long (Matt. 11:14), while on the contrary, John the Baptist himself had already denied the fact. Then, whose words were they to believe and follow? It depended upon which of the two appeared to be more believable to the people at that time.

Let us then examine how Jesus appeared to the Jewish people, from their own standpoint. Jesus was a young man of little formal education. He had been born and raised in the poor and lowly home of a carpenter. This young man emerged unknown, calling himself the Lord of the Sabbath, and yet violated the Sabbath which the Jews strictly observed (Matt. 12:1-8). Therefore, Jesus came to be known as one who wanted to abolish the Law, which was the symbol of salvation to the Jews (Matt. 5:17). Therefore, Jesus was persecuted by Jewish leaders and had to gather fishermen to be his disciples. He became a friend to tax-collectors, harlots, and sinners, eating and drinking with them (Matt. 11:19). More than that, Jesus declared that the tax-collectors and harlots would enter the Kingdom of Heaven ahead of the Jewish leaders (Matt. 21:31).

On one occasion, a woman, weeping, began to wet Jesus' feet with her tears, wipe them with her hair, kiss them and anoint them with a flask of precious ointment (Luke 7:37-38). Such conduct would not be acceptable even in today's society; and how much more unacceptable it would have been within the strict ethics of Jewish society, in which they could stone an adulterous woman to death. Nevertheless, Jesus not only accepted it, but reproached his disciples, who had rebuked the woman; in fact, he also praised her (Luke 7:44-50, Matt. 26:7-13).

Moreover, Jesus placed himself on the same level as God (John 14:9) and said that no one could enter the Kingdom of

Heaven except through him (John 14:6). He even said that people should love him more than their parents, brothers, husband or wife, and their children (Matt. 10:37, Luke 14:26).

Because of the attitude which Jesus' words and actions seemed to convey, the Jewish leaders derided him and accused him of being Beelzebub, the Prince of Demons (Matt. 12:24). From all this we can gather that Jesus was not accepted by the Jews of that time.

Next, let us investigate how John the Baptist appeared to the Jewish people. John was born to a distinguished family as a son of Zechariah, a chief priest (Luke 1:13). His birth greatly surprised the whole city because of the miracles and signs surrounding his conception. His father, burning incense in the holy place, saw the angel of the Lord, who announced that his wife would conceive a son. Upon disbelieving the angel's words, Zechariah was struck dumb, and his speech was restored only upon the birth of the child (Luke 1:9-66). Moreover, John led a brilliant life in faith and discipline, living on locusts and wild honey in the wilderness, and he appeared so admirable to the Jewish people that even the chief priests, as well as the people in general, asked him if he were the Messiah (Luke 3:15, John 1:20).

Considering the above, when we compare Jesus and John the Baptist from the standpoint of the Jewish people, whose words would they be more likely to believe? It was only natural for them to believe the words of John the Baptist. Consequently, they had to believe John's words, when he denied being Elijah, more than they believed Jesus' testimony that John the Baptist was Elijah. Since the Jewish people came to believe the words of John the Baptist, Jesus' testimony appeared to be false, and thus he was condemned as an imposter.

In this way, Jesus was condemned as a man of reckless words, and his manner was offensive to the Jewish people. Their disbelief in Jesus became aggravated by degrees. Since the Jewish people believed the words of John the Baptist rather than those of Jesus, they had to think that Elijah had not yet come; accordingly, they could not even imagine that the Messiah had arrived.

From this viewpoint, the Jews had to deny Jesus, who claimed to be the Messiah, because, from the standpoint of believers in the prophecy of Malachi, they could not believe that Elijah had come. Otherwise, they would have to deny the Scriptures, which prophesied that the coming of the Messiah would take place after the return of Elijah. In this way, the Jewish people, who could not abandon the prophecy in the Scriptures, were compelled to choose the way of disbelief in Jesus.

3. THE DISBELIEF OF JOHN THE BAPTIST

As already discussed in detail, the chief priests as well as all the Jewish people of that time respected John the Baptist to such a degree that they thought he might be the Messiah (Luke 3:15, John 1:20). Consequently, if John the Baptist had declared himself to be Elijah as Jesus testified he was, the Jewish people, who expected Elijah's return before the coming of the Messiah, would have come to Jesus, because they were accustomed to believing the testimony of John the Baptist. However, the ignorance of God's providence on the part of John the Baptist, who protested to the last moment that he was not Elijah, was the principal cause blocking the way of the people to Jesus.

John the Baptist once testified:

> I baptize you with water for repentance, but he who is coming after me is mightier than I, whose sandals I am not worthy to carry; he will baptize you with the Holy Spirit and with fire. (Matt. 3:11)

Again in John 1:33-34 he confessed, saying:

> I myself did not know him; but he [God] who sent me to baptize
> with water said to me, 'He on whom you see the Spirit descend and
> remain, this is he who baptizes with the Holy Spirit [Christ].' And I
> have seen and have borne witness that this is the Son of God.

In this way, God directly manifested to John the Baptist that Jesus was the Messiah, and even John himself testified to him as such, while in John 1:23 he said he came with the mission of making straight the way of the Messiah. In addition, he declared in John 3:28 that he was the one who had been sent before the Christ. Therefore, John the Baptist should have known through his own wisdom that he was Elijah. Even if John the Baptist had not realized on his own that he was Elijah, he should have nonetheless declared that he was Elijah in obedience to Jesus' testimony, since he knew Jesus as the Messiah through the testimony from God (John 1:33-34), and he knew that Jesus bore witness that John was Elijah.

However, John not only denied Jesus' testimony (John 1:21) from his ignorance of God's will (Matt. 11:19), but he also deviated from the direction of providence even after that. We can well imagine how sad Jesus must have been when he had to regard John the Baptist in that way, not to mention the sorrow of God, when He looked at His son who was placed in such a difficult situation.

In fact, the mission of John the Baptist as the witness ended with his baptizing of and testifying to Jesus. Then what should his mission have been after that? His father Zechariah, moved by the Holy Spirit, said about John, who had just been born: "we . . . might serve him without fear, in holiness and righteousness before him all the days of our life. And you, child, will be called the prophet of the Most High; for you will go before the Lord to prepare his ways. . ." (Luke 1:74-76), thus prophesying clearly about his mission. John the Baptist should have ministered to Jesus as a disciple, after having testified to him. Nevertheless, he went about baptizing people separately from Jesus, thus confusing the Jewish people (Luke 3:15), even the chief priests (John 1:20). Further, the disciples of Jesus and the followers of John the Baptist quarreled about "purification" among themselves, each saying that his own teacher baptized more people (John 3:25-26). Besides, John 3:30 tells us eloquently that John the Baptist did not bear the same fate with Jesus, who said, "He must increase, but I must decrease." How could he ever decrease while Jesus increased, if he shared the same destiny with Jesus? In fact, the gospel of Jesus should have been proclaimed by John the Baptist himself. But through ignorance, he could not accomplish his mission, and at last he degraded his life, which was to have been devoted to Jesus, to a thing of practically no value.

John the Baptist knew Jesus was the Messiah, and when John was on God's side, he testified to him. But when God no longer directly inspired him, and John returned to his normal state, his disbelief of Jesus became aggravated by his ignorance. John the Baptist, who did not realize that he was Elijah, regarded Jesus from the same standpoint as other people, especially after John's imprisonment. Accordingly, everything Jesus said or did seemed, from the merely human standpoint of John the Baptist, to be strange and incomprehensible. Moreover, John himself could not believe that Jesus, who had appeared before the coming of Elijah, was the Messiah. At last John sent his disciples to Jesus in an attempt to remove his doubt, by asking him, "Are you he who is to come, or shall we look for another?" (Matt. 11:3)

Jesus, so questioned, answered indignantly, with an air of admonition (Matt. 11:4-10). John the Baptist was chosen by God while he was still in his mother's womb for the mission of serving Him throughout his life (Luke 1:76), and was trained in the wilderness, leading the bitter life of an ascetic, in order to prepare the way of the Lord. When Jesus started his public ministry, God first told John who Jesus was, then had him testify to Jesus' being the Son of God. When John the Baptist, who was failing to fulfill his mission and blessing from heaven, asked Jesus such a question, Jesus did not answer straightforwardly that he was the Messiah, which should have been plain enough. He answered in a roundabout way, saying:

> Go and tell John what you hear and see! The blind receive their sight and the lame walk, lepers are cleansed and the deaf hear, and the dead are raised up, and the poor have good news preached to them. (Matt. 11:4-5)

Of course, John the Baptist was not ignorant of such miracles and wonders done by Jesus. Nevertheless, Jesus gave such a lengthy explanation in order to let him know who he was by reminding John the Baptist of what he was doing.

We must understand that when Jesus said the poor had good news preached to them (Matt. 11:5), he was indicating his grief over the disbelief of the Jewish people, and especially that of John the Baptist. The chosen people of Israel, especially John, had been richly blessed with divine love and care. Nevertheless, they betrayed Jesus, and he was compelled to wander about the seacoast of Galilee through the region of Samaria to search among the poor for those who would listen to the Gospel. The ignorant fishermen, tax-collectors and harlots were such poor people. Actually, the disciples Jesus would have preferred were not people of this kind. Jesus, having come to establish the Kingdom of Heaven on earth, was more in need of one person qualified to lead a thousand, than one thousand following him blindly. Did he not, therefore, first preach the Gospel in the temple to the chief priests and scribes in search of those who were able and well prepared?

However, as Jesus indicated in a parable, he had to call beggars roaming about on the street to the feast, because the

invited had not come. Jesus, who himself had to go about
bringing in those who were uninvited, at last uttered bitter
words of judgment in deep lamentation, saying, "Blessed is he
who takes no offense at me." (Matt. 11:6) Jesus predicted John
the Baptist's destiny by saying, indirectly, that one who took
offense at him would not be blessed, however great he might be.

On the contrary, it was John the Baptist who had offended
Jesus. How did John the Baptist offend him? John failed to
carry out his mission of serving and ministering to Jesus.

After the disciples of John the Baptist left him, Jesus said:

> Truly, I say to you, among those born of women there has risen no
> one greater than John the Baptist; yet he who is least in the kingdom
> of heaven is greater than he. (Matt. 11:11)

indicating that, from the standpoint of his ministry, John the
Baptist had come originally as the greatest of all the prophets,
but that he was failing to accomplish his mission.

All those in heaven had once been born of women and lived
their earthly lives before they died. Therefore, it would have
been natural for him who was the greatest of all those born of
women to be the greatest also in heaven. Then, why was John
the Baptist worse than he who was least in the Kingdom of
Heaven? Numerous prophets in the past had testified to the
Messiah from a distance, looking forward to his coming in the
future. But John the Baptist came with the mission of testifying
to the Messiah directly. Since it was the mission of the prophets
to testify to the Messiah, John the Baptist, who was to testify
to the Messiah directly, was greater than any of the other
prophets, who testified to him indirectly. However, seen from
the point of ministering to the Messiah, he was the least one.
This is because the least in the Kingdom of Heaven recognizes
Jesus as the Messiah and serves him, while John the Baptist,
who was called for the mission of serving him closely in person
(Luke 1:76), did not prepare the way of Jesus and failed to

serve him. Jesus went on to say, "From John the Baptist until now, the Kingdom of Heaven has suffered violence, and men of violence take it." If John the Baptist, who was chosen in the womb and trained in so difficult an ascetic life in the wilderness, had only served Jesus as he should, he would no doubt have become his chief disciple. But, since John failed to accomplish his mission of serving Jesus, Peter took the position of chief disciple.

In the passage, "From John the Baptist until now, the Kingdom of Heaven has suffered violence," Jesus was not referring to the failure of the people in general, but that of John the Baptist himself. If John had acted wisely, he would not have left Jesus, and his deeds would have remained for eternity as righteousness; but, unfortunately, he blocked the way for the Jewish people to go to Jesus, as well as his own way.

Here, we have come to understand that the greatest factor leading to the crucifixion of Jesus was the failure of John the Baptist. Paul lamented over the ignorance of the people, including John the Baptist, who crucified Jesus, saying:

> None of the rulers of this age understood this; for if they had, they would not have crucified the Lord of glory. (I Cor. 2:8)

4. THE REASON THAT JOHN THE BAPTIST WAS ELIJAH

According to what we have previously stated (cf. Sec. II, 1), we can see that John the Baptist came to succeed Elijah and accomplish the mission which Elijah had left unaccomplished on earth. As Luke 1:17 says, John was born with the mission of going before the Lord in the spirit and power of Elijah, to turn the hearts of the fathers to the children and the disobedient to the wisdom of the just, and to make ready for the Lord a people prepared. For this reason, John was the second advent of Elijah from the standpoint of their identical mission. Details will be clarified in the chapter on "Resurrection," but we know now that Elijah descended in spirit to John the Baptist. By cooperating with John the Baptist he tried to accomplish his mission, which he had left unaccomplished during his physical life on earth, through the physical body of John the Baptist. John the Baptist was in the position of representing Elijah's physical body, making himself identical with Elijah from the standpoint of their mission.

5. OUR ATTITUDE TOWARD THE BIBLE

We have learned from our study of the Bible that the ignorance and disbelief of John the Baptist brought about the disbelief of the Jewish people, which finally compelled Jesus to take the way of crucifixion. Since the time of Jesus until the present, no one has been able to reveal this heavenly secret. This is because we have hitherto read the Bible from the standpoint that John the Baptist was the greatest prophet of all. We have learned from the story of John the Baptist that we must abandon the conservative attitude of faith which has caused us to be afraid to remove old traditional concepts. If it would be unjust to believe that John the Baptist had failed to accomplish his mission when he actually succeeded, it would also no doubt be wrong to believe that he fulfilled his mission, when on the contrary he had failed to do so. We must struggle to obtain the right way of faith, both in spirit and truth.

We have now brought to light the true nature of the story of John the Baptist as demonstrated in the Bible. Any Christian who, in spiritual communication, can see John the Baptist directly in the spirit world will be able to understand the authenticity of all these things.

CHAPTER V

Resurrection

If we are to accept as literal all the prophecies contained in the Bible, we must be convinced of the possibility that, at the Second Advent of the Lord, the physical bodies of all the saints that were buried and decomposed will come back to their original state of life once more in flesh (I Thess. 4:16, Matt. 27:52). Since this prophecy is from God, men of faith must accept it. However, this prophecy cannot satisfy the intellect of modern men; our life in faith has, after all, fallen into great chaos. Therefore, it is a matter of paramount importance to elucidate the true nature of this problem.

SECTION I
Resurrection

Resurrection means to come back to life. It is because we once died that we need to come back to life. To know the true meaning of resurrection we must understand the Biblical concept of life and death.

1. BIBLICAL CONCEPT OF LIFE AND DEATH

In Luke 9:60, we read that Jesus told a disciple who wanted first to go and bury his father to "Leave the dead to bury their own dead." In these words of Jesus, we find two different concepts of life and death.

The first is the concept of life and death concerning death of the physical body, which is the expiration of physical life; this was the case of the disciple's father, who was to be buried. The life which is opposite to this kind of death is the state in which the physical body maintains its physiological functions.

The second is the concept of life and death concerning the persons—whom Jesus called "the dead"—who were gathered together for the burial of the father. Why then did Jesus indicate that the men who were actually alive were "dead"? It was because they were in a state cut off from the love of God; that is, they were under the dominion of Satan. Therefore, death does not mean the expiration of physical life, but rather the state of Satanic dominion, apart from the bosom of God's love. Accordingly, the meaning of life opposite to this kind of death is the state of actively living in the dominion of God's infinite love. Therefore, however active one's body may be, while man remains in the dominion of Satan, separated from that of God, he is dead in the true sense according to the standard of the original value endowed at the creation.

Our understanding may be further enhanced by reading Revelation 3:1, words to the people of the church in Sardis, saying, ". . . You have the name of being alive, and you are dead." On the other hand, even though one may have died physically, if his spirit abides in God's dominion in the Heavenly Kingdom of God, he is alive in the truest sense. When Jesus said, ". . . he who believes in me, though he die, yet shall he live" (John 11:25), he meant that he who believes in Jesus and lives under God's dominion is still alive, though he has physically died and turned to dust, because his spirit man remains in the dominion of God.

Jesus went on to say, "whoever lives and believes in me shall never die." This does not mean that those who believe in Jesus will never die physically, thus enjoying eternal life on the earth. Those who believe in Jesus in life remain alive not only while on earth, but even after physical death will transmigrate to the world of spirit, living there forever in the bosom of God's love, without tasting death. Jesus' statement here is an indication that man's physical death does not affect his eternal life in the spirit world.

Again, he said, "Whoever seeks to gain his life will lose it, but whoever loses his life will preserve it." (Luke 17:33) He meant that those who betray God's will in order to preserve their physical life, though they may be physically active, are dead. On the other hand, the spirit men of those who sacrifice their lives for the sake of God's will, though they may be physically dead and decomposed, will live forever in the bosom of God's love, thus remaining alive through eternity.

2. DEATH CAUSED BY THE FALL

We have learned that there are two concepts of death, each with a different meaning. Which of the two, then, would be the death brought about by the fall of the first human ancestors?

God created man to grow old and turn to dust; this would occur even if man had not fallen. Therefore, when Adam died at the Biblical age of 930 and turned to dust, this was not the death which was caused by the fall. According to the principle of creation, our flesh is like clothes to our spirit; and it is natural for us to discard our flesh when it is old and exhausted, just as we would discard worn-out clothing. Then our spirit man goes to the invisible world to live there forever. There is no single material being that can perpetuate its physical life. Man is no exception to this principle of creation; the human body cannot live forever.

If men were to live eternally on the earth, there would have been no need to create, in the beginning, the invisible world where spirit men are supposed to go after physical death. The invisible world was not created after the human fall, so that the spirits of fallen men might go there to live; rather it had been created before the creation of men, so that their spirits, after having accomplished the purpose of creation, might go and live there forever, once they had discarded their flesh, after their physical life on earth.

Fallen men are strongly attached to their physical life on earth because, due to the fall, they became ignorant of the fact that they had been created to go to live eternally in the beautiful invisible world after discarding their flesh. Our physical life on earth and our spiritual life in the invisible world may be compared to the phases of a caterpillar and butterfly. If a caterpillar living in the soil had consciousness, he would also be reluctant to die, from attachment to his life under the earth, just as man is attached to his physical life on earth. This is because the caterpillar does not know that there is another new world after his death where he can enjoy fragrant flowers and sweet honey.

The relationship between an earthly man and a spirit man is similar to that between a caterpillar and a butterfly. If man had not fallen, he would have known that discarding his flesh does not mean eternal separation from his loved ones, because the earthly men were created to communicate freely with spirit men, just as they do among themselves. Besides, if men knew what a beautiful and happy place the spirit world is, they would look forward to the day of departure from this world into the next.

If, among the two kinds of death, the physical one is not a result of the fall, we must conclude that spiritual death, signifying the degradation to Satanic dominion, is the real death caused by the fall.

Let us inquire into the question in more detail, centering on the Bible. The death caused by the fall means the death brought about by the first human ancestors' eating the fruit of the Tree of the Knowledge of Good and Evil. What kind of death must it have been? Genesis 2:17 says that God, after creating Adam and Eve, told them not to eat the fruit, because on the day they ate of it, they would surely die. Therefore, we must conclude that they did die on the day they ate the fruit, if we are to believe what God said. However, the "dead" Adam and Eve continued their physical life on earth, just as we do today, multiplying their children and finally producing a corrupted human society.

From this fact, we can clearly understand that the death caused by the fall does not mean the expiration of physical life, but the state of having fallen from the good dominion of God, to the evil dominion of Satan.

Let us then draw examples from the Bible. I John 3:14 says, ". . . He who does not love remains in death." Love here, of course, means God's love. It means that those who do not love their neighbor with God's love are dead, no matter how actively they may be living on the earth. Again, in Romans 6:23 we read, "The wages of sin is death, but the free gift of God is eternal life," and in Romans 8:6 it says, "To set the mind on the flesh is death, but to set the mind on the spirit is life and peace."

3. MEANING OF RESURRECTION

Man has hitherto entertained the wrong idea that the expiration of man's physical life is the death brought about by the fall. Consequently, we have believed that the resurrection of the passed-away saints would be realized through the restoration of their once corrupted and decomposed physical bodies to their original state.

According to the principle of creation, this kind of death was not brought about by the fall of the human ancestors. From the beginning, man's body was created to turn to dust after it ages and dies. Therefore, the human body, once it is dissolved into dust, cannot be resurrected to its original state. It is not necessary for a spirit man to resume his flesh, when there is a vast spirit world where he is supposed to go and live forever.

Therefore, "resurrection" means the phenomena occurring in the process of man's restoration, according to the providence of restoration, from the state of having fallen under Satanic dominion, back to the direct dominion of God. Accordingly, when we repent of our sins, making ourselves better and better, day by day, we are coming closer to resurrection.

To draw examples of resurrection from the Bible, we read in John 5:24, ". . . He who hears my word and believes him who sent me, has eternal life; he does not come into judgment, but has passed from death to life." This signifies that resurrection means to leave the bosom of Satan by believing in Jesus and to return to the bosom of God's love. Again, I Corinthians 15:22

says, "As in Adam all die, so also in Christ shall all be made alive," signifying that resurrection means to return to the Heavenly lineage through Christ, leaving the death of the Satanic lineage caused by the fall of Adam.

4. HOW DOES RESURRECTION CHANGE MAN?

As God predicted in Genesis 2:17, Adam and Eve, who had eaten the fruit of the Tree of the Knowledge of Good and Evil, died as a result (spiritual death). Nevertheless, there appeared to be no external change. If any, there must have been only a momentary change in their countenance, caused by fear and uneasiness from their guilty conscience. Therefore, even after fallen man has been resurrected to the original state, which existed before he ate the fruit, there will be no external change whatsoever in him. Those who are reborn through the Holy Spirit are men of resurrection to a certain degree, compared to what they were before. Let us compare a man of resurrection to a burglar. The former, being in the state of resurrection in proportion to the degree of his rebirth, belongs to the side of Heaven; while the latter, being in the state of death, belongs to Hell. There is, however, no external difference between the two.

As previously proven by examples, those who believe in God, in obedience to the words of Jesus, have surely passed from death into life. Nevertheless, there would be no detectable physical change by which we might discern a person in the state of death before his belief in Jesus from the same person after resurrection, through which he was transformed into life by believing in Jesus.

It is true that Jesus came as a man who had himself accomplished the purpose of creation (cf. "Christology"). However, Jesus, from his outward appearance, was no different from ordinary, fallen men. If he had any such difference, all his associates at that time would have surely followed him. Man leaves the Satanic dominion through resurrection, and by becoming one with God's heart he can enjoy deity.

When fallen men thus come into the dominion of God through resurrection, spiritual changes necessarily occur. The spiritual changes, in fact, would sanctify the human body, transforming it from the abode of Satan to the temple in which God may dwell. In that sense, it may be said that the physical body also is resurrected. It is similar to a building which has been used for evil purposes; when used as the temple of God, it would be turned into a sacred building, although there may be no change whatsoever in its external appearance.

SECTION II
Providence of Resurrection

1. HOW IS THE PROVIDENCE OF RESURRECTION ACCOMPLISHED?

Resurrection means the phenomena occurring in the course of fallen men's restoration to their original nature, endowed at the creation. Therefore, the "providence of resurrection" means the providence of restoration. In other words, since the providence of restoration is the providence of re-creation, the providence of resurrection is also the providence of re-creation. Consequently, the providence of resurrection is worked out in the following way, according to the principle of creation.

First, in the history of the providence of resurrection, the figures who took charge of certain responsibilities in their respective missions, though they could not fully carry out their portions of responsibility, loyally offered their best for the sake of God's will. In proportion to their accomplishments, they were able to broaden the base on which fallen men could open their relationship to God. As time goes by, people of succeeding generations can enjoy more benefit from their ages, according to the providence of restoration. The providence of resurrection, therefore, is carried out according to the benefits of the age.

Second, according to the principle of creation, man, who was created as part of God's portion of responsibility, was made to be perfected by believing in God's words and practicing them, as his own portion of responsibility. Therefore, in carrying out the providence of resurrection, there must be "words" from God for the sake of the providence, which is God's portion of responsibility. Only by believing in and practicing these words, as man's own portion of responsibility, is God's will accomplished.

Third, in light of the principle of creation, the spirit man was made to grow and become perfect only through the physical body. Thus, the resurrection of the spirit man, according to the providence of restoration, is also to be accomplished only through physical life on earth.

Fourth, man was created to be perfected by going through three orderly stages of growth, according to the principle of creation. Therefore, the providence of resurrection for fallen men is also to be accomplished through the three orderly stages of the providential period.

2. THE PROVIDENCE OF RESURRECTION FOR EARTHLY MEN

(1) The Providence for the Foundation of Resurrection

God began His providence of resurrection with Adam's family. However, the providence was prolonged due to the failure of central persons, who were in charge of God's will, to accomplish their portion of responsibility. 2,000 years later, God set up Abraham as the father of faith, and through him, the will began to be accomplished. Consequently, the 2,000-year period from Adam to Abraham resulted in the establishment of the foundation for the providence of resurrection, which was to be completed in the ages which followed. We call this period the "providential age for the foundation of resurrection.

(2) The Providence of Resurrection in the Formation Stage

During the 2,000-year period from the time of Abraham, when the providence of resurrection commenced, to Jesus, God carried out the "providential age for the formation stage resurrection." Earthly men of this period could enjoy the benefit of the age in accordance with God's providence of resurrection in the formation stage. God carried out the providence of resurrection in the formation stage in such a way that people were justified by believing in and practicing the Law of the Old Testament, which God had given them for the sake of the providence of that age, and by accomplishing their respective portions of responsibility. Therefore, we call this age the "age of justification by deeds." People of this age could attain the form-spirit stage by having their spirit men go through resurrection in the formation stage by their practice of the Law. When a man who has attained the form-spirit stage on earth leaves his physical body, his spirit goes to live in the spirit world at the form-spirit stage.

(3) The Providence of Resurrection in the Growth Stage

Due to the crucifixion of Jesus, the providence of resurrection has been left unaccomplished and has been prolonged until the time of the Second Advent. The 2,000-year period of prolongation is called the "providential age for the growth stage resurrection," because it is the age in which the providence of resurrection in the growth stage is carried out through spiritual salvation. Earthly men belonging to this age can receive the benefit of the age in accordance with the providence of resurrection in the growth stage. God carried out the providence of resurrection in the growth stage in such a way that the people of that age were justified by believing in the New Testament Words, which God had given them for the sake of the providence of that age, and by accomplishing their portions of responsibility. Therefore, that age may be called the "age of justification by faith." People of that age can attain the life-spirit stage by having their spirit men go through resurrection in the growth stage, through their faith in the Gospel. When a man who has attained the life-spirit stage leaves his physical body, he goes to Paradise, which is the spirit world for those who have attained the life-spirit stage.

(4) The Providence of Resurrection in the Perfection Stage

The age in which we complete the providence of resurrection through the resurrection of both spirit and body, through the Lord of the Second Advent, is called the "providential age for the perfection stage resurrection." Earthly people of this age can enjoy the benefit of the age through the providence of resurrection in the perfection stage. The Lord of the Second Advent is the one coming with the new Word for the fulfillment of the Old and New Testament Words (cf. Part I, Ch. III, Sec. V, 1). Therefore, God carries out the providence of resurrection in the perfection stage in such a way that people will be justified by believing in the new Word (the Completed Testament) which is given to them for the fulfillment of the Old and New Testaments, and by serving the Lord in person, thus accomplishing their portions of responsibility. Thus, this age may also be called the "age of justification by attendance." The spirit men belonging to this age can attain the divine-spirit stage of perfect resurrection in both spirit and body by believing in and serving the Lord of the Second Advent. The earthly region where the people of the divine-spirit stage live is called the Kingdom of Heaven on earth. When a perfected man, living in the Kingdom of Heaven on earth, leaves his physical body, he goes to live in the Heavenly Kingdom of God, which is the region of the spirit world belonging to divine spirits.

(5) Heaven and Paradise

Christians, up to the present, have been confused in their concepts of Heaven and Paradise because they have not known the Principle. If Jesus had accomplished the purpose of his coming on earth as the Messiah, the Kingdom of Heaven on earth would have been established at that time. If perfected man, living in the Kingdom of Heaven on earth, had gone to the spirit world as a spirit man having attained the divine-spirit stage, the Heavenly Kingdom of God would have been realized at that time.

However, the Kingdom of Heaven on earth has not been realized due to the crucifixion of Jesus, and not a single person on earth has attained the divine-spirit stage. Consequently, no spirit man has entered the Heavenly Kingdom of God, which was created for spirit men of the divine-spirit stage to live in. Therefore, the Heavenly Kingdom of God still remains vacant. Seen from the standpoint of men, who are to be its inhabitants, it may well be said that the Heavenly Kingdom has not yet been realized. Why then did Jesus say that whoever believed in him would enter the Kingdom of Heaven? This is because the original purpose of his coming to earth was to realize the Kingdom of Heaven. Nevertheless, Jesus died on the cross without having realized the Kingdom of Heaven on earth, due to the disbelief of the people.

Jesus permitted the thief who was crucified beside him to enter Paradise with him, because the thief was the only one who believed in him at the end, while the people of that time had not believed in him (Luke 23:43). Jesus emphasized the possibility of entering the Kingdom of Heaven when he still hoped to accomplish his mission as the Messiah. But upon his crucifixion, which prevented the fulfillment of the will, he expressed the fact that he was to enter Paradise. Paradise is the region of the spirit world where those spirit men who have attained the life-spirit stage by believing in Jesus while on earth go after death, and stay until the gate to the Kingdom of Heaven is opened.

(6) Spiritual Phenomena Occurring in the Last Days

Man, who fell in the perfection level of the growth stage, enters the age in which he can restore his position before the fall of the first human ancestors by restoring the perfection level of the New Testament Age (representing the growth stage), after having passed through the Old Testament Age (representing the formation stage). This age is called the Last Days.

Since this is the age in which man can communicate directly with God, just as he could right before the fall of Adam and Eve, there are many people on earth today who can communicate with the spirit world. The reason for God's promise that in the Last Days He would pour out His Spirit on all flesh (Acts 2:17) can be understood only through such a principle.

In the Last Days, a person may receive the revelation that he (or she) is a lord. In many cases, such people fail to find the right way, believing themselves to be the Lord of the Second Advent. What is the reason for this?

Originally, God created man and blessed him to be the lord and dominator of the whole creation (Gen. 1:28). Nevertheless, man failed to realize this blessing, due to the fall. When a fallen man attains the spiritual level corresponding to the position of Adam and Eve right before the fall, by having been spiritually restored to the perfection level of the growth stage through the providence of restoration, then God gives him the revelation that he is a lord, signifying that he has been restored to the position of having been blessed to be the lord of all creation.

The saints in the Last Days who have manifested such devout faith as to be entitled to the revelation that they are lords are in a position similar to that of John the Baptist, who came in the days of Jesus with the mission of making the way straight for him (John 1:23). Accordingly, in proportion to their ability, they also are given the mission of making straight the way of the Lord of the Second Advent. Thus, they receive the revelation that they are entitled to be lords because they were chosen for this mission.

Those with powers of spiritual communication are liable to become antichrists; upon receiving the revelation that they are lords they may act wrongly, as if they were the Lord of the Second Advent, since, not knowing the Principle, they are unaware of the situation. This is actually why it was prophesied that in the Last Days there would appear many antichrists.

It is common that those with powers of spiritual communication fall into conflict and confusion among themselves, because the content of their revelations and the class and level of the spirit world to which they belong differ from one another (I Cor. 15:41). These men of spiritual communication are in fact all headed for the same destination; but because of the difference in their spiritual standard, the part of the spirit world seen by each can vary, and these differences lead them into conflict.

Those who are in charge of a certain mission in the providence of restoration are often ignorant of their horizontal relationship with others who have spiritual communication, because they have only a vertical relationship with God which relates to their partial mission within the whole providence. Accordingly, they come into conflict because the will of God of which they take charge appears different to each. This kind of horizontal conflict is inevitable, because God gives each the revelation that he is a lord in order to encourage him to do his very best in carrying out the purpose of the providence of restoration. In his respective mission, which is partial and limited, the person in charge is, in fact, the only one and the best one; thus he receives such a revelation.

Meanwhile, when devout men of faith develop spiritual communication, after having attained the same spiritual level as Adam and Eve before the fall, they are apt to fall themselves through a test or temptation of the same kind which Adam and Eve failed to overcome. It is, in fact, very difficult to overcome such a temptation, as long as one remains ignorant of the Principle. It is truly regrettable that many religious men, having failed to overcome this test, have nullified in an instant the merit they gained through their long and bitter trials in the ascetic life.

How then can we prevent such confusion among men of spiritual communication? God has given a partial mission to numerous individuals in order to accomplish rapidly the purpose of the providence of restoration, with each relating vertically to Him during the process of the providence; therefore, horizontal conflict among men of spiritual communication is inevitable. Finally, at the consummation of human history, all will come to realize that their respective missions were allotted to them by God with an identical purpose: the accomplishment of the providence of restoration. By establishing horizontal relationships with each other, they will be unified in their efforts to accomplish the whole purpose of the providence of restoration through the new Words of truth God will give at the proper time. Then, all men of spiritual communication will cease their stubborn insistence that their way alone is God's will, and will gain the right understanding of their providential missions.

Thus, they will not only be able to overcome all confusion, but each will also be able to perfect his own mission in the course of his life in faith.

(7) The First Resurrection

The first resurrection is the resurrection enabling the accomplishment of the purpose of creation for the first time since the commencement of the history of God's providence of restoration. The original self will be restored by removing man's original sin through the Second Advent of the Lord.

Therefore, the hope of all Christians is to share in the first resurrection. What kind of people may share in this? Those who are the first to believe in the Lord at the Second Advent, following and serving him, will be those who participate. By doing so, they cooperate with him in setting up the condition of indemnity, on a general and worldwide basis, for the course of the providence of restoration. Thus, they fulfill the purpose of creation, having become spirit men of the divine-spirit stage, by removing the original sin before all other men. These are the people who can share in the first resurrection.

Next, let us study what "one hundred and forty-four thousand" as indicated in the Bible, means. In order for the Lord to accomplish the providence of restoration at his Second Advent, he must lay the foundation for victory over the Satanic world. He must set up horizontally, in his lifetime, the people who can restore through indemnity the positions of the saints and sages of history who have been invaded by Satan or have failed to accomplish their portions of responsibility. The total number of the saints whom the Lord of the Second Advent must find and set up for this purpose is one hundred and forty-four thousand, as written in Revelation 7:4 and 14:1-4.

In the course of God's providence of restoration, Jacob, who had the mission of restoring the family, started his mission centering on his twelve sons; and Moses started his mission of restoring a nation with twelve tribes under him. When each tribe multiplies after the pattern of the twelve sons, the total will be one hundred and forty-four. Jesus, who had the mission of restoring the world, had twelve disciples in order to restore through indemnity the number one hundred and forty-four, both spiritually and physically. But, due to his crucifixion, he has been able to work only spiritually for restoration through indemnity. Therefore, just as Jacob had twelve sons in order to restore horizontally, through indemnity, the twelve vertical generations from Noah to Abraham which had been claimed by Satan, the Lord of the Second Advent must set up a certain necessary number of saints corresponding to the number one hundred and forty-four, in order to restore this number horizontally, through indemnity, both spiritually and physically.

3. THE PROVIDENCE OF RESURRECTION FOR SPIRIT MEN

(1) The Reason and Method of the Spirit Man's Resurrection through Second Coming

According to the principle of creation, man's spirit was created to grow only through give and take action between the life element from God and the vitality element from man's physical body. Therefore, the spirit man can neither grow nor be resurrected apart from our physical body. So in order that spirit men, who passed away to the other world without having perfected themselves in their physical life on earth, might be resurrected, they must come again to earth and fulfill the responsibility they left unaccomplished in their physical life on earth, through the physical bodies of earthly men, by cooperating with the earthly saints and helping them fulfill the same mission. This is why Jude 1:14 says that in the Last Days the Lord will come "with his holy myriads."

In what manner do spirit men cooperate with earthly men to accomplish the will? When earthly saints form a reciprocal base with spirit men, through prayer and other spiritual activities, the spirit men descend and form reciprocal bases with the spirits of the earthly men, on which bases they cooperate. Thus, the spirit men pour out spiritual fire on earthly men, give them the power to heal diseases, and help them do many mighty works. More than that, they enable earthly men to see many facts in the spirit world in a state of trance, give them the gift of prophecy, and inspire them spiritually. Through such activities, substituting for the Holy Spirit, they cooperate with earthly men to fulfill the will of God.

(2) Resurrection through Second Coming of Spirit Men Who Were Christians in Their Lifetime

(i) Resurrection through Second Coming in the Growth Stage

Those form spirits of the Old Testament Age who in their lifetime had earnestly served God by observing the Law on earth all descended after the advent of the Messiah and cooperated with the earthly saints to fulfill the will, and thus enter the life-spirit stage. Spirit men who have thus come again and cooperated with earthly men can obtain the same benefit as those men; having become life spirits, they enter Paradise. We call this "resurrection through second coming in the growth stage."

Let us take some examples from the Bible. From the record that Elijah appeared, as a spirit, before Jesus and his disciples (Matt. 17:3), it is clear that Elijah is still in the spirit world. Meanwhile, Jesus called John the Baptist "Elijah." Jesus said this because Elijah descended to John the Baptist and cooperated with him to achieve the mission he left unaccomplished on earth, thus attaining the purpose of resurrection through second coming. So the physical body of John the Baptist substituted for that of Elijah, when seen from the standpoint of their mission.

On the other hand, Matthew 27:52 states that, upon the crucifixion of Jesus, the tombs were opened and many bodies of the saints who had fallen asleep were raised. This does not mean that their physical bodies, which had already decomposed in the earth, were raised. This is merely a record of the fact that the spirit men of the Old Testament Age, who had stayed in the spirit world as form spirits, descended in order to enter the life-spirit stage by cooperating with the saints on earth, who were in a position to benefit by the ransom of the cross. If the saints of the Old Testament Age had literally been raised from the tombs, they would surely have given witness to Jesus as the Messiah. Then, would not the people have believed that Jesus, who was testified to by the saints raised from the tombs, was the Messiah? Their activities would have been recorded in the Bible. But we have no such record in the Bible, other than the fact that they were raised from the tombs. From this, we may understand that these were spirit men who could be seen for a brief interval, only by those whose spiritual eyes were opened.

Compared to Paradise, which people could enter through the ransom by the cross of Jesus, the region where the spirit men of the Old Testament Age were staying was darker and full of misery; thus, it was called a "tomb."

(ii) Resurrection through Second Coming in the Perfection Stage

Those life spirits of the New Testament Age who believed in Jesus on earth and thus went to Paradise are to come again to earth after the Second Advent of the Messiah. These spirits, by cooperating with the earthly saints in believing in and serving the Lord of the Second Advent, thereby elevating them to the divine-spirit stage, would themselves become divine spirits. Thus, they can enter the Kingdom of Heaven in the spirit world with the earthly saints, who would enter this Kingdom after leaving their physical bodies. This providence of resurrection is called the "providence of resurrection through second coming in the perfection stage." Seen from the standpoint of this providence, earthly men consequently come to cooperate with spirit men, not to speak of the spirit men's cooperating with earthly men.

Hebrews 11:39-40 says, "All these [saints of the Old Testament Age], though well attested by their faith, did not receive what was promised [permission to enter the Kingdom of Heaven] since God had foreseen something better [the Kingdom of Heaven] for us [earthly men], that apart from us [earthly men] they [spirit men] should not be made perfect [citizens in the Kingdom of Heaven]." This Biblical passage demonstrates the principle that, apart from the cooperation of earthly men, the spirit men of the spirit world cannot perfect themselves. Also, in Matthew 18:18, it is said, "Whatever you [earthly saints] bind on earth shall be bound in heaven, and whatever you loose on earth shall be loosed in heaven," clarifying that whatever is bound by spirit men shall not be loosed unless the earthly saints loose it. Thus spirit men can be resurrected only by descending to the earthly saints and cooperating with them. Therefore, as we read in Matthew 16:19, Jesus gave the keys of the Kingdom of Heaven to Peter, who represented the earthly saints, so that he might open the gate of Heaven here on earth.

(3) Resurrection through Second Coming of Spirit Men Outside of Paradise

First, let us examine the manner in which spirit men who believed in religions other than Christianity in their lives can be resurrected through their second coming. In the same manner that all men, in order to accomplish a common purpose must first establish a reciprocal base, earthly men and spirit men must also establish a reciprocal base between them in order to fulfill the common purpose of the providence of restoration. Therefore, the spirit men who come again for resurrection first choose earthly men of the same religion they believed in during their earthly life as their suitable objects to work through, and then descend to the specific men of their choice. Thus, they come to enjoy the same benefits as the earthly men, by assisting them to accomplish the purpose of restoration.

Second, let us investigate in what manner the good spirit men, who in their earthly life lived conscientiously though they did not have any religion, can be resurrected through second coming. There can be no absolutely good man among fallen men, since he would have the original sin inherent in him. Therefore, by "good spirit men," we mean those in possession of more goodness than evil within themselves. This type of good spirit man descends to good earthly men, and by cooperating with them to fulfill the purpose of God's restoration, finally enjoys the same benefits with them.

Third, let us study in what manner evil spirit men can be resurrected through their second coming. In Matthew 25:41, we read about the cursed, who are liable to the eternal fire prepared for the "devil and his angels." The "angels" of the devil means the evil spirit men working under the control of the devil. The spiritual creatures commonly called "ghosts," whose real nature has not been known, are none other than such evil spirit men. These evil spirits also gain the benefit of the age by descending on earthly men.

However, not all the works of evil spirit men result in their receiving the benefit of resurrection through second coming. Their works must first of all result in establishing a condition of indemnity for God's intention to eradicate the sins of earthly men by punishment, before the evil spirit men can obtain the benefit of resurrection through second coming. Then, how do the works of evil spirits result in exercising judgment on behalf of God?

Let us consider another example. Suppose there is an earthly man who is entitled to go from the sphere of benefit of the family level to that of the tribal level, through the benefit of the age in the providence of restoration. However, if this man has a certain debt of sin, either his own or his ancestors', he cannot go to the sphere of benefit of the tribal level without having liquidated the sin by setting up a corresponding condition of indemnity. In this case, God can allow the evil spirit to torment the earthly man as punishment for his sin. Then, if this man gladly endures the torment given by the evil spirit man, he can graduate from the sphere of benefit of the family level to that of the tribal level, with his endurance as the condition of indemnity. In this case, the evil spirit man receives a share of the benefit. In this way, the providence of restoration broadens its scope in accordance with the benefit of the age, from the sphere of benefit of the family level, to that of the tribal level, national level, and finally to that of the worldwide level. Whenever he is to graduate to the next level of the sphere of benefit of the age, the person in charge of the providence must necessarily set up a condition of indemnity corresponding to the debt of sin incurred either by himself or his forefathers. There are two methods by which evil spirit men may set up a condition of indemnity for sinful earthly men.

First, there is the method in which the earthly man sets up the condition of indemnity to liquidate his sin, in which evil spirit men work directly on the earthly man, whom they obsess. The second method of setting up a condition of indemnity for the sin of an earthly man is to have an evil spirit descend to an evil earthly man; the evil spirit then influences the evil earthly man to perform substantially the evil works of his intention against the man setting up the indemnity condition.

In both cases if the man gladly endures the works of the evil spirit man (as due), he can set up a condition of indemnity for his own sin and that of his ancestors. Thus he is allowed to enter the sphere of benefit of the new age. Thus, the works of the evil spirit man result in having exercised judgment on the earthly man for his sins, on behalf of God. Through their works, evil spirit men also are allowed to enter the sphere of benefit of the new age, with the same benefits as earthly men.

4. THE THEORY OF REINCARNATION VIEWED FROM THE STANDPOINT OF RESURRECTION THROUGH SECOND COMING

For the providence of restoration, God has called many individuals and given each an appropriate share of the total mission, in order to accomplish the whole purpose. Meanwhile, each man has transferred his mission to many similar individuals in succession, until the mission is finally accomplished, having passed through many individuals throughout human history.

The providence of restoration, beginning on the individual level, is headed for the final goal of the restoration of the entire cosmos, after passing through the family level, national level and worldwide level. Therefore, the mission of a certain person, though it may be a part of the whole, would begin first as an individual mission, and then broaden in scope to a family mission, national mission, and finally to a worldwide mission. Examples of this in the Bible include: Abraham, with both an individual and family mission; Moses, with a national mission; and Jesus, with a worldwide mission.

Also, the spirit men who left their missions unaccomplished on earth descend to earthly men whose missions are similar to those with which the spirit men were charged while on earth, and cooperate with them for the accomplishment of the will. Seen from the standpoint of mission, the physical body of the earthly man serves as the body of the spirit man. The earthly man, receiving the cooperation of the spirit man, would accomplish the mission of the spirit man as well as his own. In this case, the earthly man is the "second coming" of the spirit man who cooperates with him, so he often takes on the name of the spirit man. Therefore, the earthly man frequently appears to be the reincarnation of the spirit man. To take an example from the Bible: John the Baptist, in the course of fulfilling his mission through the cooperation of Elijah, had to accomplish the mission which Elijah had left unaccomplished while on earth. Jesus called John the Baptist "Elijah" (cf. Sec. II, 3[2]) because John's body was the substitute for Elijah's body.

In the Last Days, the earthly men in charge of specific world-wide missions are in a position to succeed the spirit men who formerly had these missions on earth, and to accomplish these missions. Accordingly, these spirit men descend to earthly men of their choice and, by cooperating with them, accomplish the missions which they left unfulfilled in their earthly lives. There-fore, the earthly man, receiving the cooperation of the spirit man, is the second coming of that spirit man; he also appears to be the reincarnation of the spirit man. This is why many people in the Last Days claim to be either Christ, Buddha, Confucius, or the "Olive Tree" or the Tree of Life. The doctrine of reincar-nation, upheld by Buddhism, comes from an interpretation of external appearances, without knowing the theory of "resur-rection through second coming."

SECTION III
Unification of Religions by
Resurrection through Second Coming

1. UNIFICATION OF CHRISTIANITY BY RESURRECTION THROUGH SECOND COMING

As stated in Section II, 3(2) of this chapter, the spirit men of the life-spirit stage, Paradise, descend to the earthly saints who are capable of attaining the divine-spirit stage by believing in the

Lord of the Second Advent and ministering to him. They can finally enter the Kingdom of Heaven with the same merit as earthly saints by cooperating with them in accomplishing the will of the providence of restoration. Accordingly, in the days of the Second Advent, all the spirit men in Paradise will descend to the earthly saints and cooperate with them.

The time of the visitation may differ according to the individual's faith, his natural disposition, and his ancestors' accomplishments for the will of God. In this manner, earthly saints are sooner or later destined to attend the Lord of the Second Advent and devote themselves to the will of God, through the cooperation of the spirit men descending to them from Paradise. Therefore, Christianity is destined to realize its unification.

2. UNIFICATION OF ALL OTHER RELIGIONS BY RESURRECTION THROUGH SECOND COMING

As discussed in the "Consummation of Human History," we cannot deny the historical fact that all religions, which in fact have an identical purpose, are being absorbed gradually into the cultural sphere of Christianity. Therefore, Christianity is not a religion for Christians alone, but has the mission of accomplishing the ultimate purpose of all the religions that have appeared in the past. Naturally, the Lord of the Second Advent, who comes as the central figure of Christianity, will also play the role of Buddha, whom Buddhists believe will come again, as well as the role of the "True Man" whose appearance Confucianists anticipate, and "Chung Do Ryung" ("Herald of the Righteous Way") whom many Koreans expect to come. In addition, he will also play the role of the central figure whom all other religions await.

For this reason, the spirit men who believed in religions other than Christianity while on earth will have to come again, like the spirit men of Paradise, in order to receive the same benefit of resurrection through the Second Advent, though the time of their visitation may differ according to their spiritual positions. In this manner, they are destined to descend to the earthly men who belong to their religions and lead them to the Lord of the Second Advent, cooperating with them to believe in and serve him for the accomplishment of the will of God. Therefore, all religions will finally be unified, centering on Christianity.

3. UNIFICATION OF NON-RELIGIOUS MEN BY RESURRECTION THROUGH SECOND COMING

The spirit men who in their lifetime did not believe in any religion but lived conscientiously, also come again at permitted times in order to obtain the benefit of resurrection through second coming. In this way, they cooperate with earthly men of conscience to find and serve the Lord of the Second Advent and participate in accomplishing the will of God. The story of the three wise men coming from the East and worshipping the infant Jesus (Matt. 2:1-16) is one such example.

The ultimate purpose of God's providence of restoration is to save all mankind. Therefore, it is God's intention to abolish Hell completely, after the lapse of the period necessary for the full payment of all indemnity. If Hell remains eternally in the world of creation even after the fulfillment of God's purpose of goodness, it would result in the contradiction of an imperfect God, not to speak of the resultant imperfection in His ideal of creation and His providence of restoration.

If the hearts of parents in fallen families are saddened by the unhappiness of even one of their children, how much more would it be so with God, as the Heavenly Parent! In II Peter 3:9 we find, "The Lord . . . is forebearing toward you, not wishing that any should perish, but that all should reach repentance." Accordingly, Hell cannot remain forever in the ideal world, which is to be realized in accordance with the will of

God. Even the forces of Satan testified to Jesus' being the son of God (Matt. 8:29). When the Last Days come, even evil spirits will descend to earthly men of the same level, and by cooperating with them will take part in the fulfillment of God's will. Finally, after a due period of time, the unified purpose of creation will be attained.

CHAPTER VI

Predestination

It is true that theological controversies about "Predestination" have caused great confusion in the religious lives of many Christians. We must understand what brought this about.

In the Bible, there are many passages that could be interpreted to mean that the fortune or misfortune, happiness or misery of any individual, as well as the salvation or damnation of fallen men and the rise and fall of nations, all occur according to God's predestination. For example, the Bible says:

Those whom He predestined He also called; and those whom He called He also justified; and those whom He justified He also glorified. (Rom. 8:30)

Again it says:

> . . . 'I will have mercy on whom I have mercy, and I will have compassion on whom I have compassion.' So it depends not upon man's will or exertion, but upon God's mercy. (Rom. 9:15-16)

It again says (Rom. 9:21), "Has the potter no right over the clay, to make out of the same lump one vessel for beauty and another for menial use?" It also says (Rom. 9:11-13) that God loved Jacob and hated Esau while they were still in their mother's womb, and said the elder would serve the younger.

In this way, there are ample Biblical grounds to justify "complete predestination." But we must not forget that there are also many Biblical passages that deny complete predestination. For example, when we see that God warned the first human ancestors not to eat of the fruit (Gen. 2:17) in order to prevent them from falling, it is evident that man's fall was not God's predestination but the result of man's disobedience to God's commandment. Again we read (Gen. 6:6), that God was sorry that He had put man on earth. If man had fallen according to God's predestination, there would be no reason for Him to be sorry for His having created man, whose fall He would have predestined. John 3:16 says that whoever believes in Christ shall not perish.

When we read in Matthew 7:7, "Ask, and it will be given you; seek, and you will find; knock, and it will be opened to you," we can see well enough that all things are not accomplished merely by the predestination of God, but by human endeavor. If all things are to be accomplished solely by God's predestination, why did God so emphasize human efforts? Again, when we read that we should pray for sick brothers (James 5:14), we can understand that suffering due to sickness is not by the predestination of God. If all things were inevitably decided by

God's predestination, there would be no need for man's tearful prayers.

If we accept the traditional belief of predestination, man's prayers, evangelism, charity and other human endeavors would be of no use whatsoever to God's providence of restoration; and any such endeavor would ultimately be useless. This is because the predestination of God, who is absolute, should also be absolute, without leaving room for any change due to human effort.

Since there are sufficient Biblical grounds to justify either acceptance or rejection of the theory of predestination, controversies over the doctrine of predestination are inevitable. How, then, would the Principle solve such problems? Let us investigate the question of predestination.

SECTION I
Predestination of the Will

Let us first define "will" before discussing predestination of the will. God could not accomplish His purpose of creation due to the human fall. Therefore, the will of God, in working His providence with fallen men, is to accomplish His purpose of creation. In other words, the "will" means the fulfillment of the purpose of the providence of restoration.

Next, we must know that God first determines the will, and then works to accomplish it. Having created man, God set up His will to accomplish the purpose of creation; however, due to the human fall, He was unable to accomplish the will. Naturally, in order to accomplish it, He has to determine His will a second time, and thus He carries out the providence of restoration.

God predestines the will to be one of goodness, not of evil; then He works to accomplish it. Since God is the essence of goodness, His purpose of creation must also be one of goodness. Naturally, the purpose of His providence of restoration must be good, and His will to accomplish this purpose must also be good. God could not have predestined that which obstructs and is against the purpose of creation. Thus, we know that He could not have predetermined such things as the human fall, judgment of fallen men, or the destruction of the universe. If such evil results had been the necessary product of God's predestination, He would not have regretted the evil result of His own predestination, and we could not think of God as the subject of goodness. God, looking at fallen men, was sorry that He had made man on earth (Gen. 6:6); and, seeing King Saul's faithlessness, He repented that He had made Saul king (I Sam. 15:11). This is good evidence that these events were not the result of God's predestination. Such evil results occur from man's failure to accomplish his portion of responsibility, and from his being on the side of Satan.

To what extent does God predetermine the will to accomplish His purpose of creation? God is the absolute being—unique, eternal, and unchangeable; so God's purpose of creation must be the same. Accordingly, the will of the providence of restoration, which is to accomplish the purpose of creation, should be unique, unchangeable, and absolute (Is. 46:11). God predetermines the will to be absolute; so, when a person chosen for the will fails to accomplish it, God must go on to fulfill it, even by setting up another person in place of the one who failed.

For example, when God's will to fulfill the purpose of creation centering on Adam failed, He sent Jesus as the second Adam, attempting to fulfill the will centering on him, because His predestination of the will was absolute. When this will was again a failure, due to the disbelief of the people (cf. Part I, Ch. IV, Sec. I, 2), Jesus promised the Lord would come and fulfill the will without fail (Matt. 16:27). Again, in Adam's family,

God intended to lay the foundation to receive the Messiah through His providence centered on Cain and Abel.

However, this will ended in failure when Cain killed Abel. Then, God intended to accomplish His will through Noah's family. When Noah's family failed to accomplish this will, God had to set up Abraham to fulfill the will. In another instance, God intended to fulfill the will which Abel failed to accomplish by setting up Seth (Gen. 4:25). Also, He attempted to fulfill the will unaccomplished by Moses by choosing Joshua in his stead (Josh. 1:5); and again, He tried to fulfill the will unaccomplished due to the betrayal of Judas Iscariot by electing Matthias (Acts 1:15).

SECTION II
Predestination for the Fulfillment of the Will

As clarified in the "Principle of Creation," God's purpose of creation is to be fulfilled only by man's accomplishment of his portion of responsibility. The will for the providence of restoration, which is to fulfill this purpose, being absolute, is not for man to interfere with; however, man must accomplish his own portion of responsibility in order for the will to be accomplished. Therefore, God's purpose of creation was to be fulfilled only through man's accomplishing his portion of responsibility by not eating of the fruit of the Tree of the Knowledge of Good and Evil (Gen. 2:17).

Accordingly, even in accomplishing the purpose of the providence of restoration, the will can be fulfilled only through the accomplishment of man's responsibility by the central figure in charge of the mission. In Jesus' day, the people should have believed in Jesus absolutely, in order that he might accomplish the purpose of the providence of salvation. But due to their disbelief, they could not accomplish their portion of responsibility, and naturally, the accomplishment of the will had to be postponed to the day of the Second Advent.

Then, to what degree and to what extent would God predetermine the accomplishment of the will? As mentioned, God's will to accomplish the purpose of the providence of restoration is absolute, but the accomplishment of the will is relative. So, it is predetermined that the will is to be accomplished, but only through God's 95 percent responsibility and man's 5 percent responsibility combined. Indicating the proportion of man's responsibility as 5 percent is only to say that man's responsibility is extremely small compared to God's. Nevertheless, we must understand that, for man, it means 100 percent effort.

To cite examples: the accomplishment of the will centering on Adam and Eve was predestined to be fulfilled by the fulfillment of their own portion of responsibility, namely, by not eating of the fruit of the Tree of the Knowledge of Good and Evil. The providence of restoration centering on Noah was predestined to be fulfilled by the accomplishment of his own portion of responsibility, through his loyalty in building the ark. The providence of salvation through Jesus was predestined to be accomplished through the fulfillment of responsibility on the part of fallen men by their believing in Jesus as the Messiah and following him (John 3:16). Men have caused the prolongation of God's providence of restoration by not fulfilling even their small amount of responsibility.

The Bible says, "The prayer of faith will save the sick man" (James 5:15); "Your faith has made you well" (Mark 5:34); "For every one who asks receives, and he who seeks finds, and to him who knocks it will be opened." (Matt. 7:8) All these Biblical passages prove that the will is predestined to be fulfilled by the accomplishment of man's own portion of responsibility. We can understand well enough how small were the responsibilities men took charge of in all these instances, compared to God's responsible portion of toil and grace.

At the same time, from the fact that through their failure to accomplish their portions of responsibility, the central figures in the providence were compelled to cause the prolongation of the providence of restoration, we can well imagine how extremely difficult it was for them to fulfill even a relatively small responsibility.

SECTION III
Predestination of Man

Adam and Eve could have become good human ancestors if they had accomplished their own portion of responsibility by obeying God's injunction not to eat the fruit of the Tree of the Knowledge of Good and Evil, but they failed to do so. Therefore, God could not predestine them, absolutely, to be good human ancestors. In the case of fallen men, a chosen man could become a person of God's predestination only by accomplishing his own portion of responsibility. Therefore, God cannot predestine a certain person with absolute certainty that he will become what he is predestined to be.

Then, to what degree does God predestine man? In God's accomplishment of His will, centering on a certain person, He establishes it as an indispensable condition that the man must fulfill his own portion of responsibility. Therefore, God, in predestining a person for a certain mission, determines that the person will be what he is predestined to be only by the 100 percent accomplishment of the will centering on the person, with God's portion of 95 percent responsibility and man's portion of 5 percent responsibility accomplished together. Therefore, if the person fails to accomplish his own portion of responsibility, he cannot become the person God predestined.

For example, when God chose Moses, He predestined him to be the great leader capable of bringing the elected people to the blessed land of Canaan, but only by accomplishing his own portion of responsibility (Ex. 3:10). When in Kadesh-barnea Moses went against God's will by striking the rock twice, he failed to carry out his responsibility, thus nullifying God's predestination; he died on the way to the appointed place (Num. 20:7-12, 20:24, 27:14). Likewise, when God chose Judas Iscariot, He predestined him to be Jesus' apostle if he accomplished his own portion of responsibility with loyalty. However, since Judas failed to carry out his responsibility, God's predestination was not fulfilled and Judas turned out to be a betrayer.

When God called the Jewish people, He predestined them to be the chosen nation of glory, but only by fulfilling their portion of responsibility through their faith and service. Nevertheless, the predestination was not realized because they delivered Jesus to be crucified; and therefore, the chosen nation was scattered.

Next, let us examine the conditions and qualifications for becoming the central figure of the providence of restoration in God's predestination. The purpose of God's providence of salvation is to restore the fallen world to the original world of creation. Though the times of their salvation may differ, all fallen men are predestined to be saved (II Peter 3:9). Just as with the process of His creation, God's providence of salvation, which is the providence of re-creation, cannot be accomplished in a moment. Therefore, this providence is gradually broadening its scope to cover the whole, starting from "one." Thus, in the predestination of the providence of salvation, God first predestines the central figure and calls him to the mission.

What conditions and qualifications must this central figure have? First, he must be born out of the chosen nation, in charge of the providence of restoration. Next, even within the chosen nation, he must be the descendant of ancestors with many accomplishments of goodness. Then, even though he may be the descendant of ancestors with many good deeds, he must be endowed with the natural disposition suitable for the accomplishment of the will. Even if a man has these endowments, he must subsequently have good conditions in which to grow and work in his lifetime. Still, even among these persons, God would select first the individual most fully prepared at the appropriate time and place of God's need.

SECTION IV
Elucidation of Biblical Verses Which Justify the Theory of Predestination

We have clarified many problems concerning God's predestination. But the problem yet to be solved is how to elucidate the Biblical records, such as those enumerated in the introduction to this chapter, which are written as though all things are of God's absolute predestination.

Let us first elucidate Romans 8:29-30, which says:

> For those whom He foreknew He also predestined . . . and those whom He predestined He also called; and those whom He called He also justified; and those whom He justified He also glorified.

God, being omniscient, knows who is endowed with the qualities to be the central figure in the providence of restoration (Sec. ·III). Therefore, God predestines and calls the person He foreknew in order to fulfill the purpose of the providence of restoration. Calling the person is God's portion of responsibility, but this alone has nothing to do with the person's being justified and finally glorified in God. He must accomplish his own responsibility in the position of a person called by God before he can be justified; only after he is thus justified will he be glorified by God. It is predestined that man can enjoy glory from God only by accomplishing his own portion of responsibility. There are no words such as "man's own portion of responsibility" in the Bible, so everything appears to be accomplished merely by God's absolute predestination.

The Bible says (Rom. 9:15-16):

> . . . 'I will have mercy on whom I have mercy, and I will have compassion on whom I have compassion.' So it depends not upon man's will or exertion, but upon God's mercy.

As elucidated above, God chooses the one who is most suitable for the fulfillment of the purpose of restoration, foreknowing all his qualities. Therefore, it is God's privilege to elect such a person and to have mercy on him or have compassion for him. It depends not upon man's desire or endeavor. These Biblical verses are given in order to emphasize the power and grace of God.

It is again said (Rom. 9:21):

> Has the potter no right over the clay, to make out of the same lump one vessel for beauty and another for menial use?

It has already been said that God set up man's own portion of responsibility as the condition to exalt him to be the lord of all creation and to love him most by having man take after His creative nature. However, man fell, having violated this condition. Therefore, man became an existence deserted like trash; so this verse was given to teach people that man has no right to complain against whatever way God may handle men of this kind.

Further, the Bible states that God loved Jacob but hated Esau, and that "The elder will serve the younger." (Rom. 9:10-13) What must have been the reason that God loved Jacob and hated Esau while they were not yet born and had done nothing, either good or bad? This was to fulfill God's program in the course of the providence of restoration. Further details will be discussed in the section covering the providence of restoration centering on Abraham's family (cf. Part II, Ch. I, Sec. III). We must understand here that God gave Isaac twin sons, Esau and Jacob, because He had to restore through indemnity the will for the restoration of the birthright, which had been left unaccomplished by Cain's killing of Abel in Adam's family. This He intended to do by setting up the twin brothers, in the positions of Cain and Abel, and by having Jacob (in the position of Abel) make Esau (in the position of Cain) give in. God said this because Esau, being in the position of Cain, was liable to be hated by God, while Jacob, being in the position of Abel, was entitled to His love.

God's actually either loving or hating one or the other depended upon the fulfillment of their respective portions of responsibility. In fact, Esau, having surrendered in obedience to Jacob, received a blessing of love equal to Jacob's though he was in the position liable to be hated by God. On the other hand, Jacob, though he was in the position to be loved by God, could not have received such love if he had failed to accomplish his portion of responsibility.

It was because of ignorance about the relationship of man's portion of responsibility to God's in fulfilling the purpose of the providence of restoration that there appeared a man like Calvin, who obstinately held to his "theory of predestination," and that such a theory has been believed by so many people for so long.

CHAPTER VII

Christology

There are many questions to be resolved by fallen men who are on their way to attaining the goal of salvation. The most important of all are the questions concerning the relationship between Jesus and the Holy Spirit centered on God, the relationship between Jesus, the Holy Spirit, and fallen men, rebirth, Trinity, and others, all within the scope of Christology. Up to the present day, no one has ever completely answered these questions. With these questions still unresolved, there remains much confusion in the life in faith and doctrines of Christianity. In order to resolve these questions, we must first understand the value of the original man endowed at the creation. Let us discuss this question before dealing with the others.

SECTION I

The Value of the Man Who Has Attained the Purpose of Creation

Let us discuss the value of the man who has attained the purpose of creation—that is, the value of Adam in perfection.

First, let us discuss the relationship between God and perfected man from the standpoint of "dual characteristics." According to the principle of creation, man was created with mind and body, taking after God's dual characteristics. There are mutual relationships between God and perfected man which may be compared to the relationships between man's mind and body.

Just as the body was created as the substantial object to the invisible mind which it resembles, man was created as the substantial object to the invisible God, taking after His image. Since we cannot separate one from the other when the mind and body of a perfected man become one, centered on God, we can never sever the relationship formed when God and perfected man become one body through the four position foundation, because, in this state, man would live in perfect union with God's heart and feeling. In this way, a man who attains the purpose of creation would become the temple of God's constant abode (I Cor. 3:16), thus assuming deity (cf. Part I, Ch. I, Sec. III, 2). As Jesus said, man must become perfect as our heavenly Father (Matt. 5:48). Therefore, the man who has attained the purpose of creation would assume the divine value of God.

Second, let us consider the value of man, centering on the purpose of creating man. God's purpose in creating man was to enjoy happiness through him. Each individual has special characteristics which others do not have. However vast the number of people on earth may be, we can find no two identical in their individuality. Therefore, there is only one individual in the whole creation who can return stimulating joy to God as His substantial object, through a reciprocal base with the particular dual essentialities contained within God, which are subjective to that individual (cf. Part I, Ch. I, Sec. III, 2). The man who has attained the purpose of creation, whoever he may be, is an existence unique in the whole universe. Buddha's statement, "I am my own Lord throughout heaven and earth," is reasonable in light of this principle.

Third, let us study man's value from the standpoint of the relationship between man and the rest of creation. By understanding the relationship between man and the rest of creation, according to the principle of creation, we can better understand the value of perfected man. Man was created to rule the invisible world with his spirit, and to rule the visible world with his physical body. Therefore, the man who has attained the purpose of creation becomes the ruler of all creation (Gen. 1:28). Thus, man is to rule both the visible and the invisible worlds, with his physical body and his spirit. Thus, these two worlds form a substantial object to God by performing the action of give and take, with man as the medium.

According to the principle of creation, we know that the world of creation is the substantial development of man's dual essentialities. Accordingly, man's spirit is the substantial encapsulation of the entire invisible world, while his physical body is the substantial encapsulation of the entire visible world. Therefore, a man having fulfilled the purpose of creation is the substantial encapsulation of the entire cosmos. This is the reason man is called a microcosm. Man has the value corresponding to that of the whole macrocosm, as it is said (Matt. 16:26), "For what will it profit a man if he gains the whole world and forfeits his life?"

Suppose there is a perfect machine. If the parts of the machine are the only ones of their kind in the whole world and can neither be obtained nor made again, one part would have a value corresponding to that of the whole machine, however trivial that part may be, because without it the whole machine would not operate. Likewise, the individuality of a perfected man is unique. So, however unimportant he may seem, he in fact corresponds to the whole macrocosm in terms of his value.

SECTION II
Jesus and the Man Who Has Attained the Purpose of Creation

1. JESUS AND PERFECTED ADAM AS THE RESTORATION OF THE TREE OF LIFE

Human history is the history of the providence to establish the Kingdom of Heaven on earth by restoring the Tree of Life (Rev. 22:14), which was lost in the Garden of Eden (Gen. 3:24). We can know the relationship between Jesus and perfected Adam by understanding the relationship between the Tree of Life in the Garden of Eden (Gen. 2:9) and the Tree of Life that is to be restored at the close of the age (Rev. 22:14).

As already discussed in detail in the "Fall of Man," if Adam had become a man who had attained the ideal of creation, he would have become the Tree of Life (Gen. 2:9); and all his posterity would also have become trees of life. However, Adam fell, nullifying the will (Gen. 3:24), and ever since, it has been the hope of fallen men to restore themselves to this Tree of Life (Prov. 13:12, Rev. 22:14). Since fallen man can never restore himself as the Tree of Life by his own power, a man having attained the ideal of creation must come as the Tree of Life, and all men must be engrafted to him. Christ is the man who comes, symbolized as the Tree of Life (Rev. 22:14). Therefore, perfected Adam, symbolized by the Tree of Life in the Garden of Eden, and Jesus, who is also likened to the Tree of Life (Rev. 22:14), are identical from the standpoint of their being men who have attained the ideal of creation.

2. JESUS AND THE MAN WHO HAS ATTAINED THE PURPOSE OF CREATION

We have already explained in Section I the value of perfected man. Let us here consider the difference between Jesus and perfected man. As we well know from the previous discussion, a perfected man, in light of the purpose of creation, should become perfect, as God is perfect (Matt. 5:48); thus, he is so valuable as to even possess deity. Since God is eternal, man, who was created as His substantial object, should also become eternal, after his perfection.

Besides, the value of the existence of the whole macrocosm cannot be complete without perfected man, because he is a unique being and the lord of all creation. Therefore, man has the value of the whole macrocosm.

Jesus is truly a man of this value. However great his value may be, he cannot assume a value greater than that of a man who has attained the purpose of creation. Therefore, we cannot deny that Jesus was a man who had attained the purpose of creation.

The Principle does not deny the attitude of faith held by many Christians that Jesus is God, since it is true that a perfected man is one body with God. Furthermore, when the Principle asserts that Jesus is a man having attained the purpose of creation, this does not in the least diminish his value. However, the principle of creation sees the original value of perfected man as being equal to that of Jesus. We have explained above that Jesus was a man who had attained the purpose of creation. Then, let us look at the Biblical proof for this.

It is written in I Timothy 2:5, "For there is one God, and one mediator between God and men, the man Christ Jesus." We find in Romans 5:19, "For as by one man's [Adam's] disobedience many were made sinners, so by one man's [Jesus'] obedience many shall be made righteous." It further explains (I Cor. 15:21), "For as by a man [Adam] came death, by a man [Jesus] has come also the resurrection of the dead." The Bible also says (Acts 17:31), " . . . he has fixed a day on which he will judge the world in righteousness by a man whom he has appointed" and Luke 17:26 says, "As it was in the days of Noah, so will it be in the days of the Son of man." Thus, the Bible demonstrates most plainly that Jesus is a man. Above all, he had to come as a man in order to be the True Parent of mankind, thus giving man rebirth.

3. IS JESUS GOD HIMSELF?

When Philip asked Jesus to show him God, Jesus said to him, "He who has seen me has seen the Father; how can you say, 'Show us the Father?' Do you not believe that I am in the Father and the Father in me?" (John 14:9-10) Again the Bible says, "He was in the world, and the world was made through him, yet the world knew him not." (John 1:10) Further, it is written, "Truly, truly, I say to you, before Abraham was, I am." (John 8:58) On the grounds of all these Biblical verses, many Christians have hitherto believed that Jesus is God Himself, the Creator.

As demonstrated above, Jesus, as a man having fulfilled the purpose of creation, is one body with God. So, in light of his deity, he may well be called God. Nevertheless, he can by no means be God Himself. The relationship between God and Jesus can be compared to that between the mind and body. The body, as the substantial object which resembles the mind, is one body with the mind, so it may be called a second mind (image of the mind), but the body can by no means be the mind itself. In like manner, Jesus, being one body with God, may be called a second God (image of God), but he can by no means be God Himself. It is true that he who has seen Jesus has seen God (John 14:9-10); but Jesus did not say this to indicate that he was God Himself.

It is written (John 1:14) that Jesus is the Word made flesh. This means that Jesus is the substantiation of the Word; that is, the incarnation of the Word. Then, it is written (John 1:3) that all things were made through the Word, and again (John 1:10), that the world was made through Jesus; naturally, Jesus may well be called the Creator. According to the principle of creation, the world of creation is the substantial development of the character and form of a man of perfected individuality. So, a man who has fulfilled the purpose of creation is the substantial encapsulation of the entire cosmos, and the center of harmony in the whole creation. In that sense, it may also be said that the world was created by a man of perfection. God intended to have man, after his perfection through the fulfillment of his own portion of responsibility, stand in the position of the creator over all things, by giving him even His own creative nature. Seen from this perspective, we can understand that the Bible (John 1:10) only clarifies the fact that Jesus was a man who had perfected the purpose of creation, and does not signify that he was the Creator Himself.

Jesus was a descendant of Abraham; but since he came as the human ancestor giving rebirth to all mankind, he would become the forefather of Abraham, in light of the providence of restoration. This is why Jesus said (John 8:58), ". . . before Abraham was, I am." We must understand that this also does not signify that Jesus was God Himself. Jesus, on earth, was a man no different from us except for the fact that he was without original sin. Even in the spirit world after his resurrection, he lives as a spirit man with his disciples. The only difference between them is that Jesus abides as a spirit man of the divine spirit stage, emitting brilliant light, while his disciples are the objects who reflect this light.

Meanwhile, Jesus has been interceding for us before God even in the spirit world after his resurrection (Rom. 8:34), just as he did on earth. If Jesus is God Himself, how could he intercede for us before Himself? Moreover, we see that Jesus also called upon "God" or "Father" for help, which is good evidence that he is not God Himself (Matt. 27:46, John 17:1). If Jesus was God Himself, how could God have been tempted by Satan, and finally crucified by the evil force? Furthermore, when we find that Jesus said on the cross, "My God, my God, why hast thou forsaken me?" it becomes clear that Jesus is not God Himself.

SECTION III
Jesus and Fallen Man

Fallen man, lacking the value of the original man who has fulfilled the purpose of creation, fell to a lowly position, in which he looks up to the angels, who were created to be lower than himself. But Jesus had the value of a man who has accomplished the purpose of creation, and this qualified him to dominate the entire cosmos, including the angels (I Cor. 15:27). Meanwhile, fallen man, still having the original sin, remains susceptible to Satan's invasion. But Jesus, having no original sin, is without any such susceptibility. Fallen man does not know the heart and will of God; if he had ever had such knowledge, it would be extremely limited. However, Jesus was living in the position in which he knew God's heart completely and experienced His feeling as if it were his own.

Accordingly, man has no value as long as he remains in a fallen state; but when he is reborn through Christ, the True Parent, and when he thus becomes a child of goodness, cleansed of original sin, he is restored as a man who has fulfilled the purpose of creation, like Jesus. This is similar to the relationship of father and son, in which the original values of both do not in the least differ; only their order is different, one being the father and the other the son.

Therefore, Christ is the head of the church (Eph. 1:22), and we are his body and members (I Cor. 12:27). Accordingly, Jesus is the main temple and we are the branch temples. Jesus is the vine and we are the branches (John 15:5); and we, as wild olive shoots, should be grafted into Jesus, the true olive tree, in order to become true branches (Rom. 11:17). Thus, Jesus called us friends (John 15:14). Again, the Bible says that when Jesus appears, we shall be like him (I John 3:2). The Bible also says that Christ is the "first fruits," and we who belong to him will be the next, indicating only a difference of time and order (I Cor. 15:23).

SECTION IV
Rebirth and Trinity

The theory of Trinity has been discussed in the theological world as one of the most difficult questions to resolve. Meanwhile, another question that has been left without fundamental solution concerns the theory of Rebirth, which we will consider here.

1. REBIRTH

(1) Jesus and the Holy Spirit from the Standpoint of Rebirth

Jesus told Nicodemus, a ruler of the Jews, that unless one is born anew, he cannot see the Kingdom of God (John 3:3). "Rebirth" means to be born the second time. Let us study the reason fallen men must be born anew.

Had Adam and Eve, having fulfilled the ideal of creation, become the True Parents of mankind, their descendants would have realized the Kingdom of Heaven on earth, as children of goodness without original sin. However, having fallen, they became the evil parents of mankind and multiplied evil children, thus producing earthly Hell. Therefore, as Jesus said to Nicodemus, fallen men cannot see the Kingdom of God unless they are born anew as children without original sin.

We cannot be born without our parents. Then, who are the parents of goodness, giving us the second birth as children without original sin, capable of entering the Kingdom of God?

It would be impossible for evil parents with original sin to give birth to children of goodness without original sin. Naturally, we cannot expect to find parents of goodness among fallen men. Such parents should "descend" from Heaven. Jesus was the True Parent of mankind who came in that manner. In other words, he came as the True Father in order to realize the Kingdom of Heaven on earth by giving rebirth to fallen men as children of goodness without original sin.

Therefore, it says (I Peter 1:3), ". . . By his great mercy we have been born anew to a living hope through the resurrection of Jesus Christ from the dead." Jesus came as the True Father, the position which Adam had not fulfilled. This is why the Bible says that Jesus is the second Adam (I Cor. 15:45); that he is the "Everlasting Father" (Is. 9:6); and that God would send Elijah the prophet again and have him turn the hearts of the children (fallen men) to their father (Jesus), so that they might also become his children (Mal. 4:6). Again it is written that Jesus is to come again with his angels in the glory of his Father (Matt. 16:27).

However, a father alone cannot give birth to children. There must be a True Mother with the True Father, in order to give rebirth to fallen children as children of goodness. She is the Holy Spirit. This is why Jesus said to Nicodemus that no one can enter the Kingdom of God unless he is born anew through the Holy Spirit (John 3:5).

There are many who receive revelations indicating that the Holy Spirit is a female Spirit; this is because she came as the True Mother, that is, the second Eve. Again, since the Holy Spirit is a female Spirit, we cannot become the "bride" of Jesus unless we receive the Holy Spirit. Thus, the Holy Spirit is a female Spirit, consoling and moving the hearts of the people (I Cor. 12:3). She also cleanses the sins of the people in order to restore them, thus indemnifying the sin committed by Eve. Jesus, being male (positivity), is working in heaven, while the Holy Spirit, being female (negativity), is working on earth.

(2) Jesus and the Holy Spirit Seen from the Standpoint of the Dual Essentialities of Logos

"Logos" is a Hellenic word meaning "word" or "law." It is written (John 1:1) that Logos is in the objective position to God. In the meantime, since God, as the subject of Logos, contains dual essentialities within Himself, Logos, as His object, should also contain dual essentialities. If Logos were without dual essentialities, the things of creation, which were made through Logos (John 1:3), would not have dual essentialities either. Adam and Eve were the substantial objects of God, divided from the dual essentialities of Logos (cf. Part I, Ch. I, Sec. I, 1).

If Adam had become the Tree of Life, as a male having realized the ideal of creation, and if Eve, symbolized by the Tree of the Knowledge of Good and Evil as a female, had realized the ideal of creation in herself, and if they had thus become the True Parents of mankind, then God's three great blessings to man would have been fulfilled, thus enabling the realization of the Kingdom of Heaven on earth. However, due to their fall, the world became an earthly Hell. Therefore, Jesus came as the True Father of mankind, with the mission of the Tree of Life (Rev. 22:14); that is, as the second Adam (I Cor. 15:45). Then, it would only be logical that there should come the True Mother of mankind, with the mission of the Tree of the Knowledge of Good and Evil (Rev. 22:17); that is, the second Eve. The Holy Spirit came as the True Mother who would give rebirth to fallen man.

(3) Spiritual Rebirth through Jesus and the Holy Spirit

A baby is born through the love of his parents. As it is written (I Cor. 12:3), when we come to believe in Jesus as the Savior through the inspiration of the Holy Spirit, we receive the love of the spiritual True Parents, coming from the give and take action between Jesus, the spiritual True Father, and the Holy Spirit, the spiritual True Mother. Then, through this love, new life is infused into those who believe in Christ, and each is reborn into a new spiritual self. This is called "spiritual rebirth."

Man fell both spiritually and physically; so he must liquidate even the original sin through "physical rebirth." Therefore, Christ must come again to accomplish man's physical salvation by being born on earth.

2. TRINITY

According to the principle of creation, God's purpose of creation can be realized only through the four position foundation which is established by forming the three objective purposes through origin-division-union action. Accordingly, in order to fulfill the purpose of creation, Jesus and the Holy Spirit must establish the four position foundation centered on God, by becoming one body in unity through the action of give and take, each as the object of God, substantially divided from His dual essentialities. In this manner, Jesus and the Holy Spirit become one body centered on God; this is called "Trinity."

Originally, God's purpose of creating Adam and Eve was to form a trinity by uniting them into one body in love as the True Parents of mankind, thus establishing the four position foundation centered on God. If they had perfected themselves without the fall, forming a trinity as the True Parents centered on God, and had multiplied children of goodness, all their descendants would have grown to become married couples of goodness centered on God, each pair forming a trinity with God. Naturally, the Kingdom of Heaven on earth would have been realized centering on the first human couple, in accordance with the realization of God's three great blessings to them. However, due to the fall, Adam and Eve established the four position foundation centered on Satan, thus resulting in a trinity centered on Satan. Therefore, their descendants have also formed trinities centered on Satan, and have brought about a human society of corruption.

Therefore, God must work to have all fallen men born anew through the True Parents of mankind, Jesus and the Holy Spirit—one as the second Adam and the other as the second Eve—and then having all form respectively a trinity centered on God. But because of the undue death of Jesus, he and the Holy Spirit have fulfilled only the mission of spiritual True Parents, by forming the spiritual Trinity centered on God. Since Jesus and the Holy Spirit have undertaken the mission of spiritual rebirth only, the saints still remain in the position of their spiritual children, having been restored through the spiritual Trinity only.

Christ must come again in flesh in order that he may become the True Parent both spiritually and physically, by forming the substantial Trinity centered on God. He will then, by giving them rebirth both spiritually and physically, have all fallen men form (by couples) substantial trinities centered on God, after having liquidated the original sin. When fallen men have established the four position foundation in the original form centered on God, then the Kingdom of Heaven on earth will be restored through the realization of God's three great blessings to man.

PART II

Introduction

The "providence of restoration" means God's providence of restoring fallen man to his original state endowed at the creation, thus fulfilling the purpose of creation. As already demonstrated in Part One, man fell in the perfection level of the growth stage and has remained ever since under the dominion of Satan. In order to restore such men, God must first work the providence of separating Satan from man.

As discussed in detail in "Christology," in order that fallen man may be separated from Satan and restored to his original state before the fall, he must remove the original sin. But, man cannot remove the original sin unless he is born anew through the Messiah as his True Parent. Therefore, fallen man, having been separated from Satan, must first restore himself to the perfection level of the growth stage; that is, to the standard to which Adam and Eve had grown. On that foundation he may receive the Messiah and, through rebirth, be restored to the position before the fall of Adam and Eve. Then finally he will come to fulfill the purpose of creation. Since the providence of restoration is the providence of recreating man so he can fulfill the purpose of creation, God must work this providence according to the Principle. The principle through which restoration is worked is called the "principle of restoration." Let us further inquire into the question of how the providence of restoration is fulfilled.

I. The Principle of Restoration through Indemnity

1. RESTORATION THROUGH INDEMNITY

Before discussing the questions concerning the principle of restoration through indemnity, we must first know in what position man, due to the fall, is placed in relation to both God and Satan.

Originally, if the first human ancestors had perfected themselves without having fallen, becoming one with God in heart, they would have been in the position where they could communicate with God. But, because of their fall, through their blood relationship with Satan, they were placed in a position where they had to deal with Satan, too. Accordingly, Adam and Eve, who, though with the original sin after the fall, had not yet performed anything good or bad, were placed in the mid-position between God and Satan where they could deal with both. Their descendants were placed in the same midway position. Consequently, those of the fallen society who lead conscientious lives cannot be taken into Hell even by Satan, even though they may not have faith in Jesus, since they are in the midway position. On the other hand, however conscientious a life one may lead, God cannot bring him into Paradise, unless he believes in Jesus. Therefore, such spirit men have to remain in the midway spirit world which is neither Paradise nor Hell.

How, then, does God separate from Satan those fallen men who are in the midway position? Satan dominates fallen man, with whom he has a blood relationship, so even God cannot restore man to the side of Heaven unconditionally, unless man himself establishes the conditions which enable God to claim him.

Satan, likewise, cannot take man to Hell unconditionally, unless there is some condition in the man himself, through which Satan may invade him. Thus, fallen man can be placed on the side of God when he sets up good conditions, while he may be placed on the side of Satan when he sets up evil conditions.

It was for the purpose of placing Adam and Eve in a position where God could work the providence of restoration through their offering acceptable sacrifices, that God commanded them to offer sacrifices when Adam's family was in the midway position. However, Cain killed Abel, thus producing, on the contrary, the condition which permitted Satan to invade them. God sent Jesus to fallen men in order that they might stand on the Heavenly side by believing in him. However, against God's will, they did not believe in Jesus, and thus they stayed on Satan's side. This is the reason that Jesus is called "master of judgment," as well as the Savior.

What, then, does "restoration through indemnity" mean? When anything has lost its original position or status, certain conditions must be established in order for the original position or status to be restored. The setting up of such conditions is called "indemnity". For example, in order to restore lost honor, position, or health, we must set up the necessary conditions of sincere efforts, good qualification, and sufficient medical care. Suppose there are two people who have loved each other, but who are now on bad terms. In order for them to restore the original state of loving each other, they have to set up the condition of apologizing to each other.

In like manner, man, who lost the original position or status endowed at the creation, must set up certain necessary conditions in order to restore himself. This act of restoring the original position or status endowed at the creation is called "restoration through indemnity." The condition to be set up for restoration through indemnity is called the "condition of indemnity."

Further, the providence of restoring fallen men to their original position endowed at the creation by setting up the "condition of indemnity" is called the "providence of restoration through indemnity."

To what extent must we set up the condition of indemnity? We can give the following three instances:

The first is to set the condition of indemnity at the same amount; that is, to restore the original status by setting the condition at a value identical with that which was lost from the original position and status. For example, compensation or repayment belongs to this category. It is said (Ex. 21:23-25):

> If any harm follows, then you shall give life for life, eye for eye, tooth for tooth, hand for hand, foot for foot, burn for burn, wound for wound, stripe for stripe.

signifying this kind of condition of indemnity.

The second is the case of setting up the condition of indemnity at a lesser price; that is, to restore the original status by setting the condition at a value less than what was originally lost. For example, we may give the case of liquidating the entire amount of a debt through the creditor's grace to the debtor of a heavy debt. According to this principle, we receive the great benefit of salvation (resurrection after spiritual death), identical with that of Jesus, by setting up the condition of indemnity that we believe in the redemption through the cross. We can restore the position of having been born anew through Jesus and the Holy Spirit by setting up the condition of indemnity through baptism, merely by the sprinkling of a few drops of water on our heads. Furthermore, we may receive the valuable benefit of eating Jesus' body and drinking his blood merely by taking a piece of bread and a cup of wine at the Sacrament of Holy Communion. These are examples of lesser indemnity.

The third way is to set the condition of indemnity at a price greater than that which was originally lost. This means that when one has previously failed to meet the condition of indemnity at a smaller price, he may restore the original status by setting a condition of indemnity at a greater price. For example, Abraham, when he had failed in offering the sacrifices of dove, ram and heifer, had to offer his only son Isaac because of the additional price of the condition of indemnity. In the days of Moses, when the Israelites had failed to meet God's will in their 40 days of spying in the land of Canaan, their condition of indemnity increased and they had to wander in the wilderness for 40 years, calculated on the basis of one year for every day. (Num. 14:34).

Why then, do we have to set a greater condition when we set the condition of indemnity the second time? This is because when a central figure in the providence is to set the condition of indemnity again, he must include what was left undone due to the failure of previous persons, in addition to what he himself had to set originally.

The next thing we must know is how to set the condition of indemnity. When we are to restore anything to its original status from the circumstance of having been perverted from the original position and status, we must set a condition of indemnity, taking a course to reverse what we have gone through. For example, the chosen nation of Israel has been punished for the sin of rejecting Jesus and crucifying Him. Therefore, in order for them to be restored to the position of the elect, having been saved from sin, they must reverse their position, love Jesus, and even bear the cross and follow him (Luke 14:27). This is the reason Christianity became a religion of martyrdom. As another example, man caused grief to God by rebelling against Him and falling into corruption. Therefore, in order to be restored through indemnity, man must reverse his fallen nature and console God by restoring himself to the status of a man of the original nature endowed at the creation, by practicing God's will. The first Adam rebelled against God, thus compelling his descendants to fall into the bosom of Satan. Jesus, who came as the second Adam, therefore had to serve and honor God from the position of being abandoned by Him, in order to be able to restore mankind from the bosom of Satan to that of God. Herein lies the complex reason that God had to forsake Jesus when he was crucified (Matt. 27:46). Seen from this angle, even a nation's criminal law is a method of setting up the condition of indemnity to maintain the nation's security and order by imposing punishment on the criminals.

Who must set up the condition of indemnity? As already clarified in the principle of creation, man originally was to dominate even the angels, after having perfected himself by fulfilling his own portion of responsibility. The first human ancestors failed to do so, and, in reverse manner, fell under Satan's domination. Therefore, in order for man to be restored to the position of dominating Satan from the position of being under Satan's domination, man himself must set up the due condition of indemnity by fulfilling his own portion of responsibility.

2. THE FOUNDATION TO RECEIVE THE MESSIAH

The Messiah must come as the True Parent of mankind. He must come as the True Parent, because he must redeem mankind, born of fallen parents, from the original sin (cf. Part I, Ch. VII, Sec. IV, 1[1]). In order for fallen men to be restored to the status of the original men of creation, they must receive the Messiah on the "foundation to receive the Messiah", and thus eliminate their original sin.

Then, what kind of condition of indemnity must be set up in order for fallen men to lay the foundation to receive the Messiah? To learn this, we must first understand in what way Adam failed to accomplish the purpose of creation. The condition of indemnity must be set up through a process which will reverse the process through which man lost his original position and status.

Adam was supposed to set up two conditions in order to fulfill the purpose of creation. First he was supposed to lay the "foundation of faith," that is, he should have obeyed God's commandment not to eat the fruit of the Tree of the Knowledge of Good and Evil. Then, Adam should have passed his growth period during which time he was supposed to fulfill his own portion of responsibility by setting up this condition of faith. Meanwhile, this period represents some number of divine significance. Therefore, this period can also be called the "period of completing the number."

The second condition Adam was supposed to set up in order to fulfill the purpose of creation was to lay the "foundation of substance" (incarnation). If Adam had laid the foundation of faith by passing his growth period in faith and obedience to God's words, he could have become one body with God on that foundation. In other words, he could have laid the foundation of substance (incarnation), thus realizing the "perfect incarnation of the Word," having attained the original nature of creation (John 1:14). Adam could have attained the status of a man of perfected individuality, which was God's first blessing to man. Naturally, fallen man must lay the foundation of substance (incarnation) on the foundation of faith, through the same process, before laying the foundation to receive the Messiah.

(1) The Foundation of Faith

Adam fell due to his disobedience of God's words, so he failed to lay the foundation of faith. Having thus been unable to become the perfect incarnation of the Word, he could not attain the purpose of creation. Therefore, in order for fallen men to be restored to the basis on which they may fulfill the purpose of creation, they must first restore, through indemnity, the foundation of faith, which the first human ancestors failed to establish. Before they restore the foundation of faith, they must set up the following three conditions of indemnity.

First there should be a "central figure" to work through. Since Adam fell without becoming the person to lay the foundation of faith, God has looked, up to the present moment, for a central figure capable of restoring the foundation of faith. It was because of God's intention to set up such central figures that He had Cain and Abel offer sacrifices in Adam's family, and that He called Noah, Abraham, Isaac, Jacob, Moses, the Kings and John the Baptist.

Second, in order to restore the foundation of faith, there should be "conditional objects" for it. Through disbelief, Adam annulled God's Word, which He had given him as the condition to establish the foundation of faith. Man, who has thus fallen, was in the position where he could not directly receive God's Word for the restoration of the foundation of faith; therefore, conditional objects became necessary in place of the Word. However, fallen men were situated in the position and status in which they were deceitful above all things (Jer. 17:9), so in the age before the Old Testament, men were supposed to establish the foundation of faith by setting up the conditional objects from the created things such as offerings or the ark substituting for offerings. Therefore, the foundation of faith can also be the foundation to restore all things that were invaded by Satan because of man's disbelief. In the Old Testament Age, the conditional objects to lay this foundation were the words of the Law or the ark of the covenant, the temple, or the central figures substituting for the Word. Further, in the New Testament Age, the Gospel and Jesus, who was the "Word in substance," were the conditional objects to establish the foundation of faith. Such conditional objects which became necessary after the human fall, are for the restoration of the foundation of faith when seen from man's side. But seen from God's side, it is to decide the ownership.

Third, fallen men must have a "mathematical period of indemnity." Why, then, must there be a mathematical period of indemnity in the providence and what is it? This will be later discussed in detail (cf. Part II, Ch. III, Sec. II, 4).

(2) The Foundation of Substance

In order that a fallen man may fulfill the purpose of creation, he must realize the perfect incarnation of the Word, which the first human ancestors failed to fulfill, on the restored foundation of faith. But fallen men can never become the perfect incarnation without removing the original sin through the Messiah. A fallen man cannot receive the Messiah until he stands on the foundation to receive the Messiah, which is to be realized by establishing the foundation of substance on the restored foundation of faith. Fallen man may become a perfect incarnation (substance) only after removing his original sin through the Messiah, thus restoring the position before the fall of the first human ancestors, and then becoming one body with the Messiah, centering on God's heart; and finally passing through the growth period, which the first human couple left unaccomplished due to their fall.

Even in laying the foundation of substance, there are certain conditions of indemnity necessary for the fallen man to set up; that is, "the condition of indemnity to remove the fallen nature." The first human couple came to bear the original sin due to the fall, thus failing to realize the original nature endowed at the creation, and coming to bear the fallen nature. Therefore, in order for a fallen man to establish the foundation of substance for the restoration of his original nature by the removal of his original sin through the Messiah, he must first set up the condition of indemnity to remove the fallen nature. How to set up such conditions will be later discussed (cf. Part II, Ch. I, Sec. I, 2).

II. The Course of the Providence of Restoration

THE AGES IN THE COURSE OF THE PROVIDENCE OF RESTORATION

We will present a general overview of the ages in the entire course of the history from Adam's day up to the present.

God's providence to fulfill His purpose of creation by having fallen man lay the foundation on which to receive the Messiah began with Adam's family. However, Cain's killing of Abel frustrated the providence, and God's will was shifted to Noah's family after ten generations.

The purpose of judging the evil generation by a 40-day flood was to accomplish the providence of restoration, by having Noah's family lay the "foundation on the family level to receive the Messiah." Due to Ham's fall, the ten generations and 40 days which God had set up to elect Noah's family with the ark were invaded by Satan.

God's will was then shifted to Abraham, after the 400 years which was the period to restore through indemnity all the lost conditions to the Heavenly side. If Abraham had laid wholesomely the foundation on the family level to receive the Messiah, the "foundation on the national level to receive the Messiah" could have been established centering on the family level. Then on the foundation of the national level, he could have received the Messiah. However, the will was frustrated again by Abraham's failure in the symbolic offerings.

Therefore, the 2,000-year period after Adam, during which time God had looked for the "father of faith" to receive the Messiah, was invaded by Satan. Abraham differed from Noah in that, though he failed in the symbolic offering, he finally succeeded in laying the foundation on the family level to receive the Messiah by prolonging the duration covering three generations including Isaac's and Jacob's generations. Centering on this foundation, he multiplied God's elect in Egypt, and later he could extend nationwide the foundation to receive the Messiah. This is why Abraham is called the "father of faith."

The 2,000-year period from Adam to Abraham may well be called "the age to lay the foundation on which to start the providence of restoration by setting up Abraham, the father of faith." This is why the work of the providence of restoration is said to have started with Abraham.

Due to Abraham's failure in the symbolic offering, the 2,000-year period from Adam to Abraham was invaded by Satan, therefore there must follow the period to restore through indemnity this lost period back to the Heavenly side; this is the

2,000-year period from Abraham to the coming of Jesus. If Abraham had not failed in the symbolic offering, the Messiah could have come on the foundation on the national level to receive the Messiah which would have been laid by his descendants; so the providence of restoration would have been accomplished at that time. Likewise, if the Jewish people had set up Jesus as a living offering before God by believing and serving him, the providence of restoration could have been accomplished at that time centering on the Messiah, who had already come on the foundation on the national level, which they had laid.

However, the Jewish people failed in the offering on the national level by crucifying Jesus, just as Abraham had failed in his symbolic offering. Therefore, the 2,000-year period from Abraham to Jesus was again invaded by Satan. Then, there was to be another necessary 2,000-year period to restore through indemnity the lost 2,000-year period back to the Heavenly side; and this is the 2,000-year period from Jesus to the present day. During this period, Christians must lay the "foundation on the worldwide level to receive the Lord of the Second Advent," in the providence of restoration through the cross.

III. Division of the Ages in the Course of the Providence of Restoration

1. DIVISION OF THE AGES FROM THE STANDPOINT OF THE PROVIDENCE ACCORDING TO THE WORD

A. The 2,000-year period from Adam to Abraham was the period in which man could not yet set up the condition of indemnity enabling him to receive directly God's Word for the providence of restoration. Therefore, this was the period in which fallen man laid the foundation for the next period when the providence through the Word would be possible, by their merely setting up the condition of indemnity through offerings; so this period is called the "providential age for the foundation of the Word."

B. Again, the 2,000-year period from Abraham to Jesus was the period in which man's spiritual standard and degree of intellect grew to the formation stage through the Old Testament Word; therefore, this period is called the "Old Testament Age in the formation stage."

C. On the other hand, the 2,000-year period from Jesus to the period of the Second Advent is the period in which man's spiritual and intellectual standard should develop to the growth stage through the New Testament Word; therefore, this period is called the "New Testament Age in the growth stage."

D. The period for the completion of the providence of restoration after the Second Advent is the period in which man's spiritual and intellectual standard should grow to the perfection stage through the Completed Testament Word; therefore this period is called the "Completed Testament Age in the perfection stage."

2. DIVISION OF THE AGES FROM THE STANDPOINT OF THE PROVIDENCE OF RESURRECTION

A. The 2,000-year period from Adam to Abraham was the period in which man established through offerings the foundation for the Old Testament Age enabling the future providence of resurrection. Therefore this period is called the "providential age for the foundation of resurrection."

B. The 2,000-year period from Abraham to Jesus was the period in which man could resurrect to the form-spirit stage through the Old Testament Word and through the benefit of the age in the providence of resurrection. Therefore this period is called the "providential age for the formation stage resurrection."

C. The 2,000-year period from Jesus to the Second Advent is the period in which man is resurrected to the life-spirit stage through the New Testament Word and through the benefit of the age in the providence of restoration. Therefore this period is called the "providential age for the growth stage resurrection."

D. The period for the completion of the providence of restoration after the Second Advent is the period in which man is completely resurrected to the divine-spirit stage through the Completed Testament Word and through the benefit of the age in the providence of restoration. Therefore this period is called the "providential age for the perfection stage resurrection."

3. DIVISION OF THE AGES FROM THE STANDPOINT OF THE PROVIDENCE OF RESTORATION THROUGH INDEMNITY

A. The 2,000-year period from Adam to Abraham was the period in which man laid the foundation for the Old Testament Age, enabling the restoration through indemnity of the Satan-invaded period back to the Heavenly side, by setting up Abraham. Therefore this period is called the "providential period for the foundation of restoration through indemnity."

B. The 2,000-year period from Abraham to Jesus was the period in which to restore through indemnity the 2,000-year period from Adam (which was invaded by Satan due to Abraham's failure in the offerings) back to the Heavenly side centering on the Israelite nation. Therefore, this period is called the "providential age for restoration through indemnity."

C. The 2,000-year period from Jesus to the Second Advent is the period in which to restore again through indemnity the 2,000-year period of the Old Testament Age (which was invaded by Satan due to the crucifixion of Jesus) back to the

Heavenly side centering on the Christians. Therefore this period is called the "providential age of the prolongation of restoration through indemnity."

D. The period for the completion of the providence of restoration after the Second Advent is the period in which to restore through indemnity the entire course of the providence of restoration, which was invaded by Satan, completely back to the Heavenly side. Therefore this period is called the "providential age for the completion of restoration through indemnity."

4. DIVISION OF THE AGES FROM THE STANDPOINT OF THE EXTENT OF THE FOUNDATION TO RECEIVE THE MESSIAH

A. The 2,000-year period from Adam to Abraham was the period in which God had man establish the foundation on the family level to receive the Messiah by setting up Abraham's family through the offering. Therefore, this period is called the "providential age for the family level foundation to receive the Messiah."

B. The 2,000-year period from Abraham to Jesus was the period in which God intended to establish the foundation on the national level to receive the Messiah by setting up the Israelite nation through the Old Testament Word. Therefore this period is called the "providential age for the nationwide foundation to receive the Messiah."

C. The 2,000-year period from Jesus to the Second Advent is the period in which to establish the "worldwide foundation to receive the Messiah" by setting up the Christians worldwide through the New Testament Word. Therefore this period is called the "providential age for the worldwide foundation to receive the Messiah."

D. The period for the completion of the providence of restoration after the Second Advent is the period in which to complete the foundation on the macrocosmic level to receive the Messiah by working the providence on the cosmic level through the Completed Testament Word. Therefore this period is called the "providential age for the completion of the cosmic foundation to receive the Messiah."

5. DIVISION OF THE AGES FROM THE STANDPOINT OF THEIR RESPECTIVE PORTIONS OF RESPONSIBILITY

A. The 2,000-year period from Adam to Abraham was the period in which God laid the foundation for the providence of His own portion of responsibility to be done in the following age of the Old Testament. Therefore this period is called the "providential age for the foundation of God's portion of responsibility."

B. The 2,000-year period from Abraham to Jesus was the period in which God worked the providence of restoration on the formation level, centering on the prophets, by taking the responsibility in the Principle of His having created man, and thus taking the first responsibility of directly making Satan surrender. Therefore this period is called the "providential age for God's portion of responsibility."

C. The 2,000-year period from Jesus to the Second Advent was the period in which Jesus and the Holy Spirit, who were to fulfill the mission of Adam and Eve (who are responsible for the fall), worked the providence of restoration in the growth degree among fallen men by taking the second responsibility of making Satan surrender. Therefore this period is called the "providential age for the portion of responsibility of Jesus and the Holy Spirit."

D. The period for the completion of the providence of restoration after the Second Advent is the period in which the saints, both on earth and in heaven, should complete the providence of restoration by taking the third responsibility of making Satan, the fallen angel, surrender according to the principle of creation that man was made originally to dominate even the angels. Therefore, this period is called the "providential age for the saints' portion of responsibility."

6. DIVISION OF THE AGES FROM THE STANDPOINT OF PROVIDENTIAL TIME-IDENTITY

A. The 2,000-year period from Adam to Abraham was the period in which the conditions of indemnity to restore the foundation to receive the Messiah were set up symbolically. Therefore this period is called the "age of symbolic time-identity."

B. The 2,000-year period from Abraham to Jesus was the period in which the conditions of indemnity to restore the foundation to receive the Messiah were set up in image and likeness. Therefore this period is called the "age of image time-identity."

C. The 2,000-year period from Jesus to the Second Advent is the period in which the conditions of indemnity to restore the foundation to receive the Messiah have been set up substantially. Therefore this period is called the "age of substantial time-identity."

IV. The History of the Providence of Restoration and "I"

The individual body called "I" is, after all, a product of the history of the providence of restoration. This "I," therefore, is the personage who is to fulfill the purpose history is headed for. Therefore, "I" must stand for the will of history. In order to do this, "I" must set up horizontally, centering on "myself," all the conditions of indemnity which are demanded by the history of the providence of restoration through a long period.

Only by doing this, can "I" become the fruit desired by the history of the providence of restoration. Therefore, "I" must horizontally restore through indemnity, in my generation, centering on myself, all the missions of all the ages which the prophets and saints, elected for the purpose of the providence of restoration in the course of the history, have left unaccomplished. Otherwise, "I" cannot become the individual body having accomplished the purpose of the providence of restoration. In order for "me" to become such an historical victor, "I" must know precisely God's heart when He worked with the prophets and saints, the fundamental significance of His calling them, and the providential missions He entrusted to them.

There is no one among fallen men who can really stand in such a position all by himself. Therefore, we must understand all these things through the Lord of the Second Advent, who is to come as the completion of the providence of restoration. By believing in him and becoming one body with him, we must be in the position to set up, horizontally, all the vertical conditions of indemnity in the history of the providence of restoration.

In this manner, the way which all our predecessors, who have come to fulfill God's will in the providence of restoration, have hitherto trodden is what we ourselves must walk again today. Besides, we must walk even the ways they have left untrodden. Fallen men can never find the way of life without knowing the particulars and content of the providence of restoration. Herein lies the reason that we must know the principle of restoration in detail.

CHAPTER 1

Providential Age for the Foundation of Restoration

We have discussed (cf. Part I, Ch. III, Sec. II, 1) the fact that God has been working to save fallen men, though the human fall was brought about by man's own failure. God's providence to restore fallen men by having them lay the foundation to receive the Messiah began with Adam's family.

As discussed in the "Introduction," Adam, due to his blood relationship with Satan, was placed in the midway position where he could deal with either God or Satan. Therefore, in order that fallen man of the midway position might be separated and shifted from Satan to the Heavenly side to lay the foundation to receive the Messiah, he must by himself set up certain conditions of indemnity. Consequently, Adam's family should have set up the condition of indemnity to restore the foundation of faith and the foundation of substance (incarnation), and, on the foundation to receive the Messiah automatically laid by the previous two, should have finally received the Messiah before the providence of restoration could be realized.

1. THE FOUNDATION OF FAITH

First, in order that the foundation of faith may be laid, there must be certain conditional objects as the price of restoring it through indemnity. Originally, Adam, due to his disbelief, lost God's Word given as the condition to lay the foundation of faith. Consequently, in order for Adam, who fell into a position where he was unable to receive God's Word directly, to restore the foundation of faith, he should have set forth certain conditional objects acceptable to God's will in place of the Word, with an absolute faith. This conditional object to be set forth in Adam's family in place of the Word was the offering.

Second, there must be a central figure to restore the foundation of faith before laying the foundation at all. The central figure to restore the foundation of faith in Adam's family was, of course, Adam himself. Therefore, it was natural for Adam to offer the sacrifices. His doing so acceptably or not could decide the success or failure of laying the foundation of faith.

The Biblical record shows that Adam could not offer the sacrifices but, instead, Cain and Abel did this. What must have been the reason? According to the principle of creation, man was originally created to deal with only one master. Therefore, God cannot work His providence in the principle of creation with any being that is in the position to deal with two masters. If God should accept Adam and his offering, Satan would also try to deal with them on the basis of his having a blood relationship with Adam. In that case, Adam would be placed in the non-principled position to have to deal with two masters, God and Satan. God, not being able to work such a non-principled providence, had to conduct the providence of dividing Adam, the origin of the two characters of good and evil, into two beings; namely, the being representing good character, and the being representing evil character. For this purpose, God gave Adam two sons, respectively representing good and evil. He had each offer sacrifices by setting them in the respective positions to deal either with God or Satan; that is, He put them in the position in the principle of creation of dealing with one master.

Then who, between Cain and Abel, the sons of the same father, is supposed to stand in the position to deal with God as the representation of good, and who is to stand in the position to deal with Satan as the representation of evil? Both Cain and Abel were the fruit of Eve's fall. Consequently, this question was to be decided according to the course of the fall of Eve, who was the origin of the fall.

Eve's fall consisted of two kinds of illicit love affairs. The first one was the spiritual fall through love with the archangel. The second was the physical fall through love with Adam. Both are, of course, the same in that they are fallen actions. However, when we want to decide which is more aligned with the Principle and more forgivable, we must say that the second act is more so than the first. This is because the second act of the fall was that in which Eve had intercourse with Adam, who was going to be her spouse in the Principle, out of her desire to go back to God's side after realizing the illicit nature of the relationship with the archangel (cf. Part I, Ch. II, Sec. II, 2). The first act of the fall was that in which she had the relationship with the archangel, who was not her spouse in the Principle, out of the excessive desire to enjoy what it was not yet time for her to enjoy; that is, to become like God, with her eyes opened (Gen. 3:5).

Cain and Abel were the fruits of Eve's illicit love. Therefore, God had to discriminate conditionally between the two types of illicit acts of love committed centering on Eve, and had to set up Cain and Abel in the respective positions representing different situations. That is to say, Cain, being the fruit of the first love, was placed in the position to deal with Satan, as the representation of evil, symbolizing the first fallen act of love with the archangel. Abel, being the fruit of the second love, was placed in the position to deal with God, as the representation of good, symbolizing the second fallen act of love with Adam.

Originally, there was a standard in the Principle which provided that the first son succeed to the birthright. So, Satan also had more attachment to the elder than to the younger. Besides, Satan, being in the position of the ruler of the created world, intended to take Cain, to whom he was more attached. Therefore, God took Abel.

Let us take an example from the Bible. God said to Cain, "If you do not do well, sin is couching at the door." (Gen. 4:7) From this, we may understand that Cain was placed in a position to deal with Satan. When the Israelites fled out of Egypt, God smote not only all the first-born of the Egyptians but also of their cattle (Ex. 12:29), because they were all in the position of Satan's objects (Cain's position). On the other hand, when the Israelites were restored into Canaan, only the Levites, who were in the position of the second son Abel, could carry the ark of the covenant (Deut. 31:25). There is also a Biblical record saying that God loved the second son Jacob and hated the first son Esau while they were still in their mother's womb (Gen. 25:23). This is because only the distinction of being the first-born or the second justified their respective positions as Cain and Abel. In the case of Jacob's blessing of his grandsons, Ephraim and Manasseh, he blessed them by crossing his hands to lay the right hand on the head of Ephraim, the younger son, to whom he wanted to give priority (Gen. 48:14). This, too, is because Ephraim was in the position of Abel. According to this principle, God had Abel and Cain offer sacrifices, having set them up respectively in the positions where each could deal with only one master, either God or Satan (Gen. 4:3-5).

God accepted Abel's offering and rejected Cain's. What must have been the reason? God accepted Abel's offering (Gen. 4:4) because he offered the sacrifice acceptable to God's will through good faith, in the objective position from which God could take it (Heb. 11:4). In this way, the foundation of faith to be set up in Adam's family was laid. This was also to teach that God is ready to accept any man, though fallen, if a favorable condition is formed enabling God to take him. It was not because God really hated Cain that He rejected Cain's offering. It was because God could not accept his offering unless Cain himself set up a certain condition justifying the acceptance of the offering, for Cain was placed in a position in which he could be taken by Satan.

By this example, God showed us that, in order for a man in the position of object to Satan to return to God's side, he must set up a certain condition of indemnity. What kind of condition of indemnity should Cain have set up? This was the condition of indemnity to remove the fallen nature which we will discuss in detail later.

2. THE FOUNDATION OF SUBSTANCE

In order for Adam's family to lay the foundation of substance, Cain would have had to set up the "condition of indemnity to remove the fallen nature" so that God might be able to accept his offering with joy. How then should he have set up the condition of indemnity to remove the fallen nature?

The first human ancestors fell through the archangel, thus inheriting his fallen nature. Therefore, in order for fallen man to remove the fallen nature, he should have set up the condition of indemnity, according to the principle of restoration through indemnity, by taking a course in reverse to the way he obtained the fallen nature.

The archangel fell by failing to love Adam, whom God loved more. Therefore, the fallen nature of not taking the same position with God, came about. Consequently, in order to remove the fallen nature, Cain, who was in the position of the archangel, should have loved Abel, who was in the position of Adam, thus taking the same position with God.

Next, the archangel fell because he failed to receive God's love through Adam, who was closer to God, as the mediator. The archangel intended to take Adam's position instead. Therefore, the fallen nature of not keeping one's position came about. Consequently, in order to remove this fallen nature, Cain, who was in the position of the archangel, should have taken the position to receive God's love through Abel, who was in the position of Adam, as the mediator, so that he might be able to keep his position.

Then, the archangel fell by his domination of Adam and Eve, who were supposed to dominate him. Therefore, the fallen nature of reversing domination came about. Consequently, in order for man to remove this fallen nature, Cain, who was in the position of the archangel, should have set up the law and system of domination by standing in the place to obey Abel, who was in the position of Adam, and to be dominated by him.

The will of goodness that man should not eat the fruit of the Tree of the Knowledge of Good and Evil should have been conveyed by God to Adam, by Adam to Eve, and by Eve to the archangel, thus multiplying goodness. However, on the contrary, the archangel conveyed to Eve the will of unrighteousness that the fruit could be taken and eaten, then Eve conveyed this to Adam, thus causing the human fall. Therefore, the fallen nature of multiplying sins came about. In order to remove this type of fallen nature, Cain, who was in the position of the archangel, should have established the position to multiply goodness by standing in the position relative to Abel, who was closer to God than himself, and by receiving the will of goodness through Abel.

Now, let us draw several examples corresponding to the offerings of Cain and Abel. In our individual body, our mind, which directs us toward goodness (Rom. 7:22) is in the position of Abel, while our body, tending to serve the law of sin (Rom. 7:25), is in the position of Cain. Consequently, only when our body obeys our mind's command will our individual body be made good. However, in reality, our body always rebels against the command of our mind, thus repeating the same action in which Cain killed Abel. Therefore, our individual body becomes bad. Accordingly, life in religion may be called life to make our body obey our mind, directed toward the will of God, just as Cain should have obeyed Abel. Besides, man fell to the position of being deceitful above all things (Jer. 17:9); so he was supposed to go before God only through the created things, by setting these things in the position of Abel. This was the "offering." Man's tendency to look for good leaders and good friends, seen from the result, is derived from the desire of the divine mind to stand before God, by finding one who is in the position of Abel closer to God and by becoming one with him.

Christian faith teaches us to be gentle and humble so we may secure a position before God by finding in our daily life an Abel-type person, through these virtues. Starting from the individual to the family, the society, the race, the nation, and the world, there are always two types of persons; namely, Cain-type and Abel-type. Therefore, in order to restore all these to the original position of creation, the Cain-type person must obey and surrender to the Abel-type person. Jesus came to the world as the Abel whom the whole of mankind was to serve and obey. Therefore, he said, ". . . no one comes to the Father, but by me." (John 14:6)

If Adam's family had succeeded in setting up the condition of indemnity to remove the fallen nature through Cain's obedience to Abel, they could have set up the foundation of substance on the foundation of faith already established. They could thus have restored the four position foundation, originally designed at the creation, by receiving the Messiah on the family-level foundation to receive the Messiah. However, Cain killed Abel, repeating the original fallen nature through which the archangel caused man to fall, and thus Adam's family failed to set up the foundation of substance which was to be established then. Consequently, the providence of restoration centering on Adam's family ended in failure.

3. THE FOUNDATION TO RECEIVE THE MESSIAH IN ADAM'S FAMILY

The foundation to receive the Messiah is realized by establishing the foundation of substance on the basis of having restored through indemnity the foundation of faith. From the standpoint of offering sacrifices, the foundation of faith is to be restored by acceptably making the symbolic offering, and the foundation of substance is to be realized by acceptably offering the substantial offering. Let us then inquire into the meaning and purpose of the symbolic offering and the substantial offering.

God's three great blessings to man, the purpose of His creation, were to be realized when Adam and Eve, after having perfected their respective individualities, would become husband and wife, then multiply their children to form a family, and, further, they would come to rule the whole of creation. However, due to the fall, the three great blessings were not realized. In order to restore this, we must follow the course in reverse and establish the foundation of faith by offering the symbolic sacrifices through which both the condition of indemnity to restore the created things and the symbolic condition of indemnity to restore man can be set up at the same time.

Next, we must lay the foundation to receive the Messiah, after having set up the foundation of substance by offering the substantial sacrifices, which can be set up at the same time as the condition of indemnity to restore the children, and on this basis to restore the parents. Therefore, we may consider the meaning and purpose of the symbolic offering separately.

As we have discussed in the chapter on the "Fall of Man," Satan, who came to dominate fallen men, has also dominated all things which were supposed to be under man's dominion. It is for that reason that the Bible says all things are in travail together (Rom. 8:22). Therefore, the first purpose to give symbolic offerings with created things is to set up the condition of indemnity to restore all things, which are the symbolic substantial objects of God. Then, in order for man, who became deceitful above all things due to the fall (Jer. 17:9), to go before God, he must go through the created things, which are closer to God than himself, according to the order in the principle of creation. Accordingly, the second purpose for making symbolic offerings is to set up the symbolic condition of indemnity in order to restore substantial men before God.

Next, the substantial offering is an offering of the internal type; so, it is to be realized only on the basis of having acceptably made the symbolic offering of the external type, following the pattern of creating all things first and man afterwards.

Therefore, we must first make the symbolic offering in an acceptable manner, thus setting up the condition of indemnity to restore all things, and the symbolic condition of indemnity to restore man at the same time. On that basis we must make the substantial offerings as the condition of indemnity to restore man substantially. Substantial offering means to set up the condition of indemnity to remove the fallen nature in order to restore substantial man. If a Cain-type person should set up the condition of indemnity to restore children by making the substantial offering with the Abel-type person, this will also be reckoned as the condition of indemnity to restore parents, which will be elucidated; so, this substantial offering will become an acceptable one.

In order for Adam's family to set up the foundation to receive the Messiah, Adam himself must first lay the foundation of faith through the symbolic offering. As noted above, the offering did not begin with Adam, because if Adam should offer the sacrifices, the offering would be for both God and Satan to deal with, so it would be in a non-principled position. Besides, there is another reason from the aspect of feeling and heart. The fallen Adam in fact was the very person who caused God the grief which will last thousands of generations. Therefore, Adam could never be the object of God's heart, with whom God could directly deal in His providence of restoration.

Therefore, God had the second son Abel offer symbolic sacrifices instead of Adam. Thus the condition of indemnity to restore all things and the symbolic condition of indemnity to restore men were set up at the same time. Then, on this basis, if Cain and Abel had set up the condition of indemnity to restore children through the substantial offering, Adam, as the parent, would have stood on this foundation of substance and thus the foundation to receive the Messiah could have been realized at that time.

In order to offer the substantial sacrifices by setting up the condition of indemnity to remove the fallen nature, the central figure to offer the sacrifice should be decided first. Therefore, we must understand that Abel's symbolic offering had two purposes: first, to set up the foundation of faith in place of Adam; and, second, to decide on Abel as the central figure to make the substantial offering.

The condition of indemnity to remove the fallen nature was to be set up by Cain, and we must know how this could result in Adam's family's setting up the condition in its entirety. If the human ancestors had obeyed God's words, God's will could have been realized at that time; and, if the Jewish people had believed in Jesus, the will of Jesus could have been realized in his lifetime. In this case, too, if Cain had set up the condition of indemnity to remove the fallen nature by obeying Abel, both Cain and Abel could have stood in the position of having established the condition of indemnity to remove the fallen nature while they were children. Since Cain and Abel were substantial beings derived from the division of Adam, who was the source of good and evil, Adam, as the parent, could have stood on the foundation of substance of having separated from Satan, if they had separated from Satan by setting up the condition of indemnity to remove the fallen nature. Then, the foundation to receive the Messiah could have been laid in Adam's family. In this manner, the condition of indemnity to restore the parents could be set up through the symbolic offering and substantial offering.

Meanwhile, Abel offered an acceptable sacrifice. Thus, the condition to restore through indemnity the foundation of faith, centering on Adam, and the position of Abel as the central figure to offer the substantial offering were set up successfully. However, by Cain's killing Abel, they fell again into the same state as the archangel and Eve when they fell. Therefore, the substantial offering was a failure. They could not set up the condition of indemnity to remove the fallen nature. Thus, they also failed to lay the foundation of substance. This prevented them from establishing the foundation to receive the Messiah. Therefore, the providence of restoration centering on Adam's family came to naught.

4. THE LESSONS LEARNED FROM ADAM'S FAMILY

First, the failure of the providence of restoration centering on Adam's family showed us God's predestination for the accomplishment of the will and His attitude toward man's portion of responsibility. Originally, God's predestination of the will was supposed to be realized only when His portion of responsibility and man's portion of responsibility could be combined. God could not instruct Cain and Abel on how to offer sacrifices because Cain's decision whether or not to offer sacrifices through Abel was his portion of responsibility.

Second, after Cain killed Abel, God worked His providence through Seth. This showed us that God's predestination for the will is an absolute one whereas His predestination for man to carry out the will is relative. God so predestined that, corresponding to His portion of responsibility, Abel should accomplish his own portion of responsibility and, thus, become the central figure for the substantial offering. Therefore, when Abel failed to accomplish his portion of responsibility, God, by setting up Seth in his place, intended to carry out the will, which was predestined as absolute.

Third, the offerings of Cain and Abel showed us that any fallen man can accomplish God's will when he can find an Abel-type person and obey him in complete surrender.

Meanwhile, the providence identical to that which God intended to fulfill in Adam's family has been repeated ever since, due to the repeated failures arising from man's disbelief. Accordingly, this persists as our own course of indemnity today. The providence of restoration, centering on Adam's family, is a living lesson for us, showing us the typical course to follow.

SECTION II
The Providence of Restoration
Centering on Noah's Family

The providence of restoration centering on Adam's family was not fulfilled, because Cain killed Abel. Nevertheless, since God's will to accomplish the purpose of creation was absolute and unchangeable, He set up Seth in place of Abel on the basis of Abel's having been loyal and filial in heart (Gen. 4:25).

Then from among his descendants God chose Noah's family to substitute for Adam's family and recommenced His providence. As God said:

> I have determined to make an end of all flesh, for the earth is filled with violence through them; behold, I will destroy them with the earth. (Gen. 6:13)

He performed flood judgment. This clearly shows us that it was also the Last Days at that time. This is because God intended to fulfill the purpose of creation by sending the Messiah, on the foundation laid by Noah's family, after the flood judgment. Noah's family should have set up the condition of indemnity to restore the foundation of faith, and, based on that, they should have set up the condition of indemnity to restore the foundation of substance. By doing these things, Noah's family should have restored, through indemnity, the foundation to receive the Messiah, which Adam's family had failed to do.

1. THE FOUNDATION OF FAITH

(1) The Central Figure to Restore the Foundation of Faith

In the providence of restoration centering on Noah's family, the central figure to restore the foundation of faith was Noah. God called Noah after ten generations, or 1,600 years after Adam, in order to fulfill the will, which ended in failure with Adam. Therefore, God blessed Noah to be fruitful and multiply (Gen. 9:7), just as He did Adam (Gen. 1:28). In that sense, Noah is the second human ancestor.

Noah was called when the earth was filled with violence through men (Gen. 6:11), and he worked on the ark for 120 years on the mountain, in obedience to God's command, despite all the derision and scoffing of the people. On that condition, God could venture to judge the earth with the flood, centering on Noah's family. In this aspect, Noah is the first father of faith. We know Abraham is the father of faith, but originally it was to be Noah. Due to his son Ham's sinful act, Noah's mission as the father of faith was shifted to Abraham.

Adam was to be the central figure to restore the foundation of faith, but because of the forementioned reason, he could not offer sacrifices himself. However, Noah was called on the basis of Abel's having been faithful and filial in acceptably offering the symbolic sacrifices. Besides, as seen from his lineage, he was a descendant of Seth (Gen. 4:25) called in place of Abel. Furthermore, he was a righteous man in the sight of God (Gen. 6:9). Therefore, he could offer symbolic sacrifices directly by building the ark in obedience to God's will.

(2) The Conditional Objects to Restore the Foundation of Faith

For Noah, the conditional object by which the foundation of faith could be restored was the ark. What did the ark signify? In order for Noah to stand in Adam's position as the second human ancestor, he had to set up the condition to restore through indemnity the whole universe, which was under Satanic control due to Adam's fall. Consequently, he had to offer as sacrifices, acceptably before God, certain conditional objects symbolizing the new universe. The ark was his conditional object.

The ark consisted of three floors, to symbolize the universe created through the three stages of growth. The eight members of Noah's family who entered the ark were to restore through indemnity the eight members of Adam's family, who fell into Satan's bosom. Since the ark was the symbol of the whole universe, the master of the ark, Noah, symbolized God. His family symbolized mankind, and the animals symbolized all things.

What was the purpose of God's 40-day flood judgment, which He exercised after the completion of the ark? According to the principle of creation, man was made to serve one master. God could not work His providence in the non-principled realm by dealing with mankind, when man remained under Satan due to his own lustfulness.

Therefore, He exercised the providence of the flood judgment to destroy the men subject to Satan, and to set up the objects through whom He could exercise His providence. Why did He decide that His judgment should be 40 days? As will be discussed later (cf. Part II, Ch. III, Sec. II, 4), the number "ten" is the number of unity. Therefore, God set up Noah ten generations after Adam to restore through indemnity the will left unaccomplished because of Adam's fall. He set up the indemnity period to restore the number "ten" in the second attempt at unification. Through ten generations up to Noah, God also continued His providence of setting up each generation as the indemnity period to restore the number "four" to fulfill the purpose of the four position foundation. Consequently, the period from Adam to Noah was the indemnity period to restore the number "40". Due to the lustfulness of the people of that time, the indemnity period for the number "40" was invaded by Satan. In order that God might recommence His providence to accomplish the four position foundation through Noah's ark, He intended to restore the foundation of faith by setting up the 40-day period of judgment as the indemnity period to restore the number "40" invaded by Satan.

In this way, the number "40" became necessary as the number to separate Satan in order later to restore the foundation of faith in the providential course of restoration through indemnity. For example, we see many instances comparable to the 40-day judgment in Noah's day: the 400-year period from Noah to Abraham; the 400 years of slavery in Egypt of the Israelites; 40 years of wandering in the wilderness; Moses' 40-day fast; 40 years each of the rule of Kings Saul, David and Solomon; Elijah's 40-day fast; Jonah's 40-day prediction of the destruction of Nineveh; Jesus' 40-day fast and prayer; and his 40-day period of resurrection. All are indemnity periods for separation from Satan.

We also read in the Bible that, after the judgment, Noah sent out a raven and a dove from the ark. Let us now investigate what kind of providence for the future God foreshadowed through this, for God said, "Surely the Lord God does nothing, without revealing his secret to his servants the prophets." (Amos 3:7) The 40-day period of judgment as the condition of indemnity to restore the universe corresponds to the period of chaos (Gen. 1:2). Therefore, all the things centering on the ark after the 40 days are the symbolic representation of the entire course of history after God completed His creation of heaven and earth.

What did God foreshadow by sending from the ark a raven (Gen. 8:6-7) which flew about until the water subsided? This indicated that Satan crouched at the door of Noah's family, even after the flood judgment, to spy on the condition for invasion there, just as the archangel looked for a chance to win Eve's love right after the creation of man and just as Satan watched for the opportunity to invade Cain and Abel when they offered sacrifices (Gen. 4:7).

Next , what did God foreshadow when Noah sent a dove three times from the ark? It is recorded in the Bible that the dove was sent forth to find out if the water had subsided. However, if that had been the only purpose, we may think that Noah could look out directly through the window to learn for himself, instead of sending out the dove. Therefore, we can imagine that the purpose of sending for the dove lay in something more important than seeing if the water had dried up.

We must understand the significance of God's providence in this situation. Seven days after God announced the flood judgment through Noah (Gen. 7:10), the flood came. It was after the 40-day period of judgment that Noah first sent out the dove. The Bible says that the dove went to and fro over the water but finding no place to set her foot she returned to the ark, and Noah brought her into the ark (Gen. 8:9). The first dove symbolized the first Adam. Therefore, this story means that God created man on earth so that His ideal of creation, which had been in Him even before creation, might be realized in Adam as the perfect incarnation. But due to Adam's fall, God could not realize His ideal of creation on earth through Adam, so God had to take back His ideal from earth for the time being and postpone the realization of His will.

Seven days later, Noah sent out the dove the second time. She could not set foot on the earth then because the water had not dried up. She returned to the ark with an olive leaf in her mouth, signifying that she would be able to alight the next time (Gen. 8:10-11). The second dove symbolized Jesus, as the second Adam, who would come as the perfect incarnation of

the ideal of creation. Therefore, this second story signifies that
Jesus would come to earth in order to accomplish the providence of restoration. But in case of the Jewish people's disbelief, he would go back to God's bosom, through the cross,
leaving a promise to come again, because, with no place to "set
his feet," he could not fulfill the will on earth. Of course, this
foreshadowing indicates that, if the water had dried up so that
the dove could alight and find something to eat, she did not
have to return to the ark, but she had to go back because the
water had not yet subsided. Likewise, this indicates that if the
Jewish people were to believe in him and serve him, Jesus would
not die, being able to realize the Kingdom of Heaven on earth at
that time. But in the case of their disbelief, Jesus would have to
die on the cross and come again later at a more favorable time.

After another seven days, Noah sent out the dove the third
time. It is written that this time the dove did not come back to
the ark because the water had dried up (Gen. 8:12). The third
dove symbolized the Lord of the Second Advent who would
come as the third Adam. Consequently, this story indicates
that, when Christ comes again, he will be able to realize God's
ideal of creation on earth without fail so that the ideal will
never have to go back to God's bosom. When Noah found that
the third dove would not return, he then came down from the
ark to the earth and enjoyed the new heaven and earth. This
foreshadows that, when the ideal of creation will be realized on
earth through the third Adam, then the new Jerusalem will
descend from heaven and God's dwelling will be among men
(Rev. 21:1-3).

The story of having sent out the dove three times shows us
that, as clarified in the chapter on predestination, God's providence of restoration could be prolonged in case that man, who
is the object of the providence, could not fulfill his portion of
responsibility. This foreshadowed that, due to Adam's failure in

carrying out his responsibility because of his disbelief, Christ had to come as the second Adam, and that if the Jewish people should fail to fulfill their responsibility because of their disbelief, Jesus would have to die on the cross and thus Christ would have to come again as the third Adam. The period of seven days here shows us that, just as God's creation took seven days, it will also take a certain period in the providence to restore the lost element.

In the meantime, Noah's family could restore through indemnity the foundation of faith by acceptably setting up the ark as the condition to restore the foundation through the 40-day judgment.

2. THE FOUNDATION OF SUBSTANCE

Noah restored through indemnity the foundation of faith by succeeding in making the symbolic offering of the ark acceptable to God. By this, Noah set up, at the same time, the condition of indemnity for the restoration of all the created things and also the condition of indemnity for the restoration of men, in symbolic terms. Next, if Noah's sons, Shem and Ham, had succeeded in the substantial offering by setting up the condition of indemnity to remove the fallen nature, in the respective positions of Cain and Abel, the foundation of substance could have been established at that time.

In order for Noah's family to offer the substantial offering acceptably after the success in the symbolic offering, the second son, Ham, who was the central figure for the substantial offering, ought to have restored the position of the second son Abel, who had been the central figure for the substantial offering in Adam's family. In the case of Adam's family, Abel, the son, offered the symbolic offering in place of Adam. Therefore, when he succeeded in that offering, Abel could restore through indemnity the foundation of faith, while at the same time, he was destined to be the central figure for the substantial offering. However, in the case of Noah's family, Noah himself offered a symbolic sacrifice. In order for Ham to stand in the position of Abel, who had succeeded in the symbolic offering, he should have remained in a position of inseparable oneness with the heart and feeling of Noah, who had succeeded in the symbolic offering. Let us, then, examine how God worked His providence in order to have Ham stand in the position of inseparable oneness with Noah's heart and feeling.

We read (Gen. 9:20-26) that Ham, upon seeing his father Noah lie naked in the tent, was not only ashamed of it, but even displeased with it, and that he stirred up the same emotion among his brothers, Shem and Japheth. Then they too were agitated by Ham in the same emotion to feel ashamed of their father's nakedness; and in an effort not to see that scene, they turned their faces and walked backward to cover their father's body with a garment. However, this was such a crime that Noah cursed Ham, saying that his son Canaan should be a slave to his brothers.

Why did God work His providence in such a way, and why was the feeling of shame at Noah's nakedness such a sin? In order to understand this, let us first determine what sin is. Satan cannot emit the power of existence and action unless he finds an object with which to form a correlative base on which to have a mutual relationship of give and take. Therefore, whenever any being makes a condition for Satan to invade and thus becomes an object with which Satan can work, sin is created.

Next, we must understand why God tested Ham through Noah's nakedness. It has already been stated that the ark symbolized the whole universe and that all the things done immediately after the acceptable offering of the ark, through the 40-day judgment, therefore symbolized everything since the creation of the universe. Consequently, Noah's position right after the 40-day judgment was identical to that of Adam after the creation of the universe.

We can well imagine how unreserved and affectionate with each other Adam and Eve were after the creation, and how frank and without concealment they were before God. We can conclude this from the fact that they did not have the feeling of shame, even though they were naked (Gen. 2:25). But after the fall, they became ashamed of the nakedness of their lower parts, covered them with fig leaves and concealed themselves from God, fearing that He might see (Gen. 3:7). Therefore, their act caused by feeling ashamed of their lower parts was an expression of their feeling due to their sinful blood relationship with Satan committed through their lower parts. The action of concealing themselves by covering their lower parts was the expression of their guilty conscience, which deterred them from appearing before God after their blood relationship with Satan.

Noah, in the position of separation from Satan through the 40-day judgment, ought to have stood in the position of Adam right after the creation of the universe. In this case, God wanted to restore through indemnity the heart and feeling of joy He had experienced, looking at innocent naked man, without concealment before he committed the crime, by looking at Noah's family neither feeling shameful nor trying to hide themselves at the sight of Noah's nakedness. God had Noah lie naked in order to fulfill such a profound will. Consequently, Ham could have set up the condition of indemnity to restore the position of Adam's family, which had never known any shame before the first sin, on Ham's foundation of inseparable oneness with Noah through dealing with Noah without any sense of shame; that is, from the same position and heart as God.

However, on the contrary, Noah's sons were ashamed of their father's nakedness and covered him with a garment, thus showing that they could not appear before God because they were ashamed of their blood relationship with Satan, as was the case in Adam's family after the fall. Therefore, Satan, who had been watching to see if there was any condition for him to invade in Noah's family, as foreshadowed through the raven, did invade with Noah's sons as his objects because they had shown themselves to be Satan's lineal descendants.

In this manner, Ham's act in being ashamed of his father's nakedness became a sin, because it created a condition for Satan to invade. Thus, Ham failed to restore through indemnity the position of Abel from which to offer a substantial sacrifice, and failed to establish the foundation of substance. Thus, the providence of restoration centering on Noah ended in failure.

Would it be a sin for anyone to be ashamed of his nakedness? No. Noah had the mission of removing all the conditions which allowed Satan to invade, because Noah was substituting for Adam. Therefore, Noah's family should have set up the condition of indemnity to restore the position of Adam's family before the blood relationship with Satan, by demonstrating that they were not ashamed of nakedness and thus did not worry about covering it. In consequence, the condition of indemnity showing that they neither felt ashamed of nakedness nor cared to cover it was a condition that only Noah's family could set up, for Noah's family was in the position of Adam's family.

3. LESSONS LEARNED FROM NOAH'S FAMILY

It is not easy to understand why Noah built an ark on the mountain for 120 long years. Ham knew that Noah's family was saved due to the toils of his father—toils for which he had been mocked and criticized. Considering all these things, Ham should have regarded his father's works as good and meaningful, even though he was displeased with his father's nakedness.

Instead of trusting Noah, who was on the side of God, Ham criticized him from a self-centered perspective, and showed his displeasure in his action. Therefore, the providence centering on Noah's family, which God had set up by exercising the 40-day flood judgment 1,600 years after Adam, ended in failure. This shows us that we need patience and obedience to go the way of Heaven.

Next, God's providence through Noah's family shows us God's attitude about predestination and the accomplishment of man's own responsibility. We know well enough that Noah's family was that which God found after 1,600 years of search, which He directed for 120 years until Noah finished the ark, and which He kept intact at the sacrifice of the whole of mankind by the 40-day flood. However, when Satan invaded the family through Ham's mistake, God abandoned without reserve the entire family, which was the object of His providence of restoration, and thus His providence centering on Noah's family ended in failure.

Moreover, the providence through Noah's family shows us what God's predestination for man is like. We must not forget that, in spite of His having found Noah as the father of faith after such a long period, God abandoned the family when once it failed to accomplish its portion of responsibility, and elected Abraham's family in its place.

SECTION III
The Providence of Restoration Centering on
Abraham's Family

Due to Ham's fallen act, the providence of restoration centering on Noah's family was not fulfilled. However, since God's intention was to predestine absolutely and to fulfill the will to accomplish His purpose of creation, He called Abraham on the foundation of heart-and-zeal which Noah had established with his loyalty, and began again His providence of restoration, centering on Abraham's family.

Therefore, Abraham should have restored the foundation to receive the Messiah, which Noah's family had left unaccomplished, and should have actually received the Messiah on that foundation. Consequently, Abraham, too, should have restored through indemnity the foundation of faith, and, on it, he should have restored through indemnity the foundation of substance.

1. THE FOUNDATION OF FAITH

(1) The Central Figure to Restore the Foundation of Faith

The central figure to restore the foundation of faith in the providence of restoration centering on Abraham's family was Abraham himself. Therefore, Abraham was chosen as the central personage to succeed and fulfill God's will. Therefore, if Abraham did not restore through indemnity all the conditions invaded by Satan due to Ham's sinful act, he would fail in carrying out God's will centering on Noah, whose course he had been chosen to fulfill.

The first condition that Noah lost to Satan was the ten generations from Adam to Noah, plus the 40 days. Therefore, Abraham should have restored through indemnity that lost ten generations. Then he would have stood in the position of each of the ten, having restored the number "40" for the judgment. The calculation of 40 years for each generation to be restored through indemnity came about due to the failure of one generation (Noah's) to be restored through a 40-day period. Later, in Moses' course, the Israelites restored through indemnity the failure in the 40-day spying in Canaan by the 40-year period of wandering in the wilderness (Num. 14:34). God chose Abraham in place of Noah after the lapse of a 400-year period of indemnity through ten generations after Noah. In this way, by shortening the human life span after Noah, the age in which ten generations would be restored during a 1,600-year period was changed into an age in which ten generations could be restored during a 400-year period.

The second condition that Noah had to forfeit to Satan was the position of the father of faith plus the position of Ham, who was in the place of Abel. Therefore, Abraham could not stand in the position of Noah, unless he restored through indemnity the position of Ham and of the father of faith. In order for Abraham to stand in the position of the father of faith, replacing Noah, he should have offered a symbolic sacrifice with faith and loyalty, just as Noah did by building the ark.

As stated above, God also had to leave Ham in Satan's hands; Ham was in place of Abel, whom God loved (both were second sons playing the central roles in the substantial offerings). Therefore, God in turn had to take those who were in the position of being most loved by Satan according to the principle of restoration through indemnity. That is why God called Abraham, the first son of Terah, who was an idol-maker (Josh. 24:2-3).

Abraham was the personage of the restored Adam, because he was the substitute for Noah and, naturally, for Adam himself. Accordingly, God blessed Abraham, saying that his descendants would be multiplied, that a great nation would come from him, and that he would be the source of blessedness, just as He had earlier blessed Adam and Noah (Gen. 12:2). After this blessing, Abraham, in obedience to God's command, left his father's house in Haran and entered Canaan with his wife Sarah, his nephew Lot and all the wealth and people he could take from his homeland (Gen. 12:4-5). In this way, God set Abraham's course as the typical course for Jacob and Moses in later days; that is, to restore Canaan by taking there his wife, children and wealth, all of whom he had removed from the Satanic world (Haran and Egypt) under difficult circumstances.

This course foreshadowed the course for Jesus in future days; namely, to restore to God's world all men and things taken from the Satanic world (cf. Part II, Ch. II, Sec. I, 2).

(2) The Conditional Objects to Restore the Foundation of Faith

(i) The Symbolic Offering of Abraham

God commanded Abraham to offer sacrifices of a dove, ram, and heifer, all these being conditional things to restore the foundation of faith (Gen. 15:9). Just as Noah established his faith before offering his symbolic sacrifice of the ark, so Abraham had to first establish his faith before offering his symbolic sacrifice. The Bible does not contain any precise record of how Noah did this. However, the Bible says that Noah was a righteous man (Gen. 6:9), and we can imagine that he must have set up certain conditions of faith before he was righteous enough in God's sight to be given the divine commandment to build the ark. In fact, the providence of restoration is to be realized through faith; for faith, and he who through faith is righteous, is recognized by God (Rom. 1:17). Let us now investigate what kind of faith Abraham established before offering his symbolic sacrifice.

Abraham had to restore the position of Noah, the second human ancestor. He had to stand in the position of Adam, too. Therefore, he had first to set up the symbolic condition of indemnity for the restoration of the position of Adam's family before he offered the symbolic sacrifice.

According to the Biblical verses (Gen. 12:10), Abraham once went down to Egypt because of a famine. When the Pharaoh of Egypt wanted to take his wife Sarah, Abraham, as planned beforehand, told the Pharaoh that she was his sister, lest the King should kill him if he found out that they were husband and wife. In this way, Sarah was taken by the Pharaoh from the position of Abraham's sister, and after God's chastisement of the Pharaoh, Abraham took back his wife, and also his nephew Lot, as well as abundant wealth. Abraham went on this providential course, though unconsciously, to set up the symbolic condition to restore through indemnity the position of Adam's family.

The archangel took Eve while Adam and Eve were still in the position of brother and sister in their immaturity, thus forcing all created things, as well as their own children, to be under his dominion. In order for Abraham to set up the condition to restore through indemnity the above mentioned situation, he was deprived by Pharaoh, who symbolized Satan, of his wife Sarah, who was in the position of Abraham's sister. Then he had to take back Sarah, in the position of his wife, together with Lot, symbolizing the whole of mankind, and his wealth, symbolizing the world of creation (Gen. 14:16). Abraham's course thus was the course for Jesus to walk in later days. It was only after Abraham had set up such a condition of indemnity that he could offer the symbolic sacrifice with the dove, the ram and heifer.

What, then, does Abraham's symbolic sacrifice mean? In order for Abraham to become the father of faith, he had to restore through indemnity the position of Noah whom God intended to set up as the father of faith, and of his family. Naturally, he had to stand also in the position of Adam and his family. So, he had to offer a conditional object as a symbol enabling him to restore through indemnity all the things which were supposed to be restored in Adam's family, centering on the offerings of Cain and Abel. Further, he had to offer, as acceptable sacrifices before God, certain symbolic things to restore through indemnity all the things intended to be restored centering on the ark of Noah's family. Abraham's symbolic offerings were of such a nature.

What then, did Abraham's symbolic sacrifices, namely, the dove, ram and heifer, symbolize? These three symbolic offerings symbolized the whole universe which was created to be perfected through three stages of growth. First, the dove symbolized the formation stage. Jesus came as the perfection of the providence in the formation stage, which was represented by the doves. Therefore, when he was baptized by John the Baptist in the River Jordan, the Spirit of God descended like a dove, alighting on him (Matt. 3:16). On the other hand, Jesus came to restore Abraham's failure in the offering. Naturally, he had to stand in the position to have restored the dove which was invaded by Satan at that time. Therefore, God showed by the dove that Jesus came as the perfection of the Old Testament providence in the formation stage.

In the next place, the goat or ram symbolizes the growth stage. Jesus came to restore Abraham's failure in the offering. On the foundation of the Old Testament providence, having restored all things symbolized by the dove, he had also to restore all the things symbolized by the goat or ram, as the one who was to begin the New Testament providence in the growth stage. One day after John the Baptist had witnessed that Jesus was the perfection of the providence in the formation stage symbolized by the dove, he again gave witness to Jesus as the one who was to begin his mission in the growth stage. When he saw Jesus coming toward him, he said, "Behold the Lamb of God, who takes away the sin of the world!" (John 1:29)

The heifer symbolized perfection. We read in Judges 14:18 that, when Samson put a riddle to the Philistines, they could only answer it by having Samson's wife tempt him and press him hard for the answer. Then Samson said to them, "If you had not ploughed with my heifer, you would not have found out my riddle." In this way, Samson metaphorically called his wife a heifer. Since Jesus came as the bridegroom to all mankind, all the saints until the time of the Second Advent each become a "bride" to Jesus, the bridegroom to come. However, after the wedding feast of the Lamb, when all the saints, as the bride, are united into perfect oneness with the Lord, then all will live in the Heavenly Kingdom of God with Christ as a husband, each not merely as a bride but as a wife. Therefore, we must know that the Completed Testament Age after the Second Advent of the Lord is the age of a heifer—the age of a wife. The heifer thus symbolizes perfection. This is why many spiritually attuned people receive the revelation that today is the age of a cow or heifer.

What, then, do the three kinds of offerings restore through indemnity? Abraham, through his symbolic offerings, had to set up the symbolic condition of indemnity enabling him to restore through indemnity all the things previously left in Satan's hand, due to the failures of the restoration through indemnity by the symbolic sacrifices and the substantial offerings of Adam's and Noah's families. Therefore, the symbolic offering of Abraham was to restore at once, horizontally, through the three kinds of offerings, the symbolic condition of indemnity of the vertical providence through the three generations of Adam, Noah and Abraham.

Abraham offered sacrifices with the dove, ram, and heifer on the altar, symbolizing the three stages of formation, growth and perfection, in order to fulfill at once, in horizontal terms, the vertical providence which God intended to restore through indemnity through the three generations (seen from the viewpoint of His will): Adam symbolizing formation, Noah symbolizing growth, and Abraham symbolizing perfection. Therefore, this offering symbolically represented God's will to fulfill the whole providence of restoration at once by restoring through indemnity all the conditions represented by the number "three," which had been invaded by Satan.

We must know in what manner Abraham offered the symbolic sacrifice. We read (Gen. 15:10-13) that Abraham cut the offerings in two and laid each half over against the other, but he did not cut the doves in two. Birds of prey came down upon the carcasses and Abraham drove them away. God appeared to Abraham that evening at sunset and said to him:

> Know of a surety that your descendants will be sojourners in a land that is not theirs, and will be slaves there, and they will be oppressed for four hundred years ... (Gen. 15:13)

The birds of prey came down upon the carcasses because Abraham did not cut the doves in two. This caused the Israelites to suffer 400 years of slavery in Egypt.

Why was it such a sin not to cut the dove? This question has remained unsolved until today, and can be elucidated only through the Principle. Let us first study the reason for cutting the sacrifices. The purpose of the providence of salvation is to restore the sovereignty of goodness by separating good and evil, by destroying evil and exalting goodness. Therefore, when God required sacrifices to be offered after having separated Adam into Cain and Abel; and when He smote the evil to exalt the good through the flood judgment in Noah's days, His purpose was, without exception, to restore the sovereignty of goodness. Consequently, God intended to carry out the symbolic performances of separating good and evil, which He failed to fulfill through Adam and Noah, by having Abraham offer the sacrifices cut in two.

The act of cutting the sacrifices in two was, first, to restore the separated position of Cain and Abel in Adam's family, in order to separate Adam, the origin of good and evil, into two parts representing good and evil, respectively. Second, it was to restore the position of Noah, having separated good and evil through the 40-day flood. Third, it was to set up the symbolic condition to separate the world of good sovereignty from the world under the dominion of Satan. Fourth, it was to set up the condition of consecration by draining away the blood of death that had come through the illicit blood relationship.

Why, then, was it such a sin not to cut the sacrifice in two?

First, it was analogous to not separating Cain and Abel; so, as a result, there was no Abel-type object for God to take. Therefore, the sacrifice was unacceptable to God, and the failure in the sacrifice of Cain and Abel was not restored.

Second, it represented not having separated good and evil at the time of the flood judgment in the providence of restoration centering on Noah; as a result, there was no object of goodness which God could take and upon which He could work His providence. Therefore, it resulted in having taken the position of failure, just as the flood judgment failed.

Third, it failed to set up the symbolic condition of separating the world of good sovereignty from the world under the dominion of Satan in order for God to take it.

In the fourth place, the sacrifice was not consecrated because the blood of death was not drained, and it could not be a sacred thing for God to take and work His providence upon. In this manner, Abraham's offering the sacrifices without having cut the dove in two resulted in offering Satan's possession, as it were, and so the offering ended in the assertion that the offering was Satan's possession.

Thus, the dove, which was the offering symbolizing the formation stage, remained in Satan's possession. The ram and heifer, symbolizing growth and perfection, which were to be established on the foundation of formation, were then invaded by

Satan. Consequently, the whole symbolic offering ended up under Satan, and the act of not having cut the dove in two became a sin.

Let us next inquire into the meaning of the birds of prey alighting on the symbolic offering (Gen. 15:11). Since the fall of the first human ancestors, Satan has always been pursuing those who advocate the will of God. When Cain and Abel offered sacrifices, Satan crouched at the door (Gen. 4:7); also, in Noah's days, the raven symbolized Satan, who was looking for the opportunity to invade his family right after the judgment (Gen. 8:7). Similarly, at the time of Abraham's symbolic offering, Satan, who had been looking for the opportunity to invade the offering, saw that the dove was not cut in two and profaned it. The Bible symbolically represented this fact by describing the birds of prey alighting on the offering.

What result was brought about by this failure in the symbolic offering? Abraham's failure in the symbolic offering caused the annulment of all the conditions that were supposed to be restored through indemnity by the symbolic offering. As a result, the descendants of Abraham were put into slavery for 400 years in Egypt, the land of Pharaoh. Let us now study the reason for this.

God set up a 400-year period for the separation of Satan in order to restore through indemnity the judgment number "40" as well as the ten generations that had been invaded by Satan because of Ham's mistake, and on this basis He called Abraham and had him offer the symbolic sacrifices. Abraham's failure enabled Satan to claim the offering; therefore, the 400-year period after Noah, the period of indemnity to establish Abraham as the father of faith through the symbolic offering, was also invaded by Satan. In order to restore through indemnity both the position of Abraham before his failure in the symbolic offering and the position of Noah when he was called for the construction of the ark, God had to again set up a period of 400 years for the separation of Satan. The 400-year period of the Israelites' slavery in Egypt existed in order to put Moses on the foundation of having restored through indemnity on the national level the position of either Noah or Abraham at the time they were about to start as the father of faith. This period of slavery was the period of punishment, due to Abraham's failure in the offering, as well as the period to lay the foundation for separation from Satan for the sake of God's new providence.

It has been stated that God intended to fulfill, at the same time, the whole providence represented by formation, growth and perfection, by having Abraham offer a successful symbolic sacrifice of three kinds on one altar. When Abraham failed, God's providence was extended through him to Isaac and Jacob, three generations.

(ii) Abraham's Offering of Isaac

After Abraham's failure in the symbolic offering God ordered him to offer his only son Isaac as a burnt offering (Gen. 22:2), by which God commenced a new providence to restore through indemnity the failure of Abraham's symbolic offering. According to the theory of predestination in the Principle, God does not use for a second time a person who is called for a certain mission and fails to carry out his own portion of responsibility. How, then, could God work His providence through the offering of Isaac to restore Abraham's failure in his symbolic offering when his failure in the symbolic offering annulled the will which was to be set up through the offering?

First, concerning God's providence to restore the foundation to receive the Messiah, the providence centering on Adam's family was the first one, while the providence centering on Noah's family was the second, and that centering on Abraham's family was the third. The number "three" is the number of perfection (cf. Part II, Ch. III, Sec. II, 4), and since the providence through Abraham was the third time for the providence of restoring the foundation to receive the Messiah, there was a condition in the Principle for the fulfillment of this providence. Therefore, Abraham could restore all the objects or conditions lost symbolically, due to the failure in the symbolic offering, by offering his own son as a substantial offering, thus setting up a condition of indemnity far greater in value than the previous condition.

Second, as already noted, the position of Abraham in offering the sacrifices was that of Adam. At that time Satan invaded two generations in succession by profaning Adam and his son Cain. Naturally, according to the principle of restoration through indemnity, the providence of taking back the two generations of Abraham and his son was possible on the Heavenly side.

Third, Adam could not offer the sacrifices directly before God, but Noah, standing on the foundation of Abel's heart, which enabled the success in the symbolic offering of the formation stage while he was in the position of Adam, could directly offer the symbolic offering of the ark. In this way, Abraham was called both on the foundation of Abel, who had been successful in the symbolic offering of the formation stage, and of Noah, who had succeeded in the symbolic offering of the growth stage. On that level, he offered the symbolic offering of the perfection stage. Therefore, although Abraham failed in the symbolic offering, God could have him offer the sacrifice again, on the condition of the historical foundation of heart-and-zeal, since Abel and Noah had succeeded in the symbolic offering.

At the time of offering Isaac as the sacrifice, Abraham had set up the condition of faith for the offering of Isaac by establishing the symbolic condition of indemnity to restore Adam's family, just as he had done at the time of his symbolic offering.

Therefore, Abraham planned with his wife, Sarah, to pretend to be in the position of brother and sister. After having been deprived of his wife by Abimelech, king of Gerar, he took his wife back again from the king. This time Abraham took both his wife and slaves, symbolizing mankind, and wealth, symbolizing all things (Gen. 20:1-16).

How, then, did Abraham offer Isaac as the sacrifice? When, in obedience to God's command with an absolute faith, Abraham was about to sacrifice his only son Isaac, whom he had received as a blessing, as a burnt offering, God commanded him not to lay his hand on the lad and said, ". . . now I know that you fear God . . ." (Gen. 22:12). Abraham's heart-and-zeal toward God's will and his resolution to slay his son arising from his absolute faith, obedience and loyalty, caused him to stand in a position equal to having killed Isaac; therefore, he could separate Satan from Isaac. Accordingly, God commanded Abraham not to kill the child, because Isaac, being separated from Satan, already stood on the side of Heaven. We must know that when God said, "now I know," He emphasized the mixture of His reproach for Abraham's mistake in the symbolic offering, and His joy over his success in the offering of Isaac.

In this manner, God's providence of restoration centering on Abraham's family was to be fulfilled through Isaac by Abraham's success in the offering of Isaac.

It took a three-day period for Abraham to offer his son as a burnt sacrifice on Mt. Moriah so that he might start a new providential course by separating Isaac from Satan to the Heavenly side. This three-day period continued as a period necessary for the separation of Satan before starting a new providential course. Jacob, too, had a three-day period of separation from Satan before he started the course of restoration of Canaan on the family level by taking his family out of Haran (Gen. 31:20-22). Moses also had a three-day period of separation from Satan before he started the course of the restoration of Canaan on the national level by taking the Israelite nation out of Egypt (Ex. 8:27-29). Jesus, too, had a three-day period of separation from Satan in the tomb, before starting the course of the restoration of Canaan on the worldwide level spiritually. It is also to be noted that when the Israelites returned to Canaan, centering on Joshua, the ark of the covenant, which went before the main troops, journeyed a three-day course of separation from Satan (Num. 10:33).

(iii) The Position of Isaac from the Standpoint of the Will, and His Symbolic Offering

It has previously been discussed in detail that, despite Abraham's failure in his symbolic offering, there still remained a condition in the Principle enabling the foundation to receive the Messiah to be laid, centering on Abraham. As clarified in the chapter on "Predestination," however, the situation was such that God could not repeat His providence centering on Abraham, who had failed in carrying out his own portion of responsibility. In consequence, God had to regard Abraham in the position of not having failed, though he did fail in his symbolic offering. He had to regard the providence of restoration, prolonged after Abraham, in the position of not having been prolonged. For this purpose, God commanded Abraham to offer Isaac as a burnt offering.

God promised Abraham to call His chosen nation through Isaac, saying,

> '. . . your own son shall be your heir!' And He brought him outside and said, 'Look toward heaven and number the stars, if you are able to number them.' Then He said to him, 'So shall your descendants be.' (Gen. 15:4-5)

In consequence, Abraham's loyalty, demonstrated by his being ready to slay his son of promise upon God's command, established the same condition as if he had killed himself, invaded by Satan due to the failure in his symbolic offering. Accordingly, the fact that God had Isaac survive means that Abraham himself was resurrected from his situation of having died, by separating himself from Satan, together with Isaac. Therefore, Abraham could separate himself from Satan, who had invaded him due to the failure in his symbolic offering, by succeeding in his offering of Isaac. Further, he could stand in a position of complete oneness with Isaac, centered on the will of God.

In this way, Abraham and Isaac, who survived death, though they were two individuals, were one body centered on the will of God. If Isaac should succeed in the providence, though the providence through Abraham failed and was prolonged to Isaac, Isaac's success could equally be the success of Abraham himself, who was one body with Isaac. Accordingly, despite the fact that the providence was prolonged from Abraham to Isaac, due to Abraham's failure in his symbolic offering, it became, seen from the viewpoint of the will, as though Abraham did not fail and the providence was not prolonged.

Nobody is sure of Isaac's age at the time of the offering. But, from the fact that he could carry the wood to be used for the burnt offering (Gen. 22:6) and that he asked his father where the lamb for the burnt offering was (Gen. 22:7), Isaac apparently was old enough to understand the significance of the incident. We can again well imagine that Isaac had obeyed and cooperated with his father at the time of the burnt offering.

If Isaac, who was old enough to understand the situation, had resisted his father's willingness to kill him for the burnt offering, God would not have accepted the offering of Isaac by any means. Abraham's loyalty, combined with that of Isaac, which was not any less, caused the success of the offering of Isaac, thus enabling the separation from Satan to occur.

Consequently, centering on the offering, Abraham and Isaac both survived. First, Abraham could restore through indemnity his position before his failure in the offering, by separating himself from Satan, who invaded him because of his failure in the symbolic offering. From this position, he was able to pass on his providential mission to Isaac. Second, Isaac, who inherited the divine mission from his father Abraham, by obeying him in complete surrender to the will, thus was enabled to set up the condition of faith for offering the symbolic sacrifice later.

In this way, the divine will was transmitted from Abraham to Isaac, and Abraham offered a ram for the burnt offering in place of Isaac, as it was written:

> Abraham lifted up his eyes and looked, and behold, behind him was a ram, caught in a thicket by his horns; and Abraham went and took the ram, and offered it up as a burnt offering instead of his son. (Gen. 22:13)

This became, as it was, the symbolic offering set up in order to restore the foundation of faith centering on Isaac. From the fact that Isaac carried the bundle of wood for the burnt offering, it can be concluded that he cooperated with Abraham when he offered the ram as the burnt offering. Accordingly, even though Abraham offered the ram as the symbolic offering, the result, seen from the viewpoint of God's will, was that Isaac himself offered the sacrifice because he succeeded his father's mission by becoming one body with him. In this manner, Isaac restored through indemnity the foundation of faith by being successful in the symbolic offering, from the position of substituting for Abraham, after inheriting his mission.

2. THE FOUNDATION OF SUBSTANCE

As the central figure to restore the foundation of faith in place of Abraham, Isaac offered an acceptable symbolic sacrifice with the ram. Isaac was thus able to lay the foundation of faith. In order to establish the foundation to receive the Messiah centering on Isaac, there had to be the foundation of substance fulfilled on the condition of indemnity to remove the fallen nature. This was to be achieved by offering a substantial sacrifice with his children Esau and Jacob in the positions of Cain and Abel.

If Abraham had not failed in the symbolic offering, Isaac and his half-brother Ishmael, in place of Abel and Cain, should have set up the condition of indemnity to remove the fallen nature, which had been left unaccomplished by Cain and Abel. Because of Abraham's failure, God, by setting up Isaac in Abraham's position, and Esau and Jacob in place of Ishmael and Isaac, worked the providence to have them set up the condition of indemnity to remove the fallen nature. Therefore, Esau and Jacob, centering on Isaac, are in the position of Cain and Abel centering on Adam, and, at the same time, in the position of Shem and Ham centering on Noah.

Isaac's eldest son, Esau, and the second son, Jacob, were symbols respectively, of Abraham's first symbolic offering, which was invaded by Satan, and his second offering of Isaac, separated from Satan; they represented evil and good, having to offer substantial sacrifices in the positions, respectively, of Cain and Abel. Esau and Jacob fought, even in their mother's womb (Gen. 25:22-23), because they were in the conflicting situations of Cain and Abel, who had been separated as the representations, respectively, of evil and good. Also, God loved Jacob and hated Esau while they were still in their mother's womb (Rom. 9:11-13), because they represented good and evil respectively.

In order for Esau and Jacob to set up the condition of indemnity to remove the fallen nature through substantial offerings, Jacob first had to set up the condition to restore through indemnity the position of Abel, who was the central figure for the substantial offering.

First, Jacob had to set up a condition of victory in his struggle to restore the birthright on the individual level. Satan had occupied God's world of creation in the position of the elder son. God, from the position of the younger son, had worked His providence to take the birthright of the elder. This is why God "hated" the elder and loved the younger (Mal. 1:2-3). Meanwhile, Jacob, who had been called even in his mother's womb with the mission to restore the elder's birthright, wisely took the birthright from his elder brother Esau, with some bread and a pottage of lentils (Gen. 25:34). God had Isaac bless Jacob because he tried to restore the birthright, knowing its value (Gen. 27:27), while He did not bless Esau because he, on the contrary, thought so little of the birthright that he sold it for a pottage of lentils.

Second, Jacob went to Haran and there triumphed in his struggle to restore the birthright of the elder, centering on his family and the wealth, during the 21 years of drudgery, and then returned to Canaan.

Third, Jacob restored domination substantially over the angel by winning in the struggle with him at the ford of Jabbok, on his way back from Haran to Canaan, the land promised by God.

Jacob at last became the central figure for the substantial offering by restoring through indemnity the position of Abel.

In this way, Esau and Jacob established the positions of Cain and Abel at the time God accepted Abel's offering. Therefore, in order for them to set up the condition of indemnity to remove the fallen nature, Esau had to love Jacob, set him up as the mediator, and obey him in the position of being dominated by him, thus standing in the position to multiply goodness by inheriting the good from Jacob who had received the blessing from God. Meanwhile, Esau, in fact, loved and welcomed Jacob when he returned to Canaan with his Heavenly family and the wealth after having finished the drudgery of 21 years in Haran

(Gen. 33:4); thus, they could establish the condition of indemnity to remove the fallen nature. In this manner, they could restore through indemnity what Cain and Abel of Adam's family and Shem and Ham of Noah's family had failed to achieve in the substantial offering.

Thus, through the success in the substantial offering by Esau and Jacob, the vertical course of history, which from Adam's family had aimed to restore through indemnity the foundation of substance, was, for the first time, restored through indemnity on the horizontal basis in Isaac's family in the providential course of restoration centering on Abraham.

The Biblical record says (Rom. 9:11-13) that God hated Esau while he was still in his mother's womb. However, he could stand in the position of a restored Cain, because he fulfilled his own portion of responsibility by surrendering to Jacob, and at last he received God's love. We must understand that God hated Esau merely because he was in the position of Cain, who had been on the side of Satan in the providential course of setting up conditions of indemnity.

3. THE FOUNDATION TO RECEIVE THE MESSIAH

The foundation to receive the Messiah, which was to be set up in Adam's family, was prolonged through three generations as far as Abraham because the central figures in charge of the providence of restoration failed to fulfill their portions of responsibility. However, God's will was prolonged to Isaac, on account of the failure in the symbolic offering of Abraham, who was supposed to accomplish the will. The foundation of faith and the foundation of substance were established centering on Isaac's family, and for the first time, the foundation to receive the Messiah was established. Accordingly, the Messiah was to come at that time.

When viewing things centering on the foundation to receive the Messiah, we must first know the social background necessary for the foundation to receive the Messiah. Fallen men must first set up the foundation to receive the Messiah in order to provide the basis to restore the world, established centered on Satan, into the kingdom centered on the Messiah.

In the providence of restoration centering on Adam's family and Noah's family, there were no other families who could possibly invade the family of divine will. Therefore, the Messiah was supposed to come on the foundation on the family level to receive the Messiah, if this had been established at that time. However, at the time of Abraham, there already was a nation formed by fallen men, centering on Satan, contending with Abraham's family. The Messiah could not have come directly on the foundation on the family level to receive the Messiah though it might have been established. They could receive the Messiah only after having established the foundation on the domain of the national level which could cope with the Satanic world.

Therefore, even if Abraham had been successful, both in the symbolic offering and the substantial offering, making possible at that time the establishment of the foundation on the family level to receive the Messiah, the Messiah could not have come, unless, on the established foundation, Abraham's descendants had multiplied in the land of Canaan, thus forming the foundation on the national level to receive the Messiah.

However, Abraham failed in the symbolic offering. As punishment for this, the descendants of Isaac, though they had established the foundation on the family level to receive the Messiah, had to leave their homeland and go into a foreign nation. They were supposed to establish the foundation on the national level to receive the Messiah only after 400 years of drudgery, and after again returning to Canaan.

Who had to begin the course of indemnity left for Abraham's descendants because of his failure in the symbolic offering? It was Jacob, and not Isaac. This was because, as shown, the central figure to go through the courses of indemnity was to be of the Abel-type, being the center of the substantial offering. Therefore, Abel in Adam's family, Ham in Noah's family, Isaac in Abraham's family and Jacob in Isaac's family had to go through a course of indemnity representing their respective families.

Jacob especially had to go through the traditional course of separation from Satan, as the pattern for Jesus to walk later, because he was the Abel-type person standing on the foundation to receive the Messiah (cf. Part II, Ch. II, Sec. 1). Jacob's family was supposed to start this course of indemnity in the position of Isaac's family, because they had to fulfill the purpose of the providence of restoration centering on Abraham. To do this, Jacob's family had to bear Abraham's sin through a 400-year course of indemnity. In Isaac's family, Jacob, in the position of Abel, had taken this course of indemnity; therefore in Jacob's family, Joseph, son of Rachel (Jacob's wife on God's side), had to establish Abel's position by going into Egypt first and there following the course of indemnity.

Therefore, Joseph was sold by his brothers and brought into Egypt. After having become the prime minister of Egypt at the age of 30, what he had been taught from heaven in his dream as a child became true (Gen. 37:5-11) when Joseph's half-brothers, other sons of Jacob on the Satanic side, surrendered to him. Thus they followed the course of first entering Egypt on the part of the children, and later, his parents were led through the same course. In this way, Jacob's family started the course of indemnity to later receive the Messiah on the national level.

In this manner, the providence centering on Isaac was prolonged to the providential course centering on Jacob. Jacob, who shouldered Abraham's sin, started the course of indemnity to fulfill Isaac's will on the national level. Therefore, Abraham, Isaac and Jacob were all one body, though they differed as individuals, just as Abraham and Isaac were one body seen from the significance of the will. Accordingly, Jacob's success meant Isaac's success, and Isaac's success meant Abraham's success. Therefore, the providence of restoration centering on Abraham, though it was prolonged to Isaac and then to Jacob, is the same as if it were fulfilled in one generation without any prolongation, when it is seen from the significance of the divine will. The Biblical passage in which God said, "I am the God of your father, the God of Abraham, the God of Isaac and the God of Jacob" (Ex. 3:6) tells us that those three, though three different generations, are just the same as if they were one generation seen from the significance of the divine will, since they are all our ancestors who fulfilled one divine purpose by joint efforts.

In fact, God intended to accomplish the providence of restoration by first having Jacob's family suffer 400 years slavery in Egypt, the Satanic world, then choosing them as the elected nation and bringing them back into Canaan as He promised in His blessing to Abraham. Then God intended to have them lay the foundation on the national level to receive the Messiah, and finally He would send the Messiah on that foundation.

Therefore, the foundation to receive the Messiah, established centering on Isaac's family, became the basis to start the course of indemnity for the establishment of the foundation on the national level to receive the Messiah. Accordingly, the 2,000-year period from Adam to Abraham was that during which they established the basis to start the establishment of the foundation on the national level to receive the Messiah in the next age.

Jacob, who took charge of the course of indemnity which resulted from Abraham's failure in the symbolic offering, succeeded in the struggle on the individual level by taking the birthright from Esau, using his wisdom for the sake of the heavenly will; and he again succeeded in the 21 years of struggle to take the birthright on the family level from his mother's brother, Laban, in Haran, the Satanic world. On his way back from Haran to Canaan Jacob won in the fight with the angel and earned the name "Israel" by setting up the condition of indemnity to restore the dominion over the angel for the first time, as a fallen man, since the fall of the first human ancestors. Thus he could build the basis for the formation of the chosen nation.

Jacob returned to Canaan through such a course, and after that set up the condition of indemnity to remove the fallen nature. Therefore, Jacob successfully set the pattern for the subjugation of Satan. Moses, and Jesus, too, had to go through this typical course, and the Israelites, as a whole, also had to go through it. Therefore, the history of the Israelite nation is the historical account of this typical course, in which they subjugated Satan on the national level. This is the reason the history of the Israelite nation is the central focus of the providential history of restoration.

4. LESSONS LEARNED FROM ABRAHAM'S COURSE

The providence of restoration centering on Abraham shows us first what God's predestination of His will was like. The providence of restoration cannot be fulfilled by God's power alone, but it is to be fulfilled by man's joint action with God. Accordingly, God could not fulfill His will through Abraham, although He called Abraham to accomplish the purpose of the providence of restoration, because Abraham failed to fulfill his own portion of responsibility.

Second, it shows us what God's predestination for man was like. God predestined Abraham to be the father of faith, but, when he failed to accomplish his own portion of responsibility, his mission was transferred to Isaac and then Jacob.

Third, it shows us that the providence of restoration must necessarily be prolonged when man fails to accomplish his own portion of responsibility, and, at the same time, a greater condition of indemnity must be set up in order to restore the failure. In Abraham's case, the will was to be fulfilled by offering animal sacrifices; but, due to his mistake, it was to be fulfilled only by offering his loving son Isaac as a sacrifice.

Fourth, it shows us, through the cutting of the sacrifices, that we too must divide ourselves as a sacrifice, representing good and evil. A religious life is that in which one places himself in the position of a sacrifice and offers himself as an acceptable sacrifice to God by dividing himself in two, representing the separation of good and evil. Therefore, unless we thus separate good from evil in ourselves centered on God's will, a condition for Satan to invade is created.

CHAPTER II

Providence of Restoration Centering on Moses and Jesus

A Biblical passage says, "Surely the Lord God does nothing, without revealing his secret to his servants the prophets." (Amos 3:7) The Scriptures contain countless secrets concerning God's providence of salvation. However, without knowing the principle of God's providence, men have not been able to understand the secret meaning of the words in the Bible. Even a record of the life of a prophet in the Bible is not merely the history of the man, but is, in fact, an explanation of the way for fallen men to take. Here, we are going to study how God revealed the pattern of Jesus' providential course for the salvation of mankind by having Jacob and Moses go through the providential course of restoration.

SECTION I
Pattern for the Subjugation of Satan

In the providence of restoration centering on Isaac's family, the entire course of Jacob was a pattern for Moses' course, and also was the pattern for Jesus' eventual substantial course. This pattern also set the course for the Israelites and the whole of mankind, who were to subjugate Satan in order to fulfill the purpose of the providence of restoration.

1. WHY GOD SET UP JACOB'S COURSE AND MOSES' COURSE AS THE PATTERN FOR JESUS' COURSE

The purpose of the providence of restoration is to be fulfilled ultimately by man's becoming able to naturally subjugate Satan and to dominate him through the fulfillment of his own portion of responsibility. Jesus came with the mission of the Messiah as a perfect human ancestor, in order to pioneer the final course for the subjugation of Satan and to have all the saints follow this course.

Satan, who had not obeyed nor surrendered even to God, would by no means obey and surrender to Jesus as the human ancestor, much less to the saints. Therefore, God, taking responsibility in the Principle for His having created men, set up the symbolic course to subjugate Satan through Jacob's pattern.

Moses could subjugate Satan by going through the "image" course with Jacob's course as the pattern, because God foreshadowed through Jacob the typical course to subjugate Satan. Jesus, as well, could subjugate Satan by going through the substantial course, with the course of Moses as the pattern, for Moses had trodden the course shown by Jacob. All the saints, too, could subjugate and dominate Satan by going through the same course.

When Moses said that God would raise up a prophet like himself (Acts 3:22), he meant that Jesus would have to walk the providential course of restoring Canaan on a worldwide level, using Moses' course as the pattern. The Bible says, "The Son can do nothing of his own accord, but only what he sees the Father doing; for whatever He does, that the Son does likewise." (John 5:19) The Biblical meaning is that Jesus was going through the very course God had revealed through Moses. Thus, Moses became the model for Jesus' later actions (Acts 3:22).

2. MOSES' COURSE AND JESUS' COURSE, AFTER THE PATTERN OF JACOB'S COURSE

Jacob's course enabled him to subjugate Satan. The course to subjugate Satan must be followed in a way reverse to that in which Satan invaded. Let us now study Moses' course and Jesus' course which they went through with Jacob's course as their pattern.

(1) Man originally should have kept God's commandment not to eat of the fruit at the risk of his life. By failing to overcome the temptation offered by the archangel, he fell. In order for Jacob to complete the restoration of Canaan on the family level by restoring the foundation to receive the Messiah when he had returned to Canaan with his family and wealth from Haran, he had to win a victory by trial in fighting against Satan at the risk of his life. To overcome such a trial, Jacob fought the angel at the ford of Jabbok. By defeating the angel, he received the name of Israel (Gen. 32:25-28). God tested Jacob by placing the angel in the position of Satan. The purpose was not to drive Jacob into misery. God's purpose for the trial was to set Jacob up as the lord of the restoration on the family level, by having him establish the position of Abel with his vic-

tory in the fight to restore dominion over the angel. The angelic world, also, was to be restored through the act of the angel in playing the main role in the trial.

In the case of Moses, in order for him to become the lord of the restoration of Canaan on the national level, returning to Canaan with the Israelites, he had to overcome a trial in which God tried to kill him (Ex. 4:24). If man had been given the trial not by God but by Satan, he would fall prey to Satan if he were defeated. Therefore, we must know it is from God's love of man that He would test man from His side. Jesus, too, had to win the fight against Satan at the risk of his life in the 40 days of temptation in the wilderness (Matt. 4:1-11).

(2) Jacob had to set up the condition to remove the fallen nature, because this came about due to Satan's invasion of man's flesh and spirit. Therefore, Jacob had to restore Abel's position in setting up the condition of indemnity to remove the fallen nature by taking the birthright from Esau, at the cost of bread and the pottage of lentils (Gen. 25:34), which symbolized the flesh and spirit.

For the same purpose, God intended, in Moses' course, to have the Israelites set up the condition of indemnity on the national level to remove the fallen nature by feeding them quail and manna (Ex. 16:13), symbolizing the flesh and the spirit, and through this giving them a strong sense of gratitude and the consciousness of being God's elect so that they might obey Moses.

Jesus said:

> Your fathers ate the manna in the wilderness and they died. . . . I say to you, unless you eat the flesh of the Son of man and drink his blood, you have no life in you. (John 6:49-53)

signifying that he, too, walked in the same course as the pattern previously established by Jacob and Moses. This means that fallen men cannot restore the original nature endowed at the creation unless they serve him and minister to him as the Messiah after they set up the condition of indemnity on the worldwide level to remove the fallen nature by believing in and obeying Jesus, who was in the position of John the Baptist (cf. Part II, Ch. II, Sec. III, 2[1]).

(3) Due to man's fall, even man's dead body was invaded by Satan. Jacob's body, already sanctified with the blessing, was embalmed for 40 days to set up the condition for his body to also be separated from Satan by the victory in the battle against him (Gen. 50:3). With Moses, who walked a course after this pattern, there also was a dispute concerning the location of his body after death (Jude 9). After the death of Jesus, there also were problems concerning his body (Matt. 28:12-13).

(4) Due to the fall of the first human ancestors, Satan invaded man during his growth period. In order to restore this, through indemnity, God has worked His providence to set up the number representing the period as follows (cf. Part II, Ch. III, Sec. II, 4): there was a three-day period of separation from Satan when Jacob returned from Haran into the land of Canaan (Gen. 31:22); there was also a three-day period of the same kind when Moses returned from Egypt into Canaan leading the Israelites (Ex. 5:3); and Joshua, too, could cross the river Jordan only after the three-day period (Josh. 3:2). Jesus also had the three-day period in the tomb (Luke 18:33) for the separation from Satan in his spiritual course of the restoration of Canaan on the worldwide level.

In order to horizontally restore through indemnity, in the generation of Jacob, the vertical conditions of indemnity ranging over 12 generations from Noah to Jacob, that had been delivered into Satan's hands, Jacob had to have 12 sons (Gen. 35:22). Therefore, Moses had 12 tribes (Ex. 24:4), and Jesus had 12 disciples (Matt. 10:1).

In order to set up the condition of indemnity to separate Satan, who had invaded the 7-day period of creation, Jacob had 70 family members (Gen. 46:27), Moses had 70 elders (Ex. 24:1) and Jesus had 70 disciples, each group respectively playing the central role in each course (Luke 10:1).

(5) The staff, being a symbolic representation of the will to smite injustice, to lead the way, and to support, symbolized the Messiah to come (cf. Part II, Ch. II, Sec. II, 2[2]). Therefore, the fact that Jacob entered the land of Canaan across the Jordan leaning on the staff which had such a profound meaning (Gen. 32:10), foreshadowed that fallen men would enter the ideal world of creation traversing the sinful world by smiting injustice, following the example of the Messiah, and by being led by him and by leaning on him. Therefore, Moses led the Israelites across the Red Sea with his staff (Ex. 14:16), while Jesus, too, had to lead the whole of mankind into God's ideal world of creation across the troubled sea of this world with a rod of iron representing himself (Rev. 2:27,12:5).

(6) Eve's sin formed the root of all sin, and her sin became fruitful when Cain killed Abel. According to the principle of restoration through indemnity, a mother and a son have to effect separation from Satan in mutual cooperation, because Satan invaded man through a mother and a son, thus producing the fruit of sin.

Accordingly, Jacob could separate from Satan after the blessing, because his mother cooperated with him in a positive way (Gen. 27:43). Without his mother's cooperation, Moses, too, could not have served God's will (Ex. 2:2). Jesus, too, had the cooperation of his mother, who took refuge in Egypt, with her son, escaping from King Herod, who sought to kill him (Matt. 2:13).

(7) The central figure responsible to accomplish the will of the providence of restoration must go through the course of restoration from the Satanic world to the Heavenly world.

Therefore, Jacob walked the course of restoration from Haran, the Satanic world, into the land of Canaan (Gen. 31:17-21). Moses walked the course of restoration from Egypt, the Satanic world, into the blessed land of Canaan (Ex. 3:8). Jesus also had to take refuge in Egypt, immediately after his birth, and then returned, in order to go through the same course (Matt. 2:13).

(8) The ultimate purpose of the providence of restoration is to destroy Satan. Therefore, Jacob buried the idols under the oak tree (Gen. 35:4), while Moses burnt the idol of the golden calf with fire, ground it to powder, and scattered the powder upon the water making the people of Israel drink it (Ex. 32:20). Jesus, too, had to destroy this sinful world by subjugating Satan with his words and power (cf. Part I, Ch. III, Sec. III, 2[2]).

SECTION II
The Providence of Restoration Centering on Moses

1. THE GENERAL VIEW OF THE PROVIDENCE OF RESTORATION CENTERING ON MOSES

The providence of restoration centering on Moses was to be accomplished on the foundation to receive the Messiah, which had already been established in the providence of restoration centering on Abraham. However, Moses was no exception to the principle of restoration in that he had to build the foundation to receive the Messiah after having restored through indemnity both the foundation of faith and the foundation of substance. Since the central figures in charge of the providence changed, the new persons could not fulfill the will of the providence of restoration without carrying out their own portions of responsibility. Besides, the scope of the providence was broadened from the family level to the national level. However, in the providence of restoration centering on Moses, as shown by the following records, the contents of the condition of indemnity for the establishment of this foundation were changed greatly, compared with the previous ones.

(1) The Foundation of Faith

(i) The Central Figure to Restore the Foundation of Faith

Moses was the central figure to restore the foundation of faith in the course of the Israelites' returning to the blessed land of Canaan after the 400 years of slavery in Egypt which had come about due to Abraham's failure in the symbolic offering. Before knowing how Moses established the foundation of faith, we must first know in what respects Moses was different from other personages, such as Adam, Noah or Abraham, who had been trying to restore the foundation of faith in the providential course before Moses.

First, we should know that Moses was in the place of God, substituting for God Himself. Therefore, God told Moses that he should be as God to Aaron, the prophet of the Israelites (Ex. 4:16). Again, God told Moses that He would make him a God to Pharoah (Ex. 7:1).

Second, Moses was the model for Jesus, who was to come in the future. As discussed above, God made Moses as God before Aaron and Pharoah. However, since Jesus is God in the flesh, the expression that "God made Moses as God" signifies that God set him up to walk the course that Jesus was to later walk. In this manner, Moses was the model for Jesus and pioneered the way for Jesus, just as John the Baptist had to make straight the way of Jesus (John 1:23). Let us now study how Moses walked this course.

Moses, as a descendant of Jacob, who had established the foundation to receive the Messiah, was not only the central personage of restoration, but also the one who walked figuratively the model course of Jacob which Jesus was to walk later. Moses was also standing on the foundation established by Joseph in the course of Jacob's family's entry into Egypt.

Joseph was another model for Jesus. Joseph was the son born of Rachel, who was Jacob's wife on the Heavenly side, and was the younger brother to the sons of Leah. Joseph, who was in the position of Abel, barely escaped death when his elder brothers, who were in Cain's position, plotted to kill him. However, he was sold to a merchant; he went into Egypt ahead of all. He became the prime minister of the country at the age of 30. Then his brothers and his parents came to Egypt and bowed before him (in surrender) just as heaven had instructed in his childhood (Gen. 37:5-11). On that foundation in the providential course, the Israelites' course of slavery in Egypt for the separation from Satan began. This course of Joseph foreshadowed that Jesus would come later to the Satanic world, and, after becoming the King of Kings at the age of 30, through the way of suffering, he would subjugate the whole of mankind, including his forefathers, and separate them from the Satanic world, thus restoring them all to the Heavenly side. Thus Joseph's whole life was the very model for the path of Jesus.

On the other hand, Moses' birth, growth and death were also the model for what Jesus was to go through. Moses at birth was on the verge of being killed by Pharoah. After his mother raised him in concealment, he went into Pharaoh's palace and was brought up safely among his foes. In like manner, Jesus also was at the point of being killed by King Herod. After his mother took him into Egypt and raised him in concealment, he was brought back into the dominion of King Herod and was brought up in safety even among his foes. Further, nobody knew the whereabouts of Moses' body after his death (Deut. 34:6). This, too, was the pattern for what was going to happen to Jesus' body.

Furthermore, Moses' course of restoration into Canaan on the national level was the true model for the worldwide course of restoration into Canaan, which Jesus was going to walk later. We can well understand that Moses was thus the model for Jesus from Biblical passages, which say:

> I will raise up for them a prophet like you from among their brethren . . . and whoever will not give heed to my words which he shall speak in my name, I myself will require it of him. (Deut. 18:18-19)

Again, the Bible says (John 5:19) that Jesus can do nothing of his own accord, but only what he sees the Father doing. This also signifies that God had already shown through Moses what Jesus was going to do in the future.

(ii) Conditional Objects to Restore the Foundation of Faith

Moses, as discussed above, was standing in a position different from that of the other central figures who had restored the foundation of faith in the providential course before him. Therefore, Moses could restore through indemnity the foundation of faith, merely by having established the 40-day foundation of separation from Satan, centering on God's words, even without offering the symbolic sacrifice as Abel, Noah, or Abraham did.

First, Moses stood on the foundation of having completed the providence through symbolic offerings established by Abel's, Noah's and Isaac's having succeeded three times in the symbolic offerings.

Second, the offering was the conditional object which was set up in place of the words, because fallen men became unable to receive God's words directly. At the time of Moses, the symbolic offering for the foundation of faith became unnecessary, because the providential period for the foundation of restoration (pre-Abramic age), in which the foundation of faith was restored by setting up the offering as the conditional object, had passed into the providential age of restoration (Old Testament Age) in which man could receive God's Word directly.

Third, since the providence centering on Adam's family had been prolonged on and on, conditions had to be set up to restore through indemnity the providential age which had been thus prolonged due to the invasion of Satan. In order for Noah to establish the foundation of faith through the ark, the 40-day foundation of separation from Satan became necessary. Abraham, too, could offer the symbolic sacrifice to establish the foundation of faith only after he had placed himself on the 40-day foundation of separation from Satan, having restored through indemnity the 400-year period. The Israelite nation suffered 400 years of slavery in Egypt in order to restore through indemnity the foundation of faith invaded by Satan due to Abraham's failure in the offering, by restoring through indemnity the 40-day foundation of separation from Satan.

Thus, in the providential age of restoration, the foundation of faith was supposed to be restored if one could stand, centering on God's Word in place of offerings, on the 40-day foundation of separation from Satan.

(2) The Foundation of Substance

In the providential age for the foundation of restoration, God operated His providence of establishing the foundation of substance on the family level. However, in the providential age of restoration, God worked His providence of establishing the foundation of substance on the national level. Meanwhile, Moses, who was to restore the foundation of faith on the national level, was in the position of Jesus because he was the substitute for God (Ex. 4:16, 7:1). For that reason, Moses was in the position of parent (father) to the Israelite nation. Moses was also in the position of child to Jesus, as a prophet with the mission of pioneering the way of Jesus. Therefore, he was also able to stand in the position of Abel, as the central figure to establish the foundation of substance on the national level.

Abel could establish his own position for the substantial offering along with the foundation of faith, which Adam should have established, by being successful in his offering, because Abel offered sacrifices from the position of a parent (father) in place of Adam. According to the same principle, Moses, being in the position of both parent and child at the same time, could establish the position of Abel (who was to offer the substantial offering) from the position of a child, if and when he had restored through indemnity the foundation of faith from the position of a parent.

In this way, after Moses had established the position of Abel, if the Israelites had set up the condition of indemnity on the national level to remove the fallen nature, through Moses, from the position of Cain, the foundation of substance on the national level would have been established.

(3) The Foundation to Receive the Messiah

If and when Moses had restored through indemnity the foundation of faith on the national level and the Israelites, centering on Moses, had restored through indemnity the foundation of substance on the national level, that would have become the foundation on the national level to receive the Messiah.

If the Israelites, on that foundation, had received the Messiah, removed the original sin through rebirth, and restored the original nature endowed at the creation by becoming one body with God in heart and feeling, they would have been able to become "perfected substantial individuals."

2. THE COURSE OF RESTORATION OF CANAAN ON THE NATIONAL LEVEL CENTERING ON MOSES

Moses' course of returning to Canaan, the land of God's promise, by leading the chosen nation of the Israelites out of Egypt, the Satanic world, with miracles and signs, and then leading them across the Red Sea and detouring through the wilderness was a veritable foreshadowing of Jesus' way. Jesus was going to restore Eden in the original form of creation, as God promised, by leading the Christians, the Second Israelites, out of the sinful world with miracles and signs and by leading them across the troubled sea of the sinful world and detouring through the desert without the water of life.

Just as the course of restoration of Canaan on the national level centering on Moses had been prolonged three times due to the disbelief of the Israelites, the course of the restoration of Canaan on the worldwide level centering on Jesus was also prolonged three times due to the disbelief of the Jewish people.

Let us avoid complicated explanations and detailed comparisons between Moses' course and that of Jesus. Their relationship will be clarified by comparing this section with the next.

(1) The First Course of Restoration into Canaan on the National Level

(i) The Foundation of Faith

The period of indemnity on the national level, which had been brought about due to Abraham's failure in the symbolic offering, ended in the Israelites suffering slavery in Egypt for 400 years. Then, in order for Moses to become the central figure to restore the foundation of faith, he had to establish the 40-day foundation of separation from Satan by indemnifying again, on the individual level, the 400 years which was the period of indemnity on the national level.

For this purpose, Moses had to spend 40 years in the palace of Pharaoh, the center of the Satanic world, in order to restore through indemnity the number 40, which Adam, before the fall, had to set up for the foundation of faith (cf. Part II, Ch. III, Sec. II, 4).

Moses put an end to his 40-year period in Pharaoh's palace where he received an education from his own mother, hired in the palace as his nurse unknown to anyone. This education encouraged his strong consciousness of Israel as God's elect. With unchanging loyalty and fidelity to the lineage of the chosen nation, he left the palace, preferring to suffer with God's people rather than to enjoy the sinful ephemeral pleasure of Pharaoh's house (Heb. 11:24-25). In this way, Moses could restore through indemnity the foundation of faith, having established the 40-day foundation of separation from Satan through his 40 years of life in Pharaoh's palace.

(ii) The Foundation of Substance

Moses came to establish Abel's position in setting up the condition of indemnity on the national level to remove the fallen nature as already discussed above, at the same time as he established the foundation of faith.

The Israelites, who were in Cain's position, should have obeyed with faith and surrendered to Moses, who was in the position of Abel as their parent and at the same time as a child. By inheriting God's will from Moses, they should have multiplied goodness. Then, they could have restored through indemnity the foundation of substance on the national level, having set up the condition of indemnity on the national level to remove the fallen nature. The period in which the Israelites thus left Egypt, following Moses, and returned to Canaan became also the period for them to establish the foundation of substance.

With Moses' act of killing an Egyptian, God commenced the "providence for the start." Moses, seeing that his brethren were ill-treated by the Egyptian, could not restrain his fervent love for his brethren; he killed the Egyptian (Ex. 2:12). In fact, this was the expression of God's heartfelt resentment when He saw the misery of His people (Ex. 3:7). Whether or not the Israelites became one, centering on such a leader as Moses, was to decide whether or not they could successfully start the course of restoration into Canaan, traversing the desert under Moses' leadership.

The reason that Moses, who had been chosen by God, had to kill the Egyptian was that, through the archangel's act in causing the first human ancestors to fall and by Cain's killing Abel, Satan had formed the sinful history of mankind from the position of the eldest son. Therefore, unless the Heavenly side could set up the condition to restore through indemnity by smiting the Satanic side, which was in the position of the eldest, it could not start the course of restoration into Canaan. Also it was to have Moses cut off his attachment to Pharaoh's palace and to place him in a situation in which he was unable to return, while, at the same time, it was to make the Israelites trust Moses by showing them his patriotism. It was for this same reason that God smote all the first-born men and cattle of the Egyptians in the second course of restoration into Canaan on the national level.

If the Israelites, upon witnessing such an act of Moses, had been deeply touched by his patriotism with the same heart as God's, and if they had respected him, trusted him, served him and followed him with more ardor, they could have entered the blessed land of Canaan through the direct route by the land of the Philistines, without having to cross the Red Sea or to make a detour by way of the wilderness of Sinai, centering on Moses, who led them as God. They could have established the foundation of substance then and there. Again, this would have become the 21-day course restoring Jacob's 21-year course in Haran. It is recorded (Ex. 13:17):

> When Pharaoh let the people go, God did not lead them by way of the land of the Philistines, although that was near; for God said, "Lest the people repent when they see war, and return to Egypt."

From this we understand that God intended to have the people go the first course of restoration into Canaan on the national level through the direct way of the Philistines. But due to the Israelites' distrust of Moses, this course was annulled even before it started. At the time of the second course of restoration into Canaan on the national level, God led them across the Red Sea and through the wilderness, lest they should return to Egypt on the way of restoration into Canaan due to their disbelief.

(iii) The Failure in the First Course of Restoration into Canaan on the National Level

If the Israelites, who were in the position of Cain, had entered the land of Canaan by obeying and surrendering to Moses, who was in the position of Abel, they would have set up the condition of indemnity on the national level to remove the fallen nature and establish then the foundation of substance. However, when they saw Moses kill the Egyptian, they misunderstood him and badly publicized the fact. Pharaoh, hearing it, sought to kill Moses (Ex. 2:15). Then, Moses was compelled to escape from Pharaoh and, leaving the Israelites, fled to the wilderness of Midian. Naturally, the foundation of substance was not established and the Israelites' course of restoration into Canaan, centering on Moses, was prolonged to a second and eventually a third time.

(2) The Second Course of Restoration into Canaan on the National Level

(i) The Foundation of Faith

Due to the failure of the "first course of restoration into Canaan on the national level" caused by the disbelief of the Israelites, Moses' 40-year period in Pharaoh's palace, which he had set up as his foundation of faith, was invaded by Satan. Therefore, in order for Moses to start the second course of restoration into Canaan on the national level, he had to set up again the period to restore through indemnity his 40-year period of life in Pharaoh's palace, which had been annulled by Satanic invasion, and then had to restore the foundation of faith. The purpose of Moses' 40 years in the wilderness of Midian, after he escaped from Pharaoh, lay here. During this 40-year period the Israelite nation also led a miserable life due to their disbelief of Moses.

Moses again established the 40-day foundation of separation from Satan through his 40 years in the wilderness of Midian; thus, he could restore the foundation of faith for the second course of restoration into Canaan on the national level. Therefore, God appeared before Moses and said:

I have seen the affliction of my people who are in Egypt, and have heard their cry because of their taskmasters; I know their sufferings, and I have come down to deliver them out of the hand of the Egyptians, and to bring them up out of that land to a good and broad land, a land flowing with milk and honey, to the place of the Canaanites . . . and now, behold, the cry of the people of Israel has come to me, and I have seen the oppression with which the Egyptians oppress them. Come, I will send you to Pharaoh that you may bring forth my people, the sons of Israel, out of Egypt. (Ex. 3:7-10)

(ii) The Foundation of Substance

Moses' 40 years in the wilderness of Midian re-established the 40-day foundation of separation from Satan and restored the foundation of faith. At the same time, he established the position of Abel in setting up the condition of indemnity on the national level to remove the fallen nature. Accordingly, as in the case of the first course of restoration into Canaan on the national level, the Israelites, who were in the position of Cain, should have absolutely trusted and followed Moses, who was in the position of Abel. Then they could have entered into the land of Canaan, which flowed with milk and honey, as God had said, and there they could finally have set up the condition of indemnity on the national level to remove the fallen nature and then could have established the foundation of substance.

For the same purpose as when Moses killed the Egyptian, God had Moses smite the Egyptians by giving him the power of three great miracles and ten calamities when he was about to start his second course of restoration into Canaan on the national level. Through this, God commenced the providence for the start.

The reasons that Moses had to smite those on the side of Satan were, as already elucidated: first, to restore through indemnity the position of the eldest son which had been invaded by Satan; second, to have the Israelites cut off their attachment to Egypt; and third, to let the Israelites know that Moses was sent by God (Ex. 4:1-9). Again, there was another reason for Moses to be able to kill the Egyptian. This was because, despite the fact that the Israelites had completed the 400-year indemnity period of slavery in Egypt, caused by Abraham's failure in his symbolic offering, as God had said, they were suffering 30 years more of the slavery (Ex. 12:41); hearing their lamentation, God pitied them (Ex. 2:24-25).

What did the three great miracles foreshadow in the course of the providence of restoration?

The first miracle, which God had ordered and showed (Ex. 4:3-9), was that by Moses' command Aaron cast down his rod before Pharaoh, and it became a serpent. Pharaoh, seeing this, summoned his magicians and had them cast down their rods and their rods became serpents. However, Aaron's serpent swallowed their serpents (Ex. 7:10-12).

What, then, did the miracle foreshadow? This showed us symbolically that Jesus would come as the Savior and destroy the Satanic world. The rod which performed the miracle before Moses, who was set up in place of God Himself (Ex. 7:1), symbolized Jesus with his authority and might, who in the future would perform such a miracle before God. At the same time, a rod has the mission of supporter, of a protector, and of a righteous leader always smiting unrighteousness; therefore, it also symbolized Jesus in the aspect of his mission, because it foreshadowed that Jesus would come before the whole of mankind in the future with such a mission.

Besides, the fact that the rod symbolizing Jesus became a serpent showed us that Jesus also had to play the role of a serpent. For this very reason, Jesus likened himself to a serpent, saying, "As Moses lifted up the serpent in the wilderness, so must the Son of man be lifted up." (John 3:14) Again, Jesus told his disciples to be "wise as serpents." (Matt. 10:16) By this he meant that, since the first human ancestors in the beginning fell by the temptation of the evil serpent, Jesus, in order to restore this through indemnity, had to come as a good serpent of wisdom, to tempt and lead the evil men into goodness. Therefore, his disciples also had to follow the wisdom of Jesus, who came as a good serpent, thus leading evil men into goodness. On the other hand, the fact that Moses' serpent swallowed up the magicians' serpents showed us, symbolically, that Jesus would come as a heavenly serpent to swallow up the Satanic serpent and destroy it.

The second miracle was that, upon God's command, Moses put his hand into his bosom and it became leprous. But, upon God's second command, he again put his hand into his bosom and it was healed (Ex. 4:6-7). This miracle symbolically showed us that Jesus would come in the future as the second Adam and, with the Holy Spirit as the deity of the second Eve (cf. Part I, Ch. VII, Sec. IV, 1), would perform the work of redemption. When his hand was first put into his bosom and it became leprous, this meant that the archangel first put Eve into his bosom and men fell into a position incapable of salvation. Again, the fact that when he put his hand into his bosom the second time it was healed represented that Jesus as the father spirit of mankind would come and restore the Holy Spirit as the mother spirit of mankind (cf. Part I, Ch. VII, Sec. IV, 1); then, as a hen gathers her brood under her wings (Matt. 23:37), he would restore the whole of mankind completely by gathering them into his bosom and giving them rebirth.

The third miracle was that Moses took some water from the Nile and poured it upon the dry ground and it became blood (Ex. 4:9). This represented symbolically that a lifeless thing like water would be restored into a thing of life like blood. Water signifies the people of the world who lost their lives due to the fall (Rev. 17:15). This sign showed us that Jesus and the Holy Spirit would come in the future and restore fallen men deprived of life into the children of life.

God manifested these three powers in order to set up the symbolic condition of indemnity, in the future, enabling Jesus and the Holy Spirit to come before the Israelites as the True Parents of mankind, and to restore the whole of mankind as their children and then restore the original four position foundation taken by Satan.

When Moses asked God for one who could speak for him (for he was not eloquent), God gave him Aaron his brother (Ex. 4:14), then Miriam, the prophetess, his sister (Ex. 15:20) to assist him. This shows us figuratively (in image) that in the future, Jesus and the Holy Spirit, as the Word in substance, would come and restore men, deprived of the Word due to the fall, to the substance (incarnation) of the Word. Therefore, Aaron and Miriam exalted the will of Moses, who was in the position of God in the course of restoration into Canaan, and carried out their mission of leading the people in place of Moses. This showed figuratively (in image) that in the future, Jesus and the Holy Spirit would exalt the will of God in the worldwide course of restoration into Canaan and carry out the mission of redemption in place of God.

When Moses was going before Pharaoh with God's command, Yahweh (the Lord) appeared on the way and sought to kill him. At that time, Moses was spared his life through his wife Zipporah's circumcision of his son (Ex. 4:24-26). By Moses' having overcome the test through the circumcision, his family survived and consequently the Israelites could come out of Egypt. This also foreshadowed that even when Jesus would come in the future, God's providence of salvation would not be fulfilled unless the Israelites went through the process of circumcision.

Let us then study what the significance of circumcision is. The first human ancestors, due to the blood relationship with Satan, received the blood of death through the foreskin. Therefore, in order for fallen men to be restored as God's children, they began to circumcise themselves as the condition representing the draining the blood of death by shedding the blood from the foreskin as the condition of indemnity. The fundamental significance of circumcision is, firstly, the sign of shedding the blood of death; secondly, the sign of restoring male dominion; and thirdly, the sign of promise to restore the position of the children of original nature. There are three kinds of circumcision: the circumcision of mind (Deut. 10:16), the circumcision of the flesh (Gen. 17:10) and the circumcision of all things (Lev. 19:22-23).

Next, God saved the Israelites from the land of Egypt, by performing the signs of ten calamities through Moses (Ex. 7:10-12:36). This, too, showed that in the future Jesus would come and save God's chosen people through miracles and signs. When Jacob suffered the drudgery of 21 years in Haran, Laban deceived Jacob ten times without giving him the due wage (Gen. 31:7). Consequently, in the course of Moses, who was to go through Jacob's model course, we see that Pharaoh not only put the Israelites under more than due slavery, but also deceived them ten times without keeping his promise of liberating them. Therefore, as the condition of indemnity, God could smite Pharaoh by afflicting him with ten calamities. Let us, then, study what these ten calamities foreshadowed.

There were three days' darkness on the side of Egypt, while there were three days' light on the side of Israel, showing that, in the future when Jesus would come, there would be darkness on the side of Satan, while there would be light on the Heavenly side. Next, God smote all the first-born of the Egyptians, including the first-born of the cattle, but the Israelites could avoid the calamity with the blood of the lamb painted on their doorposts. This was to enable the second son, who was in the position of Abel, to restore the position of the first-born by God's smiting the first-born, because all the first-born on the side of Satan were in the position of Cain. This calamity also foreshadowed that, when Jesus would come, he would restore the original position of the first-born, thus resulting in the decline of the Satanic side which took initiative in the course of the providence, and in the salvation of the Heavenly side due to the redemption through the blood of Jesus. Moses also took great wealth from Egypt (Ex. 12:35-36), and this, too, foreshadowed the restoration of all things by Jesus, which was to occur in the future.

Whenever God worked miracles of calamity, He hardened Pharaoh's heart (Ex. 10:27). The first reason was to show the people that God was the God of the Israelites, by manifesting His power before Pharaoh and the Israelites (Ex. 10:12). The second reason was to make Pharaoh abandon his attachment to the Israelites even after they left Egypt. God desired that Pharaoh, after having tried his very best to catch the Israelites, realize his inability to stop them, and thus finally let them go. A third reason was to help the Israelites cut off their attachment to Egypt by causing them to have a feeling of hostility against Pharaoh.

In the first course of restoration into Canaan on the national level, God worked the "providence for the start" when Moses killed the Egyptian. However, the people distrusted Moses, and this course ended in a failure before it even started. But, the Israelite nation in the second course came to believe that Moses was their true leader, sent by God, when they saw the three signs and ten calamities which God showed them as the "providence for the start." The Israelites, by trusting and following Moses, who had established Abel's position on the foundation of faith on the national level, were able to start their second course of restoration into Canaan on the national level.

The mere fact that the Israelites obeyed and surrendered to Moses temporarily could not make possible the establishment of the condition of indemnity to remove the fallen nature. Since the providential course of establishing the condition of indemnity to remove the fallen nature had been invaded by Satan, and a long providential period was cast into the hands of Satan, the Israelites should restore through indemnity an equivalent period on the national level. Therefore, the Israelites, who were in Cain's position to Moses, could never set up the condition of indemnity on the national level to remove the fallen nature unless they believed in and followed Moses with complete obedience throughout the whole period of their journey in the wilderness. Accordingly, the foundation of substance on the national level was not to be realized before the Israelites had passed through their course in the wilderness by obeying Moses and had entered into Canaan.

In this manner, the "providence for the start" in the second course of restoration into Canaan was done with greater grace than in the first one. But, since it was due to their disbelief, the condition of indemnity that the Israelites had to establish in the second course was additionally heavy. In the first course, they would have been led directly through the land of the Philistines into the blessed land of Canaan within 21 days, the number representing the period of Jacob's course in Haran. However, in their second course, as described clearly in the Bible (Ex. 13:17), God was worried about the possibility of the people's going back to Egypt, if they were led through the land of the Philistines, by being afraid of possible war and thus falling into disbelief again as in the first course. Therefore, God did not lead them through this path but had them enter Canaan only after crossing the Red Sea and traversing the wilderness, thus spending 21 months.

In this way, the Israelites, centering on Moses, started their 21-month course through the wilderness. Let us study how this could become, as previously stated, the model course of restoration into Canaan on the worldwide level, centering on Jesus, who was to come later.

When Pharaoh, having surrendered to Moses, permitted the Israelites to offer sacrifices there, Moses deceived Pharaoh and obtained three days' permission by saying:

> It would not be right to do so; for we shall sacrifice to the Lord our God offerings abominable to the Egyptians. If we sacrifice offerings abominable to the Egyptians before their eyes, will they not stone us? We must go three days' journey into the wilderness and sacrifice to the Lord our God as he will command us. (Ex. 8:26-27)

Thus Moses led the Israelites out of Egypt.

This three-day period was truly the period which Abraham needed for the separation from Satan before offering the sacrifice of Isaac. After that, this became the period of indemnity necessary for the separation from Satan whenever anyone started any providential course. Even when Jacob was about to start his period of restoration into Canaan, he left Haran by deceiving Laban and had the three-day period of separation from Satan (Gen. 31:19-22). Likewise, Moses also, before starting his course of restoration into Canaan, had to have the three-day period of separation from Satan by deceiving Pharaoh and thus taking free action. This also showed us that later Jesus, too, would have to take the three-day period of resurrection for the separation from Satan before he could start the spiritual providence of restoration. Thus, 600,000 Israelites, mostly young, left Ramses on the fifteenth of January (Ex. 12:6-37, Num. 33:3).

After the Israelites had reached Succoth by acceptably setting up the three-day period, God gave them grace and led them by a pillar of clouds by day and a pillar of fire by night (Ex. 13:21). The pillar of cloud by day (positivity) which led the Israelites on Moses' course represented Jesus, who would later lead the Israelites through the course of restoration into Canaan on the worldwide level. The pillar of fire by night (negativity) symbolized the Holy Spirit, who was to lead them as a female spirit.

Moses, according to God's command, divided the Red Sea with his rod and crossed it as if it were land, but the pursuing Egyptian chariots were all drowned in the water (Ex. 14:21-28). As already discussed, Moses, when he went before Pharaoh, symbolized God (Ex. 7:1), and the rod in Moses' hand symbolized Jesus, who was to manifest the power of God. Therefore, this sign shows us that later when Jesus would come, Satan would come in pursuit of the believers in Jesus who would follow Jesus through the course of restoration into Canaan on the worldwide level. But Jesus, coming with the mission of a rod, would strike the bitter sea of the world lying in front of the people with the rod of iron (Rev. 2:27, Ps. 2:9). Then the bitter sea of the world would become like a smooth way before the saints, and Satan, in pursuit of the people, would perish. As already discussed in the chapter on the "Last Days" in Part I, the rod of iron signifies God's Word. Then, in a Biblical passage (Rev. 17:15) this sinful world is likened to water. From this meaning we also can call the world "the bitter sea."

The people of Israel crossed the Red Sea and came to the wilderness of Sin, on the fifteenth day of the second month after they had departed from Egypt (Ex. 16:1). God fed the people of Israel with manna and quail until they came to a habitable land (Ex. 16:35). This shows us that later Jesus would feed all men, in the course of restoration into Canaan on the worldwide level, with his flesh (manna) and blood (quail), which were the elements of life for men. Therefore, the Bible says:

> Your fathers ate the manna in the wilderness, and they died; . . . I am the living bread which came down from heaven; if anyone eats of this bread, he will live forever; . . . unless you eat the flesh of the Son of Man and drink his blood, you have no life in you. (John 6:49-54)

When the people of Israel left the wilderness of Sin and camped at Rephidim, God commanded Moses to strike the rock at Horeb so that water should come out of it for the people to drink (Ex. 17:6). Again the Bible says, "The Rock was Christ." (I Cor. 10:4) Therefore, it showed us that later Jesus would come and make the people alive with the spring of the living water (John 4:14). The two tablets of stone that Moses later received on Mount Sinai symbolized Jesus and the Holy Spirit. Moreover, the rock, being the root of the tablets of stone, also symbolized God. Since Moses struck the rock, the root of the tablets of stone, to give water to the people of Israel so that they might live, Moses, on this foundation, could receive the tablets of stone, and could make the ark of the covenant and the tabernacle.

Joshua fought with Amalek at Rephidim, and whenever Moses held up his hand, Israel prevailed. Whenever he lowered his hand, Amalek prevailed. Therefore, Aaron and Hur took a stone and put under Moses, and he sat upon it, and they held up his hands, one on one side and the other on the other side; and Joshua defeated Amalek and his people (Ex. 17:10-13). This also foreshadowed what would happen when Jesus would come in the future. Joshua was the symbol of the believers in Jesus, Amalek was that of the Satanic world, and Aaron and Hur symbolized Jesus and the Holy Spirit. Again, the fact that Joshua smote and defeated Amalek before Aaron and Hur, who held up Moses' hands, foreshadowed that the believers serving the Trinity of God, Jesus and the Holy Spirit could smite and destroy Satan.

(iii) The Providence of Restoration Centering on the Tabernacle

We must first learn the details of how the Israelites received the tablets, the tabernacle and the ark. After having triumphed in the fight against Amalek, they reached the wilderness of Sinai in the beginning of the third month (Ex. 19:1). From there,

Moses went up Mount Sinai with 70 elders and met God (Ex. 24:9-10). God called Moses to the summit of Mount Sinai, and Moses fasted for 40 days and 40 nights so that he might receive the Ten Commandments written on the tablets of stone (Ex. 24:18). While he fasted on the mountain, he received instructions about the ark and the tabernacle from God (Ex. 25-31). When he had finished the 40-day fast, Moses received from God the two tablets of stone on which were written the Ten Commandments (Ex. 31:18).

When Moses came down from Mount Sinai with the tablets of stone and went to the people of Israel, they were worshiping the golden calf, which they had Aaron make, as the god which led them out of Egypt (Ex. 32:4). Moses' anger burned hot when he saw this, and he threw the tablets to the ground and broke them at the foot of the mountain (Ex. 32:19). God appeared again to Moses and told him to cut two tablets of stone like the first, that He might write upon them the Ten Commandments that were on the first tablets which he had broken (Ex. 34:1). When Moses had finished fasting 40 days and 40 nights the second time according to God's words, God again gave him the Ten Commandments written on the tablets (Ex. 34:28). When Moses again appeared before the Israelites with the tablets of stone, the people ministered to Moses; and they, then, built the ark and the tabernacle (Ex. 35:10-12).

a) The significance and the purpose of the tablets, the tabernacle and the ark of the covenant

What do the tablets of stone signify? The fact that Moses received the two tablets of stone with the words written on them means that the providential age for the foundation of restoration, in which men, due to the fall, contacted God only through offerings, had passed; and men had entered the providential age of restoration, in which fallen men could contact

God through the words which they had thus restored. As already elucidated in the "Introduction" of Part II, if Adam and Eve, who had been created by the Word, had perfected themselves, they would have become the "perfect incarnation of the Word." However, due to the fall, they lost the Word. Now, the fact that Moses received the two tablets of stone with the words written on them through the 40-day period to separate Satan signifies that Adam and Eve, long lost in the Satanic world, were restored as the symbolic incarnation of the Word. Accordingly, the two tablets of stone with the words written on them were the symbols of restored Adam and Eve, again symbolizing Jesus and the Holy Spirit, who would later come as the incarnation of the Word. The Bible symbolized Christ as a white stone (Rev. 2:17) and also states that the Rock was Christ (I Cor. 10:4), for the same reason. The two tablets of stone, thus symbolizing Jesus and the Holy Spirit, symbolize heaven and earth as well.

Next, what is the significance of the tabernacle? Jesus likened the temple of Jerusalem to his body (John 2:21). Again, the saints who believed in him were called "God's temple". (I Cor. 3:16). Therefore, the temple is the representation in image of Jesus himself. If the Israelites, centering on Moses, had succeeded in their first course of restoration into Canaan, they would have prepared to receive the Messiah by building the temple as soon as they entered the land of Canaan. However, due to their faithlessness, they had not even started the first course. In their second course, they built a tabernacle in place of the temple, because they had to wander in the wilderness after having crossed the Red Sea. Therefore, the tabernacle was the symbolic representation of Jesus himself. For this reason, God, when He commanded Moses to build the tabernacle, said, "Let them make me a sanctuary, that I may dwell in their midst." (Ex. 25:8)

The tabernacle consisted of the "holy place" and the "most holy place" (holy of holies). The latter was the place where only the chief priest entered once a year to offer sacrifices. In it was the ark, and it was supposed to be the place of God's presence. Thus, the most holy place symbolized the spirit of Jesus. The holy place was the place where they entered ordinarily, and this symbolized Jesus' body. Consequently, it can also be said that the most holy place symbolized the invisible substantial world, while the holy place symbolized the visible substantial world. When Jesus was crucified, the curtain between the holy place and the most holy place was torn in two, from top to bottom (Matt. 27:51), meaning that by the completion of the providence of spiritual salvation through Jesus' crucifixion, the way to communicate between the spirit man and the physical man, and between heaven and earth, opened up.

Then what was the ark? The ark was that of God's covenant, which was to be enshrined in the most holy place. In it were the two tablets of stone, symbolizing Jesus and the Holy Spirit, and, naturally, heaven and earth. In the ark there was manna, which had been the food of life for the Israelites in their course in the wilderness, and symbolized Jesus' body. The manna was contained in a golden urn that symbolized the glory of God. Also included was Aaron's rod that budded, which showed God's power to the Israelites (Heb. 9:4). In this respect, the ark, generally considered, was the condensed body of the cosmos, while on the other hand it was the condensed body of the tabernacle.

The mercy seat overshadowed the ark, and God said that they should make two cherubim of hammered gold and cover the two ends of the mercy seat. Then He would meet with them there, between the two cherubim, and speak with them of all that He would give them as commandments for the people of Israel (Ex. 25:16-22). This showed us that, later, when Jesus and the Holy Spirit, represented by the tablets of stone, would come and redeem the people through the work of moving their hearts, God would appear in the mercy seat; at the same time the cherubim, which had blocked the way for Adam to attain the Tree of Life in the garden of Eden, would be separated on each side, to the right and left, and everyone would enjoy the chance of going before Jesus, as the Tree of Life, and receiving God's words.

What, then, was God's purpose in giving them the tablets of stone, the tabernacle, and the ark? The Israelites, after having finished the 400-year period of indemnity brought about by Abraham's failure in the symbolic offering, smote the Egyptians with the three signs and ten calamities, drowned the countless Egyptian soldiers and chariots pursuing them by dividing the waters of the Red Sea, and then made their way into the wilderness. The Israelites had left Egypt with much resentment and hostility. So, for the Israelites, who were in a situation which compelled them to continue their way without having to return to Egypt, the restoration into Canaan was the inevitable course which had to be followed at all costs. Therefore, God performed many miracles and signs in the "providence for the start," and He had the Israelites cross the Red Sea, thus putting them in a situation where they were incapable of returning.

Nevertheless, the Israelites all fell into faithlessness. At the end, there was danger that even Moses might possibly act faithlessly. Here, God had to set up an object of firm faith, that would never change, even though man might change. That is to say, whenever there is even one man of absolute faith, God has this man succeed to the attendance of the object of faith, thus gradually realizing the will of His providence.

By what could man, then, set up the object of faith? The tabernacle, which symbolized the Messiah, by enshrining the ark with the tablets of stone inside, was this object. Therefore, the construction of the tabernacle meant that the Messiah had already come, symbolically.

Consequently, if the Israelites, centering on Moses, had exalted the tabernacle as the Messiah with profound loyalty and thus had been restored into the blessed land of Canaan, the foundation of substance on the national level would have been realized at that time. Even though all the Israelites had fallen into faithlessness, if Moses alone had remained to keep the tabernacle, the nation could have again set up the condition of indemnity and could have been restored upon the foundation centering on Moses, who served the tabernacle. Further, even if Moses would have fallen into faithlessness, if any single man of Israel had kept the tabernacle to the end in place of Moses, it would have been possible for God to work again His providence of restoring the whole nation, which had fallen into faithlessness, by centering on the single man left.

If the Israelites had not fallen into faithlessness in their first course of restoration into Canaan on the national level, Moses' family could have played the role of the tabernacle. Moses could have substituted for the tablets of stone and the ark of the covenant, and the family law of Moses could have been the substitute for the heavenly law. Thus, they could have entered into the land of Canaan without need of the tablets of stone, the ark, and the tabernacle; and there they could have built the temple. The tablets of stone, the tabernacle, and the ark were what God gave the Israelites in order to save them, after they had fallen into faithlessness. The tabernacle, being the symbolic representation of Jesus and the Holy Spirit, was what they needed until the erection of the temple. The temple, being the image-representation of Jesus and the Holy Spirit, was what they needed until the coming of the Messiah, who was to be the substantial temple.

b) The foundation for the tabernacle

Just as the foundation to receive the Messiah must be realized in order to be able to receive the Messiah, the "foundation for the tabernacle" must be established in order to be able to receive the tabernacle, which is the symbolic Messiah. Therefore, there should be no question that they had to establish both the foundation of faith for the tabernacle, and the foundation of substance for the tabernacle, in order to establish the foundation for the tabernacle. Then, what should the Israelites have done, centering on Moses, in order to establish these two foundations?

If Moses had acceptably established the 40-day period of separation from Satan through fasting and prayer, by obeying God's words for the tabernacle, the foundation of faith for the tabernacle was to be established. And, if the Israelites had obeyed in surrender and faith to Moses, who had to set up the ideal of the tabernacle, the condition of indemnity to remove the fallen nature for the tabernacle was supposed to be set up. Accordingly, the foundation of substance for the tabernacle was also to be established. The tabernacle here means the whole thing, including the tablets of stone and the ark of the covenant.

The first foundation for the tabernacle

Man is the substantial being (incarnation) of the Word (John 1:3), and he was created on the sixth day. Therefore, in order for God to work the providence of giving man the words of re-creation for the restoration of fallen man, He had to sanctify the number "six" corresponding to the period of creation invaded by Satan. Consequently, God sanctified Mount Sinai by covering it with clouds in the glory of Yahweh for six days. Appearing in the clouds on the seventh day, He called Moses

(Ex. 24:16). From that time on, Moses fasted for 40 days and 40 nights (Ex. 24:18). This was for God to have Moses establish the foundation of faith for the tabernacle, which was the symbolic Messiah, by having him set up the 40-day period of separation from Satan, when God saw that the Israelites had again fallen into faithlessness after crossing the Red Sea.

As already discussed, the condition of indemnity to remove the fallen nature in the course of restoration into Canaan was to be fulfilled not by the Israelites' simply trusting and obeying Moses temporarily, but only by their remaining in that state until they had entered Canaan, had built the temple, and had received the Messiah. In the same manner, even in their establishing the condition of indemnity to remove the fallen nature and then the foundation of substance for the tabernacle before erecting the tabernacle, the Israelites should have trusted, served and obeyed Moses until he finished erecting the tabernacle. However, the Israelites fell into faithlessness while Moses was fasting and praying. They had Aaron make a golden calf for them, and worshipped it, saying it was their god who had led them out of the land of Egypt (Ex. 32:4). In this way, the Israelites failed in setting up the condition of indemnity to remove the fallen nature which they had to set up for the tabernacle, and naturally failed also in establishing the foundation of substance for the tabernacle.

God led the Israelites with signs and miracles. However, even God could not interfere with their action during the period in which man himself was to restore the Word by his own portion of responsibility, because it was man himself that had lost the foundation of the Word. Moses raged in anger upon seeing the people dancing before the idol, and threw the two tablets of stone at the foot of the mountain, thus breaking them (Ex. 32:19). This resulted in Satan's invasion of the foundation of faith for the tabernacle, which Moses had established through the 40-day period to separate Satan. The two tablets of stone, as already clarified above, symbolize the second Adam and the second Eve, Jesus and the Holy Spirit. The fact that Moses broke the two tablets of stone symbolizing Jesus and the Holy Spirit, because of the faithlessness of the Israelites, shows us symbolically that later, when Jesus would come, Jesus and the Holy Spirit could possibly fail to accomplish the original mission given by God, by Jesus' being crucified, if the Jewish people should fall into faithlessness.

Such faithlessness of the Israelites frustrated God's providence, which was designed to have the Israelites establish the foundation for the tabernacle. God's providence to establish the foundation for the tabernacle was prolonged to the second and the third time because of the continued faithlessness of the Israelites.

The second foundation for the tabernacle

All the Israelites centering on Moses fell into faithlessness to God's providence. Since they were already on the foundation of having drunk the water from the rock at Rephidim (Ex. 17:6), which was the root of the tablets of stone, God could appear again to Moses after he had broken the tablets of stone and tell him to cut two tablets like the first that He might write upon them the words that had been on the first tablets (Ex. 34:1). But Moses could not restore the tabernacle centering on the tablets of stone without restoring the foundation of faith for the tabernacle, by setting up again the 40-day foundation of separation from Satan. Therefore, he could restore the ideal of the tabernacle and the second tablets of stone with the words of the Ten Commandments written on them, only after the second 40 days and 40 nights of fasting (Ex. 34:28).

The fact that the tablets of stone, once broken, were restored through the fasting and prayer of 40 days and 40 nights, showed us that though Jesus was crucified, Christ could come again and commence the providence of salvation on that foundation, if and when the saints, believing in him, should set up the condition of indemnity to receive him through the 40-day foundation of separation from Satan.

During the 40-day period of separation from Satan, in which Moses restored, for the second time, the ideal of the tabernacle centering on the tablets of stone, the Israelites not only obeyed and surrendered to Moses but also created the tabernacle according to God's direction and Moses' instruction. This was on the first day of the first month in the second year (Ex. 40:17).

Thus, the chosen people of Israel erected the tabernacle on the foundation for the tabernacle which they had established by fulfilling the foundation of substance for the tabernacle, after having set up the condition of indemnity to remove the fallen nature. However, as previously discussed, the foundation of substance in their second course of restoration into Canaan on the national level was not to be established merely by erecting the tabernacle. They should have exalted and honored the tabernacle with undiminishing ardor until they entered Canaan, erected the temple, and received the Messiah.

On the 20th day of the second month in the second year, the Israelites started from the wilderness of Sinai centering on the tabernacle, under the guidance of the pillar of cloud (Num. 10:11-12). However, God burnt their camp in wrath, because the people again fell into faithlessness and bore a grudge against Moses (Num. 11:1). Nevertheless, the Israelites were not awakened to God's will, and continued to have resentment against Moses, grumbling that there was no fish and no fruit, except the manna, and that they missed the land of Egypt (Num. 11:4-6). Therefore, the foundation for the tabernacle was invaded by Satan. The providence of restoring this foundation had to be prolonged once again.

The third foundation for the tabernacle

The second foundation of faith for the tabernacle was invaded by Satan, because the people again fell into faithlessness. Due to Moses' unchanging faith and loyalty, however, the tabernacle stood firmly on the foundation of faith for the tabernacle, set up by Moses. The Israelites stood on the foundation of having drunk the water from the rock at Rephidim (Ex. 17:6); the rock was the root of the tablets of stone which were the center of the tabernacle. On these foundations, therefore, if the Israelites had succeeded in the establishment of the 40-day foundation of separation from Satan and obeyed in complete surrender to Moses, centering on the tabernacle, they should have restored through indemnity the foundation for the tabernacle for the third time. The 40-day period of spying was the condition God gave them in order to accomplish this.

God sent into the land of Canaan the twelve persons whom He had chosen, one from each tribe of the Israelites, as the chief of the tribe (Num. 13:1), and had them spy on the land for 40 days (Num. 13:25). However, all returning from the land, except Joshua and Caleb, presented faithless reports. That is, they reported that the Israelites would not be able to destroy the city and the people there, saying that the people dwelling in the land were strong and that the cities were fortified (Num. 13:28). Besides, they said that the land would devour its inhabitants and that all the people they saw in it were men of great stature alongside whom they seemed to be like grasshoppers (Num. 13:32-33). The Israelites, hearing this report, murmured against Moses and cried in lamentation, saying that they should choose a captain and go back to Egypt.

Nevertheless, Joshua and Caleb cried out, saying that they should not rebel against the Lord, that they should attack the people dwelling in the land without fear. They proclaimed that the Lord was with the Israelites, and that the Canaanites would become their prey, since their protection was removed from them (Num. 14:9). But the congregation tried to stone Joshua and Caleb (Num. 14:10). Then the glory of the Lord appeared to all the people, and the Lord said to Moses:

> How long will this people despise me? And how long will they not believe in me, in spite of all the signs which I have wrought among them? (Num. 14:11)

He again said:

> But your little ones, who you said would become a prey, I will bring in, and they shall know the land which you have despised. But as for you, your dead bodies shall fall in this wilderness. And your children shall be shepherds in the wilderness forty years and shall suffer for your faithlessness, until the last of your dead bodies lies in the wilderness. According to the number of the days in which you spied out the land, forty days, for every day a year, you shall bear your iniquity, forty years, and you shall know my displeasure. (Num. 14:31-34)

In this way, the third foundation for the tabernacle was unable to be restored, and their second course in the wilderness of 21 months was prolonged to a third course in the wilderness of 40 years.

(iv) The Failure in the Second Course of Restoration into Canaan on the National Level

Due to the faithlessness of the Israelites, the foundation for the tabernacle was invaded by Satan for the third time. Therefore, the establishment of the condition of indemnity on the national level to remove the fallen nature in the second course of restoration into Canaan on the national level was a failure. In consequence, they failed in the establishment of the foundation of substance, which they were to set up for the second time;

naturally the second course of restoration into Canaan on the national level was a failure, and it was prolonged into the third course of restoration into Canaan on the national level.

(3) The Third Course of Restoration into Canaan on the National Level

(i) The Foundation of Faith

Due to the faithlessness of the Israelites, the second course of restoration into Canaan on the national level ended in failure. Therefore, the 40-year period in the wilderness of Midian, which Moses had established in order to restore the foundation of faith in that course, was again invaded by Satan. Because the Israelites failed to set up the 40-day period of spying in faith and obedience, it took them 40 years, each day calculated as a year, to wander in the wilderness and to return to Kadesh-barnea. This 40-year period was for Moses to separate Satan, who had invaded the foundation of faith in the second course, and to restore through indemnity the foundation of faith for the third course. Moses, who had kept and exalted the tabernacle in utter faith and loyalty during the 40-year period of wandering in the wilderness until his return to Kadesh-barnea, succeeded in establishing the foundation of faith for the third course of restoration into Canaan on the national level. Accordingly, the position of Abel for the substantial offering on the national level of this course was firmly established.

(ii) The Foundation of Substance

Due to the Israelites' failure, through faithlessness and rebellion, in setting up the 40-day course of spying, the foundation for the tabernacle remained invaded by Satan. Therefore, the foundation of substance for the second course was not established. However, the foundation of faith for the tabernacle, set up by Moses, who had exalted and kept the tabernacle with loyalty, remained a success. On this basis, if the Israelites had established the foundation of separation from Satan, who invaded the 40-day period of spying, by obeying Moses who was exalting the tabernacle in an unchanging faith during their 40-year period of wandering in the wilderness, they could have established both the foundation of substance for the tabernacle and the foundation for the tabernacle, at that time. If the Israelites had, on this foundation, entered Canaan honoring Moses, centering on the tabernacle through faith and obedience, the foundation of substance in the third course of restoration into Canaan on the national level would have been established at that time.

For Moses, the 40-year period of wandering in the wilderness was the period for the establishment of the foundation of faith in the third course. For the Israelites, it was the period to fulfill the "providence for the start" in the third course, by restoring their position of having honored Moses, who had erected the tabernacle in the second course.

The foundation of substance centering on Moses

It was previously clarified that the Israelites received the tablets of stone, the tabernacle, and the ark because they fell into faithlessness in the wilderness. Their faithlessness enabled Satan to invade the three great signs, which God manifested before them as the "providence for the start," in their second course of restoration into Canaan on the national level. Therefore, God had them go through the 40-day trial period, in order to restore through indemnity what they failed to do, and then granted them the three great gifts of the tablets of stone, the tabernacle, and the ark.

Again, God performed the ten calamities in order to restore through indemnity the fact that Laban had deceived Jacob ten times when Jacob was going to return from Haran into the land of Canaan. But the Israelites again fell into faithlessness, and God gave them the Ten Commandments to restore it through indemnity. Therefore, if and when the Israelites had kept the Ten Commandments and the three gifts by exalting the tablets of stone, the tabernacle, and the ark, they were supposed to restore the position of having started from Egypt by the aid of the three great miracles and ten calamities in their second course. The tablets of stone were the condensed body of the ark, and the ark was that of the tabernacle, so the tablets of stone were the condensed body of the tabernacle. Therefore, the ark and the tabernacle could be represented either with the tablets of stone or with the rock, their root. Consequently, the third course of restoration into Canaan on the national level would begin by starting from Kadesh-barnea according to the "providence for the start," centering on the rock.

How, then, did God intend to fulfill the "providence for the start," centering on the rock? In order to give life to the Israelites, who were falling into faithlessness without having acceptably set up the 40-year period in the wilderness (Num. 20:4-5), God had Moses strike the rock with his rod before the congregation of the Israelites, to have water and to let them drink (Num. 20:8). Had Moses' first strike against the rock, bringing water and giving drink to the Israelites, made them awe-stricken with God's power to such an extent that they all became one, centering on their leader, they could have stood on the foundation for the tabernacle, together with Moses; on that foundation, they could have fulfilled the "providence for the start," centering on the rock. If they had trusted and obeyed Moses from that time on and entered Canaan under his leadership, they could have set up the condition of indemnity on the national level to remove the fallen nature, and could then have also established the foundation of substance, centering on Moses, for their third course. However, Moses, upon seeing the people murmur in resentment against him for having no water, raged in such an anger that he struck the rock twice with his rod. Therefore, God said:

> Because you did not believe in me, to sanctify me in the eyes of the people of Israel, therefore you shall not bring this assembly into the land which I have given them. (Num. 20:12)

Moses thus failed to fulfill the "providence for the start" centering on the rock by striking it twice, when he should have struck just once. Therefore, he could never enter the blessed land of Canaan, the land of promise, although it was in his sight (Num. 20:24, 27:12-14).

We now must understand why Moses should have struck the rock just once and how his striking it twice became such a crime. Christ is symbolized as a white stone (Rev. 2:17); again it is said that the Rock was Christ (I Cor. 10:4). Meanwhile, as clarified in the chapter on the Fall of Man, Christ came as the Tree of Life (Rev. 22:14). Naturally, the Rock is also the Tree of Life. On the other hand, the Tree of Life was the symbol of Adam in perfection in the Garden of Eden. Since this Tree of Life is symbolized by the Rock, the Rock is also the symbol of Adam in perfection.

In the Garden of Eden, Satan struck Adam, who was supposed to become the Rock. Consequently, Adam could not attain the Tree of Life (Gen. 3:24). Accordingly, he also failed to become the Rock that would yield the "water of life" from God, which his descendants would drink forever. Therefore, the rock, before Moses struck it, that had not yielded water, symbolized fallen Adam. Satan, by once striking Adam and causing him to fall, made him "Adam as the rock not capable of yielding water." Therefore, God intended to set up the condition to restore through indemnity "Adam as the rock capable of yielding water," by once striking the rock representing Adam incapable of yielding water and by bringing water from it. Consequently, the rock which Moses struck once to bring water symbolized Jesus, who was to come and give the drink of the water of life to all fallen men. Therefore, Jesus said:

> Whoever drinks of the water that I shall give him will never thirst, the water that I shall give him will become in him a spring of water welling up to eternal life. (John 4:14)

God allowed Moses to strike the rock only once, as the condition to restore through indemnity the first Adam of the fall into the second Adam of perfection, or Jesus. But Moses' act of striking the rock the second time became the action representing the possibility of striking Jesus, who was to come as the restored Rock and give the drink of the water of life to all mankind. In this way, the faithlessness of the Israelites and the act of Moses' twice striking the rock in rage established a condition which enabled Satan to come directly before Jesus, the "Rock in substance," if and when the Israelites would ever fall into faithlessness later, at the coming of Jesus. Therefore, Moses' act became a crime.

Moses' act of breaking the tablets of stone once could be restored, but his mistake of twice striking the rock could not be restored. We must study the reason for this.

Seen from the viewpoint of the providence of restoration, the tablets of stone and the rock have the relationship of the external and the internal. The tablets of stone, with the Ten Commandments written on them, were the center of Moses' law, and accordingly, the center of the Old Testament. The Israelites of the Old Testament Age could enter the sphere of salvation of this age by believing in the ideal of the tablets of stone. In this respect, the tablets of stone were the external representation of Jesus, who was to come later.

According to the passage "the Rock was Christ" (I Cor. 10:4), the rock symbolizes Jesus, and at the same time forms the root (origin) of the tablets of stone. Therefore, it also symbolizes God, who is the root (origin) of Jesus, the substantial tablets of stone. In that sense, the tablets of stone are external while the rock is internal. If we liken the tablets of stone to our body, the rock corresponds to our mind. If we liken the tablets of stone to the holy place, the rock can be likened to the most holy place. Further, if we liken the tablets of stone to the earth, the rock corresponds to heaven. Therefore, the rock is the internal representation of Jesus and bears a greater value than the tablets of stone.

Since the tablets of stone are the external representation of Jesus, they also symbolize Aaron, who was set up as the external representation of Jesus, before Moses, the symbol of God (Ex. 4:16, 7:1). Meanwhile, the Israelites had Aaron make a calf of gold (Ex. 32:4). Thus Aaron became a failure, together with the tablets of stone. Nevertheless, Aaron could revive through repentance on the foundation of having drunk the water of life from the rock at Rephidim. Therefore, the tablets of stone symbolizing Aaron could also be restored by again setting up the condition of indemnity on the internal foundation of the water of life from the rock. However, the rock representing the root of the tablets of stone symbolizes both Christ and God, who is his root. Therefore, the act of striking them could never be recovered.

What kind of result did Moses' act of striking the rock twice bring about? Moses' act of striking the rock a second time was caused by his impatience and anger against the Israelites' falling into faithlessness (Ps. 106:32-33). This act was what he did from the standpoint of Satan. Consequently God's "providence for the start," which He had intended to fulfill through the rock, resulted in the invasion by Satan.

Thus, Moses' external act of having struck the rock twice was an act of Satan; but in the internal reality, the Israelites were given drink from the spring of water coming from the rock. Therefore, the external Israelites who had come out of Egypt could not enter Canaan, God's promised land, except Joshua and Caleb. Moses, too, died at the age of 120 with the land of hope and desire within his sight (Deut. 34:4-5). In place of Moses (Num. 27:18-20), Joshua entered Canaan leading the internal Israelites, who had been born in their course in the wilderness, where they had drunk of the water from the rock and exalted the tabernacle (Num. 32:11-12).

If Moses' act of twice striking the rock had resulted in Satan's invasion, the rock could not have yielded the water. How, then, could the rock yield water? In their second course of restoration into Canaan on the national level, Moses already had provided the base by which to bring water from the rock, by obeying God's command at Rephidim, by striking the rock to bring water, and by giving drink to the Israelites (Ex. 17:6). The tablets of stone, the tabernacle and the ark, which were set up on this foundation, were passed on to the third course of restoration into Canaan on the national level, because of the faith of a single man, Moses, who had kept God's command firmly on the foundation of faith for the tabernacle that he had set up through the 40-day fast and prayer, even when the Israelites all fell into faithlessness. Later, even Moses fell into the state of faithlessness in the rage against the people, but his heart-and-zeal toward heaven were unchangeable. Furthermore, Joshua kept and exalted the tablets of stone, the tabernacle and the ark with unchanging faith on the foundation for the tabernacle which he had set up through his 40-day spying in Canaan. Therefore, the foundation of the spring from the rock set up at Rephidim also remained intact, centering on Joshua.

In this manner, even though Moses' external act of faithlessness resulted in Satan's external invasion of the second rock, the water was yielded from the rock internally so that the people drank it, due to the internal basis of Moses' unchanging heart and Joshua's faith and loyalty.

Moses' act of twice striking the rock resulted in his taking the position of Satan. Satan therefore took possession of the stone. It was for this reason that Jesus, who came as the substantial stone, went into the wilderness, when the Jewish people fell into faithlessness in their worldwide course of restoration into Canaan, in order to find and restore the stone that had been lost in the wilderness. That is why he first suffered the temptation of being told by Satan to make bread out of stone.

Due to Moses' twice striking the rock externally in rage against the faithlessness of the Israelites, his flesh was invaded by Satan and he died in the wilderness, but internally, he could bring water from the rock and gave drink to the people because of his unchanging heart-and-zeal. That made it possible for him to enter Canaan spiritually. This foreshadowed the possibility that when Jesus, the substantial Rock, would come, his flesh might be invaded by Satan by the crucifixion, because of the people's disbelief, thus leaving unaccomplished the worldwide restoration into Canaan physically. In this case, he would accomplish it only spiritually.

After Moses had struck the rock twice, God sent fiery serpents to the Israelites, who were falling into faithlessness, and the serpents bit them to death (Num. 21:6). When the Israelites came to repent, God had Moses make a bronze serpent and set it on a pole, so that if a serpent had bitten any man, the man might look at the bronze serpent and live (Num. 21:9). The fiery serpent symbolized Satan, the ancient serpent, who had caused Eve to fall (Rev. 12:9), and the bronze serpent set on the pole symbolized Jesus, who would later come as the heavenly serpent (John 3:14). This foreshadowed for us that, just as God had put the Israelites into the hands of the Satanic serpent when they had fallen into faithlessness, and had brought them into life again when they repented and restored their faith, similar things would happen in the time of Jesus. That is, if the Jewish people fell into faithlessness, God would have to put them into the hands of Satan; then, Jesus would be compelled to die on the cross, as the heavenly serpent, in order that the whole of mankind might live. Whoever repented of his faithlessness and believed in the redemption through the cross would be saved. Therefore, Jesus said, "As Moses lifted up the serpent in the wilderness, so must the Son of man be lifted up." (John 3:14) This, in fact, became a remote cause that made Jesus start his spiritual course through the cross, in the third worldwide course of restoration into Canaan, centering on Jesus.

When Moses had struck the rock twice, God predicted that Moses would not be able to enter the land of Canaan (Num. 20:12). Moses then prayed to God to let him enter Canaan (Deut. 3:25), but he finally died with the promised land in his sight. After his death, he was buried in a valley in the land of Moab, but no man knows the place of his burial to this day (Deut. 34:6). This foreshadowed that later, Jesus also might die on the cross if the Jewish people fell into faithlessness. Though he might pray with ardor that God would let the cup of death pass from him, that he might fulfill the worldwide restoration into Canaan, he would finally die without realizing this will, and the whereabouts of his body would be unknown.

The foundation of substance centering on Joshua

Because Moses struck the rock twice, God's will for the Israelites to enter Canaan with the "providence for the start" centering on the rock was not fulfilled. Due to Moses' striking the rock twice (Num. 20:1-13), Satan could invade externally, but due to the foundation of having brought water from the rock at Rephidim, Moses could give drink internally to the

Israelites. This showed us another course of God's providence. That is, those belonging to the "external Israelites," who had been born in Egypt (the Satanic world) and had fallen into faithlessness in the wilderness, all died in the wilderness except for Joshua and Caleb, who had set up the 40-day period of spying in good faith. Only the "internal Israelites," born during their life in the wilderness when the people drank the water from the rock and exalted the tabernacle, entered Canaan, centering on Joshua in place of Moses (Num. 32:11-12). Therefore, God said to Moses:

> Take Joshua, the son of Nun, a man in whom is the spirit, and lay your hand upon him; cause him to stand before Eleazar the priest and all the congregation, and you shall commission him in their sight. You shall invest him with some of your authority, that all the congregation of the people of Israel may obey. (Num. 27:18-20)

Joshua was one of the two who, in contrast to the Israelites who fell into faithlessness during the 40-day period of spying, stood firmly on the foundation of faith for the tabernacle, set up by Moses. Joshua was thus able to establish the foundation for the tabernacle with unchanging faith and loyalty, exalting the tabernacle to the end. In this way, even though Moses had fallen into faithlessness, the tablets of stone, the tabernacle and the ark remained intact on the foundation for the tabernacle, set up by Joshua.

Therefore, God intended to fulfill the "providence for the start," centering on the water from the rock, by setting up Joshua in place of Moses, and having the internal Israelites obey him and stand with him on the foundation for the tabernacle. In accordance with this providence, God intended to have the people enter the land of Canaan, establish the condition of indemnity on the national level to remove the fallen nature, and accomplish the foundation of substance centering on Joshua in their third course.

Therefore, God said:

> He [Joshua] shall go over [into Canaan] at the head of this people,
> and he shall put them in possession of the land which you [Moses]
> shall see. (Deut. 3:28)

Then God said to Joshua:

> . . . as I was with Moses, so I will be with you; I will not fail you or
> forsake you. Be strong and of good courage; for you shall cause this
> people to inherit the land which I swore to their fathers to give
> them. (Josh. 1:5-6)

When Moses had accomplished, according to God's will, the
40-year period in the wilderness of Midian, God appeared to
Moses and commanded him to lead the Israelites into the land
of Canaan, the land flowing with milk and honey (Ex. 3:8-10).
Likewise, God called Joshua, in place of Moses, and commanded
him saying:

> Moses my servant is dead; now therefore arise, go over this Jordan,
> you and all the people, into the land which I am giving to them, to
> the people of Israel. (Josh. 1:2)

Joshua, in obedience to God's command, called the officers
of the people and conveyed God's will (Joshua 1:10-11). Then
they answered him saying:

> All that you have commanded us we will do, and wherever you send
> us we will go. . . . Whoever rebels against your commandment and
> disobeys your words, whatever you command him, shall be put to
> death. Only be strong and of good courage. (Josh. 1:16-18)

Thus they were determined to follow Joshua at the risk of their
lives. In this way, Joshua, who had the mission of substituting
for Moses, can be viewed as a symbol of the Lord of the Second
Advent, who comes in order to succeed and fulfill the mission

of Jesus. Therefore, the course of Joshua, who was to restore through indemnity the course of Moses, was the course representing the way of the Lord of the Second Advent, who is to restore through indemnity, both spiritually and physically, the course of spiritual restoration by Jesus.

There were 12 men whom Moses sent, in their second course into Canaan, to spy on the land (Num. 13:1-2). Of these, only two accomplished their mission in unchanging loyalty. On the foundation of their heart-and-zeal, Joshua sent two men into Jericho to spy on the city (Josh. 2:1). After having accomplished their mission the two men reported in faith, saying, "Truly the Lord has given all the land into our hands; and moreover all the inhabitants of the land are fainthearted because of us." (Josh. 2:24) Then, all the descendants of Israel born in the wilderness believed the words of the spies. Through their faith, they could indemnify the sin of their forefathers, who had not been able to accomplish their 40-day spying in accordance with God's will.

In this manner, the internal Israelites, having pledged at the risk of their lives to obey Joshua who stood on the foundation for the tabernacle, could also stand on the same foundation with Joshua. Thus, through the "providence for the start," which they had established centering on the spring of water from the rock, they restored the position of their forefathers, centering on Moses, who had fulfilled the "providence for the start," through the three great signs and ten calamities in their second course. Therefore, just as the Israelites, centering on Moses, had accomplished the three-day course before crossing the Red Sea, the Israelites, centering on Joshua, also accomplished the three-day course before crossing the Jordan (Josh. 3:2). Meanwhile, just as the Israelites, after their three-day course, had been led to the Red Sea by the pillar of clouds and the pillar of fire, the Israelites centering on Joshua, also after their three-day course, were led to the Jordan by the ark of the covenant (Josh. 3:3, 3:8), which symbolized Jesus and the Holy Spirit, representing the pillar of clouds and the pillar of fire.

Just as the Red Sea had been split by the rod, opening the way for Moses and the people, the waters of the Jordan, overflowing the bank, were separated when the priests bearing the ark entered the stream (Josh. 3:16), and all Israel passed over the river on dry ground (Josh. 3:17). The rod was a representation of Jesus who was to come. The ark of the covenant, containing the two tablets of stone, together with manna and Aaron's rod, was the substance symbolizing Jesus and the Holy Spirit. The fact that in the presence of the ark, the waters of the Jordan were separated and the Israelites were restored into the land of Canaan without difficulty foreshadowed that later, in the presence of Jesus and the Holy Spirit, the sinful world, symbolized by waters (Rev. 17:15), would be separated through judgment, and all the saints would accomplish the worldwide restoration into Canaan.

At this time, God commanded Joshua, saying:

> Take twelve men from the people, from each tribe a man, and command them, 'Take twelve stones from here out of the midst of the Jordan, from the very place where the priests' feet stood, and carry them over with you, and lay them down in the place where you lodge tonight.' (Josh. 4:2-3)

> The people came up out of the Jordan on the tenth day of the first month, and they encamped in Gilgal, on the east border of Jericho. And those twelve stones, which they took out of the Jordan, Joshua set up in Gilgal. (Josh. 4:19-20)

What did this foreshadow? As already discussed, the stone symbolized Jesus, who was to come. Therefore, the fact that the twelve men representing the twelve tribes honored the twelve stones, taken in the midst of the Jordan where the waters were cut off by the ark, showed that later the twelve disciples of Jesus, elected as representatives of the twelve tribes, should honor Jesus, in the midst of a sinful world, separated into good and evil, according to the words of Jesus.

After they had taken the twelve stones and set them up in the camp in the land of Canaan, Joshua said:

> ... so that all the people of the earth may know that the hand of the Lord is mighty; that you may fear the Lord your God for ever. (Josh. 4:24)

This foreshadowed that only when the twelve disciples of Jesus later should become one, in one place, with complete unity of mind and will, would the worldwide restoration be accomplished, and the almightiness of God be praised through eternity.

Just as Jacob had set up the altar of stone wherever he had been, the representatives of the twelve tribes, who were the descendants of Jacob's twelve sons, also set up the altar of prayer to praise God by gathering twelve stones, showing that later a temple would be erected in a like manner. This showed us truly that the twelve disciples of Jesus ought to honor and serve Jesus, as the Temple, with all their zeal put together. Later, when his disciples failed to become one, Jesus said, "Destroy this temple, and in three days I will raise it up." (John 2:19) In fact, the twelve disciples failed to become one in harmony, and the betrayal of Judas Iscariot caused the destruction of Jesus, the Temple, through crucifixion; and in three days he was raised from death, and gathered again his scattered disciples. Then his disciples served and honored the resurrected Jesus only as the spiritual Temple. The substantial Temple will be established at the time of the Second Advent.

Just as the Israelites, when they commenced their second course towards the land of Canaan, observed the feast of Passover on the 14th day of the first month of the year before they journeyed (Ex. 12:17-18), the Israelites, centering on Joshua, who encamped in Gilgal, also observed the feast of Passover on the 14th day of the first month of the year before journeying toward the fortified city of Jericho. When they began to live on the products of the land, God stopped feeding them with manna, after His 40 long years of care for them. From then on, they had to rely on what they cultivated by their own sweat. Even during the moment of breaking through the last toll-gate to the Satanic city, they had to fulfill their own portion of responsibility, which was man's part. According to God's commandment to the Israelites, 40,000 soldiers were in the vanguard, followed by seven chief priests marching with seven trumpets, who preceded the ark of the covenant, carried by the Levite priests (Josh. 3:3). Then, the entire host of the Israelites marched in the rear line (Josh. 6:8-9).

As God had commanded them, the Israelites marched around the city in this formation for six days, making one tour each day; but there was no change caused in the city. They had to restore through indemnity in utter patience and obedience the six-day period of creation which had been invaded by Satan. After having set up the six days through such obedience, on the seventh day, the seven priests with the seven trumpets marched around the city seven times blowing the trumpets, and Joshua said to the people, "Shout; for the Lord has given you the city!" Upon his command the people raised a great shout, and the walls crumbled (Josh. 6).

This course showed us that later, through the power of Jesus and his disciples, the Satanic barrier between heaven and earth would fall down. Therefore, Joshua said:

> Cursed before the Lord be the man that raises up and rebuilds the city, Jericho. At the cost of his firstborn shall he lay its foundation, and at the cost of his youngest son shall he set up its gates. (Josh. 6:26)

because this Satanic barrier was never to be set up again.

Thus Joshua destroyed the enemy with an irresistible force, defeating 31 kings altogether (Joshua 12:9-24). This also foreshadowed that Jesus would come as the King of Kings and establish the earthly Kingdom of God, in unity, by destroying all the gentile kings, and unifying the peoples of the whole world.

(iii) The Foundation to Receive the Messiah

The Israelites failed in their second course of restoration into Canaan on the national level because they could not set up the 40-day spying period for the separation from Satan. Then, in order to indemnify this period again, they started their third course of restoration into Canaan on the national level, and after 40 years of wandering in the wilderness they came back to Kadesh-barnea. At this time, Moses could establish the foundation of faith for the third course and the Israelites could stand on the foundation for the tabernacle.

However, due to the faithlessness of the Israelites, and Moses' striking the rock twice, both foundations were invaded by Satan. Therefore, the external Israelites who had left Egypt centering on Moses were all destroyed in the wilderness; but Joshua and Caleb could establish the foundation for the tabernacle, because they set up the 40-day spying period of separation from Satan with faith and loyalty, based upon the foundation of faith and the foundation of faith for the tabernacle, which had been established by Moses in the second course. Thus, the external Israelites, centering on Moses, all died in the wilderness. But the internal Israelites, born during their life in the wilderness when they exalted and served the tabernacle, could cross the Jordan bearing the ark of the covenant in utter loyalty, centering on Joshua in place of Moses. Then, having destroyed the city of Jericho, they entered Canaan, the land of their desire.

Thus the foundation of substance in the third course of restoration into Canaan on the national level was established. Accordingly, the foundation to receive the Messiah for this course was also laid. After the foundation to receive the Messiah on the family level, established by Abraham, and after the indemnity course of the 400-year slavery in Egypt, caused by Abraham's failure in the offering, the foundation to receive the Messiah on the national level was established. Meanwhile, fallen men at that time erected a powerful kingdom; that is, Egypt, centering on Satan, and they held their stand against the heavenly providence of restoration. As already discussed (cf. Part II, Ch. I, Sec. III, 3), the Messiah could not come before the kingdom was built on the side of God, which could cope with Satan, even though the foundation to receive the Messiah on the national level centering on Joshua had been established. However, the internal Israelites, having entered Canaan, again fell into faithlessness, and the providence was prolonged again, until the time of Jesus.

3. LESSONS LEARNED FROM MOSES' COURSE

In the long course of history since the time of Moses up to the present moment, numerous saints, serving the divine will, have repeatedly read the Biblical record with respect to Moses. However, they thought these words were merely the record of Moses' history, and there has not been a single man among them who knew that God intended to teach us, through Moses, certain secrets concerning His providence of restoration. Even Jesus only intimated it by saying, "Truly, truly, I say to you, the Son can do nothing of his own accord, but only what he sees the Father doing" (John 5:19), and left unclarified the fundamental meaning of Moses' course (John 16:12).

We have clarified already how Moses went through the typical or formulary course for the providence of restoration.

The fact that his course foreshadowed the course which Jesus was later to tread will be made clearer in comparison with Section III of this chapter. Looking into God's providence centering on Moses, alone, we cannot deny the fact that God is behind human history, leading it toward one absolute purpose.

Next, Moses' course shows us that the degree of man's accomplishment of his own portion of responsibility would decide the success or failure of God's predestination. Even God's predestined will could not succeed, centering on a particular person, if and when the person set up for the predestination should fail to accomplish his own portion of responsibility. God predestined His will to have Moses lead the people of Israel into the land of Canaan, flowing with milk and honey, and commanded Moses to do so. Nevertheless, when he and his people had failed to accomplish their responsibility, only Joshua and Caleb, out of all the Israelites who had left Egypt, entered Canaan, and the rest of them all died in the wilderness.

Moses' course also shows us that God does not interfere in man's portion of responsibility, but deals only with the result. God had led the Israelites with wonderful miracles and signs, but He interfered in neither the people's act of making the idol of the golden calf while Moses was on the mountain receiving the tablets of stone, nor in Moses' act of striking the rock twice, because these were their own portions of responsibility which they had to accomplish by themselves.

On the other hand, God showed us, through Moses' course, the absoluteness of His predestined will. It is positive and absolute for God to fulfill the will He once predestined. Therefore, when Moses failed to fulfill his responsibility, God set up Joshua in his place and finally fulfilled the will He once predestined. In this way, if a person whom God has set up in the position of Abel should fail to accomplish his mission, the person who has been loyal in the position of Cain would replace him, succeeding the mission of Abel. Jesus meant this when he said, ". . . the kingdom of heaven has suffered violence, and men of violence take it by force." (Matt. 11:12)

Still another lesson that Moses' course teaches us is that the greater a man's mission, the heavier the temptations he may be offered. Since the first human couple fell by not believing in God and by rebelling against Him, the personage in charge of restoration of the foundation of faith had to overcome the temptation or suffering of God's deserting him without care. Therefore, Moses was entitled to be the leader of the Israelites only after he had overcome the trial of God's seeking to kill him (Ex. 4:24).

Even God cannot grant man grace unconditionally, because, originally, Satan came to possess man under the condition of the fall, and could accuse God of unfairness if grace were given without a corresponding temptation. Therefore, when God grants man grace, He is sure to give him a temptation, either preceding or following (or both) the grace, in order to prevent Satan's accusation. To take examples from Moses' course: Moses was granted the grace of the first Exodus only after his suffering of 40 years in Pharaoh's palace. He was again granted the grace of the second Exodus only after suffering 40 years in the wilderness of Midian (Ex. 4:20). God granted Moses the three great signs and the miracles of ten calamities (Ex. 7:1–10:2) only after the trial of God's seeking to kill him (Ex. 4:24-25). There came the grace of the pillar of clouds and the pillar of fire (Ex. 13:21) only after the suffering of the three-day course (Ex. 10: 22). On the other hand, only after the suffering while crossing the Red Sea (Ex. 14:21-22) could the gift of manna and quail come (Ex. 16:13), and only after the suffering through the fight against the Amalekites (Ex. 17:10) came the grace of the tablets of stone, the tabernacle, and the ark of the covenant (Ex. 31:18–40:38). Again, only after the suffering of 40 years wandering in the wilderness (Num. 14:33) was there the grace of the water from the rock, (Num. 20:8) and only after the suffering of the fiery serpent (Num. 21:6) was there the grace of the bronze serpent (Num. 21:9). Thus we can see that Moses' course teaches us many lessons.

SECTION III
The Providence of Restoration Centering on Jesus

In the beginning, Adam, who was supposed to dominate the angels (I Cor. 6:3), brought about Hell by being dominated by Satan. Therefore, in order to restore Adam's domination, through indemnity, Jesus, who came as the second Adam, was supposed to subjugate Satan and restore the Kingdom of God. As stated in Section I, Satan, who had not surrendered even to God, could not be made to surrender to Jesus and his followers. Therefore, taking the responsibility in the Principle for creating man, God, by setting up Jacob and Moses, established the model course for Jesus to subjugate Satan in the future.

Jacob went through the symbolic course of subjugating Satan, while Moses walked the image-course of subjugating Satan, then, Jesus had to go through the substantial course. Therefore, Jesus had to accomplish the worldwide course of the restoration into Canaan by subjugating Satan, following the model of the nationwide course of restoration into Canaan, in which Moses had subjugated Satan.

God said to Moses:

> I will raise up for them a prophet like you from among their breth-ren; and I will put my words in his mouth, and he shall speak to them all that I command him. (Deut. 18:18)

By "a prophet like you" (Moses), God meant Jesus, who would go through the same course as that of Moses. Again, Jesus said ". . . the Son can do nothing of his own accord, but only what he sees the Father [God] doing . . ."(John 5:19), signifying that Jesus was treading the model course which God had fore-shadowed through Moses. Details were already discussed in the providence of restoration centering on Moses, but here, let us discuss the providence of restoration centering on Jesus by com-paring and contrasting the entire outline of the three courses of nationwide restoration into Canaan centering on Moses, and the three courses of worldwide restoration into Canaan centering on Jesus.

1. THE FIRST WORLDWIDE COURSE OF RESTORATION INTO CANAAN

(1) The Foundation of Faith

The central figure to restore the foundation of faith in the first worldwide course of restoration into Canaan was John the Baptist. In what position was John the Baptist to accom-plish his mission? It was discussed in "Moses' Course" that his acts of breaking the tablets of stone, and of striking the rock twice in the course of nationwide restoration into Canaan, cen-tering on Moses, allowed Satan the possibility of striking Jesus, if the Jewish people, who should have centered on Jesus, would fall into faithlessness.

In order for Jesus to avoid this condition, the chosen people of Israel, who were preparing the foundation for his coming, should have become one in harmony, centering on the temple, which was the image-entity of the Messiah. However, the Israel-ites repeatedly fell into faithlessness, thus creating the condition for Satan to invade Jesus, who was to come in the future. In order to prevent this condition, Elijah, the prophet, came and worked for the separation from Satan by destroying 850 false prophets, including Baal and Ashera (I Kings 18:19), and finally ascended into heaven (II Kings 2:11). However, since Elijah's mission was not entirely realized, he had to come again to accomplish the rest of his mission (Mal. 4:5). The prophet who came as Elijah to succeed and accomplish the mission of separating from Satan, which had been left unfulfilled by Elijah, and to make straight the way of the Messiah (John 1:23), was John the Baptist (Matt. 11:14, 17:10-13).

The Israelites were suffering the 400-year slavery in Egypt, without a prophet to lead them, and while doing so, they met with one man, Moses, as the personage who could lead them into the land of Canaan and help them meet the Messiah. Likewise, the Jewish people also were suffering slavery under the gentile nations of Persia, Greece, Egypt, Syria, and Rome, during the 400 years of the preparation period for the coming of the Messiah, since the time of the prophet Malachi, without even a single prophet to guide them. While doing so, they finally met John the Baptist as the personage able to lead them to the Messiah who should come for the worldwide restoration into Canaan.

Moses, who had been set up on the foundation of separation from Satan of the 400-year slavery in Egypt, learned the way of loyalty and filial piety in Pharaoh's palace. John the Baptist, who was placed on the foundation of separation from Satan of the 400-year period of preparation for the coming of the Messiah, also learned the way of loyalty and filial piety toward God, in order to receive the Messiah, while living on locusts and wild honey in the wilderness. Therefore, the Jewish people, including the high priests (John 1:19), thought that John the Baptist might be the Messiah (Luke 3:15). In this way, John the Baptist stood on the 40-day foundation of separation from

Satan, and he could lay the foundation of faith for the first worldwide restoration of Canaan.

(2) The Foundation of Substance

John the Baptist, set up in the position of Moses, was, for the Jewish people, in the position of both the parent and the child. From the position of the parent, he could restore, through indemnity, the foundation of faith for the first worldwide restoration of Canaan. At the same time, he could establish the position of Abel in setting up the condition of indemnity on the worldwide level to remove the fallen nature, from the position of the child (cf. Part II, Ch. II, Sec. II, 1[2]). Consequently, John the Baptist stood on the foundation which he established on the worldwide level, magnifying the position of Moses, who, after the 40 years of indemnity in Pharaoh's palace, laid the foundation of faith for the first restoration on the nationwide level.

At the time of Moses, God intended to fulfill the "providence for the start," by having the people of Israel trust Moses, after seeing him kill the Egyptian. The Israelites of that time had to leave Egypt, the Satanic nation, and go into the land of Canaan; whereas the Jewish people, centering on John the Baptist, instead of leaving the Roman Empire to move into another land, had to remain under the regime and subjugate it, restoring the empire to Heaven. Therefore, God showed the people the signs and miracles centering on John the Baptist, and by having the Jewish people believe him, He intended to fulfill the "providence for the start."

Through the wondrous prediction of the angel concerning the conception of John the Baptist, through the miracle of his father's becoming dumb when he did not believe in this, and through many other miracles which God showed the Israelites at the time of John's birth, they knew from the time of his birth that John was the prophet God had sent to them. This is just as the Bible says:

> Fear came on all their neighbors. And all these things were talked about through all the hill country of Judea; and all who heard them laid them up in their hearts, saying, 'What then will this child be?' For the hand of the Lord was with him. (Luke 1:65-66)

Furthermore, because of his brilliant career of asceticism, and his life of prayer in the wilderness, the chief priests (John 1:19) and all the Jewish people (Luke 3:15) esteemed him so highly that they mistook him for the Messiah.

Moses slew the Egyptian after the 40-year period of indemnity in Pharaoh's palace. Then, if the Israelites, moved by his patriotism, had believed and followed him, they could have gone straight into Canaan through the direct way of the Philistines, without having to cross the Red Sea, without making a detour by way of the wilderness, and without need of the tablets of stone, the tabernacle, or the ark of the covenant. If the Jewish people of Jesus' day, also, had believed and followed John the Baptist, whom God had set up for them to believe, through the miracles and signs, they could have restored the foundation of substance by establishing the condition of indemnity to remove the fallen nature, and on it they could have restored the foundation to receive the Messiah.

(3) The Failure in the First Course of Restoration into Canaan on the Worldwide Level

The Jewish people were in the position of believing and following John the Baptist on the foundation of faith established by him (John 1:19, Luke 3:15). Therefore, they could terminate the Old Testament Age and start their new course of restoration into Canaan on the worldwide level. However, as already stated (cf. Part I, Ch. IV, Sec. II), John the Baptist, though he himself testified to Jesus as the Messiah, finally doubted him (Matt. 11:3). By denying that he had come as Elijah, he not only blocked the way for the Jewish people to go before Jesus, but caused them to betray Jesus. Therefore, John the Baptist left the position of Abel in laying the foundation of substance and, in consequence, the Jewish people failed to establish the condition of indemnity on the worldwide level to remove the fallen nature.

In this way, the foundation to receive the Messiah was not established because the Jewish people failed to lay the foundation of substance. Therefore, the first course of restoration into Canaan on the worldwide level ended in failure, foreshadowing a second, or even a third prolongation, just as at the time of Moses.

2. THE SECOND COURSE OF RESTORATION INTO CANAAN ON THE WORLDWIDE LEVEL

(1) The Foundation of Faith

(i) Jesus Succeeds the Mission of John the Baptist

John the Baptist was a personage in the position of a restored Adam before Jesus, who came as a perfected Adam. Therefore, John the Baptist had to establish the foundation to receive the Messiah by completing all the missions left unaccomplished by all the central figures who had come in the course of providential history until then with the purpose of restoring the foundation of faith and the foundation of substance. Then, leading the Jewish people, who would believe and follow him on this foundation, he would have handed them all over to Jesus, together with the whole foundation of the providence. After this, he himself should have followed Jesus with the utmost faith and loyalty.

John the Baptist baptized Jesus at the River Jordan (Matt. 3:16) without knowing the significance of the deed, but it was a ceremony of handing over to him all that John had done for the will of God.

Nevertheless, John the Baptist later became gradually more skeptical about Jesus and at last betrayed him. Naturally, the Jewish people, who believed and followed John the Baptist as the Messiah (Luke 3:15) were forced to stand in the position of disbelieving Jesus (cf. Part I, Ch. IV, Sec. II). Accordingly, the foundation of faith that John the Baptist had set up for the first worldwide course for the restoration of Canaan was, in the end, invaded by Satan. Therefore, Jesus himself was compelled to restore through indemnity that foundation of faith, succeeding the mission of John the Baptist and thus starting the second worldwide course for the restoration of Canaan. Jesus separated himself from Satan by fasting 40 days in the wilderness, and this was to restore through indemnity the foundation of faith from the position of John the Baptist.

Jesus, who came as the Son of God and the Lord of Glory, originally should not have walked the path of tribulation (I Cor. 2:8). However, John the Baptist, who was born with the mission of preparing his way (John 1:23, Luke 1:76), failed to accomplish his mission. So Jesus, himself, had to suffer the tribulations which John the Baptist had to suffer in preparing the way for Jesus. Thus, Jesus, though being the Messiah, succeeded John the Baptist in starting the course of the providence of restoration. Therefore, he told his disciples not to make public the fact that he was the Messiah (Matt. 16:20).

(ii) Jesus' Forty-day Fast and Prayer in the Wilderness and His Three Great Temptations

We must first know the remote and primary courses of Jesus' 40-day fast and prayer and his three great temptations. In the course of the nationwide restoration of Canaan, Moses, who stood before the rock, became faithless and struck it twice. Therefore, the rock, symbolizing Christ (I Cor. 10:4), suffered Satan's invasion. This became an act showing that later, even in the course of Jesus, who would have to walk with Moses' course as a pattern, it would be possible for Satan to invade if John the Baptist, who would come in order to make straight the way of Jesus, should become faithless. Consequently, this action also showed that Satan could invade the foundation of faith centering on John the Baptist, who was to come before the Messiah. Therefore, Moses' action of striking the rock twice became the remote cause compelling Jesus to go into the wilderness and suffer the 40-day fast and the three great temptations from the position succeeding John the Baptist in order to restore the foundation of faith, in case that John the Baptist should lose faith.

John the Baptist became faithless (cf. Part I, Ch. IV, Sec. II, 3), and Satan invaded the foundation of faith which he had laid. With this as the immediate cause, Jesus had to suffer the 40-day fast and the three great temptations in the position of John the Baptist, in order that he might restore through indemnity the foundation of faith by setting up the 40-day foundation to separate Satan.

Then, what was Satan's purpose in offering Jesus the three great temptations? In the Bible (Matt. 4:1-10) we read that Satan showed him stones and told him to command them to become loaves of bread. Then he took him to the pinnacle of the temple and told him to throw himself down. Finally he took him to a very high mountain and told Jesus that he would give him the whole world if Jesus would fall down and worship him, thus giving Jesus three temptations.

In the beginning, God created man and blessed him in three ways: the perfection of individuality, multiplication of children, and dominion over the world of creation (Gen. 1:28). God's purpose of creation was for man to accomplish all of these. However, Satan caused man to fall, making him fail to accomplish the three blessings. So the purpose of creation remained unfulfilled. Jesus came to fulfill God's purpose of creation by restoring these three blessings that God had promised. Therefore, Satan tried to prevent him from fulfilling the purpose of creation, by offering him the three temptations in order to block the way of restoring the blessings.

How then did Jesus confront and overcome these three great temptations? Let us first examine how Satan as a subjective being tempted Jesus. We have already clarified the fact that in the course of the nationwide restoration of Canaan centering on Moses, Satan came to stand in the subject position to the Israelites centered on Moses, by taking (due to the Israelites' disbelief and Moses' failure) the rock and the two tablets of stone, symbolizing Jesus and the Holy Spirit. Then, in the course of the worldwide restoration of Canaan, John the Baptist, who had come with the mission of making straight the way of the Messiah (John 1:23) by separating Satan, failed to fulfill his responsibility, and the Israelites again fell into faithlessness and disobedience as in the time of Moses. Consequently, just as God had already foreshadowed in Moses' course, Satan came to stand in the subject position, which enabled him to tempt Jesus. Let us study these temptations in greater detail.

After Jesus fasted 40 days, Satan appeared before him and tempted him, saying, "If you are the Son of God, command these stones to become loaves of bread." (Matt. 4:3) Meanwhile, the stone was in Satan's possession, due to Moses' action of breaking the tablets of stone and of striking the rock, and due to the disbelief of John the Baptist. Therefore, in order to restore the stone, Jesus had to go into the wilderness and separate Satan by fasting for 40 days. Satan knew well enough that Jesus had come into the wilderness to restore the stone. This temptation signified that Satan would hold possession of the stone forever, if Jesus, in his wilderness course for the worldwide restoration of Canaan, should become faithless and choose to command the stone to become loaves of bread in order to fill his hungry stomach without trying to restore the stone—just as in previous days, the Israelites could not endure hunger and had fallen into faithlessness, in the nationwide restoration of Canaan.

Jesus' answer to this temptation was, "Man shall not live by bread alone, but by every word that proceeds from the mouth of God" (Matt. 4:4). Originally, man was created to live on two kinds of nutriments. That is to say, man's physical body lives on the nutriments taken from the natural world, while his spirit lives by the words proceeding from the mouth of God. However, fallen men became unable to receive God's Word directly and their spirits live by the words of Christ, who came to earth as the incarnation of God's Word, as is written in the Bible (John 1:14). Therefore, Jesus said, "I am the bread of life" (John 6:48), and went on to say, "Truly, truly I say to you, unless you eat the flesh of the Son of man and drink his blood, you have no life in you." (John 6:53) Therefore, even if man's physical body may have life by eating bread, he cannot enjoy a wholesome life with that alone. Man can become wholesome if, in addition, he lives by Christ, who came as the incarnation of God's Word and as man's food of life.

However, the stone became Satan's possession by Moses' twice striking the rock, which was the root of the tablets of stone. The stone in Satan's hand now truly was the rock and the tablets of stone which Moses had lost. Therefore, the stone, after all, symbolized Jesus himself, who was under Satan's temptation. This becomes even more apparent when we read about a stone symbolizing Christ (Rev. 2:17) and that "the

Rock was Christ." (I Cor. 10:4) Therefore, Jesus' answer to Satan's first temptation signified that even if he were then at the point of starvation, the bread for the physical body was not a question; and he himself had to triumph from the position of receiving Satan's temptation and become the food of God's Word that could save the spiritual bodies of all mankind. The first temptation was set up so that Jesus could establish the position of the Messiah, with perfected individuality, by over-coming the temptation from the position of John the Baptist. Satan was at last defeated by such words of Jesus, who con-fronted him with God's will from the position of the Principle. Jesus, by overcoming the first temptation and thus setting up the condition enabling the restoration of his individuality, laid the foundation for the restoration of God's first blessing.

Next, Satan set Jesus on the pinnacle of the temple and said, "If you are the Son of God, throw yourself down." (Matt. 4:5-6) Jesus called himself the temple (John 2:19-21), and the saints were called the temple of God (I Cor. 3:16). It is also recorded that the saints are the members of the body of Christ (I Cor. 12:27). Therefore, we can understand that Jesus is the main temple and the saints are the branch temples. Thus Jesus came as the master of the temple, and even Satan could not help but recognize his authority. So he set Jesus on the pinnacle of the temple; then he told Jesus to throw himself down from there. This signified that if Jesus threw himself down from the position of master to that of fallen man, Satan would occupy the position of the dominator of the temple in place of Jesus.

At this point Jesus answered him saying, "You shall not tempt the Lord your God." (Matt. 4:7) Originally, angels were created to be dominated by a man of the original state of crea-tion; therefore, a fallen angel was naturally to be dominated by Jesus. Consequently, the angel's attempt to stand in the position of the lord of the temple was a non-principled act.

Therefore, he should not have stood in the position of tempting God with such a non-principled act, by tempting Jesus, the body of God, who works His providence by the Principle alone. Moreover, Jesus, by overcoming the first temptation, firmly established his position as master of the temple, as the substantial temple, with his individuality restored. Therefore, he was not in any position whatsoever to be tempted by Satan; Satan should have left without tempting Jesus again.

Thus, by overcoming his second temptation, Jesus, who came as the main temple and bridegroom, and the True Parent of mankind, set up the condition enabling him to restore all the saints to the position of his branch temples and brides, and true children, thus creating the foundation for the restoration of God's second blessing.

Next, Satan led Jesus to a very high mountain, and, showing all the kingdoms of the world and their glory, tempted him, saying, "All these I will give you, if you will fall down and worship me." (Matt. 4:9) Originally, Adam, due to his fall, lost his authority as the master of all creation, being dominated by Satan, and naturally Satan became the dominator of all creation in place of Adam (Rom. 8:20). Jesus, who came in the capacity of a perfected Adam, was the dominator of all the creation, since it is written that God put all things in subjection under Christ (I Cor. 15:27). Therefore, Satan, who knew this principle, led Jesus to a mountain top, putting him in the position of the master of all things, and then tempted him in order that Jesus, the second Adam, also might yield before him, just as Adam had yielded in the beginning.

Jesus answered this, saying, "You shall worship the Lord your God, and Him only shall you serve." (Matt. 4:10) Originally, an angel was a ministering spirit (Heb. 1:14), and was supposed to worship and serve God, his Creator. Jesus answered, signifying that it was the Principle that Satan, the fallen angel, should also worship and serve God. Naturally, it is the Principle for Satan to also worship and serve Jesus, who appeared as the body of God, the Creator. Moreover, Jesus had already established the foundation enabling him to restore God's first and second blessings, by overcoming the first two temptations. Therefore, it was natural for him to dominate all creation by restoring God's third blessing on that foundation. So he answered in accordance with the Principle, signifying that there was no reason to be further involved with temptations concerning the creation, which already stood on the victorious foundation.

Thus, Jesus overcame the third temptation to restore his domination over the whole world of creation, through which he established the foundation for the restoration of God's third blessing.

(iii) The Result of Separation from Satan by the Forty-Day Fast and the Three Great Temptations

According to the principle of creation, God's purpose of creation is to be realized only when man establishes the four position foundation, after going through the three-stage process of origin, division, and union. However, man had not been able to realize the purpose of creation, because he had been invaded by Satan, in his course of establishing the four positions. Therefore, God also intended to restore through indemnity all the lost things, by establishing the 40-day foundation of separation from Satan, through the three stages of prolongation of the providence.

Meanwhile, Jesus, though he was the Messiah, established the 40-day foundation of separation from Satan, by overcoming the three stages of temptation from the position of John the Baptist. Accordingly, Jesus could restore through indemnity all the conditions at once which God had intended to restore by establishing the 40-day foundation of separation from Satan through the three-stage prolongation of His providence of restoration.

First, Jesus could restore, through indemnity, all that was to be restored in order to establish the foundation of faith, through the providential course up to that time. Namely, he restored through indemnity the offerings by Cain and Abel, Noah's ark, Abraham's offering, Moses' tabernacle, and Solomon's temple. Besides, Jesus at once horizontally restored through indemnity all the 40-day foundations of separation from Satan which had been lost due to the failures of the central figures whose mission had been to restore the foundation of faith, through the vertical course of history during the 4,000 years since Adam. Namely, he restored through indemnity Noah's 40-day flood judgment; Moses' three 40-year periods and two 40-day fasts; the 40 days of spying in Canaan; the Israelites' 40-year course in the wilderness; the 400 years from Noah to Abraham; the 400 years of slavery in Egypt; and all other "number 40" periods lost after that, until his own time.

Second, Jesus could set up the condition enabling him to realize God's three great blessings and to restore through indemnity the four position foundation, because he came from the position of John the Baptist to stand in the position of the Messiah. Consequently, Jesus became a substantial being having fulfilled the offering, and he could stand as the substantial being of the tablets of stone, of the tabernacle, the ark of the covenant, the rock, and the temple.

(2) The Foundation of Substance

Jesus came as the True Parent of mankind and restored through indemnity the 40-day foundation of separation from Satan from the position of John the Baptist. Therefore, he could restore the foundation of faith from the position of a parent, and at the same time he could establish the position of

Abel in setting up the worldwide condition of indemnity to remove the fallen nature from the position of a child. Accordingly, Jesus came to stand in the position of having restored through indemnity on the worldwide base, the position of Moses who had established the foundation of faith for the second nationwide restoration of Canaan by going through the 40-year period of indemnity in the wilderness of Midian.

In the second course of the nationwide restoration of Canaan, God worked His "providence for the start" with the three great miracles and ten calamities. Later in the third course of the nationwide restoration of Canaan, God worked His "providence for the start" by setting up the three great graces of the tablets of stone, the tabernacle and the ark of the covenant—and the Ten Commandments, to restore through indemnity the three great miracles and ten calamities in Egypt, which were annulled because of the disbelief of the Israelites.

Since Jesus was the substantial being of the Ten Commandments and the three great graces (the tablets of stone, the tabernacle, and the ark of the covenant), he worked the "providence for the start" by his own words and miracles and signs in the second course of worldwide restoration of Canaan. If, in accordance with the "providence for the start," the Jewish people in the position of Cain had believed and followed Jesus in the position of Abel, they could have set up the condition of indemnity to remove the fallen nature and could have restored the foundation of substance, thus establishing the foundation to receive the Messiah. If so, Jesus, shifting from the position of John the Baptist, could have stood as the Messiah. Then, if all mankind had been engrafted to him (Rom. 11:17), had been reborn, cleansed of the original sin, and had become one body in heart with God, they could have restored the original nature endowed at the creation, thus realizing the Kingdom of God on earth at that time.

(3) The Failure of the Second Course of the Worldwide Restoration of Canaan

When, due to the disbelief of John the Baptist, the first providence of the worldwide restoration of Canaan ended in a
failure, Jesus restored through indemnity the foundation of
faith for the second worldwide restoration of Canaan by suffering by himself the 40-day tribulation in the wilderness, succeeding the mission of John the Baptist. Meanwhile, Satan, who was
defeated in the three great temptations, departed from Jesus
until an opportune time (Luke 4:13). Satan's having departed
from him "until an opportune time" implies that he did not
leave Jesus completely, but could come again before Jesus. As a
matter of fact, Satan confronted Jesus, working through the
Jewish people, centering on the chief priests and scribes
who had fallen faithless, and especially through Judas Iscariot,
the disciple who betrayed Jesus.

In this manner, due to the faithlessness of the Jewish people,
the foundation of substance for the second course of the worldwide restoration of Canaan resulted in a failure; accordingly, the
foundation to receive the Messiah for this providence was a
failure. Naturally, the second course of the worldwide restoration of Canaan also failed.

3. THE THIRD COURSE OF THE WORLDWIDE RESTORATION OF CANAAN

(1) The Course of the Spiritual Restoration of Canaan, Centering on Jesus

Before discussing the problems concerning the third course of
the worldwide restoration, we must first know in what respect
it differs from the third course of nationwide restoration of
Canaan. As already discussed in detail, the center of the Israelite
faith in the third course of the nationwide restoration of

Canaan was the tabernacle, which was the symbolic body of the Messiah. Thus, even when the Israelite nation fell into faithlessness, this tabernacle remained intact, standing on the foundation of faith for the tabernacle, which Moses had set up by his 40-day fast. When Moses, too, fell into faithlessness, it remained standing, centering on Joshua, who continued to serve the will on the foundation for the tabernacle, which had been established by Joshua's 40-day spying period to separate Satan on the foundation of faith that Moses had set up.

However, the object of faith of the Jewish people, in their course of the worldwide restoration of Canaan, was Jesus himself, who came as the substantial body of the temple. When even his disciples fell into disbelief, Jesus was forced to go the way of death, by giving his physical body to the cross, as it was written, "As Moses lifted up the serpent in the wilderness, so must the Son of man be lifted up." (John 3:14) In this way, the Jewish people lost their object of faith, both in spirit and flesh. Therefore, they could not start their third course of the worldwide restoration of Canaan directly as a substantial course. But the Christians as the Second Israel started first a spiritual course, by setting up the resurrected Jesus as their object of faith.

Here lies the reason Jesus said, "Destroy this temple (Jesus himself), and in three days I will raise it up." (John 2:19) The Lord will come and, succeeding the mission of Jesus, he will accomplish, both spiritually and physically, the third course of the worldwide restoration of Canaan, just as Joshua had accomplished the third course of the nationwide restoration of Canaan, succeeding Moses' mission.

Seeing such a providential course of restoration alone, we can well understand that unless the Lord would come again in flesh, as in the time of Jesus, he cannot succeed and fulfill the purpose of the providence of restoration which he intended to accomplish at the first coming.

(i) The Spiritual Foundation of Faith

Since the second course of the worldwide restoration of Canaan ended in failure due to the Israelite's betrayal of Jesus, the foundation of faith which Jesus had set up, through the 40-day fast from the position of John the Baptist, was helplessly handed over to Satan. Therefore, after giving his physical body to Satan, through the cross, Jesus set up the spiritual foundation of separation from Satan by his 40-day resurrection period, from the position of the spiritual mission-bearer of John the Baptist. By doing this, he could restore the spiritual foundation of faith for the spiritual course of the third worldwide restoration of Canaan. There has not been even a single man, until today, who knew that this was the reason the 40-day resurrection period was set up after Jesus' crucifixion. How then did Jesus establish the spiritual foundation of faith?

God had been with the chosen nation of Israel until the time when Jesus appeared as the Messiah. Nevertheless, from the moment of their rebellion against Jesus, who appeared as the Messiah, God was compelled to deliver them, His elect, into the hands of Satan. Thus, God, together with His son, who was betrayed by the Israelites, had to abandon and turn against His chosen nation. Nevertheless, God's purpose of sending the Messiah was to save not only the chosen nation but also the whole of mankind. Therefore, God intended to save the whole of mankind, even though He might have to deliver Jesus into the hands of Satan. On the other hand, Satan tried to kill one man, Jesus, the Messiah, even if he might have to hand over to God the whole of mankind, including the chosen nation, which was now on his side. This was because Satan thought that he could break the purpose of the whole providence of God by killing the Messiah, for he knew that the first purpose of God's 4,000-year providence of restoration had been to set up one man, the Messiah. Thus, God finally handed Jesus over to Satan, as the condition of indemnity, in order to save the whole of mankind, including the Jewish people, who turned against Jesus, and were now on Satan's side.

Satan thus attained what he had intended through the 4,000-year course of history, by crucifying Jesus, with the exercise of his maximum power. God, who thus handed over Jesus into Satan's hands, could, at that price, set up the condition to save the whole of mankind, including the Israelites.

How, then, did God come to be able to save sinful men? Since Satan had killed Jesus by exercising his maximum power, the position for God now to exercise His maximum power was created, according to the principle of restoration through indemnity. The exercise of maximum power on God's part was to bring the dead back to life, while that of Satan was to kill man. Here God exercised His maximum power as the condition of indemnity against Satan's act of killing Jesus through the exercise of his maximum power, and He brought Jesus back to life. By grafting the whole of mankind into the resurrected Jesus (Rom. 11:24) and giving them rebirth, God intended to save all mankind.

As we well know through the Bible, Jesus after the resurrection was not the same Jesus who had lived with his disciples before his crucifixion. He was no longer a man seen through physical eyes, because he was a being transcendent of time and space. He once suddenly appeared in a closed room where his disciples were gathered (John 20:19), while in another instance he appeared before two disciples going to Emmaus, and accompanied them for a long distance. But their eyes were kept from recognizing Jesus, who appeared before them (Luke 24:15-16); and Jesus, who appeared, would again disappear suddenly. Jesus, in order to save mankind, had established the spiritual foundation of faith through the 40-day resurrection period to separate Satan, after giving up his physical body to the cross as a sacrifice. By doing this, he pioneered the way for the redemption of the sins of all men.

(ii) The Spiritual Foundation of Substance

Jesus, by establishing the spiritual 40-day foundation to separate Satan through resurrection, from the position of the spiritual mission-bearer of John the Baptist, could then restore the spiritual foundation of faith from the position of a spiritual parent. At the same time, he also established the position of a spiritual Abel in setting up the worldwide condition of indemnity to remove the fallen nature from the position of a spiritual child. Thus, Jesus could establish a spiritual foundation of faith for the third worldwide restoration of Canaan, just as Moses could establish the foundation of faith for the third nationwide restoration of Canaan, by going through the indemnity period of the 40-year wandering in the wilderness while leading the Israelites.

At the time of Moses, God worked His "providence for the start" by having him establish the foundation for the tabernacle. However, the resurrected Jesus worked the "providence for the start" by gathering his disciples, scattered in Galilee, and giving them the power to perform miracles and signs, since he himself was the spiritual substantial body of the tablets of stone, tabernacle, and the ark (Matt. 28:16-20).

Now, the saints in the position of Cain came to restore the spiritual foundation of substance by setting up the spiritual condition of indemnity to remove the fallen nature, through their believing, serving, and following the resurrected Jesus, who was spiritually in the position of Abel, as the spiritual mission-bearer of John the Baptist.

(iii) The Spiritual Foundation to Receive the Messiah

After Jesus' crucifixion, the remaining eleven disciples scattered in utter helplessness. Jesus, after his resurrection, gathered them again in one place and started his new providence of the spiritual restoration of Canaan. The disciples chose Matthias in place of Judas Iscariot to fill the number of 12 disciples, and believed, served, and followed the resurrected Jesus, thus establishing the spiritual foundation of substance. By doing this, they could restore the spiritual foundation to receive the Messiah.

On this foundation, Jesus could establish the position of the spiritual Messiah from the position of spiritual mission-bearer of John the Baptist and restore the Holy Spirit. By doing this, he became the spiritual True Parent and came to perform the work of rebirth. That is, as it is written in the Bible (Acts 2:1-4), after the advent of the Holy Spirit at Pentecost, the resurrected Jesus became the spiritual True Father and, working in oneness with the Holy Spirit as the spiritual True Mother, spiritually grafted the saints to them, thus beginning the work of spiritual rebirth. By doing this, Jesus could accomplish the providence of spiritual salvation (cf. Part I, Ch. IV, Sec. I, 4). Consequently, in the sphere of the resurrected Jesus, Satan's spiritual condition for accusation was completely liquidated, and thus, spiritually, this became a sphere inviolable by Satan.

Fallen man's physical salvation would remain unaccomplished, though he may in faith become one with Jesus, because his body is still in the position of being invaded by Satan, just like Jesus himself. However, if we believe in the resurrected Jesus, we will be with Jesus spiritually in the sphere inviolable by Satan, and thus we will be able to accomplish spiritual salvation free from the spiritual condition of accusation by Satan.

(iv) The Spiritual Restoration of Canaan

Christians could accomplish only the spiritual restoration of Canaan by believing and serving Jesus, who came to stand as the spiritual Messiah, on the spiritual foundation to receive the

Messiah. Thus the physical bodies of the saints, who were in the sphere of grace for the spiritual restoration of Canaan, stood in the same position as the physical body of Jesus, invaded by Satan through the cross. Therefore, they were being invaded by Satan, just as in the time before the coming of Jesus, with original sin still remaining in them (Rom. 7:25). Naturally, the saints also had to go through the course of separating from Satan again for the Second Advent of the Lord (cf. Part I, Ch. IV, Sec. I, 4).

The ideal of the tabernacle in the nationwide course of the restoration of Canaan, through which God worked His providence centering on Moses, came now to be realized on the worldwide base centering on the spiritual temple of the resurrected Jesus. The most holy place and the holy place were spiritually realized by the spirit man and the physical body of Jesus. Since the ideal of the mercy seat was realized through the work of Jesus and the Holy Spirit, God could appear and speak. Thus, in the mercy seat, where God's words were heard, the cherubim that had blocked the way since the fall of the first human ancestors would be put aside, so that one might enter the ark to meet Jesus, the Tree of Life, to eat the manna given by God, and to manifest the power of God represented by Aaron's rod that budded (Heb. 9:4-5). In this way, we can understand that the crucifixion of Jesus and the Second Advent was not a determined providence, when seen through Moses' course.

(2) The Course of the Substantial Restoration of Canaan Centering on the Lord of the Second Advent

We have discussed why God's chosen people started the third course of the worldwide restoration of Canaan as a spiritual course, not being able to start it as a substantial course as they had done in their third course of the nationwide restoration of

Canaan. The spiritual providence of the third worldwide restoration of Canaan, which they started on the spiritual foundation for the Messiah, by believing and obeying Jesus, the spiritual Messiah, has today broadened its spiritual territory, on a worldwide basis, after having passed the 2,000-year course of history.

Just as Joshua, who substituted for Moses in the spiritual course of the restoration of Canaan, accomplished the nationwide restoration of Canaan by going through the substantial course, so the Lord of the Second Advent has to realize the earthly Kingdom of God, by coming to walk the spiritual course of the restoration of Canaan as a substantial course, and by accomplishing the worldwide restoration of Canaan. In this manner, the Lord of the Second Advent, who is to realize the same Kingdom of God on earth as God intended to realize substantially at the time of Jesus, must be born on earth as a substantial man in flesh (cf. Part I, Ch. VI, Sec. II, 2).

The Lord of the Second Advent must restore through indemnity the providential course of restoration left unachieved at the time of the first coming. Therefore, just as Jesus had to walk the bitter course of the spiritual providence of restoration, due to the faithlessness of the Jewish people, the Lord must restore through indemnity the spiritual course of tribulation, this time substantially in flesh, if and when Christians, the Second Israel, should fall into faithlessness. Jesus said, "But first he [Christ] must suffer many things and be rejected by this generation." (Luke 17:25)

Therefore, just as Jesus from the time of his coming onwards, had to walk anew on his spiritual course of providence by abandoning the First Israel of God's summons and by setting up Christians as his second chosen nation, the Lord of the Second Advent, may have to achieve the providential course, substantially, by abandoning the Christians of the second summons, and calling anew the Third Israel, if the Christians should fall into faithlessness. If, at the Second Advent, the heralds, coming with the mission of John the Baptist (John 1:23), to make his way straight should fail in carrying out their mission, just as at the first coming, the Lord of the Second Advent himself must establish substantially the foundation of faith for the third providence of the worldwide restoration of Canaan from the position of John the Baptist, thus having to walk the path of tribulation.

However bitter a way he may walk, the Lord of the Second Advent will never come to die, not fulfilling the providence of restoration, as in the time of Jesus. This is because God's providence to fulfill His purpose of creation, through the True Parents of mankind, has come down from Adam through Jesus, to the Lord of the Second Advent, and in the third instance, the providence will not fail to be realized. Further, as will be later discussed (cf. Part II, Ch. VI, Sec. IV), the spiritual providence of restoration for the 2,000 years after Jesus has achieved the age of democracy in order to create the society beneficial for the providence. Jesus was killed after being branded as a rebel against Judaism, but in the democratic society at the Second Advent, the Lord cannot walk the path of death, even though he may be bitterly persecuted as a heretic.

Therefore, however difficult a way the Lord of the Second Advent may walk, there will gather saints believing and serving him absolutely on the substantial foundation of faith which he will establish; and it will be certain that they will be able to set up the substantial foundation to receive the Messiah by setting up the foundation of substance, for the sake of the substantial course of the third worldwide restoration of Canaan.

In the third nationwide course of the restoration of Canaan, at the time of Moses, God was to work His "providence for the start," centering on the rock. At the time of Joshua, He worked His "providence for the start," centering on the water, which was more internal than the rock. In a like manner, Jesus worked the "providence for the start" by the miracles and signs at the first coming, but at the Second Advent, Christ will work the "providence for the start," centering on the Word, which is internal. That is because, as discussed earlier (cf. Part I, Ch. III, Sec. III, 2), man, who was created by the Word (John 1:3), failed to accomplish the purpose of the Word due to the fall. God, who has been working His providence of restoration by setting up the external condition of the Word, in order to accomplish the purpose of the Word, must send Christ, who is the substance of the Word (John 1:14), at the close of providential history, and must work His providence of salvation, centering on the Word.

When we see God's purpose of creation, centering on the connection of heart, God, as the spiritual Parent, created men as His substantial children. Adam and Eve, who were created first as the substantial objects in the image and likeness of God's dual essentialities, are God's first substantial objects and the first parents of mankind. Thus, by joining as husband and wife and multiplying children, they should have established a family connected and united in the hearts of the parents, couple, and children, representing parental love, conjugal love and children's love. This is truly the four position foundation which has realized the three objective purposes (cf. Part I, Ch. I, Sec. II, 3).

In this manner, God intended to establish the Kingdom of God on earth, with His children of direct descent. However, as discussed in the "Fall of Man," all men, due to the first human ancestor's blood relationship with the archangel Lucifer, have become the children of the devil, inheriting Satan's blood lineage (Matt. 3:7, 23:33, John 8:44). Thus, the first human ancestors fell into a position in which they were cut off from the lineage of God, and this is the fall (cf. Part I, Ch. II).

Therefore, the purpose of God's providence of restoration is to restore the fallen men who were cut off from the lineage of God and to set them up as the children of God's direct line. Let us find out God's secret of the providence of restoration in the Bible.

As was previously discussed, Adam's family, which was so degraded as to commit murder, was cut off from a relationship with God. At the time of Noah the direct relationship with God could not be restored, due to the failure of Ham, the second son, who was in the position of Abel. However, man could stand in the position of the slave of slaves (Gen. 9:25), because there was the foundation of Noah's loyalty. Thus, man could have an indirect relationship with God. This was the actual relationship of God and man in the period before the Old Testament Age.

In his own time Abraham, the father of faith, could set up God's elect by establishing the family-level foundation to receive the Messiah. Thus, for the first time, the position of God's servant was restored (Lev. 25:55). This was the relationship of God and man in the Old Testament Age. After the coming of Jesus, his disciples, who stood on the foundation of faith which he had established from the position of John the Baptist, were for the first time restored from the position of servants of the Old Testament Age to the position of adopted children. In order for them to become children of God's direct lineage, they had to establish the foundation to receive the Messiah by setting up the foundation of substance in absolute obedience to Jesus; and by grafting (Rom. 11:17) themselves both spiritually and physically into Jesus, who stood on that foundation, they had to become one body with him.

Jesus came as the Son of God, without original sin, from God's direct lineage, and by making the whole of fallen mankind into one body by engrafting them to him, he was to restore them to be the children of God's direct lineage, having removed the original sin. Jesus and the Holy Spirit came as the spiritual True Parents to make men restore their lineal connection with God, as endowed at the creation, by having the fallen men remove their original sin by engrafting them to themselves. We call the work of Jesus and the Holy Spirit "Rebirth" (cf. Part I, Ch. VII, Sec. IV). Therefore, we must know that Jesus came as the center, the true olive tree, in order to engraft fallen men, who are the branches of wild olive trees, to himself.

Nevertheless, even his disciples fell into faithlessness, and so, Jesus was crucified in the position of John the Baptist, without being able to perform the duties of the Messiah. In this way, the resurrected Jesus had established the spiritual foundation of faith through the 40-day resurrection period to separate Satan, set up from the position of the spiritual John the Baptist. After that the spiritual foundation of substance was set up by the faith and loyalty of his disciples, who returned to him in repentence; and hence, the spiritual foundation to receive the Messiah was established for the first time. Finally, on that spiritual foundation the saints came to stand as spiritual children by being spiritually engrafted to Jesus, who stands as the spiritual Messiah. This has been the relationship of God and fallen men, according to the spiritual providence of restoration after Jesus, up to the present moment. Therefore, fallen men can as yet stand only as spiritual objects of God, because the spiritual providence of restoration after Jesus has been to restore the spirit world first, just as God had created the spirit world first. Accordingly, however devout a Christian may be, since he has not been able to liquidate original sin coming down through the flesh, no difference is found between him and the saints of the Old Testament Age in light of their both not having been able to remove themselves from the lineage of Satan (cf. Part I, Ch. IV, Sec. I, 4). Christians are at best adopted sons before

God, because they are children of a different lineage. For that very reason, Paul said:

> Not only the creation, but we ourselves, who have the first fruits of the spirit, groan inwardly as we wait for adoption as sons . . . (Rom. 8:23)

Therefore, the Lord of the Second Advent must come to restore the whole of mankind to be children of God's direct lineage. Consequently, he must be born on earth, in flesh, as Jesus was. By so doing he must restore through indemnity the course of Jesus, by walking it again. Therefore, the Lord of the Second Advent must establish, substantially, the foundation to receive the Messiah, according to the "providence for the start," centering on the Word; and by engrafting the whole of mankind both spiritually and physically on this foundation, he must restore them to be children of God's direct lineage, having removed the original sin.

Jesus established the family-level foundation by setting up twelve apostles centering on the three main ones, and then broadened it to the tribe-level foundation by setting up the 70 disciples, in order to restore through indemnity the position of Jacob, who had been the central figure of the family-level foundation for the Messiah. In the same manner, the Lord of the Second Advent, must also restore the foundation to receive the Messiah substantially, starting from family level, and gradually broadening it to tribal level, racial level, national level, world level and then to the cosmic level. On that foundation, he must finally be able to establish the Kingdom of Heaven on earth.

God, by setting up the chosen nation of the First Israel, prepared the base for Jesus to come and fulfill rapidly the purpose of erecting the Kingdom of Heaven, but due to their rebellion, He had to set up anew the Christians as the Second Israel. Likewise, if the Christians, who have been set up as the Second Israel for the ideal of the erection of the Kingdom of Heaven by the Lord of the Second Advent, should also turn against him, God will be compelled to abandon His elect of the Second Israel and choose anew His elect of the Third Israel. Therefore, Christians of the Last Days, like the Jewish people of the days of Jesus, are situated in very blessed circumstances, but on the other hand, are in the position where they are liable to become very miserable.

4. LESSONS LEARNED FROM JESUS' COURSE

First, in this case, God showed us what His predestination of His will was like. God always predestines His will to be absolutely fulfilled in the end. When John the Baptist failed to accomplish his mission, Jesus himself, who came as the Messiah, intended to fulfill the will even by substituting for John. Since the earthly Kingdom of Heaven was not realized due to faithlessness of the Jewish people, Christ will come again to fulfill this will.

In the next place, God showed us that His predestination concerning the fulfillment of the will, centering on a certain individual or a nation of His elect, is not absolute, but relative. That is to say, though God may have set up a certain individual or a nation to fulfill the purpose of His providence of restoration, He would set up a new mission-bearer to succeed in the work, if the former should fail to carry out his portion of responsibility. Jesus had chosen John the Baptist as his main disciple, but when he failed to carry out his responsibility, Jesus chose Peter in his place. In another case, he chose Judas Iscariot as one of his 12 disciples, but when Judas failed to fulfill his responsibility, Jesus chose Matthias in his place (Acts 1:26). In a like manner, God chose the Jewish people to fulfill the purpose of His providence of restoration, but when they failed to carry out their responsibility, He shifted the mission to the Gentiles (Acts 13:46, Matt. 21:33-43). In this way, even though God may have chosen a certain man to fulfill His will, He can never absolutely predestine the fulfillment of the will centering on any one person.

Third, God showed us that He does not interfere with man's own portion of responsibility, but dominates only its result. When John the Baptist or Judas Iscariot fell into faithlessness, it was not that God did not know it nor that He was unable to stop it, but He did not interfere at all with their faith, but dominated only the result of their deeds.

Finally, God showed us that the greater the mission of the person, the more bitter the trial facing him. Since Adam turned against God in faithlessness, Jesus, who came as the second Adam, in order to fulfill the purpose of the providence of restoration, had to restore through indemnity the position before the fall by showing good faith, from the position where he is abandoned by God in place of Adam. Therefore, Jesus had to go through Satan's temptations in the wilderness, and had to suffer on the cross, completely abandoned by God (Matt. 27:46).

/

CHAPTER III

Formation and Length of Each Age in the History of Providence

SECTION I
The Age of Providential Time-Identity

What is the "age of providential time-identity"? When we look into the course of human history, we often find that a certain historical course, similar to that of a past age, is repeated in later ages, although there may be some difference in degree and scope. Historians, seeing such phenomena, say that history progresses in a spiral of repeating identical patterns. They never know the cause, however. If a certain age is a repetition of the historical course of the previous age, that age is called the "age of providential time-identity." The reason for calling this the age of providential time-identity will be explained later in detail, but it is mainly because all those phenomena are originally based on God's providence of restoration through indemnity.

Why then does the age of providential time-identity occur? All the facts occurring in the course of fulfilling the purpose of God's providence of restoration have formed human history. However, when a certain central figure who has been walking the providential course fails to carry out his portion of responsibility, the age of providence centering on that person comes to an end. Nevertheless, since God's predestination for the will is absolute (cf. Part I, Ch. VI), God would set up another person in place of the former, and establish a new age to restore through indemnity the foundation to receive the Messiah. Since this new age is one of restoration through indemnity of the historical course of the previous age, the same course of history needs to be repeated, and thus the age of providential time-identity is formed.

Meanwhile, the persons in charge of the providence of restoration must restore horizontally through indemnity all the vertical conditions of indemnity belonging to the previous age. Therefore, as the vertical conditions of indemnity increase with the prolongation of the providence of restoration, the conditions of indemnity to be set up horizontally become heavier and heavier. Accordingly, the age of providential time-identity will also gradually become different in its content and extent. This is the reason the forms of the respective ages of providential time-identity are not exactly the same.

In the meantime, when we classify the three stages of the period of growth by type, the formation stage is the symbolic type, the growth stage is the image type, and the perfection stage is the substantial type. Therefore, the ages in the providential course of restoration identically repeating these types have reproduced similar types of history. That is, when we divide the whole period of the providential history of restoration from the viewpoint of time-identity by type, the providential age for the foundation of restoration is the age of symbolic time-identity, while the providential age of restoration is the age of image time-identity, and the providential age of the prolongation of restoration is the period of substantial time-identity.

Next, we must know the factors which form the age of providential time-identity. The ages of time-identity repeat themselves because the providence to restore the foundation to receive the Messiah is being repeated. Accordingly, we may first list, as the factors which help to create the age of providential time-identity, three conditions for the restoration of the foundation of faith: the central figure for this foundation, the necessary conditional objects, and the mathematical length of the period. Secondly, we can list the condition of indemnity to remove the fallen nature in order to restore the foundation of substance.

The ages of providential time-identity formed by such factors exhibit the following two characteristics:

First, the providential time-identity is formed by the factor of the number of the years or generations which make up the mathematical period of indemnity to restore the foundation of faith. The providential history of restoration was the history of God's providence (through men), which involved repeatedly restoring through indemnity the foundation of faith. This foundation had been lost because the central figures in charge of the providence failed in carrying out their portions of responsibility. Thus it has been necessary to repeat the providence to restore through indemnity the mathematical period of faith. After all, the ages of providential time-identity have repeatedly formed identical types through the repetition of certain numbers of years or generations. The purpose of this chapter is to handle the questions concerning this process.

Second, the providential time-identity is formed by the factors of the historical facts in the providence such as: the central figure and the conditional objects to restore the foundation of faith, and the condition of indemnity to remove the fallen nature for the restoration of the foundation of substance. Since the purpose of the providence of restoration is to establish the foundation to receive the Messiah, the providence to restore this foundation should repeat itself if the providence is prolonged.

Meanwhile, the foundation to receive the Messiah can be established only by restoring first the foundation of faith through the symbolic offering, and then the foundation of substance through the substantial offering. Consequently, the history of the providence of restoration has been a repetition of the providence of restoring the symbolic offering and the substantial offering. Therefore, the age of providential time-identity is formed centering on the historical facts in the providence, which have been efforts to restore these two kinds of offerings. Questions concerning this will be discussed in detail in the following chapter.

SECTION II

The Formation of the Number of Years and Generations in the Providential Age for the Foundation of Restoration

1. WHY AND HOW IS THE PROVIDENCE OF RESTORATION PROLONGED?

We have previously discussed the fact that God's providence of restoration had been prolonged from Adam to Noah, to

Abraham, to Moses, finally coming down to Jesus. Due to the faithlessness of the people, Jesus died without completely accomplishing his purpose. The providence of restoration is therefore being prolonged to the time of the Second Advent.

Why then is the providence of restoration prolonged? This is a question to be solved only by the theory of predestination. According to the theory of predestination, God's will is pre-destined to be fulfilled as an absolute. Therefore, the will, once set up, must eventually be fulfilled. However, since the fulfill-ment of the will centering on any person is relative, the will would be fulfilled only when God's portion of responsibility and man's portion are combined. Accordingly, when God's will is not fulfilled, because the person with the mission of fulfilling the will fails to accomplish his own portion of responsibility, God will set up another person, in a different age, in his place. Then He will work His providence of fulfilling the will without fail. Thus, the providence of restoration is prolonged.

Next, we must know the manner in which the providence of restoration is prolonged. According to the principle of creation, God is a being of the number "three," and all things created in His image and likeness present themselves through courses in the number three, either in their aspect of existence, their move-ment, or their process of growth. Therefore, to fulfill the purpose of creation by establishing the four position foundation and performing circular movement, they must pass three points, by fulfilling the three objective purposes according to the three-stage action of origin, division and union. Meanwhile, the providence of restoring the purpose of creation is that of re-creation through the Word, so it may be prolonged to as many as three stages in the prolongation of the providence of restora-tion, according to the principle of creation.

In Adam's family, when the "substantial offering" by Cain and Abel ended in failure, the will was prolonged three times, through Noah to Abraham. Upon Abraham's failure in his "symbolic offering," the will was prolonged through Isaac to Jacob. The courses of the restoration of Canaan centering on Moses or Jesus were prolonged three times each. The ideal of erecting the temple, due to King Saul's mistake, was prolonged through King David to King Solomon. God's ideal of creation, left unfulfilled through Adam, was prolonged three times, through Jesus, the second Adam, to the time of the Second Advent. One proverb says, "If not done at first attempt, it will be sure at the third," thus verifying the principle found in our actual life.

2. THE VERTICAL CONDITION OF INDEMNITY AND HORIZONTAL RESTORATION THROUGH INDEMNITY

The central figure in charge of the will of the providence of restoration cannot succeed and accomplish the mission of his predecessors unless he can restore through indemnity, in his time, all the conditions of indemnity which the persons in charge of the same missions, in the providential course until his time, tried to set up. Accordingly, when this person again fails to accomplish this mission, the conditions of indemnity which he failed to set up would be handed on to the next person with that mission. Those conditions, historically accumulated and added to by the failure of the persons in charge of the providence in the providential course of restoration, are called "vertical conditions of indemnity." When they are restored through indemnity centering on one who has a specific mission, we call this "horizontal restoration through indemnity."

For example, in order for Abraham to accomplish his mission, he would have had to horizontally restore through indemnity all the vertical conditions of indemnity which Adam's and Noah's families had tried to set up. Abraham's sacrifices with the three offerings at once on the altar were to horizontally restore through indemnity the vertical conditions of indemnity, which had been prolonged through the three stages of Adam, Noah, and Abraham. Consequently, the three offerings symbolized all the conditions which Adam and Noah had failed to set up, and which Abraham himself was to set up.

Since Jacob had to set up the condition of restoring through indemnity, at once and horizontally, the vertical conditions of indemnity for the 12 generations from Noah down to himself, he had 12 sons and multiplied them into 12 tribes. Likewise, Jesus also had to restore through indemnity, horizontally and at one time, centering on himself, all the vertical conditions of indemnity left by the numerous prophets in charge of the providence of restoration in the course of the 4,000 years of providential history.

For example, Jesus set up the 12 apostles and 70 disciples to restore through indemnity, centering on himself, the vertical conditions of indemnity belonging to Jacob's course, in which God worked His providence, centering on the 12 sons and 70 kinsmen, and Moses' course, in which God worked His providence centering on 12 tribes and 70 elders. Again, Jesus' 40 days of fasting and prayer were to restore through indemnity (at once and horizontally centering on himself) all the vertical conditions of indemnity in setting up the 40-day separation from Satan necessary to establish the foundation of faith. Seen from this aspect, a person in charge of the providence of restoration stands not only as an individual, but also as the representation of all the saints and prophets who have previously been on earth with the same mission. At the same time he represents the sum total of the historical fruit of all of them.

3. HORIZONTAL RESTORATION THROUGH INDEMNITY CARRIED OUT VERTICALLY

Next, let us study what horizontal restoration through indemnity carried out vertically is. As already stated in detail in the section on the providence of restoration centering on Abraham's family, Abraham's case corresponded to the third one in the providence to restore the family level foundation for the Messiah. Accordingly, Abraham was, at that time, under the condition in the Principle to fulfill the will by all means. Therefore, he had to restore through indemnity, at once and horizontally, all the vertical conditions of indemnity accumulated by the failure of Adam's and Noah's family. However, Abraham failed in his symbolic offering, and the mission had to be prolonged to the next stage. Here, God had to set up Abraham, who failed, in the position of having succeeded, and also had to set up the vertical prolongation of the providence of restoration, in the position as if it were horizontally restored through indemnity, without any prolongation. In order to work His providence in such a way, God had Abraham, Isaac, and Jacob set up the condition of indemnity, all as a unity centering on the will, though they were three different individuals, as was discussed in the section on the providence of restoration centering on Abraham. Thus Abraham, Isaac and Jacob formed a unity, seen from the will. Therefore, Jacob's success was Isaac's success, while it was also Abraham's success. Consequently, even though the will centering on Abraham was prolonged vertically to Isaac and then to Jacob, it was regarded as being horizontally restored through indemnity, centering on Abraham, without any prolongation, when we see it from the viewpoint of the will.

Therefore, we must regard Abraham, Isaac, and Jacob as the one man, Abraham, centering on the will. In consequence, it was as if the will was fulfilled in the one generation of Abraham. In the Bible (Ex. 3:6), God is called "the God of Abraham, the God of Isaac, and the God of Jacob," thus indicating that those three generations were one when seen from such a viewpoint.

In this way, when Abraham failed to set up the horizontal condition of indemnity centering on himself due to his failure in the symbolic offering, God, after all, put the case in the position as if the vertical conditions of indemnity, set up while vertically prolonging the program through the three generations of Abraham, Isaac, and Jacob, were horizontally restored through indemnity within one generation, centering on Abraham. Therefore, it is called the "horizontal restoration through indemnity carried out vertically."

4. THE MATHEMATICAL PERIOD OF INDEMNITY TO RESTORE THE FOUNDATION OF FAITH

In the "Introduction" to Part II, we discussed that in order for the central figure, who is to set up faith, to restore the foundation of faith, he must restore the mathematical period of indemnity for it. Let us here study the reason for this.

God's form is also mathematical. Therefore, the world of creation, centering on man, is the substantial object of God, with His dual essentialities mathematically developed. For this reason, the development of science, which is searching for the principle of created things on the horizontal plane, is possible only by mathematical research. The first human ancestor, thus created, was to become a substantial being, mathematically perfected, by setting up the foundation of faith, only after having undergone the mathematical period of growth. Since the world of creation, as such, fell into Satan's dominion, man, in order to restore it, must restore through indemnity the foundation of faith, by setting up conditional objects symbolizing the world of creation, and then setting up the mathematical period of indemnity to restore the number invaded by Satan.

Then, by what number was the human ancestor, before the fall, to set up the foundation of faith originally, and what kind of mathematically perfected substantial being was he to become? According to the principle of creation, nothing can exist without establishing the four position foundation. Accordingly, Adam and Eve, who were in the period of immaturity, also continued their existence by establishing the four position foundation. Meanwhile, this four position foundation, with each position undergoing three stages of growth, producing the total number "12", would altogether fulfill 12 objective purposes. Accordingly, the period of growth, which was the period for Adam's establishing the foundation of faith, was truly the period for the completion of the number "12".

Therefore, first, the first human ancestors, who were in the period of immaturity, had to establish the foundation of faith by the number "12". Thus, by completing the 12 objective purposes, they had to become substantial beings having perfected the number "12". However, due to their fall, this was invaded by Satan. Therefore, the central figure who is to restore this through indemnity in the historical course of the providence of restoration, cannot establish the foundation of substance to restore the substantial being having perfected the number "12", unless he can restore through indemnity the foundation of faith by setting up the period of indemnity to restore the number "12".

For example, the 120-year period of Noah's building the ark, the 120-year period of the providence of restoration of Canaan, centering on Moses, the 120 years from the time Abraham was called until the time when Jacob set up the condition enabling him to restore the birthright from Esau, the 120 years of the United Kingdom in the Old Testament Age for the restoration through indemnity of the previous period, and the 120-year period of the Christian Kingdom in the New Testament Age are, without exception, periods of indemnity to restore the number "12".

Next, Adam and Eve, in their immaturity before the fall, were supposed to complete the four position foundation by entering the sphere of God's direct dominion, the fourth stage, only after having undergone the three stages of the period of growth. Consequently, the period of growth, in which they were to establish the foundation of faith, was also the period for the completion of the number "4".

Therefore, the first human ancestors, who were in their immaturity, should have become the substantial beings having perfected the number "4", by setting up the foundation of faith through the number "4" and by accomplishing the four position foundation. However, due to their fall, this was also invaded by Satan. Therefore, the central figure to restore this through indemnity, in the historical course of the providence of restoration, cannot establish the foundation of substance to restore the substantial being having perfected the number "4", unless he can restore through indemnity the foundation of faith by setting up the indemnity period to restore the number "4".

As already discussed in detail (cf. Part II, Ch. I, Sec. II, 1[2]), the 40-day judgment concerning Noah's ark, Moses' 40-day fast, the 40-day period of spying in Canaan, the 40-day fast and 40-day resurrection of Jesus were all periods of indemnity for the restoration of the number "4", to restore the foundation of faith.

Again, the period of growth is also the period for the perfection of the number "21". Therefore, the first human ancestors, in their immaturity, had to become the substantial beings having perfected the number 21, by establishing the foundation of faith through the number 21, and thus fulfilling the purpose of creation. However, due to their fall, this also was invaded by Satan. Therefore, the central figure to restore this through indemnity, in the historical course of the providence of restoration, cannot establish the foundation of substance to restore the substantial being having perfected the number 21, unless he can restore through indemnity the foundation of faith, by setting up the period of indemnity to restore the number "21".

Let us then study why the period of growth becomes the period for the perfection of the number "21". In order to know the meaning of the number "21", we must first understand the significance in the Principle of the numbers "3", "4" and "7". God, who is the subjective being with the dual essentialities combined (and perfected), is a being of the number "3". The perfection of a creature means to establish the four positions by becoming one body with God. Therefore, in order for an individual man to be perfected, he must establish the four position foundation by forming a trinity with his mind and body combined, in harmony, centered on God. Likewise, in order for a couple to be perfected, they must establish the four position foundation by forming a trinity with the man and woman united, centered on God. And, in order for the world of creation to be perfected, all things must establish the four position foundation, by forming a trinity with men and all things combined, in harmony, centered on God. Also, in order for the created things to establish the four position foundation by becoming one centered on God, they have to undergo the three stages of growth, thus fulfilling the three objective purposes. For this reason, we call the number "3" either the "heavenly number" or the "number of perfection."

Thus, when a subject and an object form a trinity by becoming one harmonious united body centered on God, the individual body then decides his position, as a creature furnished with the four directions of north, south, east and west, by establishing the four position foundation. In that sense, we call the number "4" the "earthly number."

Thus, when a creature establishes the four position foundation by going through the growth period of three stages and is perfected as an existence with a nature in time and space, he becomes a substantial being who has perfected the number "7", the sum total of the heavenly number and earthly number. This is why the whole period of the creation of heaven and earth became 7 days. When we see the whole period of creation as one period, it becomes the period for the perfection of the number "7". Therefore, we may regard a certain period for anything to be perfected, as the period for the perfection of the number "7". Thus, if we regard the three stages (formation, growth, and perfection) forming the period of growth each as a single period, each period would become the period for the perfection of the number "7". We can then understand that the whole period is also the period for the perfection of the number "21".

The following are examples of the indemnity period of the number "21", which the central figures for the foundation of faith set up. During the period of the flood in Noah's day, God had Noah send out the doves three times in order to foreshadow His providence of three stages. By making the time spaces 7 days each, the whole period seen from the will became 21 days (Gen. 7:4, 8:10, 8:12). When Jacob set up the providential period of going into Haran and again returning to Canaan, in order to set up the course of the restoration of Canaan on the family level, he needed also 21 years, that is, three times seven years. Further, for the period of restoring through indemnity Jacob's 21 years, the period of the Israelites' captivity in Babylon and their return encompassed 210 years. The period of the popes' captivity and return also took 210 years.

The period of growth is also the period for the perfection of the number "40". Therefore, fourth, the first human ancestors, in their immaturity before the fall, had to become the substantial beings having perfected the number "40", by setting up the foundation of faith through the number "40", thus accomplishing the purpose of creation. Nevertheless, this was invaded by Satan due to their fall. Therefore, the central figure to restore this through indemnity could not establish the foundation of substance to restore the substantial being having perfected the number "40", unless he could restore through indemnity the foundation of faith, by setting up the period of indemnity to restore the number "40".

Let us then study why the period of growth becomes the period for the perfection of the number "40". Before we can know this, we must first understand the significance of the number "10". If we divide the three stages of the period of growth into three stages each, it makes a total of nine stages. The basis in the Principle of the number "9" lies here. Incidentally, the things of creation which were divided as God's substantial object through the mathematical development of His invisible dual essentialities can fulfill the purpose of creation only when they become one body with God, by returning into the sphere of God's direct dominion, the tenth stage, after passing through the nine stages of the period of growth. Therefore, we call the number "10" the "returning number." God set up Noah ten generations after Adam to set up the period of indemnity for the restoration of the number "10" in order to have him return again to God.

Meanwhile, the four position foundation centered on Adam and Eve would become the foundation which had perfected the number "40", by each position going through the "10" stages of the period of growth and thus completing the mathematical period of growth of the number "40" in total. Therefore, the period of growth is also the period for the perfection of the number "40".

Some examples of the indemnity period of the number "40" set up for the restoration of this foundation, in the historical course of the providence of restoration, are: the 40-day period from the time when Noah's ark came to rest on Mount Ararat until he sent out the doves; Moses' 40 years in Pharaoh's palace; his 40 years in the wilderness of Midian; the 40 years in the wilderness for the nationwide restoration of Canaan, and so on.

Here, we can understand that the number "40" in the providential course of restoration through indemnity has two kinds of character. One is the number "40", with the number "10", which is the returning number, multiplied by the number "4", which fallen man must restore through indemnity. The other is the number "40" to restore through indemnity what Adam, before the fall, had to set up, as previously discussed.

Meanwhile, the 40 years in the wilderness for the restoration of Canaan on the national level was the period to restore through indemnity Moses' 40 years in Pharaoh's palace and his other 40 years in the wilderness of Midian. At the same time, it was also the period to restore through indemnity the 40-day spying and Moses' 40-day fast. Accordingly, this 40-year period, as discussed above, was to restore through indemnity both numbers "40" of different characters at the same time. This phenomenon occurs when the central figure to set up the foundation of faith horizontally restores through indemnity all the vertical conditions of indemnity at the same time. And, when the providence to restore through indemnity the number "40" is prolonged, it can be lengthened either to the number "400" or to the number "4,000", according to the rule of multiplication by a multiple of the number "10". The 400 years from Noah to Abraham, the 400-year slavery in Egypt, and the 4,000 years from Adam to Jesus are such examples.

According to what we previously discussed, let us summarize what kind of mathematical period of indemnity must be set up in order for the central figure in the providence of restoration to restore the foundation of faith. The first human ancestors should have fulfilled the purpose of creation, by setting up the foundation of faith according to the numbers "12", "4", "21", and "40", and by becoming the substantial beings who had perfected these numbers. However, due to their fall, all these were invaded by Satan. Therefore, the central figure to restore these through indemnity in the historical course of the providence of restoration cannot establish the foundation of substance for the restoration of the substantial being who had perfected all such numbers by restoring the foundation of faith, unless he sets up a mathematical period of indemnity to restore the numbers "12", "4", "21" and "40".

5. THE PERIOD OF TIME-IDENTITY CENTERING ON THE NUMBER OF GENERATIONS

God chose Noah 10 generations (1600 years) after Adam, and set him up as the central figure to restore the foundation of faith. We must understand the significance of the "1600 years" and the "10 generations" as the indemnity period to restore certain numbers.

We have previously discussed that the number "10" is the "returning number," and that the period of growth is also the period for the perfection of the number "10". Therefore, the first human ancestors should have become the substantial beings having perfected the number "10" by going through the period for the perfection of the number "10" through the accomplishment of their own portions of responsibility. However, due to their fall, all these things were invaded by Satan. Therefore, in order to work His providence of restoration for the substantial being who has perfected the number "10", the number which enables man to return to God, God must have the central figure set up the period of indemnity to restore the number "10". In order to have man set up this period of indemnity to restore the number "10", God called Noah ten generations after Adam, and set him up as the central figure for His providence of restoration.

We have previously discussed that the first human ancestors could have become the substantial beings having perfected the number "40" only by undergoing the whole period of growth which served as a condition for perfection of the number "40". Incidentally, fallen man cannot be set up as the central figure to restore the substantial being having perfected the number "40", unless, by establishing the four position foundation, he sets up the period of indemnity to restore the number "40", which Adam should have set up. Consequently, each position of the four position foundation must set up the period of indemnity to restore the number "40". Therefore, all those must become the period of indemnity to restore the number "160", and since this must be set up during 10 generations as the returning number, all those must be the period of indemnity to restore the number "1600". It was because the fallen men had to set up such a period of indemnity to restore the number "1600", that God chose Noah 1600 years—which was "10" generations—after Adam.

After His providence of restoration centering on Noah's family had ended in failure, God again chose Abraham after "400" years, which was "10" generations, and set him up as the central figure for His providence of restoration. Consequently, the period from Noah to Abraham was the period of time-identity to restore through indemnity the period from Adam to Noah, centering on the number of generations.

We have already discussed how this period became "400" years (cf. Part I, Ch. I, Sec. III, 1). God had Noah set up the 40-day judgment period to accomplish the whole purpose of the mathematical restoration through indemnity, by the 1600 years or ten generations. However, this 40-day judgment period was invaded by Satan due to Ham's mistake. God was therefore compelled to have the central figure in charge of His providence of restoration set up again the period of indemnity to restore this. Since God had worked to restore the indemnity period for the restoration of the number "160" in each generation after Adam, having it continue for ten generations until

Noah, He also had to set up, as the indemnity period to restore the judgment number "40", each of the ten generations from Noah to Abraham, which formed the period identical to the former.

However, because He could not set up the indemnity period for one generation with only 40 days, God had His people set up the indemnity period for one generation with 40 years, in order to indemnify the failure in the 40-day judgment with the 40-year period, according to the law of indemnity. This was similar to the Israelites' restoration through indemnity of their failure in the 40 days of spying with the 40-year period of wandering in the wilderness (Num. 14:34). Since God's providence of having the people set up the one generation with 40 years lasted for 10 generations, 400 years were needed for the whole period of indemnity.

6. THE PROVIDENTIAL PERIOD OF HORIZONTAL RESTORATION THROUGH INDEMNITY CARRIED OUT VERTICALLY

As already clarified above, the central figure in charge of the providence of restoration must horizontally restore through indemnity all the vertical conditions of indemnity. Therefore, the longer the providential history is prolonged, the heavier become the horizontal conditions of indemnity which the person of a later generation in charge of the providence of restoration must set up.

In the providence of restoration centering on Adam's family, God started His providence of restoration for the first time. Naturally there was no vertical condition of indemnity as yet. Accordingly, they could establish the foundation to receive the Messiah very simply, by Cain and Abel offering the symbolic sacrifices, and by Cain's offering substantial sacrifices through establishing the condition of indemnity to remove the fallen nature in obedience to Abel. Consequently, they could also restore the mathematical period of indemnity to restore the foundation of faith, by the period of offering symbolic sacrifices and substantial sacrifices. Because the mathematical periods of indemnity remained as the vertical condition of indemnity, as a result of the prolongation of the period for the providence of restoration due to the failure of the offerings in Adam's family, the central figure who had to set up faith after Adam had to establish the mathematical period of indemnity to restore the numbers of "12", "4", "21", and "40" in order to restore the foundation of faith.

Accordingly, Noah was in the position, horizontally, to restore through indemnity that condition of indemnity. Therefore, for the mathematical period of indemnity to restore the foundation of faith, he had to set up the following periods: the 120 years for the period to build the ark, the 40 days for the period of flood judgment, the 21-day period (three times seven days) which he set up in order to send out the doves (Gen. 7:4, 8:10, 8:12), and the 40-day period from the time when the ark rested on Mount Ararat until he sent out the doves (Gen. 8:8-12).

Due to Ham's failure, such mathematical periods of indemnity, set up by Noah, were again invaded by Satan, thus remaining as vertical conditions of indemnity. Therefore, Abraham had to restore that period through indemnity, horizontally and at once, through a symbolic offering. However, Abraham also failed in the symbolic offering, and could not restore those periods through indemnity. Thus, in order to restore this period as the horizontal period of indemnity carried out vertically, God again had to set up the period of indemnity corresponding to each number of "12", "4", "21", and "40" by extending the fulfillment of His will to Isaac and Jacob.

The providence of restoration centering on Abraham lists the following: 120 years from the time Abraham left Haran, until the time when Jacob took the birthright from Esau; the 40

years after that, until Jacob was blessed by Isaac with the birthright, and then again by God on his way to Haran (Gen.
28:10-14); the 21 years after that until the time he returned to
Canaan with his wives, children and his wealth after having
completed his drudgery in Haran (Gen. 31:41); and the 40 years
from Jacob's return to Canaan, until he went into Egypt to visit
Joseph who had been sold. All these were the horizontal periods
of indemnity carried out vertically to restore the foundation of
faith. In this way, the length of the period of horizontal restoration through indemnity carried out vertically was decided.

Section III
The Formation and Length of Each Period in the
Providential Age of Restoration

The providential age of restoration is the age to restore
through indemnity, as the image time-identity, the providential
age for the foundation of restoration, which is the age of symbolic time-identity. Let us now study the formation and length
of each period.

1. THE FOUR HUNDRED YEAR PERIOD OF SLAVERY IN EGYPT

Noah established the foundation of faith on the foundation
of separation from Satan by the 40-day judgment. This foundation was nullified because of Ham's failure, and God, in order to
set up Abraham in the same position, commanded him to offer
symbolic sacrifices on the foundation of having restored
through indemnity the 400 years. However, due to Abraham's
failure in the offering, the foundation was again invaded by
Satan. Thus, God had the Israelites undergo the 400-year
slavery in Egypt for the separation from Satan again, in order
to restore the 400-year foundation invaded by Satan (Gen.

15:13). This period we call the "period of slavery in Egypt" (cf. Part II, Ch. I, Sec. III, 1). This period was that in which to restore through indemnity, by the image time-identity, the 1600 years from Adam to Noah, out of the period of symbolic time-identity.

2. THE FOUR HUNDRED YEAR PERIOD OF JUDGES

In I Kings (6:1) it says,

In the four hundred and eightieth year after the people of Israel came out of the land of Egypt, in the fourth year of Solomon's reign over Israel, in the month of Ziv, which is the second month, he began to build the house of the Lord.

When we see that the fourth year of King Solomon after the 40-year reign of King Saul and the 40-year reign of King David was said to be the 480th year after the people of Israel came out of the land of Egypt, we can understand that it was approximately a 400-year period after the Israelites' return from Egypt into Canaan, until the time King Saul was enthroned. This period we call the "period of Judges."

The Israelites, centering on Moses, had to stand on the foundation of separation from Satan by the 400-year slavery in Egypt, in order to restore on a national level the position of Abraham, who had been set up on the foundation of separation from Satan by the 400 years from Noah. But, due to the faithlessness of the Israelites who returned to Canaan centering on Joshua in place of Moses, this foundation was again invaded by Satan. Because of this, the Israelites had to separate themselves from Satan again so that they could restore through indemnity again the foundation of the 400-year slavery in Egypt, which was invaded by Satan. The period set up again for that reason was the 400 years of the period of the Judges, from the Israelites' return into Canaan until the time King Saul was enthroned.

This period could restore by indemnity, as the image time-identity, the 400-year period from Noah to Abraham.

3. THE ONE HUNDRED AND TWENTY YEAR PERIOD OF THE UNITED KINGDOM

With the development of the providential age of restoration in order to restore by indemnity the providential age for the foundation of restoration, Abraham, who started this providential course, was in the position of Adam, while Moses was in Noah's position, and King Saul in Abraham's position. Abraham was the person to complete the providential period for the foundation of restoration, and at the same time was the person to start the providential period of restoration. Therefore, Abraham had to set up first the family level foundation to receive the Messiah and, on this, he had to set up the nationwide foundation to receive the Messiah. Just as God had to realize, by all means, the family level foundation to receive the Messiah at the time of Abraham, because it was His third attempt, He now had to realize, by all means, His providence to set up the nationwide foundation for the Messiah at the time of King Saul, because it was also His third attempt.

Abraham did not realize this will since he failed in his attempt to horizontally restore by indemnity, centering on the symbolic offering, the periods of 120 years, 40 days, 21 days, and 40 days, which were the mathematical periods of indemnity to restore the foundation of faith, set up at the time of Noah. Now, in order to restore these as the horizontal period of indemnity carried out vertically, Abraham again set up the 120 years, 40 years, 21 years and 40 years. Likewise, King Saul, who, nationwide, restored by indemnity the position of Abraham, also tried to restore horizontally by indemnity, by erecting the temple and centering on it, the periods of 120 years

(Moses' life consisted of three 40-year periods), 40 days (period of fasting), 21 days (period of the first nationwide restoration of Canaan), and 40 years (period in the wilderness), which were the mathematical periods of indemnity to restore the foundation of faith of Moses' time.

However, King Saul also fell into faithlessness, thus failing to fulfill this will (I Sam. 15:11-23). In order to restore those periods as the horizontal period of indemnity carried out vertically, as in the time of Abraham, God set up the 120 years of the period of the United Kingdom, the 400-year period of the Divided Kingdoms of North and South, the 210-year period of the Israelites' captivity and return, and the 400-year period of preparation for the coming of the Messiah, finally to receive the Messiah.

Therefore, the period of the United Kingdom was the period to restore by indemnity the 120 years in which Moses set up, three times, the foundation of faith for the nationwide restoration of Canaan.

Let us study this more concretely. After the Israelites centering on Moses had stood upon the foundation of separation from Satan by the 400-year slavery in Egypt, Moses set up the foundation of faith by his 40-year life in Pharaoh's palace. Then he attempted to lead the Israelites into Canaan to erect the holy temple. But, due to the faithlessness of the Israelites, this course was prolonged to Moses' 40 years in the wilderness of Midian, and then to the 40-year period of wandering in the wilderness.

Likewise, after the Israelites had stood on the foundation of having restored the 400 years of slavery in Egypt through the 400 years of Judges, King Saul had to set up the foundation of faith by restoring, with his 40-year reign, the 40-year life of Moses in Pharaoh's palace; then he had to erect the temple. However, King Saul fell into faithlessness (I Sam. 15:11-23), and as in the time of Moses, the will of erecting the temple was prolonged to the 40 years of King David, and to another 40 years of King Solomon, thus making the 120-year period of the United Kingdom.

This period was the period to restore by indemnity, as the image time-identity, the 120 years from the time of Abraham's departure from Haran until Jacob took the birthright from Esau. Accordingly, just as the will for Abraham was prolonged to Isaac, and then to Jacob, when it was realized, King Saul's ideal of the temple was also prolonged to King David, and then to King Solomon, when it was finally fulfilled.

4. THE FOUR HUNDRED YEAR PERIOD OF THE DIVIDED KINGDOMS OF NORTH AND SOUTH

King Saul attempted to horizontally restore by indemnity Moses' 40-day fast for the restoration of the words, by realizing the ideal of erecting the temple during the period of his 40-year reign.

However, due to his faithlessness, this period had to be restored as a horizontal period of indemnity carried out vertically. This was the providence behind the 400-year period of the divided kingdoms of Northern Israel and Southern Judah, which lasted until the Israelites became captive in Babylon.

This period could restore by indemnity, as the image time-identity, the 40-year period from the time when Jacob had set up the condition of taking the birthright from Esau by some bread and pottage of lentils until he again received the blessing from Isaac and from God (Gen. 28:13) and entered Haran.

5. THE TWO HUNDRED AND TEN YEAR PERIOD OF THE JEWISH PEOPLE'S CAPTIVITY AND RETURN

The Northern Kingdom of Israel, due to the people's faithlessness, was taken captive by Assyria. After that, the Southern

Kingdom of Judah, due to its faithlessness, was also taken captive by Nebuchadnezzar, king of Babylonia. After spending 70 years as captives in Babylon, they were at last liberated by a royal decree from Cyrus, the king of Persia, after Babylon's fall to Persia. The Jewish people later returned to Jerusalem, and Nehemiah, leading the remaining Jews, returned and built the walls again. They then entered the period for the preparation to receive the Messiah, centering on Malachi the prophet, according to Malachi's prophecy (Mal. 4:5). This was the 210th year from their captivity in Babylon, and about the 140th year from the time of their liberation. The sum of those periods is known as the "period of the captivity and return of the Jewish people."

By realizing the ideal of the temple, King Saul tried to horizontally restore by indemnity the 21-day period in which Moses first attempted to lead the Israelites into Canaan. However, since he failed, due to his disbelief, the 210-year period for the Jewish people's captivity and return came about in order to restore this period as the horizontal period of indemnity, carried out vertically.

Meanwhile, this period was that in which it was possible to restore by indemnity, as the image time-identity, the 21-year period of Jacob's drudgery in Haran (Gen. 31:41). The first 7 years Jacob spent in order to take Leah, the second 7 years in order to take Rachel, and the third 7 years from then until the time he returned to Canaan.

6. THE FOUR HUNDRED YEAR PERIOD OF PREPARATION FOR THE COMING OF THE MESSIAH

The Jewish people, after having returned to Canaan, their homeland, rebuilt the temples and walls, and thus stood as a nation to receive the Messiah according to the prophecy of Malachi the prophet. The 400-year period from that time until the birth of Jesus we call the "period of preparation for the coming of the Messiah."

King Saul attempted to horizontally restore by indemnity the 40-year period in the wilderness which the Israelites, centering on Moses, spent in their third course of restoration into Canaan, by realizing his ideal of the temple. But, due to his faithlessness, this again ended in failure, and the 400-year period of preparation for the coming of the Messiah was set up, in order to restore this period as the horizontal period of indemnity, carried out vertically.

This period was again that in which to restore by indemnity, as the image time-identity, the 40-year period from Jacob's return from Haran into Canaan until he visited Egypt to meet Joseph, who had been sold by his brothers.

SECTION IV
The Formation and Length of
Each Period in the Providential Age of the
Prolongation of Restoration

The providential age of the prolongation of restoration is that in which it is possible to restore by indemnity, as the substantial time-identity, the providential age of restoration, which is the age of image time-identity. Therefore, in this age, each unit of time and its length forming the providential age of restoration is restored by indemnity.

1. THE FOUR HUNDRED YEAR PERIOD OF PERSECUTION BY THE ROMAN EMPIRE

Jesus came to fulfill the will for Abraham, the father of faith. We know that the Israelites had separated themselves from

Satan through their 400 years of slavery in Egypt in order to restore by indemnity, on the nationwide base, the foundation of faith which Abraham had failed to establish, due to his mistake in the symbolic offering.

Likewise, the Christians had to endure a period similar to the period of slavery in Egypt, in order to restore by indemnity the foundation of faith left unaccomplished, due to the Jewish people's failure in offering Jesus as a living sacrifice. This was the reason for the 400-year period of persecution by the Roman Empire. In 313 A.D. after bitter persecution by the Roman Empire, the Emperor Constantine publicly recognized Christianity. In 392 A.D. Theodocius I declared Christianity as the state religion. Therefore, this period was that in which to restore by indemnity, as substantial time-identity, the 400-year period of the Israelites' slavery in Egypt out of the period of the image time-identity.

2. THE FOUR HUNDRED YEAR PERIOD OF CHRISTIAN CHURCHES UNDER THE PATRIARCHAL SYSTEM

The 400-year period of Judges occurred in the period of the providence of restoration, the period of the image time-identity. During this period the people of Israel were ruled by the Judges. Therefore, during the providential age for the prolongation of restoration, the period of substantial time-identity, there also had to occur the period in which to restore by indemnity this 400-year period of Judges. This was actually the 400-year period of Christian churches under the patriarchal system, in which the people were led by the Patriarchs, corresponding to the Judges. It lasted from the time when Christianity had been publicly recognized by the Roman Empire as the national religion, until the time of the enthronement of the Emperor Charlemagne in 800 A.D. Therefore, this period was that in which to restore by indemnity, as the substantial time-identity, the 400-year period of Judges out of the period of the image time-identity.

3. THE ONE HUNDRED AND TWENTY YEAR PERIOD OF THE CHRISTIAN KINGDOM

In the providential age of restoration, the people of Israel established a kingdom for the first time, centering on King Saul. After that, they formed the period of the United Kingdom for 120 years from King Saul through King David and King Solomon. Accordingly, in order to restore this age by indemnity, the period of the Christian Kingdom came about. It covered the 120 years from the enthronement of the Emperor Charlemagne in 800 A.D., until his royal heritage ceased, and Henry I was elected as King of Germany in 919 A.D. Therefore, this period was that which restored by indemnity, as the substantial time-identity, the 120-year period of the United Kingdom, out of the period of the image time-identity.

4. THE FOUR HUNDRED YEAR PERIOD OF THE DIVIDED KINGDOMS OF EAST AND WEST

During the period of the United Kingdom in the period of the providence of restoration, the holy temple failed to stand in God's will. Finally the kingdom was divided into North and South, thus beginning the 400-year period of the divided kingdoms. Therefore, in the providential age for the prolongation of restoration also, there had to occur a period to restore this period by indemnity.

This was the 400-year period of the divided kingdoms of East and West, which lasted from the time when the period of the Christian Kingdom was finished until the Vatican moved to Avignon in Southern France in 1309. At first the Christian Kingdom was divided into the three kingdoms of the East

Franks, West Franks and Italy. But, since Italy was under the rule of the East Franks, who had succeeded the Holy Roman Empire, the kingdom was in fact divided into two kingdoms of East and West. Therefore, this period served to restore by indemnity, as the substantial time-identity, the 400-year period of the divided kingdoms of North and South, out of the period of the image time-identity.

5. THE TWO HUNDRED AND TEN YEAR PERIOD OF PAPAL CAPTIVITY AND RETURN

During the period of the divided kingdoms of North and South, the idol-worshipping Northern Kingdom of Israel was destroyed by Assyria, and the Southern Kingdom of Judah also fell into faithlessness and failed to rebuild the ideal of the temple. Therefore, 210 years elapsed from the time when the Jews were taken captive in Babylon, the Satanic world, until they again set up the temple after their return. Consequently, in order to restore this period by indemnity, there came about the 210-year period of papal captivity and return. It lasted from the time when Pope Clement V moved the Holy See in 1309 from Rome to Avignon in Southern France, until the popes returned to Rome and later saw the religious revolution in 1517. Therefore, this period served to restore by indemnity, as the substantial time-identity, the 210-year period of the Jewish captivity and their return, out of the period of the image time-identity.

6. THE FOUR HUNDRED YEAR PERIOD OF PREPARATION FOR THE SECOND ADVENT OF THE MESSIAH

The Jewish people, who returned to Jerusalem after their liberation from captivity in Babylon, rose in action for the renewal of the politics and religion, centering on Malachi the prophet. According to his prophecy (Mal. 4:5), they began to make preparation to receive the Messiah; and, after the 400-year period, they finally received the Messiah.

Therefore, in order to restore the period by indemnity, even in the providential age of the prolongation of restoration, there had to be a 400-year period, from the time when the religious revolution broke out in 1517, centering on Luther after the Pope had returned to Rome from his imprisonment in Avignon, before we can ever receive the Lord of the Second Advent. This period is the period of preparation for the Second Advent of the Messiah. Therefore, this period serves to restore by indemnity, as the substantial time-identity, the 400-year period of preparation for the coming of the Messiah, out of the period of the image time-identity.

Chart of the Age of Providential Time-Identity

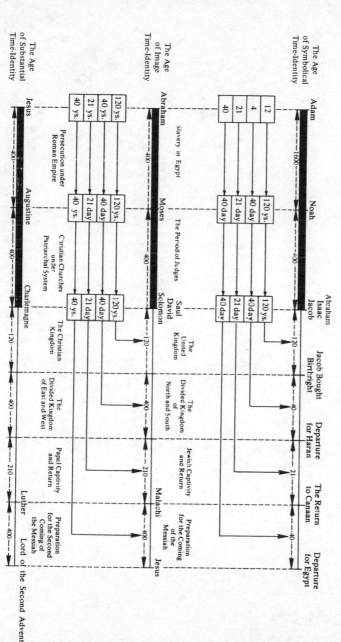

Providential Age of Restoration and Age of the Prolongation of Restoration from the Standpoint of Providential Time-Identity

As already stated above, the purpose of the providence of restoration is ultimately to establish the foundation to receive the Messiah. Therefore, as the providence is prolonged, the providence to restore that foundation must repeat itself. Meanwhile, in order to establish the foundation to receive the Messiah, first, the central figure in the providence of restoration must set up the foundation of faith by offering symbolic sacrifices, acceptable to God, by using certain conditional objects, during certain periods of time; second, he must establish the foundation of substance by offering substantial sacrifices, acceptable to God, after laying the condition of indemnity to remove the fallen nature.

Therefore, the course of the providence of restoration, the repetition of the providence to restore the foundation to receive the Messiah, was, after all, the repetition of the providence to restore, by indemnity, the symbolic offering and the substantial offering. Consequently, the age of the providential time-identity, formed by the repetition of the providential course to restore the foundation to receive the Messiah, was, after all, formed by the historical facts in the providence to restore, by indemnity, the two offerings mentioned above.

Let us now study the character of each providential age in accordance with such principles. To grasp the character of the age, we need an understanding of the central nation in charge of the providence, and the central historical sources concerning it. The history of mankind has been formed by the histories of numerous nations. Meanwhile, God, by choosing a special nation from among all the nations, and having it walk the typical providential course of restoration to establish the foundation to receive the Messiah, directs the chosen nation to be the center of His providence and to lead the history of mankind. The nation chosen for such a mission is called the "nation of God's elect," or "God's chosen people."

The nation of God's elect consisted originally of the descendants of Abraham, who established the family-level foundation to receive the Messiah. Therefore, the central nation, having fulfilled God's providence in the providential age of restoration, was Israel, the chosen nation. Therefore, the history of the Israelite nation becomes the historical material of the providential history of restoration in this age.

However, after the Israelites had delivered Jesus to his crucifixion, they lost their qualifications as the chosen nation. Jesus, who foresaw this, once told them so in the parable of the vineyard, and concluded, ". . . the Kingdom of God will be taken away from you and given to a nation producing the fruits of it." (Matt. 21:43) Paul also said that not all who are descended from Israel belong to Israel, but the people of God's will and promise are the "Israel." (Rom. 9:6-8) In reality, the central nation, which has fulfilled the dispensation of the providential age of the prolongation of restoration beginning with Jesus, has not been the Israelite nation, but the Christians, who inherited God's providence of restoration left unaccomplished. Consequently, Christian history becomes the historical source for the providential history of restoration in this age. In that sense, if we call Abraham's lineal posterity of the Old Testament Age the "First Israel," the Christians of the New Testament Age may be called the "Second Israel."

When we compare the Old Testament with the New Testament, the five books of law (Genesis to Deuteronomy), twelve books of history (Joshua to Esther), five books of verses (Job to the Song of Solomon) and seventeen books of prophecy (Isaiah to Malachi) in the Old Testament correspond to the Gospels, Acts, Letters of the Apostles, and Revelation, respectively. However, in the books of history of the Old Testament, the whole 2000-year history of the "First Israel" is recorded while, in Acts of the New Testament, only the history of the "Second Israel" (Christians) of Jesus' day is written. In order to study and comprehend the divine providence of God from the time of Jesus to the present, we must refer to the history of Christianity as a source of reference, in addition to "Acts" of the New Testament. Therefore, Christian history becomes the historical source which comprises the providential history of restoration after Jesus. By comparing the characters of each period which has formed the providential age of restoration, and the providential age of the prolongation of restoration, connected by the time-identity centering on the histories of the "First Israel" and the "Second Israel," we can understand more clearly that human history has been created according to a consistent, formal providence of the living God.

SECTION I

The Period of Slavery in Egypt and the Period of Persecution by the Roman Empire

The 400-year period from Noah to Abraham was invaded by Satan, because of Abraham's failure in the offering. Therefore, during the period of slavery in Egypt, to restore by indemnity this 400-year period, the posterity of Jacob were miserably persecuted by the Egyptians for the 400 years after he and the 70 kinsmen, centering on his 12 sons, had entered Egypt. In the period of the persecution under the Roman Empire to restore this period by indemnity, the 12 apostles, the 70 disciples, and the Christians centering on Jesus, because of his crucifixion, had to undergo miserable persecution by the Roman Empire for 400 years in order to restore, by indemnity, the 400-year period of preparation for the coming of the Messiah which had been invaded by Satan.

In the period of slavery in Egypt, the First Israel, the chosen nation, separated itself from Satan, who invaded because of Abraham's failure in the offering, by circumcising (Ex. 4:25), offering sacrifices (Ex. 5:3), and keeping the Sabbath (Ex. 16:23). Therefore, during the period of persecution by the Roman Empire also, the Second Israel, the chosen nation, had to separate itself from Satan by performing the Sacraments of Holy Communion and Baptism, offering the saints as living sacrifices, and keeping the Sabbath.

After the 400-year period of slavery in Egypt had ended, Moses subjugated Satan by the powers of the three great miracles and ten calamities, and headed for the land of Canaan, leading the First Israel, the chosen nation, out of Egypt. Likewise, in the period of persecution by the Roman Empire, after the 400-year persecution of the Second Israel ended, Jesus influenced Emperor Constantine spiritually, and moved him to recognize Christianity publicly in 313, and finally could have Theodocius I declare Christianity the national religion.

In this way, Christians came to be restored, spiritually, into Canaan, out of the Satanic world. In the Old Testament Age in which God had worked His providence by external conditions of indemnity, according to the law, God subjugated Pharaoh by giving Moses external miracles and signs. But, since the New Testament Age is the period in which God worked His providence with internal conditions of indemnity, according to the Word, God then worked through spiritual reformation.

After the period of slavery in Egypt had ended, Moses set up the center of the Old Testament by receiving the Ten Commandments and words on Mount Sinai. By receiving the tablets of stone, the tabernacle and the ark of the covenant, the First Israel, the chosen nation, came to set up the will to receive the Messiah. Likewise, after the period of persecution by the Roman Empire, the Second Israel, the chosen nation, decided on the New Testament by collecting the records of the apostles as the words to fulfill spiritually the Ten Commandments and the ideal of the temple of the Old Testament Age. They thus broadened the ground to receive the Lord of the Second Advent by establishing churches centering on the words. In the period after the coming of Jesus, Jesus and the Holy Spirit have been leading Christians directly, so God has not set up any one person as the central figure of the whole providence, substituting for God, as He did in the previous period of providence.

SECTION II
The Period of Judges and the Period of
Christian Churches under the Patriarchal System

The period of Judges is the 400-year period in which the 15 judges including 12 judges beginning with Othniel and the succeeding three (Samson, Eli and Samuel) were guiding the Israelites. These judges were each filling multiple functions as prophet, chief priest, and king, which were shared by several individuals in the next period. Therefore, the feudal society of Judaism began from that time. In the period of Christian churches under the patriarchal system of the New Testament Age, the patriarchs held duties corresponding to those of the judges in respect to leading the Christians.

In the period before Jesus, the patriarchs were establishing the foundation to receive the Messiah both spiritually and physically, centering on the First Israel. Therefore, the politics, economy, and religion of that time were under the guidance of a single leader. However, in the course after Jesus, they were creating the spiritual kingdom centering on Jesus, the spiritual King of Kings, on the spiritual foundation to receive the Messiah already established. Therefore, the Christian world or society as the "Second Israel" is a spiritual kingdom without land, with the resurrected Jesus as its king.

Since the patriarchs had the mission of the judges in erecting the spiritual kingdom, they had, at times, to become prophets, chief priests, or kings ruling the parish. As a result, the Christian feudal society began from this time.

In the period of the judges, after the Israelites, led by Joshua and Caleb, entered the blessed land of Canaan, they formed a new nation of God's elect, centering on the judges in the new land allotted to each tribe. Thus they established the foundation of the Israelite feudal society. Likewise, in the period of Christian churches under the patriarchal system, Christianity, after its liberation from the Roman Empire (the Satanic world), spread the gospel to the Germanic tribes, who had moved to Western Europe because of the invasion by the Huns in the 4th century. By setting up the Germanic people as a new people of God's elect in the new land of Western Europe, they established the foundation of the Christian feudal society.

We have already discussed in detail, in the section on the providence of restoration centering on Moses, the fact that, in the course of restoration into Canaan by the people of Israel, they set up the tabernacle as the symbolic being of the Messiah and at the same time as the conditional object substituting for Abel, in order to establish the foundation of substance. Therefore, the Israelite nation in the period of judges should have exalted the will of the tabernacle under the leadership of the Judges. But, by living among the seven tribes of Canaan without destroying them, the Israelites came to worship their idols after their evil customs, thus bringing about great chaos in their faith.

Likewise, in the period of Christian churches under the patriarchal system, the Christians should have exalted the will of the church as the image-entity of the Messiah, and, should have exalted it at the same time, as the conditional object substituting for Abel, under the leadership of the patriarchs. But, partially due to the influence of the many miscellaneous religions of the German people, there came about a great confusion in their faith.

SECTION III
The Period of the United Kingdom and the
Period of the Christian Kingdom

Upon entering the period of the United Kingdom, the period in which the judges led the First Israel was over. The prophets under direct command of God, the chief priests serving the tabernacle and the temple, and the king ruling the people were in a triangular position, each having to accomplish his leading mission centering on the purpose of the providence of restoration. Therefore, in the period of the Christian Kingdom, which restored this period by indemnity as the substantial time-identity also, the period of the patriarchs' leading the Second Israel was over; and the monasteries corresponding to the prophets, the popes corresponding to the chief priests, and the kings ruling the people had to lead the Second Israel, centering on the purpose of the providence of restoration. Christianity at that time was divided into the five great parishes of Jerusalem, Antioch, Alexandria, Constantinople, and Rome. The Roman patriarch, holding the superior position among them, was supervising other parishes, and he was called by the special title of "Pope."

In the period of the United Kingdom, Moses' "ideal of the tabernacle" presented itself as the "ideal of the temple," centering on the king, thus establishing a kingdom. This was the image-course, showing that in the future Jesus would come as the substantial temple, and erect a kingdom as a King of Kings (Is. 9:6). Likewise, in the period of the Christian Kingdom, the *City of God* written by St. Augustine as his Christian ideal at the time of the Christians' liberation from the Roman Empire, was at this time realized by the Emperor Charlemagne in the form of the Christian Kingdom which was the Kingdom of the Franks from the time of Emperor Charlemagne. This was the image-course, showing that in the future Christ would come again as King of Kings, and erect a kingdom. Therefore, in this period, the king and the pope should have realized the Christian ideal in perfect oneness centering on God's will. Thus, the spiritual kingdom without land established centering on the pope and the substantial kingdom centering on the king should have become one, centering on the Christian ideal. If so, at that time, religion, politics, and economy would have become one, and the foundation to receive the Messiah of the Second Advent would have been realized then.

The central figure to restore the foundation of faith in the period of the United Kingdom was the king, who was to realize God's Word, given by means of the prophets. Prophets and chief priests, being in the position of substituting for God's Word, would stand in the position of Abel in their age. However, in the course of the providence of restoration, they had to restore the substantial world from the position of the archangel, representing the spiritual world. Therefore, after having ordained a king on the spiritual foundation which they established for him, they had to stand in the position of Cain before him. Accordingly, the king must rule the nation according to the words of prophets, and the prophets must obey the king from their position as his subjects. Therefore, the central figure to restore the foundation of faith in this period was the king.

In reality, in the 800th year from Abraham, the prophet Samuel ordained Saul under God's command, making him the first king of the First Israel, the chosen nation of God (Sam. 8:19-22, 10:1-24). If King Saul, standing on the 400-year foundation of the period of judges, had accomplished his 40-year reign in a way acceptable to God, he could have stood in the position of having restored, by indemnity, the 400-year period of slavery in Egypt and Moses' 40-year period in Pharaoh's palace, thus being able to establish the foundation of faith on the 40-day foundation of separation from Satan. Accordingly, if Saul had erected the temple as the image of the Messiah on that foundation, and exalted it, he could have stood in the position of Moses, having succeeded in the first nationwide restoration of Canaan, finally erecting the temple and exalting it. Again, if the chosen people of Israel had absolutely obeyed the king, exalting the temple on the foundation of faith centering on King Saul, they could have established the foundation of substance, thus laying the foundation to receive the Messiah. However, King Saul, having rebelled against God's command, given through the prophet Samuel (I Sam. 15:1-23), failed to erect the temple. King Saul, who thus failed to erect the temple, was placed in the position of Moses, having failed in the first nation-wide restoration of Canaan.

In this way, the providence of restoration centering on King Saul was prolonged through the 40-year period of King David to the 40-year period of King Solomon. Just as Abraham's will had been realized at the time of Jacob after passing through that of Isaac, the will of erecting the temple by King Saul, who was also in the position of Abraham, was realized at the time of King Solomon after passing through that of King David. Nevertheless, since King Solomon left the position of Abel for the substantial offering by falling into lust, the foundation of substance became a failure. Accordingly, the foundation to receive the Messiah, which was to be established in the period of the United Kingdom, was also a failure.

In the period of the Christian Kingdom, all the conditions belonging to the period of the United Kingdom had to be restored by indemnity, as substantial time-identity. Therefore, the central figure to restore by indemnity the foundation of faith of this period was the king, who was to realize the Christian ideal of the monastery and the pope. The pope was in the position of the chief priest, who had exalted the will of the prophets in the period of the United Kingdom. Therefore, after having ordained the king on the spiritual foundation he had set up for the king to realize the Christian ideal, he had to obey the king from the position of his subject, while the king had to rule the people by exalting the pope's ideal. In reality, for this purpose of the providence, Pope Leo III ordained and crowned Emperor Charlemagne in 800 A.D., thus making him the first king of the Second Israel, "the chosen nation of God."

Emperor Charlemagne, who stood on the 400-year foundation of the period of Christian churches under the patriarchal system, having restored by indemnity the 400-year period of judges as substantial time-identity, now stood on the 40-day foundation of separation from Satan like King Saul. Consequently, the foundation of faith of this period was supposed to be established when Emperor Charlemagne practiced the Christian ideal by exalting the words of Christ on this foundation. In reality, Emperor Charlemagne could establish this foundation by becoming king, ordained by the pope. Therefore, if the Second Israel of that time had absolutely trusted and obeyed the king, standing in such a position, the foundation of substance could have been established then, and the foundation to receive the Messiah of the Second Advent also could have been accomplished. By doing this, the spiritual kingdom which was established centering on the Pope and the substantial kingdom centering on the king could have become one on the spiritual foundation to receive the Messiah, and the Lord could have come again on that foundation, thus establishing the kingdom of the Messiah. Nevertheless, the king left Abel's position of offering the substantial sacrifice, by failing to exalt God's will, and the foundation of substance was not established. Accordingly, the foundation to receive the Messiah of the Second Advent was also a failure.

SECTION IV
The Period of the Divided Kingdoms of North and South and the Period of the Divided Kingdoms of East and West

The period of the United Kingdom began with King Saul and continued through King David and King Solomon. But because

King Solomon worshipped the gentile gods that his wives had been worshipping (I Kings 11:4-9), it was divided after three generations into the Northern Kingdom of Israel, centering on the ten tribes in the position of Cain, and the Southern Kingdom of Judah, centering on the two tribes in the position of Abel. Thus came the period of the divided kingdoms of North and South.

Likewise, the Christian Kingdom, established by Emperor Charlemagne, also was divided into three—the East Franks, the West Franks, and Italy—at the third generation because his three grandsons quarreled with one another. However, since Italy was under the rule of the East Franks, it was actually divided into East and West. Meanwhile, the East Franks rose greatly under King Otto I, calling themselves the Holy Roman Empire. The Empire ruled over West Europe in the name of the Roman Emperor, trying to secure both political and religious power. Thus the East Franks stood in the position of Abel against the West Franks.

The Northern Kingdom of Israel, centering on Jeroboam, the exile from the Kingdom of Solomon, had 19 kings in 260 years. Through their killing one another, the royal families changed 9 times, and not one king was righteous. Consequently, God destroyed 850 prophets of Baal and Ashera by showering fires over the altar on Mount Carmel through the prophet Elijah, sent from the Southern Kingdom of Judah (I Kings 18:19-40). He also sent many other prophets like Elisha, Jonah, Hosea and Amos, having them evangelize at the risk of their lives. Nevertheless, the Northern Kingdom of Israel continued to worship evil spirits without repenting, so God delivered them into the hands of Assyrians to be destroyed. They were completely deprived of the qualification of God's elect for eternity (II Kings 17:17-23).

Meanwhile, the Southern Kingdom of Judah, centering on Rehoboam, the Son of Solomon, continued from King David to

King Zedekiah in one orthodox line, producing many righteous kings out of the 20 who ruled for 394 years. After King Josiah, many unrighteous kings appeared in succession and, by falling into idol worship influenced by the Northern Kingdom, they were taken captive to Babylon.

Whenever the people of Israel stood in the position contrary to the ideal of the temple, God continued to send prophets, four major and twelve minor ones in all, encouraging them to arouse movements of internal reformation. However, the people did not repent, even at the prophets' advice, and God had to work His providence of external chastisement by delivering them into the hands of the Gentiles, such as Chaldea, Syria, and Babylon.

In the period of the divided kingdoms of East and West, which restored this period by indemnity as substantial time-identity, the Vatican was corrupted; and renowned monastics, such as Thomas Aquinas, St. Bernard and St. Francis, aroused the movement of internal reformation by giving advice. However, the rulers still tended to fall and be corrupted without repentance, and God worked His providence of external purge by delivering them into the hands of the Gentiles. This was the providence behind the Crusades. When the Holy Land of Jerusalem belonged to the Caliph, the Christian pilgrims were received with hospitality. But after the occupation of Jerusalem by the Seljuk Turks upon the fall of the Caliphate, they were persecuted, and the successive kings, in rage, raised the Crusades to restore the Holy Land. The Crusades, which began in 1096, had seven expeditions in about 200 years, but they were defeated again and again.

In the period of the divided kingdoms of North and South, the peoples of the Northern Kingdom of Israel and the Southern Kingdom of Judah were all taken captive by the Gentiles. Thus the autocratic society of Israel finally collapsed. Likewise, in the period of the divided kingdoms of East and

West, the papal power completely lost its authority and supremacy with the defeat of the Crusades, and the national spirit lost its center. Besides, due to the deaths of the many feudal lords and knights who maintained the feudal society, the people lost their political base. Also, the tremendous amount of war expenditures as a result of the repeated loss of battles left them utterly impoverished. At this point, the Christian autocratic society finally began to collapse.

SECTION V

The Period of Jewish Captivity and Return and the Period of Papal Captivity and Return

The Jewish people, by falling into faithlessness without repentance, failed to restore the ideal of the temple. Therefore, in order to fulfill this will again, God allowed the Jewish people to be taken captive into Babylon, the Satanic world, to suffer slavery there just as He had let the Israelites go into Egypt, the Satanic world, to suffer slavery in order to restore by indemnity the failure of Abraham in his offering.

Likewise, as already discussed above, God established the period of the Christian Kingdom in order to build the Kingdom of the Messiah. This kingdom could be built by establishing the foundation to receive the Messiah of the Second Advent, centering on the pope and the king, and by handing over the throne and the kingdom to the King of Kings who would come again as the Messiah on that foundation (Is. 9:6, Luke 1:33). But the kings and the popes who were to establish the spiritual foundation on which to set up the king as the central figure of the foundation of substance, fell into corruption without ever repenting. They therefore failed to establish the foundation to receive the Messiah of the Second Advent. God, in order to work anew His providence of restoring this foundation, allowed the Pope to be taken captive and suffer slavery.

In the period of the Jewish captivity and return, there was the 70-year period in which King Jehoiakim, Daniel, and other members of royalty, together with the ministers of the government, officials, craftsmen, and many other Jewish people, were taken captive by Nebuchadnezzar the king of Babylon (Jer. 39:1-10, II Chron. 36:11-23, II Kings 24 and 25). There was also the 140-year period which lasted from the time of the Jews' liberation by King Cyrus' royal decree after Persia had destroyed Babylon until the time when they could return to their land for the third time to set themselves up as the nation centering on the prophet Malachi to prepare for the Messiah. In the period of papal captivity and return, which restored this period by indemnity as substantial time-identity, they had to walk a similar course.

Because of their immorality, popes and priests gradually lost the confidence of the people. The defeat of the Crusades also resulted in the collapse of papal authority. Meanwhile, after the Crusades, the feudal system collapsed, and the modern state was established. With gradual expansion of the royal power, the conflict between pope and king became violent. Thus Pope Boniface VIII came into conflict with the French King Philip IV, and was even imprisoned by him for a time. One generation later, Clement V, who was elected as pope in 1305, moved the Vatican from Rome to Avignon of Southern France in 1309. There the successive popes lived as captives for 70 long years, under the restraint of the French kings. After that, Pope Gregory XI returned to Rome in 1377.

After his death, the cardinals elected Urban VI, the Archbishop of Bari in Italy, as Pope. However, the cardinals, being mostly Frenchmen, repelled Urban VI before long and set up another Vatican in Avignon of Southern France by electing Clement VII as Pope. This division continued until the next century, when the reformation council solved the problem. The cardinals held a conference in Pisa, Italy, in 1409 and dismissed both popes, designating Alexander V as the lawful Pope. However, the two popes opposed the dismissal, and the three popes stood in triangular positions for the time being. Afterwards, they held the General Council of Constance, with many members present, such as the Bishops and Archbishops, including theologians, royalty, and envoys, and dismissed the three popes at once, electing Martin V as Pope.

Thus the cardinals were deprived of their right to elect the pope, and it was shifted to that conference, which insisted upon holding the sovereign power of the Roman Church (1418). This conference was later held in Basel, Switzerland, for the purpose of making the organization of the Roman Church into the body of a constitutional monarchy. Nevertheless, the pope did not like the idea of the congregation having the controlling power. Not only was he not present at the conference, but he even tried to adjourn the meeting. Despite the fact, the assembly members held the meeting, but it was automatically dismissed in 1449. Thus, the plan to establish the body of a constitutional monarchy in the Roman Church came to naught, and absolute papal monarchy, lost since 1309, restored its function.

Leaders of many conferences held in the 14th century tried to remove the corrupted popes and priests by setting up the laymen as representatives and giving this conference the supreme power and authority. Nevertheless, the papal power resumed the status prior to the popes' imprisonment, and they condemned to capital punishment all the leaders of the Reformation, such as Wycliffe and Huss. It was from this moment that the Protestant movement of Religious Reformation began to spread. Thus, the period of approximately 210 years from the time when the pope was taken captive into Avignon in 1309 A.D. until the Religious Reformation took place in 1517, centering on Luther, was the period in which to restore by indemnity, as the substantial time-identity, the 210-year period from the time of the Jewish captivity for 70 years in Babylon until they aroused both political and religious reformation centering on Malachi.

SECTION VI
The Period of Preparation for the Coming of the Messiah and the Period of Preparation for the Second Coming of the Messiah

The Israelites received Jesus only after the 400-year period of preparation for the coming of the Messiah, after their return to Jerusalem from Babylon. Therefore, in order to restore this by indemnity, Christians also can receive the Lord of the Second Advent only after the 400-year period of preparation for the Second Coming of the Messiah, which began with the Pope's return to Rome from his life of captivity in Avignon.

The vertical condition of indemnity for the 4000-year history of the providence of restoration since Adam, in which the providence to restore the foundation of faith through the 40-day period of separation from Satan was prolonged again and again by continual invasion of Satan, was to be restored by indemnity horizontally in this final period of providential history. For this, there came the period of preparation for the coming of the Messiah. Therefore, in order to restore this period, by indemnity, as the substantial time-identity, there must be the period of preparation for the Second Coming of the Messiah in which to restore by indemnity, horizontally, in this final period of providential history, the vertical condition of indemnity for the 6000-year history of the providence of restoration since Adam.

The Israelites, who had returned from their captivity in Babylon, were restoring the foundation of faith by erecting the temple destroyed by King Nebuchadnezzar and by studying the law, thus arousing the movement of reformation in their faith under the guidance of the prophet Malachi, in repentance of their past sin of having worshipped evil spirits. Likewise, the medieval Christians after the pope's return to Rome were restoring the foundation of faith by arousing the movement of religious reformation centering on Luther, and by pioneering a new way of faith, according to the light of the gospel, breaking through the gloom of the medieval Dark Ages.

The period of preparation for the coming of the Messiah was the period in which to restore by indemnity as the image time-identity, the approximately 40 years of preparation period, from the time of Jacob's return from Haran to Canaan until his entering into Egypt. The period of preparation for the Second Coming of the Messiah is the period in which to restore this period by indemnity, as the substantial time-identity.

Accordingly, all the Christians of this age had to walk the way of many hardships and tribulations, just like Jacob's family until they met Joseph in Egypt, or the Israelites until they met Jesus. Since the providential age of restoration was the age in which to set up the faith toward God by the external conditions of the Law and offerings, the First Israel, in the period of preparation for the coming of the Messiah, walked the way of external tribulations under the rule of the Gentile nations such as Persia, Greece, Egypt, Syria, and Rome. However, since the providential age of the prolongation of restoration was the period in which to set up faith toward God by the internal conditions of prayer and faith centering on Jesus' words, the Second Israel, in the period of preparation for the Second Coming of the Messiah, had to walk the way of internal tribulations. In this period, as a result of humanism, which was the leading ideology of Renaissance (the ideology of Enlightenment following it), and the freedom of faith propagated after the Religious Reformation, religion and ideology experienced a great chaos. Also, the Christians had to suffer unspeakable internal trials.

Thus, in order to restore by indemnity, as the substantial time-identity, the 400-year period of preparation for the coming of the Messiah, the 400-year period of preparation for the Second Coming of the Messiah came about. Let us here study how the background and environment were formed in each of the two periods which were the preparation periods to receive the Messiah.

At the time of the first coming of the Messiah, God sent the prophet Malachi to His chosen nation 430 years in advance, having him prophesy the coming of the Messiah. He reformed Judaism, preparing Israel as the chosen nation to receive the Messiah. Meanwhile, among the Gentiles, at about the same time, God had Gautama Buddha of India (565-485 B.C.) pioneer a new base for Buddhism by improving Hinduism, and had Socrates of Greece (470-399 B.C.) pioneer the period of Hellenic culture. In the Orient, He had Confucius (552-479 B.C.) set up human ethics and morality through Confucianism, thus having them establish the culture and religion suitable for the place and people in order that they may make necessary spiritual preparation to receive the coming Messiah. Jesus, coming on this prepared basis, intended to unify all the regions of various religions and cultures into one sphere of Christian culture by absorbing and winning over Judaism, Hellenism, Buddhism, Confucianism, and all the rest of the religions.

The period of the Renaissance occurred in order to restore by indemnity, as the substantial time-identity, the period of making the environment which God provided to prepare for the coming of the Messiah, when his coming was imminent. Therefore, the period of the Renaissance served to establish the background and environment of the period for the Second Coming of the Messiah. Accordingly, the rapid progress in politics, economy, culture, science and all other aspects of human endeavor as we see today began abruptly in the period of the Renaissance. This progress developed the background and environment of the period so that we may today receive the Messiah. In Jesus' day, the vast political territory formed around the Mediterranean Sea by the rise of the Roman Empire with its ease of communication in any direction and the vast cultural territory formed centering on the Hellenic language could establish the level foundation on which to be able to expand rapidly the idea of the Messiah—from Israel centering on Christ, to Rome centering on Israel, and then to the world centering on Rome.

Likewise, since today is the day of the Second Coming, the democratic political sphere, based on freedom, is covering almost every corner of the earth with the rise of the great powers. The distance between East and West is extremely shortened owing to the rapid progress in transportation and communication, and due to the free interchange of languages and cultures, the ideology for the Second Advent of the Messiah can freely and swiftly flow into the hearts of all mankind. All these are the level territory perfectly provided by God. There is no question of this becoming the best foundation on which to make the truth and ideology of the Messiah worldwide within the shortest possible time by rapidly spreading it, when the Lord of the Second Advent comes.

SECTION VII
The Development of History from the Standpoint of the Providence of Restoration

As already discussed in the "Principle of Creation," the Kingdom of Heaven on earth is a world made in the image of a perfected man. In consequence, the fallen world may be regarded as an image of fallen man. Therefore, we can understand the movement in the whole of mankind's sinful history by observing the life of fallen man.

We cannot deny the fact that fallen man possesses the original mind headed for good and the evil mind headed for bad in rebellion against the commands of the original mind, constantly at war with each other. Nor can we deny that the good deeds following the commands of the original mind and the bad deeds following the commands of the evil mind are in conflict with one another in one body. Thus, human society, where the individual bodies which have bitter fights going on in themselves live in disharmonized horizontal relationships, is a society of struggle and conflict. Meanwhile, human history is nothing other than men's social lives interwoven with struggles flowing down vertically and experiencing constant change as time goes by. Naturally, this history must necessarily unfold with struggles and wars.

Nevertheless, man is ever struggling in the midst of the persistent fight between his original mind and his evil mind to follow goodness by repelling evil. Accordingly, his deeds also assume the direction of good conduct gradually by resisting bad conduct. Even in the fallen man there is the original mind in action heading for good. Therefore, he can participate in God's providence of restoration, fulfilling by degrees the purpose of goodness.

Consequently, it is evident that history made by such men, has been heading for good by repelling evil, even in the vortex of the mixture of good and evil. Therefore, the ultimate world for which history is headed can be none other than the Kingdom of Heaven in which the purpose of goodness is realized. So we must understand the fact that struggles and wars are also phenomena in the course of separating good from evil, in order to fulfill the purpose of goodness. Therefore, though at times the battle may result in the temporary triumph of evil, history, after all, will be changed into the providential course of fulfilling the purpose of greater good. From this viewpoint, we may understand the fact that human history has developed toward good by constantly repeating its action of separation of good from evil, according to God's providence of restoration.

Meanwhile, due to man's lineal relationship with Satan, Satan has realized in advance, centering on fallen men, the type of world similar to that which God intends to realize in the future. As a result, human history has formed a non-principled world in the pseudo-form of the Principle. Consequently, at the close of the sinful history of mankind, the non-principled world in the pseudo-form of the Principle, centering on Satan, will be realized before God will restore the Kingdom of Heaven on earth; this is the world of communism. Thus, Satan realizes, in a non-principled way prior to God, what God intends to realize. We see from this that in the providential course of restoration, false things present themselves in the form of true ones before the true ones appear. The Bible verses prophesying the appearance of the false Christ before the coming of the true one can be elucidated only by such a principle.

1. THE DEVELOPMENT OF HISTORY IN THE PROVIDENTIAL AGE OF RESTORATION

The society first formed by fallen men was a primitive collective society. This was a society in which men fulfilled each other's needs, centering on Satan. This was what Satan realized in a non-principled way in advance of the collective-cooperative society which God intended to realize centering on perfected men. If there were no struggles and divisions in such a society of Satan, it would continue forever, and God's providence of restoration would never be realized.

Nevertheless, as explained above, there are two minds at war in every fallen man and this conflict within the mind, appearing in men's actions, would create conflicts between individuals. Therefore, the primitive collective society could not maintain peace. Moreover, as that society developed into a society in which the financial interests of the people mutually differed, the struggle has naturally developed to a greater scale. Thus, by the action of the original mind of man which tended toward taking part in God's providence of restoration, division was created through the fights from the early days of primitive collective society centering on Satan.

Seeing the course of the development of the sinful history of mankind centering on Satan, we find that following the primitive collective society, the clan society was formed, and feudal society grew out of that. Feudal society finally expanded its territory and sovereignty to form a monarchic society. This is because God intended to call good individuals out of the sinful world and establish a clan society of goodness centering on them, next forming a good feudal society which would finally become the kingdom of goodness with its territory and sovereignty of goodness able to receive the Messiah. Satan, knowing this in advance, walked such a course ahead of God.

In reality, God called Abraham out of such a sinful world to be the center of goodness. By having him multiply offspring with the capacity of serving God's will, He established the Israelite clan society. Later, the descendants of Abraham went into Egypt and developed there from a clan to a tribe. After their return to Canaan, they formed a period of Judges, and the society centering on the Judges was the Israelite feudal society. Why then do we call it a feudal society? The primary characteristics of a feudal society are, first, its political system with the relationship of master and servant, on the assumption of the latter's serving and obeying the former; and second, its economic system of self-supply within the territory of the blockade. The period of Judges formed a society with these characteristics. That is, a portion of land was allocated to each tribe of the Israelite nation which had returned into the land of Canaan, and the tribes formed a feudal society, centering on the Judge, who was in the position of a feudal lord. Therefore, we call this the Israelite feudal society.

The character of the feudal society compelled its people to obey, in absolute submission, the ideology and leadership of their feudal lord. Accordingly, as long as their lord stood in God's will, the people naturally stood on the side of God. In addition, being in such a relationship, they could live in circumstances in which they suffered no Satanic invasion. Consequently, the significance of the clan society's having developed into feudal society was to prevent Satanic invasion by taking Satan's possession back to the Heavenly side and forming greater territory belonging to divine sovereignty. Since this is God's providence, Satan counter-planned in order to maintain his sovereignty by forming a Satanic feudal society in advance, since he was aware of God's will.

Meanwhile, the feudal society came in order to establish the foundation for the monarchic society with greater sovereignty and territory. That is, with the Israelite feudal society, God formed small units of territory with their sovereignty, people, and economy belonging to the Heavenly side, able to prevent Satanic invasion. Then, in order to strengthen and expand into greater heavenly sovereignty for its people and territory, by uniting the small units of territory, there came the Israelite monarchic society, which was the period of the United Kingdom, beginning with King Saul.

As already mentioned, Jesus came as the King of Kings, in all respects (Rev. 11:15). Therefore, God formed the Israelite monarchic society in order to provide the foundation on which the Messiah could come and reign as King of Kings.

God intended to establish the Israelite monarchic society under this providence, so Satan attempted to prevent God's providence by forming a monarchic society, centering on him, ahead of God. Therefore, we see that before the period of the United Kingdom, the kingdom of Egypt erected its first dynasty on the side of Satan more than twenty centuries before Christ; this kingdom lasted for 30 dynasties. The ancient kingdom of Babylon had already unified the whole of Mesopotamia at the time of King Hamurabi in the 18th century B.C.; and the kingdom of the Hittites became the greatest power in the East centering on Syria in the 14th century B.C. Thus in the Satanic world, according to the action of the original mind of man in correlation to God's providence, a kingdom higher in standard of goodness and another more evil fought constantly, resulting in the separation of good and evil. Therefore, if at that time King Solomon had served God's will to the end, he could have unified all the Eastern countries by showing his excellent political ability, after having absorbed the three great civilizations of Egypt, Mesopotamia, and Crete (Minoan). Further, he could have formed a worldwide territory enabling the Messianic ideal to be realized. However, due to the fall of King Solomon, God had to work His providence of tearing down this monarchic society.

Thus, the kings of the period of the United Kingdom failed to provide the foundation on which to restore God's sovereignty by establishing the foundation of faith. Therefore, God finally divided the kingdom into those of North and South. God let the Northern kingdom be destroyed by the Gentile nation of Assyria (Assyria became the strongest, erecting the first "World Empire" by conquering the central part of the Mideast including Egypt in the 8th. century B.C.). When the Southern kingdom of Judah, having served God's will, soon rebelled against Him, God allowed it to fall into the hands of New Babylon (after the fall of the Empire of Assyria, the Chaldeans erected the kingdom of New Babylon or Kingdom of Chaldea with Babylon as its capital).

After the fall of the Kingdom of Judah, God kept the Jewish throne vacant until the coming of the Messiah by having the Jewish people belong to many gentile nations. Especially, by having the Jewish people belong to the sphere of Hellenic civilization, which was going to be the foundation of democracy, God provided a society of a democratic type (around his elect) so that later, if the Jewish people should receive the Messiah upon his coming, he might become their king, according to the will of the people. However, since the will of the Jewish people was to crucify Jesus instead of enthroning him, the purpose of God's 2000-year providence of restoration, which He intended to realize centering on Abraham's lineal descendants, was fulfilled only spiritually.

2. THE DEVELOPMENT OF HISTORY IN THE PROVIDENTIAL AGE OF THE PROLONGATION OF RESTORATION

(1) The Providence of Restoration and European History

The Roman Empire, which had persecuted Christianity, finally surrendered before the crucified Jesus at the end of the 4th century and decreed Christianity as its national religion. However, if in the beginning the Jewish people had become one in faith and service to Jesus as the Messiah, the ancient united world on the Mediterranean Sea, centering on the Roman

Empire, would necessarily have been moved and inspired by Jesus in his lifetime, and they would have erected a kingdom centering on Jerusalem, exalting Jesus as their king. However, due to the Israelites' faithlessness, the Jewish nation was destroyed, and the Roman Empire, which was to be the foundation for the kingdom of the Messiah, began to decline until in 476 Western Rome was destroyed by Odoacer, chieftain of Heruls. Thus, God's providence of restoration was shifted from Judea, the land of bitter grief, to West Europe, which was the territory of Western Rome. Accordingly, the spiritual providence of restoration by Christianity, after Jesus, has been accomplished with Western Europe as the basis. Therefore, the providential history of restoration of this age developed only in Western Europe. For this reason, the course of development of history discussed by historical materialism is applicable only to the history of Western Europe. In this way, the Christian history centering on Western Europe became the central historical source for the formation of the providential age of the prolongation of restoration.

(2) Mutual Relations Between the History of Religion, History of Economy, and History of Politics

We have already studied in the "Principle of Creation" that God created man with the dual aspects of physical man and spirit man in order to have him dominate the two worlds; namely, the visible world and invisible world. Therefore, if man had not fallen, his spirit man and physical man could have grown and been perfected together; and his intellect, both spiritual and physical, could have formed a perfect harmony at the same time in man's physical life. However, due to the fall, man fell into ignorance of both the spiritual side and the physical side. From this point, man's spiritual ignorance has been enlightened by religion while his ignorance of physical reality has been overcome by science, as already discussed (cf. Part I, Ch. III, Sec. V, 1).

As stated, man's spiritual ignorance has gradually been overcome as he searched for the invisible "world of cause" through religion. Since religion does not fulfill everyone's immediate needs, the development on the spiritual side may be active (by leaps) with specific persons, but it is usually very slow with the rest. We can see this from the fact that even today, when religion is popularized worldwide, there are many people whose spiritual aspect is no better than that of ancient men.

On the other hand, man's physical ignorance has been greatly overcome by the scientific research of the "world of result," the natural (or physical) world which is familiar to everyone. Science is of immediate necessity to everyone because it develops our everyday life. Therefore, the way out of the ignorance of physical reality is rapid and broad, and open to many. Thus, in religion, the object we search for is the invisible world of cause, which is transcendent, while in science we search for the visible world of result, which is tangible. Therefore, up to the present, religion and science have been in conflict with each other as forces which admit to no logical compromise. Besides, Satan, who is holding sovereignty over the world of creation, is constantly invading and undermining men in their everyday lives. Therefore, the way of religion, until now, has been thought to be something man cannot go through without abandoning his everyday life. Naturally, religion has not been in harmony with science, which is pursuing the benefit of the physical world. God originally created, first, man's physical body, which is external, and then his spirit, which is internal (Gen. 2:7). Therefore, as we will discuss precisely in Section I of the next chapter, His providence of restoration, according to the principle of re-creation, must also undergo the process of providence, from the external to the internal. Seen from such a principle of providence, it is evident that religion and science have trodden the course of development disharmonized with each other.

This kind of dissonance is also found in the relationship between religion and economy. That is because the economy, like science, belongs to the physical world, and it develops in an especially close relationship with the progress of science. Regarding this relationship, the history of religion is in accordance with God's internal providence, and the history of economy is in accordance with His external providence. However, religion and economy cannot help differing from each other in their direction and rate of developmental progress. Therefore, in order that we may grasp the development of history in Western Europe, which has undergone the course patterned after God's providence of restoration, we must study the history of Christianity and economy separately.

However, as in the case of religion and science, religion and the economy also cannot develop freely without a relationship, because these two have the divided missions to restore the internal and external lives of fallen men. Therefore, like religion and science, religion and economy have formed respective histories of Christianity and economy by their relationships with our social life, although they may have conflicted with each other in some aspects. Religion and economy relate to our social life through politics. This is especially evident in Western Europe, which was strongly Christianized. Politics in Western Europe should have harmonized through social life, the economic development following the radical development of science and the movement of Christianity, which had not yet been able to take any clear direction in the providence of restoration. Therefore, the political history of Western Europe headed for a new direction. Consequently, in order to grasp accurately the historical development for the providence of restoration, we must study separately the political history also. As an example, let us study the course of development of the history of Western Europe toward the end of the 17th century.

Seen from the history of religion, Christian democratic society was already formed in this period. With the collapse of the spiritual kingdom under the pope's absolute authority, which took place due to the Religious Reformation in 1517, medieval men were liberated from the life of faith, and their subjection to the pope, and everyone could lead the life of faith freely, centering on the Bible. However, politically, this period saw the rise of the absolute monarchic society, while seen from the aspect of the history of economy, the feudal society existed under the sytem of the manor. Thus the society in this period was a democratic society in the aspect of religion, a monarchic society in the aspect of politics, and a feudal society in the aspect of economy. So in order to grasp the character of this age from the viewpoint of the providence of restoration, we must consider their courses of development separately.

Then, we must know why the historical development in the period of the providence of restoration (the Old Testament Age) had not undergone such a process. In the ancient society, since science was at a standstill, the development of economics was stagnated. The Israelites of the Old Testament Age, when their mode of life was the same for all, led a simple life under a social system of the master-servant relationship in which they had to obey the strict law at the command of their leader. Therefore, their religious life was, actually, their social life. Accordingly, in this period, religion, politics, and economy could not enjoy separate development.

(3) The Clan Society

Let us now study the manner in which history developed, seen from the standpoints of religion, politics, and economics, in the providential age of the prolongation of restoration (New Testament Age).

We have already clarified above that the clan society on the Heavenly side was formed by the division of Satanic primitive collective society by the tendency of man's original mind in relation to God's providence of restoration, which brought about the separation of the men of God's will. Likewise, with the crucifixion of Jesus, God's chosen nation fell to Satan, and God could not work His providence of restoration with the society as it was. Consequently, God divided the society, and by calling upon devout Christians, He established the Christian clan society.

Just as in the Old Testament Age the 70 people centering on Jacob's 12 sons had started their providential course by forming the Israelite clan society, the 70 disciples and 12 apostles centering on Jesus started their providential course by forming the Christian clan society. Since the Christian clan society was a primitive Christian society, there was no need of any organized system in its politics and economy at that period. Accordingly, in this period, religion, politics and economy could not enjoy any separate development.

Christian clan society gradually prospered while being persecuted bitterly by the Roman Empire, finally forming Christian tribal society. Then, the Western Roman Empire fell at last in 476 A.D., due to the great movement of nations which began in the latter part of the 4th century. When Christianity spread among the German people, a vast Christian society was established.

(4) Feudal Society

Following the clan society in the course of development of history is the feudal society. Feudal society was born when, around the time of the fall of the Western Roman Empire, royal power diminished and nations fell into a state of disorder. From this time, Christian society of Western Europe began to have its religion, politics, and economy differentiated, each having its own separate course of development. Feudal society was made of a political system according to the master-servant relationship created among the major, middle, and minor feudal lords and the knights under the premise of obedience and service, and of the economic system of self-sufficiency of the manor system. The land was divided among the lords. The king, as one of the feudal lords, had his power decentralized. Each lord held possession of a certain allocation of land, granted by his king, and having his independent land, he could exercise even the authority of judicial right. In consequence, the land was almost like a private possession apart from the national power over it. Such private possession of land was called a manor.

Some lower grade nobility donated private lands to certain feudal lords or temples in order to be protected by the ruler, and they were given the land again in the form of loan. This was another type of manor. Thus, manors existed all over the country. Knights of the lowest class received an allocation of a manor, each serving his feudal lord as a private soldier, while the king or the lord possessed hundreds or even thousands of manors.

The religious aspect also developed toward the same direction as the feudal society discussed above, centering on Christianity. This is called Christian feudal society. That is, the patriarch, the archbishop, and the bishop had positions, each corresponding to a major lord, medium lord, and minor lord; just as the king was one of the feudal lords, the pope was also one of the patriarchs. There also was a religious type of governmental system under an absolute master-servant relationship. The bishops, possessing the feudal lands donated by the believers, were similar to the feudal lords, who enjoyed a powerful position among the many classes of feudal society.

Next, studied from the economic aspect, this period was that in which the ancient slavery system was shifted to the manor system. Accordingly, common people came to possess land from this time. Thus, the social position of the people under the land system of this period was separated roughly into four classes: the nobility, the yeoman, the serf and the slave.

In this way, God could provide the foundation in which to erect, later, the kingdom on the Heavenly side by establishing the feudal society around the Germanic people whom He had elected, and by strengthening the small units of heavenly territory in the three aspects of religion, politics, and economy on the foundation of the fallen Western Roman Empire.

(5) Monarchic Society and Imperialistic Society

Monarchic society came after the feudal society in the course of the development of history. Then, in what way was the monarchic society, seen from the political aspect of Western Europe, formed? Each of the states erected by the Germans who had moved into West Europe existed for a short period except the kingdom of the Franks, which continued for a long time. The Franks were a tribe of West Germans, who, after having established the Merovingian kingdom, united with Christianity. By absorbing Roman civilization, they formed in West Europe a Roman world with a Germanic heritage. After the fall of that kingdom, Charles Martel expanded his power by expelling the Moors, who had invaded in the southwest, while his son Pepin erected the Carolingian kingdom. Charlemagne, Pepin's son, who had thought highly of St. Augustine's theory of theocracy, intended to establish a monarchic nation with that theory as the national ideology as soon as he became king. Charlemagne established a powerful kingdom of the Franks by unifying Central Europe and stabilizing the security of West Europe, which was in chaos because of the great movement of the nations.

The Christian monarchic society that followed the Christian feudal society in the religious aspect was a society of the spiritual kingdom without land, established centering on the pope on the spiritual foundation to receive the Messiah. Pope Leo III ordained Charlemagne in 800 A.D., crowning him as the emperor and giving him the divine right. Thus, the spiritual kingdom which had been established centering on the pope, and the kingdom of the Franks which had been erected politically, united with each other and formed the Christian Kingdom.

The period of the Christian Kingdom was the period of time-identity with the period of the United Kingdom in the Old Testament Age. The purpose of the monarchic period's following the feudal period was to form a greater heavenly sovereignty for its people and its territory by uniting the feudal society. Accordingly, if the pope, who had been establishing the foundation to restore the substantial world from the standpoint of the archangel, had obeyed the king from the position of Cain after his blessing of the king, and if the king had established the Christian Kingdom completely in God's will by running the government to realize the Messianic ideal, following the pope's ideology, this very period could have become the Last Days, in which they could receive the Messiah. Thus, if the truth that could solve completely the conflicting problems of religion and science through one unified theme had appeared at that time, the foundation to receive the Messiah of the Second Advent could have been established then on that foundation through the religion, politics, and economy developing at that time toward a direction with one accord, centering on one ideology.

Therefore, the feudal society should have ended completely at that time with the coming of the period of the Christian

Kingdom. Nevertheless, since the popes and kings acted apart from God's will, the original ideal of Charlemagne failed to be realized and the strong foundation of the feudal system did not collapse, continuing until long after that. Accordingly, religion, politics, and economics were still separated from one another; the spiritual kingdom centering on the pope and the substantial kingdom centering on the king took contradictory positions, and separated.

In this way, Charlemagene, who had erected the kingdom on the foundation of the matured feudal system, could not tear down the barriers of feudalism. Therefore, he was, in fact, in the position of no more than a great feudal lord. The Christian Kingdom thus having failed to establish the kingdom capable of receiving the Messiah of the Second Advent, the feudal system was more and more strengthened; the feudal society of many classes in the aspect of politics, saw its prime until the rise of the society of absolute monarchy. As the feudal classes began to decline from the middle of the 17th century, the power of the feudal lords, which had been decentralized, was centralized around the king. In this way, the king, enthroned with "the divine right of kings" as his political ideology, came to enjoy absolute power. It may be regarded to have happened between the middle of the 17th century and the French Revolution in 1789 that the king actually formed the monarchic society in the political aspect, apart from the position of a feudal lord in the feudal class society.

Next, what was the consequence of the Christian monarchic society seen from the position of the history of religion? Since the popes of this age were secularized, without being able to stand in God's will, they gradually walked the way of spiritual decline. Moreover, the dignity of the Pope dropped due to the failure of the Crusades, and the papacy fell into a titular position by the Pope's imprisonment in Avignon in southern

France. Thus, the Christian monarchic society, which was the spiritual kingdom centering on the Pope, continued until the outbreak of the Religious Reformation in 1517.

As for the course of economic development in this period, the feudal system of economy persisted, even in the absolute monarchic society in which the political system was centralized after the decline of the feudal system. Thus, not only in the aspect of agricultural economy, but also in the other economic spheres which had been turning to capitalism, the economic system until the French Revolution could not transcend the limits of the feudalism. That is, even the independent farmers (yeomen), who relied on the power of the king in order to resist the rule of the feudal lord, could not remove themselves from the limitations of the feudal system, while the manufacturers, who conspired with the king, knowing the disadvantage of the feudalistic division, finally ended up by becoming feudalistic mercantilists themselves.

If feudal society is followed by monarchic society in terms of political structure, then what would follow feudalism in terms of economy? This would be the capitalistic society, and the imperialistic society following it. The centralization of capital is a characteristic of capitalism, especially of imperialism, just as centralization of power in politics is a characteristic of monarchism. Capitalism began to bud out from the beginning of the absolute monarchic society in the middle of the 17th century and gradually entered its maturity after the period of the industrial revolution in England.

In this way, capitalistic society arose in order to develop the small-unit economic foundation which had been secured through the feudalistic economic system into a large-unit foundation. Further, in order to restore a worldwide foundation of economy, capitalism moved to the stage of imperialism. What we must remember here is that the pattern of God's providence of restoration had been formed centering on Western Europe. Accordingly, the imperialism discussed here also indicates what has developed centering on West Europe.

The imperialistic idea which had expanded in West Europe motivated the Christian nations of West Europe to obtain colonies all over the world, before and after World War I. Thus, the world progressed, radically, into the Christian cultural sphere.

(6) Democracy and Socialism

The age of democracy followed the age of monarchism. Meanwhile, the reason that the age of monarchism came was to erect the kingdom capable of receiving the Messiah as King. However, this age having failed to fulfill such a mission, God destroyed this society and set up democracy in order to work a new providence for the reconstruction of the Messianic kingdom.

Democracy is a principle under which the people are given the sovereignty of running the government for themselves by their own will. Consequently, the purpose of democracy is to break down Satanic dictatorship and to set up a new political system, enabling the fulfillment of the providence of restoration to receive the Messiah as King. As history goes on, man's spirit becomes brighter and brighter, under the benevolent influence of the age through the providence of restoration. Therefore, man's original mind, in correlation with that providence, comes to seek after religion unconsciously. This original mind in search of religion, after all, inquires into Christianity, which God provided as the final and ultimate religion.

This is, in fact, the reason that today's world is on the way to form one sphere of Christian culture. Naturally, as history draws near its consummation, the will of the people inclines to be Christian-like, and the democratic government following the will of the people is also forced to be changed into that of Christianity. Thus, when the Messiah comes again into the society under the democratic government well matured by the Christian spirit, he will be able to set up God's sovereignty on the earth by the will of the people, thus restoring the Kingdom of Heaven on earth. We must know, therefore, that democracy is, ultimately the political principle of God's final providence to annihilate the dictatorship on Satan's side and to restore, according to the will of the people, the sovereignty of God centering on the Lord of the Second Advent. Thus, the democratic spirit that arose against the absolute monarchism in the late 18th century motivated the democratic revolutions in England, America and France, collapsing the monarchic society and establishing the foundation of democratic society. We have studied democracy from the viewpoint of the development of history, but democracy seen from the providential progress of the Hebraic and Hellenic ideals will be handled in the next chapter.

Next, concerning the course of the development of history in the religious sphere, we have seen that the coming of the age of Christian Democracy, after the Religious Reformation of 1517 A.D., caused the collapse of the spiritual kingdom without land centering on the pope. The Christian democracy, through religious reformation, caused the collapse of the spiritual kingdom that had been under the pope's dictatorship. Originally, that kingdom centering on the pope, as discussed above, should have realized a kingdom capable of receiving the Messiah of the Second Advent by the pope's becoming one with the king. However, the pope failed to carry out this mission. Just as democracy was brought about in order to break down the dictatorial sovereignty of the absolute monarchic society, so the Christian democracy came in order to tear down the dictatorial sovereignty of the pope, who was proceeding apart from God's will. It was natural that after the Religious Reformation, there came the age of Christian democracy in which everybody could freely seek God, centering on the Bible, without having to go through the medium of the pope or the priests. In this way, in the aspect of religion, too, they entered the age in which believers could seek their way of religious faith, according to their free will, without being subjected to anybody or anything. Thus, Christian democracy came to create a Christian-like social environment in which people could freely go, at a future time, to the Messiah of the Second Advent in whatever manner and form he might come again.

On the other hand, in the course of the development of economic history, socialism came about in order to break imperialism and to establish a democratic economic society by the same law of development. Thus, World War I may be regarded as the war for the imperialistic nations to obtain colonies, while toward the end of World War II, national democracy made its appearance to tear down imperialistic colonial policies, forcing the great powers to abandon their colonial policies and to liberate the lesser powers. Accordingly, the age of capitalistic economy was shifted into the age of socialistic economy, with the collapse of imperialism as the turning point.

It is only too natural for the Satanic world, which is headed toward a communistic society, to advocate socialism. This is because Satan would attempt to realize, in advance, the course of the Heavenly side going toward the socialistic system of economy, though the directions and contents of the two may utterly differ from each other.

Seen from God's principle of creation, man's original value endowed at the creation must be equal between any two individuals. Consequently, God intends to give everyone an equal environment and equal conditions of life, just as human parents would to their children. Therefore, production, distribution, and consumption must have the same organic relationship with one another as that between the stomach, heart and lungs of the human body. So there should not be any competition over the market because of excessive production, nor any accumulation or excessive consumption which would bring obstruction to the purpose of the life of the whole, due to unfair distribution. There must be a necessary and sufficient amount of production, distribution in fair and proper quantities, and reasonable consumption for the general purpose, just as in the liver of the human body there should be an appropriate reserve for the smooth operation of the entire body.

Man, having been created with such an ideal, cannot help demanding such a socialistic system of life since he quite naturally searches for his original nature, striving after the democratic freedom at the consummation of the providential history which will enable the restoration of the original ideal. If the will of the people should demand this, the politics according to the will of the people must also go in the same direction. Therefore, there will ultimately have to come a socialistic society centering on God. We can find a socialistic idea even in ancient Christian society, while the ideal of "Utopia" by Thomas More of England in the 16th Century was also socialism, and the ideology based on Owen's humanism in the period of the industrial revolution of England was also as such, together with the Catholic socialism and Protestant socialism, brought about by the Christian idea of Kingsley of England. All these must be regarded as coming from the natural expression of man's original nature, which is headed for the ideal of creation.

(7) The Principle of Coexistence, Co-prosperity, Common-cause—and Communism

The benevolent influence of the age of God's providence of restoration helps to develop man's original nature endowed at the creation, which was prevented from displaying itself by Satan's invasion. Therefore, in accordance with such spontaneous desires, endowed at the creation, men unconsciously search for the world of God's ideal of creation with ardent aspiration. Consequently, man's original mind, headed for a socialistic society of the Heavenly side, comes after all to advocate the principle of coexistence, co-prosperity and common-cause, finally realizing the ideal world in which God's purpose of creation is actualized. This is the true Kingdom of Heaven on earth centering on the Lord of the Second Advent.

Satan, always trying to realize God's providence in advance, is steering his way toward the world of communism by advocating so-called "scientific socialism" based on materialism. Communists say that human history, having developed from a primitive communistic society, is now going back to a communistic society, but without knowing its cause. God, having once promised man to realize the Kingdom of Heaven on earth after His creating man, permits Satan, who had his blood relationship with man first, to realize his non-principled world in a pseudo-form of the Principle centering on the fallen men. The communist world is none other than this non-principled world in a pseudo-form of the Principle in which Satan realized in advance the imitation of the Kingdom of Heaven on earth, which God is going to restore.

Democracy came about in order to replace the political dictatorship of monarchism and to win the sovereignty back to the hands of the people. Likewise, the Heavenly side is trying to realize the principle of coexistence, co-prosperity and common-cause, after going through socialism, in order to break down the imperialistic system of economy in which the state property is monopolized by a certain individual or class, and to establish a system of economy in which all people may equally enjoy the wealth. Meanwhile, the Satanic side is trying to realize communism, in advance of God. Accordingly, socialism presents itself to realize an economic society of a truly democratic type.

We have previously clarified the fact that the history of the providence of restoration, centering on Western Europe, has been separated into the three aspects of religious history, political history, and economic history, each developing through a formulary course. How, then, will these be able to provide the foundation for the ideal of the Second Advent by completing the providential history, in which they unite with one another on the same course of history? We have also clarified above that the development of history has been made in three divisions because religion and science, which were to overcome man's spiritual and physical ignorance were not unified as one theme. Accordingly, in order that history, having thus developed under three different aspects, may be concluded into one focal point in which to realize one ideal, the new truth, which can solve the problems of religion and science under one unified theme, must manifest itself.

Then there will come a political society in which all mankind, having been unified into the heart and bosom of God through the religion based on the truth, will realize the ideal of creation on the economic foundation centering on God's ideal. This is the true Messianic Kingdom based on the principles of co-existence, co-prosperity and common-cause.

Chart of the Development of History from the Standpoint of the Providence of Restoration

The Providential Age for the Foundation of Restoration

Adam — Noah — Abraham — Jacob — Joseph

1600 --- 400 --- 400 --- 400 --- 120 --- 40 --- 21 --- 40

The Providential Age of Restoration

Abraham .... *Jesus*

	Slavery in Egypt	The Period of Judges	The United Kingdom	The Divided Kingdom of North and South	Jewish Captivity and Return	Preparation for the Coming of the Messiah
	400	400	120	400	210	400
History of Religion	The Israelite Clan Society	The Israelite Feudal Society	The Israelite Monarchic Society			The Israelite Democratic-Type Society

The Providential Age of the Prolongation of Restoration

Jesus .... *The Lord of Second Advent*

	Persecution under Roman Empire	Christian Churches under Patriarchal System	The Christian Kingdom	The Divided Kingdom of East and West	Papal Captivity and Return	The Preparation for the Second Coming of the Messiah
	400	400	120	400	210	400
History of Religion	The Early Church System Society	The Christian Clan Society	The Christian Feudal Society	The Christian Monarchic Society		The Christian Democratic Society
History of Politics	The Slavery System Society	Feudal Society		The Christian Feudal Society → The Middle of 17C	The Absolute Monarchic Society — 1789 (French Revolution)	Democratic Society
History of Economy	The Slavery System Society	The Manor System (Feudalism)			1789 (English Industrial Revolution) — Capitalistic Society	Imperialistic Society / The Society of Socialism

CHAPTER V

Preparation Period for the Second Advent of the Messiah

The preparation period for the Second Advent of the Messiah is the 400-year period from the Religious Reformation of 1517 to the end of World War I in 1918. The summary of the character of this period was already discussed in the section comparing it with the preparation period for the coming of the Messiah viewed from time-identity, but a more detailed study will be made here. Seen from the viewpoint of the providence of restoration, this era is divided into three periods: the period of religious reformation, the period of struggle between religion and ideology, and the period of maturity for politics, economy, and ideology.

SECTION I
The Period of Religious Reformation (1517-1648)

The 130-year period, from the time when Luther held the banner of religious reformation in Germany in 1517 to when the fight between the two religious sects of old and new was ended by the treaty of Westphalia in 1648 is called the "period of Religious Reformation." The character of this period was formed by the Renaissance and the Religious Reformation as the products of medieval feudal society. When the purpose of God's providence which He intended to fulfill through the medieval society became a failure, the Renaissance and Religious Reformation carried out the leading mission of establishing the foundation to receive the Messiah of the Second Advent, by turning it in the new direction of the providential history. Consequently, we cannot grasp the character of this period without knowing this.

If the Renaissance and Religious Reformation are the products of medieval feudal society, what kind of influence did medieval society exert upon the original nature of the medieval people, bringing about these two new developments?

Because of the social environment of the feudal system and the secular degradation of Roman Catholicism in the medieval ages, the original nature of man was restrained and its free development was restricted. Faith, the way each must go in search of God, can only be realized by a vertical relationship directly between the individual and God. The intervention of the pope and priests together with formal religious ceremonies and laws fettered the religious freedom of that age, while the strict system of the feudalistic classes restrained man's independent religious activities. Besides, through buying and selling of the priesthood and the exploitation of the people by the priests, the priests' lives inclined to be luxurious and hedonistic. In consequence, the papal authority came to stand in a position of no credibility whatsoever in the same manner as the authorities of the general society, and it was unable to lead the life in faith of the people.

Thus, the social environment of the medieval feudalistic age blocked man's way toward restoring his original nature endowed at the creation. Therefore, medieval men, who were under the bondage of such an environment, moved spontaneously in the direction of restoring man's original nature by breaking down the environment. The original nature of man presented itself with the character and tendency of both the internal aspect and external aspect. Let us now study where its ground is in the principle of creation.

According to the principle of creation, man, being God's substantial object in the image of His dual essentialities, resembles His essential character and form. This character and form have internal and external relationships. Man is created to live by the give and take action between this internal character and external form. Therefore, man's original nature was created also in pursuit of two desires, one of internal aspect and the other of external aspect. In working His providence of restoration with such men, God is compelled to work in correlation with the two pursuits of man's original nature.

God, who originally created man's body (external) first and then his spirit (internal) next (Gen. 2:7), works His providence of restoration for the re-creation of man by restoring first what is external and next what is internal. As was already discussed (cf. Part II, Ch. I), fallen man had to first offer an external symbolic sacrifice before he could offer an internal substantial sacrifice. Only by succeeding in making the internal substantial sacrifice could the more internal foundation to receive the Messiah be realized. Accordingly, in restoring fallen man, God first let man restore his position as a "slave of slaves" (Gen. 9:25), through the offerings in the pre-Old Testament Age. Then, in the Old Testament Age, He let man restore his position as a servant (Lev. 25:55), through the law. In the New Testament Age, He let man restore his position as an adopted son (Rom. 8:23), through faith. In the Completed Testament Age, He is guiding man to restore his position as a true son, through heart-and-zeal, always progressing from that which is external to that which is internal (cf. Part II, Ch. II, Sec. III, 2).

For the same reason, God let man first restore the external social environment through science while working His providence to restore the internal spirit of man through religion. Observing the order of the creation of the archangel and man, we find that God first created the archangel, who is external, and then created man, who is internal. Accordingly, in restoring the angel and fallen man, God has been working His providence by first restoring the external substantial world, centering on man's physical body, through the cooperative works of the angelic world, which is external, and then by restoring the internal invisible world centering on man's spirit.

Medieval men were to separate from Satan, who invaded them due to the degradation of the popes, whose internal mission had been to restore the foundation of faith, and who were thus to restore their original nature endowed at the creation. They divided the leading spirit of medieval men into the two movements to restore the two ideologies, one of Cain-type and the other of Abel-type, according to the internal and external pursuits of their original nature. First came the movement to restore Hellenism, which was the Cain-type, and next came the movement to restore Hebraism, which was Abel-type. The movement to restore Hellenism caused the Renaissance, which was an expression of humanism, while the movement to restore Hebraism aroused the Religious Reformation for the revival of theism. Let us, therefore, study how the streams of

Hellenism and Hebraism have historically interchanged, finally reaching the present age.

About 2000 B.C. the Minoan civilization was formed, centering on the island of Crete in the Mediterranean Sea. This civilization, spreading into Greece, formed the Hellenistic cultural sphere of the Cain-type in the 11th century B.C., of which the leading spirit was Hellenism, centering on humanism. About the same time in Western Asia, the Hebraic cultural sphere of the Abel-type was formed, of which the leading spirit was Hebraism, centering on theism. This was the period of the United Kingdom.

If the Israelite kings of that age had set up the foundation to receive the Messiah, thus receiving the Messiah at that time, the Hebraic cultural sphere could have absorbed the Hellenic cultural sphere, thus forming one worldwide cultural sphere. However, the kings failed to unite with the will of God, leaving it unfulfilled. Thus, the period from the time of their subjection to Greece in 333 B.C. after their having returned from their captivity in Babylon until Jesus' coming at the time of their subjection to Rome, which belonged to the Hellenic cultural sphere, was the period during which Hebraism was placed in the situation of being controlled by Hellenism.

As already discussed in the previous chapter, if the Jewish people had become one centering on Jesus by believing in him, the Roman Empire of that time could have become the Messianic kingdom centering on Jesus. If so, Hebraism could have absorbed Hellenism, thus forming a worldwide Hebraic cultural sphere at that time. Nevertheless, this will was not fulfilled because of the Jewish people's betrayal of Jesus, and Hebraism remained under the control of Hellenism. After Constantine the Great had officially recognized Christianity in the Milan Decree in 313 A.D., Hebraism began gradually to overcome Hellenism, finally forming the two great cultural spheres of Greek Orthodoxy and of Western European Christianity in the 700's A.D.

If in medieval society the popes and the kings, who were the central figures to restore the foundation of faith, had not become corrupted, the foundation for the Messiah of the Second Advent could have been established at that time, and Hebraism could have completely absorbed Hellenism, forming one cultural sphere for the whole world. However, as discussed above, their degradation caused a Satanic invasion of the leading spirit of medieval men, centering on Hebraism. Hence, God had to work His providence of separating Satan. Therefore, God, just as He had divided Adam into Cain and Abel in order to separate Satan, who had invaded Adam, again worked His providence of separating the leading spirit of that time into two ideologies. These were the movements to restore Cain-type Hellenism and Abel-type Hebraism. These finally presented themselves in the form of the Renaissance and the Religious Reformation.

In this age, since the Renaissance occurred with humanism as its leading ideology, Hellenism was placed in a position of having control over Hebraism. Thus, this period becomes that in which to restore by indemnity, as the substantial time-identity, the period in which Hellenism held control over Hebraism due to the Jewish people's subjection under Greece during the period of preparation for the coming of the Messiah. We know that by Cain's surrendering in obedience to Abel and thus separating from Satan, who had invaded Adam, the foundation of substance to receive the Messiah could be established. Only by the Cain-type Hellenism surrendering completely to the Abel-type ideology of Hebraism and thus separating from Satan, who had invaded the leading spirit of medieval men, could the foundation of substance to receive the Lord of the Second Advent have been accomplished at that time.

1. THE RENAISSANCE

According to the external pursuit of man's original nature by the men of medieval society, the movement to restore Hellenism was aroused. By this movement, the Renaissance was born. Let us then study what this external pursuit of man's original nature was and how and why man came to pursue this course.

The principle of creation tells us that man was created to become perfect by carrying out by his free will his own portion of responsibility, in which process even God could not intervene. Therefore, it is man's original nature to pursue freedom. It is from man's original nature that he would pursue the independence of his personality because man was created to enjoy the absolute independence of his personality by carrying out his own portion of responsibility with his free will and thus by becoming one with God and perfecting his individuality.

Man was created as a man of perfected individuality to know God's will through his intelligence and reason and to live in accordance with it, even though he might not receive any revelation from God. Therefore, it is man's original nature to follow and develop his intelligence and reason. Man is also created to dominate the natural world. Therefore, he must pioneer the environment of his everyday life by discovering, through science, the principles latent in nature. Accordingly, man's original nature demands that he pursue nature, reality, and science.

Men of the medieval society whose original nature had been oppressed by the social environment of the feudal system, were more ardently in pursuit of the above-mentioned things due to the external desire of their original nature. Medieval people also came to study the classics of Hellenism, imported from the East. The old spirit of Hellas was an external pursuit of man's original nature: the pursuit of human freedom, the independence of personality, the dignity of human intellect and reason, estimation of nature, emphasis on reality, and exaltation of science. Therefore it agreed with the desire of the people's original nature; the movement to restore Hellenism occurred with great ardor, finally leading it to the emergence of humanism.

Renaissance, in French, means "rebirth" or revival. The Renaissance developed as early as the 14th century, in Italy, which was the Mecca of the classical research on Hellenism. This movement of humanism, which at first began as a movement to have medieval men return to ancient Greece in imitation of the Hellenic spirit, advanced to become a movement to reform medieval social life by reproducing this classic culture. Going beyond the culture, it expanded to become a movement of reform, covering all the problems of society, such as politics, economy, and religion. It also became the external driving force which formed the modern society. The Renaissance is a phenomenon which developed in the form of an external reformation movement covering the whole of the feudal society and centering on humanism, which was the current thought of the age directed toward fulfilling the external desire of man's original nature.

2. RELIGIOUS REFORMATION

The providence of restoration, centering on the popes of the medieval age, ended in failure due to the secular degradation of the popes and the priests. Medieval men, as they came to advocate humanism, resisted formal religious ceremonies and rules. They went against the feudal system of classes and the papal authority which repressed man's autonomy. They also repulsed the obstinate life of faith of the age, in which man's reason and intellect were disregarded and everything was thought to be solved only by having it subjected to the pope.

The people came to repel the seclusive, other-worldly, and ascetic attitude of faith which ignored nature, reality, and science. Thus, medieval Christians finally rebelled against the papacy.

In this way, as medieval men pursued the external desire of their original nature, they came to advocate the restoration of the early Christian spirit in which the people, centering on the apostles, were very earnest in following God's will. This was actually the movement of restoration of Hebraism in the Medieval age. In the 14th century, John Wycliffe, a professor of theology at Oxford University in England, translated the Bible into English, insisting that the standard of faith be put not upon the popes and priests but upon the Bible itself. At the same time, he denounced the degradation of the priesthood, and their exploitation and abuse of power over the people, testifying to the fact that the system, ceremonies, and rules of the church had no scriptural grounds.

In this way, the movement of Religious Reformation quickly developed in England as early as the 14th century, after the papal dignity had fallen. The same movement occurred in Italy also but failed. Later, in 1517, Pope Leo X began to sell "indulgences", propagating that they were the token of redemption and salvation after death, in order to raise funds for the erection of St. Peter's Basilica. The movement against its ill effect became the incentive for action and the Religious Reformation exploded, centering on Martin Luther, who was a professor of theology at the University of Wittenberg in Germany. The fire of this revolutionary movement spread and developed actively in France, centering on Calvin, and in Switzerland, centering on Zwingli, gradually expanding into England, Holland and many other countries.

The international conflict which burst out around the Protestant movement continued for more than 100 years until the fight between the old and new religious sects was once settled by the Thirty Years' War. This war was waged, centering on Germany, and finally ended in 1648, with the Treaty of Westphalia. As a result, the struggle ended in Northern Europe with the victory of Protestantism, centering on the Germanic nation. Southern Europe remained as the territory of Roman Catholicism, centering on the Latin peoples.

The Thirty Years' War broke out between the believers in Protestanism and Catholicism, centering on Germany. However, this war did not end up as a simple religious fight, but it was altogether a political civil war which decided the existence of the German Empire. Accordingly, the peace treaty of Westphalia which ended this war was a religious conference and also an international political conference which solved territorial problems among many countries like Germany, France, Spain and Sweden.

SECTION II
The Period of Struggle among Religions and Ideologies
(1648—1789)

This is the period of the 140 years from the success of the Protestant movement by the treaty of Westphalia in 1648 until the French Revolution in 1789. Modern men, who came to pioneer the way in pursuit of the internal and external desires of their original human nature, could not avoid the division of doctrine and the fight among philosophies that came from the freedom of religion and ideology.

As was repeatedly discussed in Part II, the providence of restoration has been woven by the works of division into the Cain-type and Abel-type from the individual level to the world-wide level during the long period of history. Consequently, at the consummation of history, this world of corruption is to be divided into the communistic world of the Cain-type and democratic world of the Abel-type. Just as the foundation of substance could only have been realized by Cain's obedience in surrender to Abel, at this time also the worldwide foundation of substance to receive the Lord of the Second Advent is to be realized only by the Cain-type world's surrender to the Abel-type world. Thus, one world will be restored. In order for the two types of world to be realized, two types of the view of life must be established; in reality, these two types of the view of life were established during this period.

1. THE CAIN-TYPE VIEW OF LIFE

The external pursuit of the original human nature aroused the movement of restoration of Hellenism, giving birth to humanism. The anti-medieval movement of the Renaissance, which occurred with humanism as its backing, made light of conversion to God and dedication to religion, replacing everything with nature and humanism. That is, it abandoned the medieval view of life under which the people were so obedient to God as to regard nature and the physical body of men as base and even sinful, and established the view of life exalting the value and dignity of these things. Man and nature came to be recognized through rational criticism by reason and experience, and through demonstrative analysis. This view of life has gone through the two forms of methodology of cognition and speculation. These form the two great currents of modern philosophy: "rationalism" by the deductive method and "empiricism" by the inductive method.

Rationalism, whose father was Descartes of France (1596-1650), maintained that all truths could be researched only by "reason," with which man was endowed from the moment of his birth. Rationalism broke down the historical tradition and set up the proposition of "I think, therefore, I am" by the deductive method. Deducing from this point, rationalists intended to affirm the external world. Accordingly, they tried to deny God, the world, and even themselves. On the other hand, empiricism, whose father was Francis Bacon of England (1561-1626), held that all truths could be researched only by experience. Empiricism held that the human mind, like pure-white paper, should be removed from any preoccupation whatever and could only come to comprehend any new truth through experience and observation. Thus, the rationalistic ideology which valued human reason apart from God and the realistic ideology centering on man while based on experience both rejected mysticism and visions. By rationalizing and focusing only on human life, both separated man and nature from God.

In this way, the Renaissance, on the two currents flowing from humanism, gave birth to a view of life which prevented man from going the way to God in accordance with his internal trend and opened the way of the Satanic side by following the external trend alone. This was actually the Cain-type view of life. This Cain-type view of life, upon entering the 18th century, broke down history and tradition, judged every human endeavor by reason and by actualism, thoroughly repulsed that which was unreasonable and unrealistic, and denied God, emphasizing the rational reality of life. This was the thought of the Enlightenment. The Enlightenment, which bloomed in the mainstream of empiricism and rationalism, became the motivating power for the French Revolution.

Influenced by this Cain-type view of life, there occurred in England the doctrine of deism, originated by Edward Herbert (1583-1648). Compared to the theology which had developed, since Thomas Aquinas, on the basis of harmony of revelation and reason, deism intended to establish a theology simply on the basis of reason. Deists confined their view of God to the significance of His having created man and the universe, and they maintained that God's revelations and miracles were not necessary to man.

In the beginning of the 19th century, Hegel, of Germany (1770-1831), made a comprehensive compilation of the philosophy of idealism. But Hegel's philosophy, when influenced by the atheism and materialism that emerged in France on the basis of the Enlightenment, gave rise to left-wing Hegelianism. The Left-Hegelians overturned his logic and systematized the philosophy of dialectical materialism, which motivates the communist world of today. D.F. Straus, a Left-Hegelian, wrote *The Biography of Jesus* denying the miracles in the Bible as posthumous fabrication, while Feuerbach (1804-1872), in his *Essence of Christianity* argued that social or economic conditions cause the emergence of religions. This theory became the backing for materialism. Karl Marx (1818-1883) and Friedrich Engels (1820-1895) were influenced by Straus and Feuerbach, but they were more greatly influenced by the socialistic ideology of France. By advocating dialectical materialism, they combined atheism and materialism, which had begun to bud after the Renaissance and had developed as the tidal current of the Enlightenment. Afterwards, the Cain-type view of life matured to form the communist world of today.

2. THE ABEL-TYPE VIEW OF LIFE

We are inclined to regard the flow of history from the medieval society to the modern one as the course of separating man or making him independent from God or religion. This is because we have seen it based on the Cain-type view of life, which occurred in accordance with the external pursuit of man's original nature by medieval men.

However, the pursuit of man's original nature by medieval men was not confined only to that which was external, but also included that which was more internal. Internal pursuit of the original nature aroused the movement to restore Hebraism, which motivated the Religious Reformation. Through this movement, philosophy and religion came to establish a vertical view of life headed for man's original nature endowed at the creation; this we call the Abel-type view of life. Consequently, this Abel-type view of life led medieval men to progress toward God at a higher level, while the Cain-type view of life led them in the direction of separation, making them independent from God or faith in Him.

Kant, of Germany (1724-1804), introduced "critical philosophy" by assimilating empiricism and rationalism, which had conflicted with each other. Through critical philosophy, he analyzed philosophically the desire of man's original nature in pursuit of both internal and external goals, thus pioneering the Abel-type view of life from a philosophical angle. According to Kant, our various sensations occur by contact with external objects. This alone may give us the content of cognition, but cannot actualize the cognition itself. In order to actualize the cognition, there must be a certain form to unify the various contents (which are subsequent and empirical) according to one solid relationship. This form is the very subjectivity of oneself. Therefore, cognition is said to be actualized when the various sensations coming from the objects are integrated and unified by one's subjective form (inherent and transcendent), according to the spontaneous action of one's thinking power or one's spiritual awareness. Thus, Kant overturned the existing theory of facsimile which said that subjectivity is determined by the object, establishing a new theory that subjectivity determines the object. Succeeding Kant's theory there appeared a number of philosophers such as Fichte, his first successor (1762-1814), and Hegel (1770-1831). Hegel especially pioneered a new aspect of philosophy. Their idealism formed the Abel-type view of life, in the realm of philosophy.

In the religious world, the Abel-type view opposed the inclination of the time, which was influenced by the current of rationalism; there emerged a new movement which emphasized mystical experiences more than doctrines or formalities, attaching importance to religious passion and man's inner life. To draw a representative example we can first name Pietism, which occurred centering on Philipp Spener (1635-1705) of Germany with a strong conservative trend to follow the orthodox faith, putting stress on mystical experiences. This movement of Pietism spread in England and, inspiring the religious awareness of the people, it gave birth to Methodism, centering on the Wesley brothers. This denomination thus aroused a great revival in the religious world of England, which was in a depressed condition.

In England, there also emerged the Quakers, with the mystic George Fox (1624-1690) as founder. Fox claimed that Christ is the inner light, illuminating the souls of the believers. He also insisted that unless we experience the inner light, receive the Holy Spirit, and unite mystically with Christ, we can never know the true meaning of the Bible. This denomination spread its missionary work, suffering persecution especially on the American continent. Next, the famous spiritually sensitive Swedish scientist, Emanuel Swedenborg (1688-1772), disclosed many heavenly secrets, with his spiritual eyes opened. His announcement has long been ignored in the theological world; but quite recently, with the increase of man's communication with the spirit world, its value is gradually being recognized.

In this manner, the Abel-type view of life has matured to form the democratic world today.

SECTION III
The Period of Maturity of
Politics, Economy, and Ideology (1789-1918)

The struggle among religions and ideologies of the previous period resulted in the establishment of Cain- and Abel-type views of life. Upon entering this period, these two views of life matured in their respective directions. As they matured, two types of worlds, one of Cain and the other of Abel, were formed while the structure of society was arranged to have a social shape based on these two views of life. The politics, economy, and ideology also developed to a stage prior to their conversion into the ideal society. The period beginning after the French Revolution through the Industrial Revolution and continuing until the end of the First World War was the period for such providence.

1. DEMOCRACY

In the previous chapter we discussed democracy from the standpoint of the development of history. However, this discussion examined only the external circumstances causing democracy to appear. Now let us examine the internal circumstances of how and on which ideological tide, in the surging flow of history, today's democracy came.

As already discussed (cf. Part II, Ch. IV, Sec. VII), if in the period of the United Kingdom, the spiritual kingdom centering on the pope and the substantial kingdom centering on the king had become one, realizing the monarchic society capable of receiving the Messiah and thus establishing the foundation to receive the Messiah, the feudalistic society would have ended at that time. However, since this providence was a failure, this period was prolonged; the political, religious and economic history came to develop through separate respective courses.

Political power, decentralized to the local lords of the medieval feudalistic period, began to decline after the Crusades and became more emaciated upon entering the period of the Enlightenment, after having gone through the Renaissance and Religious Reformation. Then, in the middle of the 17th century, the feudal lords established unified states with many small nations as a unit; by consolidating them under the king, they formed an absolute state with the centralization of administrative power. This was the period of absolute monarchy when, influenced by the idea of the "divine right of kings," the kings were endowed with absolute power. From the social aspect, let us now examine the cause that brought about this period. First, it was for the class of citizens united with the king to resist the feudalistic class. Second, it was because they needed a strong national identity apart from the feudal system in order to control trade in their economic activities, and because they needed the mercantile economic policy under strong protection and supervision by the state for the welfare of the people.

On the other hand, seen from the standpoint of the development of the history of the providence of restoration, monarchic society on the Heavenly side should have been realized after the feudalistic society. The popes and kings of this age, however, failed to become one; the society on the Heavenly side was not realized. In reverse manner, the society centering on the pope turned out to be the society of absolute monarchy on the Satanic side, following the course that Satan had laid out in advance.

Again, from the standpoint of the providence of restoration, let us consider the trends of the society of absolute monarchy. Since the medieval feudalistic society ran counter to both Hebraism and Hellenism, these two ideologies worked together in breaking down the society and established two types of society based on the two views of life—Cain-like and Abel-like. Likewise, the society of absolute monarchy developed through the following course. The society of absolute monarchy, which fettered the freedom of faith under the Christian democracy since the Religious Reformation, went contrary to the attainment of the purpose of the Abel-type view of life. The feudalistic system which had still remained in that society became an obstacle to the development of the citizen class under the leadership of the atheists and materialists and thus also contradicted the attainment of the purpose of the Cain-type view of life. Therefore, both of the two views of life tended to break down the society and finally formed two types of society—one of communism and the other of democracy based on the two types of democracy, Cain-like and Abel-like.

(1) Cain-Type Democracy

Cain-type democracy grew out of the French Revolution. In order to discuss this problem, we must first discuss the French Revolution. France in that day was in a period which saw the expansion of the idea of Enlightenment, being led into atheism and materialism by the Cain-type view of life. The citizens, thus influenced by the idea of Enlightenment, were awakened to the contradiction of absolutism, and naturally their desire to break down the remnant of the old system, still rooted deep in the society under absolutism, attained a zenith.

Here in 1789, in accordance with the high tide of the idea of Enlightenment, the citizens broke down the feudalistic ruling-class of the absolute monarchic society and at the same time rose to advocate democracy for the freedom, equality, and liberation of the third class (citizens). This was actually the French Revolution. As a result of this revolution, the "Declaration of the Rights of Man" was officially announced; thus, democracy was established in France. However, because the democracy born out of the French Revolution came about when the idea of Enlightenment, which developed into the ideology of materialism, broke down the society of absolutism in order to set up the Cain-type view of life, we call it the Cain-type democracy. Therefore, Denis Diderot (1713-1784) and D'Alembert (1717-1783), the thinkers of the French Revolution, were scholars from either the line of atheism or materialism.

As we may see from the particulars of this revolution, it was true that the democracy of France inclined toward totalitarianism rather than the equality and freedom of individuality. In this way, the Cain-type view of life formed the Cain-type democracy by establishing the idea of Enlightenment and thus giving rise to the French Revolution. This completely blocked the way of man's internal pursuit of his original nature for God, only developing externally more and more. Once systematized into the Marxism of Germany and the Leninism of Russia, the Cain-type view of life finally formed the communist world.

(2) Abel-Type Democracy

The democracy realized in England and the United States is different, even in its origin, from the democracy that was born out of the great revolution of France. The former was the Abel-type democracy realized by ardent Christians, who were the fruits of the Abel-type view of life, through their victory over absolutism, against which they had fought for the sake of their freedom of faith. The latter was the Cain-type democracy, realized by the advocates of atheism and materialism, who were the products of the Cain-type view of life, through the breakdown of the society of absolutism.

Let us then study how the Abel-type democracy was established in England and the United States. In England, as Charles I strengthened absolutism and national religion, many Puritans moved into other European countries or the New Continent in search of freedom of faith. Previously, in Scotland, some of the Puritans who had been under religious persecution passed the People's Pact, resisting the king (1640). Again in England, the

Puritans, who were the nuclear members of Parliament, launched the Puritan Revolution, centering on Cromwell (1642). Besides, as the absolutism and strengthening of the national religion by James II were intensified, William of Orange, his son-in-law, who was at that time Stadholder of the Netherlands, landed in England with his army in 1688 in order to protect the freedom of faith and civil rights and ascended the throne bloodlessly. Upon his enthronement, William recognized the independent rights of Parliament by approving the "Declaration of Right" reported by Parliament. This became the basis of the constitution of England. Since this revolution was a bloodless success, we call it the Glorious Revolution. This revolution in England also had its cause in the endeavor by the citizens class to obtain freedom and liberation from the class of great landowners such as the nobles and priests, but the main cause was to obtain, through such a revolution, the internal liberation and freedom of faith.

Then the Puritans, who had been suppressed under the imperial regime of absolutism in England, went to the new continent of America in order to obtain freedom of faith, and in 1776 they founded an independent nation there. Thus, they came to establish American democracy. The democracy established in England and America is called the Abel-type democracy because it was set up through revolution to reform the society of absolutism in order to obtain freedom of faith centering on the Abel-type view of life. In this way, the Abel-type democracy has formed today's world of democracy.

2. THE SIGNIFICANCE IN THE PRINCIPLE OF THE SEPARATION OF THREE POWERS

The idea of the separation of the three powers was advocated by Montesquieu, who was an authority in the school of the Enlightenment. The separation of powers was to decentralize national power and prevent it from being concentrated in a specific individual or organization as had been done in the political system under absolutism.

Originally this separation of the three powers was the structure of the ideal society designed by the Heavenly side, but as it always had been with all the courses in the providence of restoration, this also had been realized in advance by the Satanic side, in a pseudo-form of the Principle. Let us here study what the structure of the ideal society is like.

As we have clarified in the "Principle of Creation," the world of creation was made with the structure of a perfect man as the model. The ideal world, consisting of perfect men, would have resembled the structure and function of a perfect man. Just as all the organs of a human body would move according to the command of the brain, all the organizations of the ideal world must work under the command of God alone. Just as all the commands from the brain would be transmitted to all the members of the body through the medium of the peripheral nerve system centering on the spine, the commands from God must reach the entire society, without omission, through the medium of the saints, corresponding to the peripheral nerve system, centering on Christ, who corresponds to the spine. Again, the peripheral nerve system centering on the spine in the human body corresponds to the political parties of the state, so the function corresponding to the political parties of an ideal society must be performed by the saints centering on Christ.

Just as the lungs, heart and stomach maintain smooth give and take action without any conflict, according to the commands of the brain which are transmitted through the peripheral nerve system, the three organs—legislative, executive and judiciary—of the ideal society, which correspond to the three human organs, also must be able to have a relationship of give and take action in the Principle according to the commands of God, which are transmitted through the saints centering on

Christ, corresponding to the political parties. Just as the limbs of the human body move for the purpose of living according to the command of the brain, so the economic structure, corresponding to the limbs, must move toward establishment of the purpose of ideal society according to the command of God. Just as the liver in the human body saves nutrition for the whole body, in the ideal society, too, there must always be a reserve for the accomplishment of the purpose of the whole.

Since each of the limbs and all parts of the human body have a vertical relationship with the brain, the horizontal relationship among the members is automatically established, forming an inseparable organism. In the same way, since men of the ideal society have a vertical relationship with God, the horizontal relationship among them is automatically established, forming an organism which shares all feelings. Therefore, in this society one cannot commit crime because harming others results in harming oneself.

Let us next study how the providence of restoration has restored the social structure. There was in the course of historical development of Western Europe a period in which the king shouldered all the functions of the three powers of legislative, executive and judiciary, and of the political parties. However, this changed into another period in which the king held the three powers and churches centering on the pope took charge of the mission of the political parties. The political system of this age was again divided into the three powers—of legislative, executive and judiciary—due to the French Revolution, and political parties came to bear a marked political mission. Thus, by establishing the constitutional political system in democracy, they could at least realize the pattern of the system of an ideal society.

In this way, the political system has changed through the long period of history because the society of fallen men has been restored into an ideal society which resembles the structure and function of a perfect man, according to the providence of restoration. In this manner, today's democratic government is divided into three powers and produces many political parties, thus making itself finally resemble the structure of a human body. But this is, after all, like a fallen man who has not been restored, and naturally cannot display the original function endowed at the creation.

That is to say, the political parties, without knowing God's will, may be compared to a peripheral nervous system centering on the spine that has lost the function of transmitting the command of the brain. Since the constitution is not made of God's words, the three organs of legislative, executive and judiciary become like three organs of a human body which are rendered unable, due to the severance of the nervous system, to feel and respond to commands from the brain; they cannot help opposing and conflicting with one another, and lack mutual harmony and order.

Therefore, the purpose of the ideal of the Second Advent of the Messiah is to make the present political system resembling the structure of a fallen man—display perfectly its original function centering on God's will by connecting it to the perfect central nerve.

3. THE SIGNIFICANCE OF THE INDUSTRIAL REVOLUTION

God's ideal of creation will not be realized simply by forming a human society without sin. Man, to fulfill God's blessing of dominion over all creation (Gen. 1:28), must realize a blessed social environment by finding out the principles hidden in the created world and by developing science to the utmost degree. As already discussed in Part I, religion and science have respectively been in charge of overcoming the two aspects of ignorance of fallen men, one spiritual and the other physical, thus gradually restoring the ideal society. Therefore, at the consummation of history, the Word that can completely remove our spiritual ignorance must appear, while science must be so developed as to be capable of removing completely man's ignorance of physical reality, thus realizing a scientific society of a stage prior to the emergence of the ideal society. Seen from this providence of God, we can understand that the Industrial Revolution of England came from the providence of restoring the living environment for the ideal society.

The economic organization of the ideal society must also resemble the structure of the perfect human body. Therefore, as previously mentioned, production, distribution and consumption in that society must have an organic relationship of give and take action, such as that among the stomach, the heart and the lungs in the human body. Consequently there should not be the destructive competition for the market—caused by excessive production—nor accumulation nor consumption that hinder the whole living-purpose by partial distribution. Production sufficient to fill man's needs, fair distribution—neither excessive nor insufficient—and rational consumption for the purpose of the whole must occur.

Meanwhile, mass production after the Industrial Revolution stimulated England to rapidly pioneer the settlement of vast colonies as her markets and sources of supply of raw materials. In this way, the Industrial Revolution carried out not only the mission of restoring the external environment for the ideal society, but also that of the internal providence of restoration by providing a vast territory for the propagation of the gospel.

4. THE STRENGTHENING OF THE POWERS, AND THE PARTITION OF COLONIES

Since the Renaissance, the view of life which had matured in two types, one of Cain and the other of Abel, aroused two respective types of political revolutions and established two types of democracy. These two types of democracy, both influenced by the Industrial Revolution of England, were rapidly strengthened and finally came to form two worlds of different factions—the democratic world and the communist world.

The industrial development coming from the rapid progress of science which followed the Industrial Revolution brought about an economic society characterized by over-production. As a result, the grave necessity to pioneer new regions for markets for the excessive production and for sources of industrial materials caused great world powers to rapidly strengthen themselves in order to continue their scramble for colonies. Thus, the currents of the two views of life (the Cain-type and the Abel-type) and the economic development following scientific progress finally divided the world, politically, into two worlds: the democratic world and the communist world.

5. THE REVOLUTION OF RELIGION, POLITICS AND INDUSTRY FOLLOWING THE RENAISSANCE

The anti-medieval movement of the restoration of Hellenism, which was of the Cain-type, gave birth to humanism through the Renaissance. This, having developed more on the side of Satan, evolved into the Enlightenment, which could be regarded as a second renaissance. Then the Enlightenment, having matured more on the Satanic side, gave birth to historical materialism, which could be taken as the third renaissance. Finally, this matured into the communist ideology.

Since the Satanic side always realizes God's providence in advance, three periods of revolution in religion, politics and industry followed. The first religious reformation centering on Luther followed the first renaissance. In the religious world, a new spiritual movement which became the second movement of religious reformation rose centering around Wesley, Fox and Swedenborg, under unspeakable persecution after the second renaissance. Therefore, seen from the course of the development of history, it is natural that the third religious reformation will come following the third renaissance. In fact, the state of today's Christianity reveals an urgent need for such reformation.

On the other hand, three stages of reformation have also occurred in the political aspect. The medieval feudal society collapsed under the influence of the first renaissance and the first religious reformation, while the absolute monarchic society collapsed under the influence of the second renaissance and the second religious reformation. Then, the communist society was formed by the political revolution brought by the third renaissance. Now, through the third religious reformation to come, the democratic world of the Heavenly side will subjugate with ideology the communist world of the Satanic side. These two worlds will necessarily be united into one Kingdom of Heaven on earth, centering on God.

We can also notice the fact that the economic reformation following the religious and political reformation has also developed through the course of three stages. The first industrial revolution originated in England as a result of industrial development through steam. Immediately afterward the second industrial revolution, through electricity and gasoline, broke out in many advanced countries. Now a third industrial revolution, based on atomic energy, will arise, and this will create throughout the world a very blessed social environment for the ideal world. These three stages of revolution, covering the three fields of religion, politics and industry, which followed the three stages of Renaissance in the period of preparation for the second advent of the Messiah, are the necessary course for the realization of the ideal society, in accordance with the three stages of the law of development.

SECTION IV
The Great World Wars

1. THE CAUSE OF THE GREAT WORLD WARS VIEWED FROM THE PROVIDENCE OF RESTORATION THROUGH INDEMNITY

Wars always break out because of political, economic and ideological causes. But these are no more than external causes. We must know that there are internal causes, just as there are both internal and external causes in human action. That is, human action is decided not only by man's external free will, which tends to cope with the reality with which he is confronted, but also by man's internal free will, which tends to adjust to God's will by heading for the purpose of the providence of restoration. Therefore, the good or evil of human actions must not be judged by the external cause alone. The worldwide conflict between opposing actions, both of which occur in accordance with men's free will, has resulted in the great world wars, so we must know that also, in this case, there should be both internal and external causes. Consequently, we can never grasp the providential significance of the great world wars if we consider only the external causes such as politics, economy and ideology.

What, then, must be the internal cause of the great world wars, as interpreted by the providence of restoration by indemnity? First, the great world wars broke out because of the last struggle of Satan trying not to let his opponent take away his sovereignty. As we have already seen, due to the fall of the first human ancestors, Satan has always realized, in advance, the non-principled world in the pattern of the Principle, imitating the world of Principle God was going to realize. God, working after him, has performed His providence to restore His world of Principle, gradually broadening the territory of goodness out of the non-principled world that had been under Satanic domination. In the course of the providence of restoration, a false one would always appear before the true one comes. As a representative example, the Bible says an antichrist would come before the true Christ.

The history of evil sovereignty centering on Satan will end with the appearance of the Lord of the Second Advent, and the history of evil sovereignty will be changed into the history of good sovereignty centered on God. Therefore, Satan at this time will put up his last struggle. In the nationwide course of the restoration into Canaan centering on Moses, Satan caused Pharaoh to display his last struggle against the chosen people of Israel who were going to leave Egypt. Therefore, the Heavenly side smote him with three great miracles, thus letting the people leave. Likewise, in the consummation of history, Satan would display his last struggle against the people of the Heavenly side who are to start their worldwide course of restoration into Canaan. Therefore, the act of smiting Satan three times appeared in the three great world wars.

Second, as Satan has realized in advance the type of world in which God would have fulfilled His three great blessings to men in a non-principled way, the great world wars are inevitable in order to set up the worldwide condition of indemnity to restore God's three great blessings. God created man and blessed him with three great blessings: that he should perfect his individuality, that he should multiply, and that he should dominate the world of creation (Gen. 1:28). Consequently, man should have realized the Kingdom of Heaven on Earth by fulfilling these great blessings.

Since God, having created man, blessed him with such blessings, He could not annul the blessings, even though man fell. So, He could not but allow fallen men to realize in advance the non-principled world in the pattern of the blessings, centering on Satan. Accordingly, at the close of human history there is to be realized a non-principled world which follows the pattern of having perfected the three great blessings: that is, the individuality centering on Satan, multiplication centering on Satan, and domination of the created world centering on Satan. Therefore, in order to set up the worldwide condition of indemnity to restore God's three great blessings, three great world wars must occur to smite, through the three stages of formation, growth and perfection, the non-principled world which follows the pattern of fulfilling the three great blessings, centering on Satan.

Third, great world wars are inevitable in order for earthly men to overcome Satan's three temptations to Jesus on the worldwide base. Christians should overcome the three temptations which Jesus suffered in the wilderness on the individual, family, national and worldwide levels. Therefore, three great world wars occurred so that mankind may overcome the three temptations of Jesus three times on the worldwide level.

Fourth, great world wars are inevitable in order to set up the worldwide condition of indemnity for the restoration of the heavenly sovereignty. If man had perfected himself through the three stages of the growth period without falling, the world under the sovereignty of God would have been realized. Therefore, God has to wage the last war to restore the world of heavenly sovereignty by dividing this fallen world into the two types—the Cain-type and the Abel-type—and by having the Heavenly world of the Abel-type smite the Satanic world of the Cain-type, thus restoring worldwide, by indemnity, the act of Cain's having killed Abel. Even in doing that, the three stages must be undergone and thus, three great world wars are inevitable. Therefore, the great world wars are the last wars in which to restore by indemnity, horizontally, the purpose of all the wars that have been waged for the restoration of heavenly sovereignty in the vertical course of the providence.

2. THE FIRST GREAT WORLD WAR

(1) Summary of the Providence for the First World War

Government under absolute monarchy collapsed as the consequence of two types of democratic revolution, the Cain-type and the Abel-type, which had been brought about by the two views-of-life. The Industrial Revolution, which followed, led the feudalistic society into a capitalistic one, finally giving birth to imperialistic society. Therefore, the first world war, seen from the political aspect, was the war between the democratic government heading for the providence of restoration according to Abel-type democracy, and the totalitarian government which was against the purpose of the providence of restoration, according to Cain-type democracy.

Seen from the economic aspect, it was a war between imperialism of the Heavenly side and that of the Satanic side. This great world war was, in a certain respect, also a war waged between advanced capitalistic nations and the less advanced ones, to obtain colonies.

The First Great World War, seen from the ideological aspect, was a war between the Cain-type nations such as Turkey, the Moslem nation persecuting Christianity at that time, together with Germany and Austria-Hungary, who supported Turkey, and the Abel-type nations, such as England, America, and France, who believed in Christianity. To conclude, the First World War was one in which democracy, which was to realize the purpose of the Abel-type view of life, could create the basis of victory on the formation level.

(2) What Decides the Heavenly Side and the Satanic Side?

The Heavenly side and Satanic side are decided according to standard of direction of God's providence of restoration. The position of taking the same direction as that of God's providence of restoration and at least of acting in concert with that direction, even in an indirect way, is called the "Heavenly side," and a position contrary to it is called the "Satanic side." Therefore, its position on the Heavenly side or the Satanic side may not necessarily agree with our common sense, conscience or judgment. The fact that Moses killed the Egyptian may be considered evil by those who do not know God's providence. Nevertheless, when seen from the standpoint of the providence of restoration, it was good. Besides, when seen from the standpoint of not knowing God's providence, we must also regard as evil the Israelites' invasion of the land of Canaan, during which they destroyed all the gentiles without reason. However, this was also good when seen from the standpoint of the providence of restoration. Although there may have been among the Canaanites those who were more conscientious than the Israelites, the Canaanites at that time were uniformly on the Satanic side while the Israelites were uniformly on the Heavenly side.

Further, let us take an example from the religious viewpoint. All religions, having their purpose equally in "goodness," are on the Heavenly side. However, when a certain religion should block the way of another religion closer to God, seen from its mission, that religion may belong to the Satanic side. Since every religion has a certain mission in its age, any religion is apt to fall on the Satanic side when, after having passed its mission-period, it should stand in the way, as an obstacle, to the religion that would appear to carry on a new mission of the next age. Before the coming of Jesus, Judaism and the Jewish people were all on the Heavenly side. But, when they persecuted Jesus, who had come with a new mission in order to fulfill the purpose of Judaism, they fell on the side of Satan, regardless of how well they may have served God in the past.

Since the modern age, all the lineage of the Abel-type view of life is on the Heavenly side, while all other lineage of the Cain-type view of life is on the Satanic side. In that sense, materialists, being the fruit of the Cain-type view of life, are on the Satanic side, no matter how conscientious and devoted to others they may seem from the humanistic point of view. Accordingly, the communist world belongs to the Satanic side. On the other hand, the democratic world where freedom of faith is allowed, being the world existing under the Abel-type view of life, is on the Heavenly side.

As already discussed in Part I, Christianity was set up as the central religion with the final mission to fulfill the purpose of all religions. Therefore, seen from the standpoint of the providence of restoration, anything blocking the way of Christianity toward fulfilling the purpose of this providence belongs to the Satanic side. Consequently, any nation persecuting Christianity or blocking its development, either directly or indirectly, belongs to the Satanic side. Therefore, in World War I, the leading nations on the side of the Allies, such as England, America, France and Russia, were not only the Christian nations, but also the nations who tried to liberate the Christians under persecution in Turkey, the Moslem nation. So, all came out belonging to the Heavenly side. The other leading nations, such as Germany and Austria-Hungary, those who supported Turkey, the Moslem nation that persecuted Christianity, all belonged to the Satanic side, together with Turkey herself.

(3) The Cause of World War I Viewed from the Providence of Restoration

Seen from the providence of restoration, the internal cause of World War I was, first, to set up, worldwide, the condition of indemnity on the formation level to restore God's three great blessings to man. As already clarified above, Satan has realized, in advance, a type of world similar to that which God intended to realize centering on Adam. Therefore, at the consummation of history, there will necessarily appear a non-principled world imitating the formation-degree fulfillment of the three great blessings, centering on the Adam-type personage on Satan's side. In consequence, God's side must smite this world, and set up, worldwide, the condition of indemnity in the formation degree to restore the principled world having perfected the three blessings centered on God. The First World War occurred for that purpose.

Therefore, the Kaiser of Germany, who provoked the First World War, was the personage of the Adamic model, with perfected individuality in the formation stage on Satan's side, and fulfilled the pattern of multiplying children by advocating Pan-Germanism. He then realized the pattern of dominating the whole creation by setting up the policy of world conquest, thus realizing the non-principled world in the type of perfection in formation stage of the three great blessings, centering on Satan. Therefore, in order for the Heavenly side to attain victory by smiting the Satanic side and to set up, worldwide, the condition of indemnity in the formation level to restore the world having perfected the three great blessings centering on God, the First World War was inevitable.

Second, in order to have an earthly man of the Heavenly side overcome Satan's first temptation of Jesus on the worldwide basis, there had to be the First World War. Therefore, seen from the viewpoint centering on the temptation that Jesus had undergone, God's side had to set up the condition of indemnity to restore, worldwide, God's first blessing to man by winning the victory in the First World War. Jesus had established the foundation of restoring his perfect individuality and restored the stone as himself represented in it by overcoming the first temptation in the wilderness. Likewise, God's side had to destroy the

Satanic world, with its central figure, by winning the victory in the First World War and had to establish the world of the Heavenly side with the Lord of the Second Advent as the center, thus laying the foundation for him to restore his perfect individuality.

Third, the First World War was inevitable in order to establish the foundation in the formation stage to restore the Heavenly sovereignty. As we have already discussed (cf. Part II, Ch. IV, Sec. VII, 2[6]) the democratic system appeared as the final type of government to restore God's sovereignty, after having subjugated the society under absolutism. As the facts later proved, nations on the Heavenly side won the victory in the First World War and Christianized the world by broadening their political territory. Thus they established the foundation in the formation stage for democracy and at the same time laid the foundation in the formation stage to restore the Heavenly sovereignty by forming a wide and firm basis of politics and economy on the Heavenly side.

(4) Result of World War I Viewed from the Providence of Restoration

Due to the victory of the Heavenly side in World War I, there was established the condition of indemnity in the formation stage to restore, worldwide, God's three great blessings to man. Seen from the viewpoint of overcoming on the worldwide level Satan's temptation to Jesus, the condition of indemnity to restore, worldwide, God's first blessing to man was established. Then through the democratic nations' victory, the foundation in the formation stage to restore Heavenly sovereignty was established. With the fall of the Satanic world and of the Kaiser who reigned over that world, the foundation of victory in the formation stage in the world on the Heavenly side was established; the foundation was established on which the Lord of the Second Advent could be born as the King of the World on the Heavenly side.

Following this, the communist world rose, centering on Stalin, who was the symbolic representation of the Lord of the Second Advent on the Satanic side. The Satanic side intended to realize the pseudo-form of the Kingdom of Heaven on earth centering on a personage in the pattern of the Lord of the Second Advent on the Satanic side in order to realize, in advance, the ideal of the Heavenly side before the Lord of the Second Advent establishes the ideal of the Kingdom of Heaven on earth under the principles of coexistence, co-prosperity, and common-cause. Therefore, with the victory of the Heavenly side in the First World War, the foundation for the Second Advent of the Messiah was established. From that time began the formation period for the ministry of the Second Advent.

3. THE SECOND WORLD WAR

(1) Providential Outline Concerning World War II

As we have already noticed in history after the Medieval Age, the fundamental spirit of democracy is to realize the purpose of the Abel-type view of life. Therefore democracy is necessarily in pursuit of the world under the ideal of creation, following the natural tendency of the two characteristics, internal and external, of the original nature of man. Naturally, the Second World War was the war in which democracy established the foundation of victory in the growth stage by conquering totalitarianism, which blocked the way of the original nature of man.

(2) What is Totalitarianism?

When the economic panic overwhelmed the whole world in the 1930's, nations such as Germany, Japan and Italy who, under circumstances of isolation, found it difficult to overcome such an adversity, tried to find in totalitarianism a way to break through their difficulty.

What is totalitarianism? Totalitarianism is a political ideology which denies the dignity of man's individuality and the freedom of speech, publication, meeting and association, together with the basic human rights regarding the state and the parliamentary system—which are the bases of the democratic political ideology of the modern nations—and it insists that any individual or group should exist for the benefit and development of the whole nation or state. Therefore, freedom under this system may be defined not as a right for any individual to claim and enjoy, but as a duty or a sacrifice one should pay for the whole.

The guiding principle of totalitarianism does not put any authority on the majority but one one man, the ruler. The will of the ruler, then, becomes the ideology of the whole nation or state. To draw some examples of such totalitarian political systems, there have been those of Mussolini in Italy, Hitler in Germany, and the dictatorial government of the militarists of Japan.

(3) Nations on the Heavenly Side and Those on the Satanic Side During World War II

World War II was a war between the nations on the Heavenly side—U.S.A., England, France—in alliance with one another under democracy, and the nations on the Satanic side—Germany, Japan, Italy—in alliance with one another under totalitarianism. Why, then, is the former on the Heavenly side and the latter on the Satanic side?

The former were on the Heavenly side because they had democracy as their fundamental ideology, which had been built as the political ideology of the final stage of the providence of restoration, centering on the Abel-type view of life. The latter were on the Satanic side because they were the anti-democratic totalitarian nations whose political ideology was centered on the Cain-type view of life. Again, the former were the nations in support of Christianity, while the latter were those standing in an anti-Christian position, thus naturally separating themselves into the Heavenly side and the Satanic side.

Let us now further clarify the details. Germany, which was the center of the Axis Powers of that time, deprived the people of their fundamental freedom, and her control of ideologies exerted its influence even in the religious field. That is, Hitler imposed the strict primitive Germanic religious ideology by concluding a pact with the Pope of Rome, thus founding a national religion, and then tried to control all Protestantism under the supervision of bishops throughout the country. Therefore, the Catholics as well as the Protestants were strongly opposed to Hitler. Furthermore, Hitler massacred six million Jews.

Japanese militarists during the world war forced every Korean church to install a Kamidana (household altar) of Japanese Shintoism, and they compelled the Christians to worship at Japanese shrines. Whoever was against this was imprisoned or killed. They especially massacred Korean Christians who had emmigrated into Manchuria to escape the bondage of Japan and to find freedom. Thus, the policy of annihilating Korean Christianity, which they enforced even into the latter part of the great war, was most atrocious. Italy also became an Axis power by conspiring with Germany, who was on the Satanic side. Mussolini purposely set up Catholicism as the national religion in order to unify the ideology of his people, thus proceeding to go against God's providence of restoration. Upon such a ground we may describe Germany, Japan, and Italy of that day as the nations on the Satanic side.

(4) The Reason the Heavenly Side and the Satanic Side Confronted, with Three Great Powers on Each Side

The Second World War broke out in order to set up, worldwide, the condition of indemnity of the growth level to restore God's three great blessings, left unfulfilled, centering on Jesus.

Originally, it was due to the fall of the three beings, Adam, Eve and the archangel, that God's three great blessings were not fulfilled. Therefore, in restoring the three great blessings, there had to be the participation of three beings in order to restore the three blessings through indemnity. So God fulfilled the spiritual providence of salvation by combining the three beings—Jesus who came as the second Adam, the Holy Spirit who came as the deity of Eve (cf. Part I, Ch. VII, Sec. IV, 1), and the archangel—thus spiritually restoring His three great blessings. Accordingly, the Second World War, which was to set up, worldwide, the condition of indemnity on the growth level to restore the three blessings centered on Jesus, also had to set up the condition to restore the three blessings through indemnity with the nations on the Heavenly side symbolizing Adam, Eve and the archangel winning victory over the nations on the Satanic side, which had a similar pattern. Therefore, Satan, who knew this, mustered beforehand the nations in the patterns of Adam, Eve and the archangel of the Satanic side, ahead of this providence, and had them attack the nations of such patterns on the Heavenly side.

Incidentally, the United States, as a man-type nation, symbolized Adam of the Heavenly side, while England, as a woman-type nation, symbolized Eve on the Heavenly side, and France, as an intermediate type of nation, symbolized the archangel of the Heavenly side. On the other hand, Germany, as a man-type nation, symbolized Adam of the Satanic side, while Japan, as a woman-type nation, symbolized Eve of the Satanic side, and Italy, as an intermediate type of nation, symbolized the archangel of the Satanic side. Before this, the United States, England, France, and Germany, Austria, Turkey in World War I were also nations either on the Heavenly side or on the Satanic side, as the symbolic patterns on the formation level, composed in groups of similar types.

Why did the Soviet Union, which was a nation on the Satanic side, join the Heavenly side? When the medieval society of

Western Europe, centering on the pope, stood in a position never to attain the purpose of the providence of restoration, God had to work His providence to realize the two worlds—of communism and of democracy—by dividing the society into the two worlds based respectively on the Cain-type view of life and the Abel-type view. Meanwhile, the Feudal society and the Monarchic society, or the Imperialistic society, blocked the way of the Heavenly side and at the same time barred the ultimate way of the Satanic side in fulfilling such providence. Therefore, the Heavenly side and the Satanic side united to break that society. The providence of restoration develops with the flow of the age. Accordingly, even the non-principled world, which realizes in the pseudo-form God's providence of restoration ahead of Him, has to develop towards the Satanic purpose with the flow of the age. Therefore, even in the Satanic world, there must be struggle to liquidate the old society because it is an obstacle to the progressive society.

In accordance with such an historical trend, totalitarianism during the Second World War also became an obstacle in the way of the Satanic side, as it did on the Heavenly side. Meanwhile, God had to allow, even temporarily in the providence of restoration, the Satanic side to realize the communist world. Therefore, God let the communist world rapidly bear its own fruit through the Soviet Union's breaking the totalitarian nations in cooperation with the nations on the Heavenly side. However, as soon as the Second World War was over, the two worlds of democracy and communism were divided like water and oil.

(5) The Cause of World War II Viewed from the Providence of Restoration

Seen from the providence of restoration, the first of the internal causes leading to the Second World War was to set up, worldwide, the condition of indemnity on the growth level to restore God's three great blessings. Because of Adam's fall, God, by sending Jesus, the second Adam, tried to restore the world with His three great blessings fulfilled, centering on Jesus. Nevertheless, Jesus fulfilled this only spiritually, by his crucifixion, due to the faithlessness of the Jewish people. On the other hand, Satan always realizes, beforehand, the world in a pattern similar to the world which Jesus intended to realize. Therefore, at the consummation of history, there will no doubt be realized a non-principled world in the pattern of the three great blessings fulfilled on the growth level, centering on a Jesus-type personage on the Satanic side. Consequently, God has to set up, worldwide, the condition of indemnity on the growth level for the restoration of the world in the Principle with the blessings realized, centering on God, by smiting that Satanic world. For this purpose the Second World War came about.

The Jesus-type personage on the Satanic side was Hitler. Therefore, the life of Hitler was very similar to that of Jesus in the aspects of his thinking on a worldwide scale, his single life, his miserable death, and his missing corpse, though his will was exactly opposite to Jesus'. Consequently, Hitler of Germany, who provoked the Second World War, was the Adam-type personage on the Satanic side, while he fulfilled the pattern of multiplying children by advocating Pan-Germanism and realized the pattern of dominating the whole creation by establishing the policy of world hegemony. Thus, he realized the non-principled world in the pattern of having perfected the three great blessings on the growth level, centering on Satan. Now the Heavenly side had to set up, worldwide, the condition of indemnity on the growth level to restore the world, having perfected the three great blessings by winning victory in the Second World War.

Second, World War II came in order to have the earthly men of the Heavenly side undergo and overcome, worldwide, Satan's second temptation to Jesus. Therefore, when we see this from the temptation which Jesus had undergone, the Heavenly side had to set up, on the worldwide level, the condition of indemnity to restore God's second blessing to man by winning victory in the Second World War. Just as Jesus established the foundation for the restoration of the children by overcoming the second temptation in the wilderness, the world on the Heavenly side had to establish the foundation of democracy on the growth level by winning the victory in the Second World War, having men of the Heavenly side thus lay the worldwide foundation for it.

Third, World War II came in order to establish the foundation on the growth level for the restoration of sovereignty. Because of the victory of the Heavenly side in the First World War, the democratic world came to enjoy its foundation on the formation level while, following this, even the Satanic world which had been realizing the Cain-type world could subjugate "imperialism" and establish the foundation, on the formation level, for the communist world. Therefore, the Second World War, as the resultant facts revealed, had completely separated the two worlds of democracy and communism, each having laid its foundation on the growth level. As the democratic world came to enjoy its foundation on the growth level, the restoration of the heavenly sovereignty would come to establish its foundation on the growth level.

(6) Result of World War II Viewed from the Providence of Restoration

The victory of the Heavenly side in the Second World War enabled the establishment of the condition of indemnity on the growth level to restore, worldwide, God's three great blessings to man. Seen from the standpoint of undergoing, worldwide, Satan's temptations to Jesus, the condition of indemnity to restore God's second blessing worldwide was set up. At the same time, the foundation on the growth level for the restoration of sovereignty was established, as the democratic world could lay the basis on the growth level.

Then, seen from the principle of restoration by indemnity, the fact that Hitler (the Jesus-type personage on the Satanic side) and his country were destroyed, and the communist world centering on Stalin (the person in the pattern of the Lord of the Second Advent on the Satanic side) appeared on the worldwide basis foreshadowed that the age in which man has erected the spiritual kingdom centering on the resurrected Jesus had passed, and that the time had come to build a new heaven and a new earth (Rev. 21:1-7), centering on the Lord of the Second Advent.

Thus, after World War II, we entered the growth stage for the ministry of the Second Advent. Many people have therefore received revelations concerning Christ coming again, and spiritual works occur all over the world. At the same time, all the established religions will be secularized in increasing chaos and division, losing their religious power. This is a latter-day phenomenon occurring due to God's final providence for the unification of all the religions through a new and ultimate truth.

4. THE THIRD WORLD WAR

(1) Is the Third World War Inevitable?

In the beginning, God created the first human ancestors and blessed them to dominate the whole world (Gen. 1:28). Therefore, God could not but allow Satan to realize the non-principled world in the pattern of having fulfilled this blessing, with fallen men in front. On the other hand, God, according to His providence of restoration, has worked to take all men back to the Heavenly side, always following Satan from behind. Therefore, at the consummation of human history, both the Heavenly side and the Satanic side must come to dominate the world in their respective ways. Thus, the two worlds of democracy and communism will stand together. For the final separation and unification of these two worlds, there should come world wars. The First and the Second World War having been the wars to divide the world into the two worlds of democracy and of communism, the war for the unification of these two separate worlds must come next. This is the veritable Third World War. Therefore, the Third World War will inevitably come. However, there are two ways for that war to be fought.

First, there is the way to subjugate and unify the Satanic side by weapons. However, the ideal world to come after unification, being that in which the whole of mankind should rejoice, will never be realized by subjugating the enemy only externally by the use of weapons. Therefore they must afterwards be subjugated internally, and come to truly rejoice from the bottom of their hearts. In order to do this, there must be an absolutely perfect ideology that is able to satisfy the desire of man's original nature.

Then, the second way this war may be fought is to subjugate and unify the Satanic world directly by a wholly internal fight through ideology without any external fight by weapons. Men are rational beings. Therefore, the world of perfect oneness will be realized only when they are subjugated and united by reason. The question of which kind of war will actualize one world will be decided according to the success or failure of man's carrying out his own portion of responsibility. Where, then, will the new-world ideology necessary to establish one world come from?

The ideology that may lead the whole of mankind into one ideal world cannot be expected to come from the communist world established by the Cain-type view of life, for the Cain-type view of life is blocking the internal development of man's original nature. Therefore, this ideology should come out of the democratic world which is established by the Abel-type view of life. However, it is a fact, historically proven, that there has not been one ideology among the many existing in the democratic world that can subjugate the communist ideology.

Then, this ideology must newly emerge from the democratic world. In order for this new ideology to come out, there must appear a new truth. This new truth should, of course, be the foundation of the Abel-type view of life, and, naturally, be the foundation of democracy. Just as it was with the course of historical development in which men have pursued newer truth until now, such a new truth, when it should come, will conflict with the old ones which many people have until now believed to be true. So, even in today's democracy, people will be divided into two groups of the different standpoints of Cain and Abel, fighting with each other. Nevertheless, when this new truth establishes a victorious basis in the democratic world and further subjugates the communist ideology, the one world under this one truth will finally be realized.

Satan, knowing in advance God's providence of giving men this new truth to unify them under one ideology, has set forth a false ideology imitating the true one in his attempt to unify the whole of mankind centering on himself. This Satanic "truth" is dialectical materialism. Dialectical materialism attempts to destroy any spiritual being by setting up its own rational ground. The position of this materialism, trying to prove that there is no God, fell into a state of self-destruction, and assumed the logic of denying the existence of Satan himself. Moreover, Satan knows well enough that he himself will perish at the consummation of (evil) history. Realizing his inevitable end, when he will no longer be exalted, he rose to deny God at the risk of sacrificing himself. This denial is actually the core of "dialectical materialism." Therefore, the Heavenly side will never be able to escape from the attack of Satan's theory, unless the democratic world can set forth the truth which will subjugate his ideology. Here lies the historical ground in the providence of restoration that the Heavenly side must proclaim the perfect and absolute truth.

(2) Providential Summary of the Third World War

The Third World War is going to be that in which God intends to restore, as the final measure since He began the providence of restoration, the ideal world by having the democratic world subjugate the communist world. Seen from the viewpoint of the providence of restoration: through World War I, the Heavenly side established a democratic foundation on the formation level with the broadening of the political, economic territory by securing colonies all over the world; through World War II, the territory of the democratic world was stabilized by establishing, worldwide, the democratic foundation of the growth level. Now, through World War III they must build the democratic foundation of the perfection level by setting up the perfect Abel-type view of life, according to the new truth, and on this foundation they must lead all mankind into one world.

Therefore, the Third World War is the final war, in which the Heavenly side should restore through indemnity, horizontally, at the consummation of history, all that it was compelled to hand over to Satan after having tried to fulfill the heavenly will by making the three stages of prolongation in the historical course of the providence of restoration.

(3) The Cause of the Third World War Viewed from the Providence of Restoration

As discussed above, the question of whether the Third World War is to be waged by force of arms or by an ideological battle will be decided according to the success or failure of man's carrying out his own portion of responsibility in fulfilling God's providence of restoration. However, regardless of the type of battle to be fought, there will undoubtedly be one more worldwide war.

Then what would be the internal cause of the Third World War, as seen from the providence of restoration? First, it is to set up worldwide the condition of indemnity on the perfection level to restore God's three great blessings to man. Due to the faithlessness of the Jewish people, the providence of restoration centering on Jesus was fulfilled only spiritually. Therefore Christ must come again on earth to restore the world, both spiritually and physically, in which God's three great blessings are fulfilled. Therefore Satan again attempts to realize the non-principled world in the pattern similar to the world which the Lord is to bring about at the time of the Second Advent. Accordingly, at the close of history, there will be realized the non-principled world in the pattern of having restored the three great blessings, centering on a personage in the pattern of the Lord of the Second Advent on the Satanic side. Therefore, the Heavenly side must set up, worldwide, the condition of indemnity on the perfection level to restore the world having fulfilled the three great blessings centering on God by subjugating that world centering on Satan. For this purpose, there must come the Third World War.

Stalin was the actual personage in the pattern of the Lord of the Second Advent on the Satanic side. Accordingly, Stalin, as the personage in the pattern of having perfected his individuality on the Satanic side, fulfilled the pattern of having multiplied children by advocating the combined efforts of the farmers, fishermen, and laborers in resistance against the democratic world. He also realized the pattern of dominating all things by establishing the policy of Bolshevizing the world, thus fulfilling the pattern of the three great blessings. Therefore, we must know that the communist world is the non-principled world in which Satan has attempted to realize the world of coexistence, co-prosperity, and common-cause which shall be realized in the future, centering on God.

Second, the Third World War will come in order to have men of the Heavenly side overcome, worldwide, the third temptation of Jesus by Satan. Therefore, centering on the temptation which Jesus suffered, the Heavenly side must set up the condition of indemnity to restore, worldwide, God's third blessing by winning the victory in the Third World War. This is because, just as Jesus established the foundation to restore the dominion over all things by overcoming the third temptation in the wilderness, the Heavenly side must restore man's domination over the whole world of creation by winning a victory in the Third World War.

Third, the Third World War must come in order to establish the foundation on the perfection level for the restoration of sovereignty. This is because the Heavenly side must realize the ideal world under the macrocosmic Principle by destroying the communist world, and by having all the sovereignty returned to God through victory in the Third World War.

(4) Result of the Third World War Viewed from the Providence of Restoration

God at first intended to work His providence of restoration by setting up Cain and Abel in Adam's family. Nevertheless, due to Cain's murder of Abel, the sinful history of mankind began. God's work of separating good and evil to restore Adam's family by indemnity began on the individual level. After expanding through the levels of home, tribe, society, race and nation, it has now widened its scope to that of the worldwide level. God intends to restore by indemnity the whole of the providential course which has been prolonged as many as three stages by winning victory in the three world wars, which are the final works of the providence of restoration.

In the beginning, the first human ancestors lost the heart-and-feeling toward God by having been trapped by Satan's words of temptation, and due to the internal spiritual fall and external physical fall they succeeded in Satan's lineage. Therefore the providence of restoration will be fulfilled when all fallen men are restored and succeeded in God's lineage by restoring their heart-and-feeling towards God through His words of life, and by receiving both spiritual and physical salvation (cf. Part II, Ch. II, Sec. III, 3[2]).

The victory of the Heavenly side in these three World Wars will finally enable the realization of the ideal world originally designed at the creation, which God has tried to fulfill through the long, long period of history since the fall of man, by completely restoring through indemnity all the foundations for the providence of restoration.

CHAPTER VI

Second Advent

Jesus clearly spoke about the Second Advent (Matt. 16:27). But he said that no one knew of that day and hour, not even the angels of heaven (Matt. 24:36). Therefore, up to the present, it has been thought reckless even to try to know when, where and how the Lord would come.

By examining the words of Jesus, "Only the Father knows," (Matt. 24:36) and the verse, "Surely the Lord God does nothing without revealing his secret to his servants the prophets," (Amos 3:7) we can understand that God, who knows of the day and hour, will surely let His prophets know all the secrets concerning the Second Advent of the Lord before actualizing it.

Therefore, Jesus said that the Lord would come like a thief (Rev. 3:3), while, on another occasion, he said that, for those in the light, the Lord would not come as a thief (I Thess. 5:4). It was true that Jesus came as a thief to the chief priests and scribes, who were in darkness, but, to the home of John the Baptist, which was in light, God revealed Jesus' birth beforehand. At the time of his birth He revealed the fact to the wise men of the east, Simon, Anna, and the shepherds. Again, Jesus warned the people, telling them to watch at all times, praying that they might have the strength to escape all those things that would take place, because the day of the Second Advent would come upon them suddenly like a snare; so, it is evident that He will reveal it beforehand to the saints who are in the light, so that they may prepare for the coming day of the Lord.

From the examples appearing in the course of the providence of restoration, we can see that God always did things after having revealed the facts to His prophets beforehand; for example: the judgment in Noah's time, His destruction of Sodom and Gomorrah, and the Messiah's coming. Therefore, it is evident that, at the Second Coming of the Lord, God will speak to those who have ears to hear and eyes to see so that they may be enlightened by the saints about what would take place, as He promised that in the Last Days He would pour out His Spirit (Acts 2:17).

SECTION I
When Will Christ Come Again?

We call the time of the Lord's Second Advent the "Last Days." We have already clarified, in the "Consummation of Human History," in Part I, that we are at present in the Last Days. Accordingly, we know that now is truly the time for

Christ to come again. We find in the history of the providence of restoration that Jesus came after the 2000 years of the "providential age of restoration by indemnity." Therefore, seen from the principle of restoration through indemnity, we may understand that the Lord will come at about the end of the 2000 years of the "providential age of the prolongation of restoration through indemnity" (the New Testament Age), which restores through indemnity the previous period, through the substantial time-identity.

As we have discussed in detail concerning World War I, Kaiser Wilhelm II, the Adam-type personage on the side of Satan, perished with the defeat of Germany in the First World War, and Stalin, the personage in the type of the Lord of the Second Advent on the side of Satan, realized the world of communism; this fact foreshadowed that Christ would come again, and restore through indemnity the world under the principle of coexistence, co-prosperity and common-cause. Consequently, we can understand that the period for the Second Advent began right after the First World War.

SECTION II
In What Manner Will Christ Come Again?

1. VIEWPOINT CONCERNING THE BIBLE

God has always revealed important matters of His will in parables and symbols, so that by looking for what would come in the future, any person might understand the demand of the age of God's providence, according to the degree of his intellect and spirituality (John 16:25). Therefore, the Bible has caused the establishment of many different viewpoints by various interpreters. The main cause for denominational divisions lies here.

Consequently, the most important matter of all is the viewpoint from which one interprets the Bible.

The matters concerning John the Baptist supply us with a good example (cf. Part I, Ch. IV, Sec. II, 3). Since we have viewed the Bible for the 2000 years since Jesus from the standpoint that John the Baptist fulfilled his responsibility, the Bible has consequently appeared to support this. But when we consider the Bible again from a different standpoint, we can clearly understand that John the Baptist failed to accomplish his responsibility (cf. Part I, Ch. IV, Sec. II, 3). Likewise, since we have viewed the Bible from the standpoint that the Lord must come on the clouds by literally interpreting that the Bible says this, the Bible has appeared to us only in that way, up to the present time. However, since it is absolutely incomprehensible to the intellect of modern men that the Lord would come on the clouds, it is necessary for us to consider the Bible in detail a second time, from a different standpoint, in order to grasp the true meaning of what the Bible literally says.

We propose a new viewpoint in the section in the Bible concerning John the Baptist. Malachi prophesied that Elijah, who had ascended into heaven, would come before the advent of the Messiah (Mal. 4:5). Consequently, the Jewish people of Jesus' day believed that the very person of Elijah, who had once ascended into heaven, would come again, and they were looking forward to the day of his coming down from heaven. But, most unexpectedly, Jesus said that John the Baptist, the son of Zechariah (Luke 1:13), was Elijah (Matt. 11:14). Here, we came to know, according to the testimony of Jesus himself, that the second advent of Elijah was realized by the birth of John the Baptist, not by his coming down from heaven, as the Jewish people of that time had all expected. In like manner, although many Christians up to the present have believed that Jesus would come on the clouds, there are no grounds to deny the possibility of the Lord being born in the flesh on the earth at the Second Advent, just as the fulfillment of Elijah's second advent by the birth of John the Baptist has shown us. At this point, we need to consider, once again, the numerous Biblical records concerning the Second Advent from the viewpoint that the Lord might come on the earth by being born in the flesh.

At the time of Jesus' coming, many scholars knew that the Messiah would be born in Bethlehem of Judea as the offspring of David (Matt. 2:5-6). But on the other hand, it is not difficult to imagine that there were many saints who believed that the Messiah would come on the clouds, according to the Biblical record that said, "I saw in the night visions, and behold, with the clouds of heaven there came one like a son of man . . ." (Dan. 7:13). Therefore, the Jewish people, even after the crucifixion of Jesus, aroused an anti-Christian movement, saying that Jesus, born in the flesh on the earth, could not be the Messiah. The apostle John named "antichrists" all those who denied that Jesus was born in the flesh, saying:

> For many deceivers have gone out into the world, men who will not acknowledge the coming of Jesus Christ in the flesh. Such a one is the deceiver and the antichrist. (II John 7:8)

There are scholars who insist that Daniel 7:13 is the prophecy of what was going to happen at the Second Coming of the Lord. However, in the Old Testament Age, God was working His providence to fulfill the whole purpose of the providence of restoration with the coming of the Messiah, as we may clearly see from the words, "For all the prophets and the law prophesied until John" (Matt. 11:13), and also "For Christ is the end of the law, that every one who has faith may be justified." (Rom. 10:4) Therefore, it was the situation that no one could ever imagine the second coming of the Messiah, who had once come, until Jesus himself later said that the Lord would come again. In consequence, none of the Jews of Jesus' day could ever think that the prophecy of Daniel 7:13 was concerned with the Second Coming of the Messiah. Therefore, the Jewish people of that time thought that this prophecy would be that which was going to happen at the first coming of the Lord. In this way, even at the time of Jesus' coming, there were many believers who had believed that the Lord would come on the clouds, from Biblical grounds. However, Jesus was actually born in the flesh on earth, and we are compelled by this knowledge to study the Bible from the viewpoint that the Lord may come again in a like manner.

2. THE LORD'S SECOND ADVENT WILL BE REALIZED BY HIS BIRTH ON THE EARTH

We read in the Bible (Luke 17:25) that Jesus, anticipating what was going to happen at the Lord's Second Coming, said, "But first he must suffer many things and be rejected by this generation." If the Lord should come again, as the Bible literally says, on clouds from heaven, in the glory of God, with the trumpet call of the archangel (Matt. 24:30-31), would there be any man who would not serve and exalt the Lord coming in such a manner, no matter how sinful a generation this may be? Therefore, if the Lord should come on the clouds, it could never happen that he would suffer many things and be rejected by this generation.

Why, then, did Jesus say that the Lord would become so miserable at the time of the Second Advent? The Jewish people of Jesus' day were looking forward to the day when Elijah would come again from heaven before the Messiah. Consequently, Jesus, who was seemingly insignificant, suddenly appeared as the Messiah, like a thief, when the Jewish people had not yet heard of the news of Elijah's coming. Therefore, they despised Jesus and treated him badly (cf. Part I, Ch. IV, Sec. II, 2). Jesus, who knew he was in such a situation, anticipated that if, at the Second Advent, the Lord is born as a man and appears like a thief to the Christians, who, waiting for the Messiah, would be looking at the sky alone, just as the Jews did at the coming of Jesus, the Son of man would again be condemned as a heretic and suffer many trials. Therefore, Jesus said that the Lord would be rejected by that generation. Accordingly, we must know that this Biblical verse would only be fulfilled when Christ would come again in the flesh, and never if he should come on the clouds.

Again we read in Luke 18:8 that Jesus said:

> I tell you, he will vindicate them speedily. Nevertheless, when the Son of man comes, will he find faith on earth?

Why should the saints fall into such faithlessness where no faith could even be found when the Lord would appear on the clouds, in the glory of God, with the archangel's trumpet call? This verse, too, can never be fulfilled if the Lord comes on the clouds. Let us recall the situation in Jesus' day. The Jewish people believed that the Messiah would be born as their King in Bethlehem (Matt. 2:6) only after Elijah would come down from heaven. Meanwhile, though Elijah had not yet come, a young man, born and raised as the son of a carpenter in Nazareth, suddenly appeared, calling himself the Messiah. It is understandable that there was not to be found among the Jews any so devout that they would follow him at the risk of their lives. Jesus, who grieved over the situation, lamented in such a manner, anticipating that when the Lord would again appear on the earth in the flesh, the people would also fall into faithlessness to such a degree that nothing like faith would be found, as in the case of the Jewish people, because at the Second Advent all the saints would also be looking up at the sky alone, believing that Christ would come again on the clouds. Therefore, Jesus' words in Luke 18:8 could never be fulfilled unless Christ is born on the earth.

Meanwhile, there are some scholars who interpret the verse to mean that this situation is going to occur because the tribulations for the latter day saints to suffer will be so bitter as to cause them all to fall into faithlessness. But, in the course of restoration, no tribulation could ever block the way of the saints' faith. Then, how much less will it be in the Last Days, when the saints will go through the last barrier of faith? We must understand that it is the reality of our life in faith that the more bitter our tribulations and trials become, the greater the ardor of our search for God and for the saving grace of heaven.

We again read (Matt. 7:22-23) that Jesus said:

> On that day many will say to me, 'Lord, Lord, did we not prophesy in your name, and cast out demons in your name, and do many mighty works in your name?' And then will I declare to them, 'I never knew you; depart from me, you evildoers.'

For the saints with such good faith as to be able to perform miracles and signs in the name of the Lord, would it not be that they would follow and serve the Lord as well when he comes on the clouds in the great glory? Why, then, did Jesus say that they would be rejected by the Lord in such a way? If saints of such devout faith should be rejected by the Lord, there will not be a single saint in the Last Days that can be saved. Consequently, this too will never be fulfilled if the Lord should come on the clouds.

Even in Jesus' day, there must have been many saints whose faith was so ardent as to be able to perform miracles and signs. However, the people who believed that Elijah would first come from heaven before the Messiah did not recognize John the Baptist as the Elijah whom they had long awaited (John 1:21);

they even rejected the Messiah, who had already come. Therefore, Jesus also had to reject them, in tears. In like manner, at the time of the Second Advent, the saints with the faith that the Lord would come on the clouds would also certainly reject the Lord born on earth. Therefore, Jesus said that however ardent the saints might have been in faith, they would be rejected as evildoers by the Lord.

The view on the consummation recorded in Luke 17:20 also could not be fulfilled if Christ would come again on the clouds. Consequently, only under the premise that the Lord will be born on earth could the following Biblical verses be interpreted fully. Let us then closely study the contents of these verses.

"The Kingdom of God is not coming with signs to be observed." (Luke 17:20) If the Lord comes on the clouds, the Kingdom of God would come with signs to be observed. However, even at the time of Jesus, it was true that the Kingdom had already come with the birth of Jesus, but the Jewish people, who had believed and waited for Elijah to come again from heaven, were unable to believe in Jesus and failed to see the Kingdom that came at long last. Likewise, at the time of the Second Advent, the Kingdom of God will come with the birth of the Lord on earth, but the Christians who believe that he will come again on the clouds will not believe in the Lord, who will have come again in the flesh on earth, and thus they will not be able to see the Kingdom.

"The Kingdom of God is in the midst of you." (Luke 17:21) At the time of Jesus, those who believed him to be the Messiah and who followed and served him had already realized the Kingdom of God in their hearts. In the same manner, at the Second Advent, the Lord will be born on earth. Therefore, centering on those saints who will recognize and serve him first, the Kingdom of Heaven will first be realized in their hearts, and when such individuals increase in number, forming societies and nations, the Kingdom of God will gradually appear as a world with signs to be observed. Therefore, we must know that the Lord will not come on the clouds, realizing a Kingdom of God to be observed all of a sudden.

"You will desire to see one of the days of the Son of man and you will not see it." (Luke 17:22) If the Lord comes on the clouds, with the trumpet call of the archangel, everybody will see him, so there will be no reason why they will not see the day of the Son of man. Why then did Jesus say that they would not see the day of the Son of man? At Jesus' coming, the day of the Son of man had already come with his birth on earth, but the Jewish people, who fell into faithlessness, failed to see the day. In the same manner, at the time of the Second Advent, the day of the Son of man will come with his birth on earth, but the Christians, who believe that the Lord will come on the clouds, will not believe in and follow him as the Messiah, even though they may see the Lord. Therefore, it is true that, though the day of the Son of man may have already come, they will not be able to see that day as "the day."

"And they will say to you, 'Lo, there!' or 'Lo, here!' Do not go, do not follow them." (Luke 17:23) As we have already discussed in "Resurrection," the latter day saints whose spiritual standards have reached a certain point may receive a revelation saying "you are the Lord," but, if they don't know the principle of how they came to receive such a revelation, each would call himself the "Lord of the Second Advent," thus becoming an antichrist before the Lord to come. Therefore, Jesus warned the people with these words in order that they might not be tempted by such people.

"As the lightning flashes and lights up the sky from one side to the other, so will the Son of man be in his day." (Luke 17:24) When Jesus was born, the news that the King of the Jews was born reached even to King Herod in the Satanic world, and the whole of Jerusalem was troubled, as the Bible says (Matt. 2:2-3). At the time of the Second Advent, the news of Christ's coming will be transmitted between East and West as rapidly as a flash of lightning, because, at that time, the means of transportation and communication will be highly developed.

We have previously discussed the verse, Luke 17:25. "As it was in the days of Noah, so will it be in the days of the Son of man." (Luke 17:26) Noah, who knew that the flood judgment was coming, called to the people to repent, but they would not listen to him, and finally all were destroyed. In the same manner, Christ will come again in the flesh on earth and call to the people to come into the ark of truth. Nevertheless, the saints who are looking up at the heavens alone for the Lord to come on the clouds will not listen to the words coming from him on the earth; by repelling him as a heretic, they will all fall into the position of having failed to serve the will of God's providence, just as the people in the days of Noah failed.

"Whoever seeks to gain his life will lose it, but whoever loses his life will preserve it." (Luke 17:33) There would be no reason to risk our lives if the Lord were coming again on the clouds of glory, with the trumpet call of the archangel. Since Christ will come again, born in flesh on earth, he will look like a heretic to the saints who believe in his coming again on the clouds. Therefore, anyone believing in and following him will have to risk his life. When anyone is ready to believe in and follow him with such resolution, he will preserve his life, but those who repel him as a heretic, in cooperation with unfavorable circumstances, turning their backs to him in search of present life, will fall into the darkness of death.

"Where the body is, there the eagles will be gathered together." (Luke 17:37) Thus Jesus answered the Pharisees who asked him about the place of the Second Advent. We recall that a bird of prey alighted on the pigeon not cut in two on

Abraham's altar (Gen. 15:11). This indicates that Satan is always looking for an opportunity to take anything that is not sanctified. Therefore, this last answer of Jesus signifies that, just as the evil spirits will be gathered where there is a body of death, the Lord, who is the source of life, will come where there is life. This means that the Lord will appear among the devout saints. As already discussed in the "Resurrection," at the time of the Lord's Second Advent many devout saints will be gathered together in one place through the cooperation of many spirit men. This will be the place of life where the Lord will appear. At the First Advent, Jesus was born among the chosen people who had best served God, and he appeared as the Messiah especially to his disciples, who believed in him and followed him.

Concerning the fact that Christ will come again, born in the flesh on the earth, the Bible says, "She brought forth a male child, one who was to rule all the nations with a rod of iron, but her child was caught up to God and to his throne." (Rev. 12:5) A rod of iron here signifies the Word of God, with which to judge the sinful world and to restore the Kingdom of God on earth. As we have stated in detail in the "Consummation of Human History," judgment by fire is judgment by the tongue; that is, the judgment with words (James 3:6). Therefore, it is said that the words Jesus has spoken will be man's judge in the Last Days (John 12:48), that by the same Word, the heavens and earth that now exist have been reserved unto fire (II Peter 3:7), and that the Lord Jesus will slay the lawless one with the breath of his mouth (II Thess. 2:8). Therefore, the rod of iron is veritably the rod of Jesus' mouth. It is the breath of his lips and tongue, or the very word Jesus speaks (Is. 11:4). That is why it is said, "He shall rule them with a rod of iron, as when earthen pots are broken in pieces." (Rev. 2:27) It is clearly said that this male child is born of a woman and is caught up to God and to His throne. Then, who could be the male child who is born of a woman with the qualification of sitting on the throne of God, and who will rule all the nations with the words of God? This can be none other than the Lord of the Second Advent who is to be born on the earth as the King of Kings, and who will realize the Kingdom of God on earth.

Up to the present, there have been many people interpreting the woman in the above-mentioned Biblical verse (Rev. 12:5) as the "Church." They could not but interpret it as the church, trying to interpret this Biblical verse under the premise that Christ would come on the clouds. In a following passage, "The rest of her offspring" (Rev. 12:17) means those who bear testimony to the Lord by believing in him; that is, the saints in the capacity of adopted sons (Rom. 8:23).

As for the Second Advent of the Lord, some scholars believe that his Second Advent is when Jesus comes through the Holy Spirit (Acts 8:16-17), to live in our individual hearts (John 14:20). In that case, since Jesus would be present in the heart of any faithful believer from the time of the coming of the Holy Spirit at Pentecost to the present, we must believe that if this is really the Second Advent, then it has already taken place in the remote past, some 2000 years ago.

Some Christian denominations believe that Jesus will come again in a spiritual body. However, immediately after his resurrection from the tomb three days after his death, he visited his disciples, assuming the same appearance without a bit of difference from that of his lifetime (Matt. 28:9); and from that time until the present date, he has freely visited and taught, at any moment, any believer with a high spiritual standard. Therefore, we must think that this type of Second Advent also took place 2000 years ago. If this was the Second Advent, it would not be necessary for us now to look forward anew to the day of the Second Advent of the Lord as the historical day of our utmost desire.

From the fact that the disciples of Jesus were waiting for the day of the Second Coming even though they could meet him in spirit at any moment, we know that they did not envision the Second Advent which they were so eagerly looking forward to as his return in a spiritual body. Jesus said, "Surely I am coming soon," (Rev. 22:20) to the apostle John, whom he often met in spirit. John, who heard this, answered him saying, "Amen. Come, Lord Jesus!" Here, we find that Jesus, himself, well expressed that his coming in a spiritual body was not the Second Advent, and it is evident that the apostle John also did not regard his appearing in spirit as the Second Advent. Therefore, if the Second Advent is not Jesus' coming again in a spiritual body, it is an undeniable fact the Christ must come again in the flesh, just as in the first coming.

As stated in detail in the "Principle of Creation," God created both the invisible and the visible worlds, and created man to have both spirit and body, in order to have him dominate the two worlds, according to His words of blessing. Nevertheless, due to Adam's fall, man failed to enjoy dominion over these two worlds. Therefore, the creation, which had lost the dominator, came to wait in lamentation for the revealing of the sons of God, who could dominate it (Rom. 8:19-22). Therefore, Jesus, having come as a perfect dominator of these two worlds, in the capacity of a perfected Adam (I Cor. 15:27), intended to make all his saints (believers) the dominators over the whole creation, making them one body with himself by engrafting them to his body (Rom. 11:17). Nevertheless, due to the Jewish people's rebellion against him, the physical body of Jesus was delivered into the hands of Satan as the condition of ransom for the restoration of the Jews and the whole of mankind back to God's bosom; his body was invaded by Satan. Naturally, the physical salvation of mankind was left unfulfilled, and Jesus died, promising it would be realized when the Lord would come again (cf. Part I, Ch. IV, Sec. I, 4). Therefore, up to the present there has not been a single man who, having become perfect both spiritually and physically on the earth, could help harmonize the invisible world and the visible world by dominating both.

In consequence, the Lord, who is to come as a perfect substantial being on that standard, will not come in a spiritual body alone. As in Jesus' coming, he must come as a man perfected both spiritually and physically. Making the whole of mankind become one body with him by engrafting them to him both spiritually and physically (Rom. 11:17), he must make them become perfect both spiritually and physically, thus making them able to dominate both the invisible and the visible worlds.

Jesus, by restoring the Kingdom of God on earth, should have become the True Parent of restored mankind and the King of the Kingdom on earth (Is. 9:6, Luke 1:31-33). Nevertheless, he failed to fulfill this will due to the faithlessness of the people; he died on the cross, promising the Lord would come again later and surely fulfill it. Consequently, at the Second Advent, he must realize the Kingdom of God on earth as intended at Jesus' coming and become the True Parent of mankind and the King of the Kingdom as well. Naturally, even at the Second Advent, the Lord must be born in the flesh on the earth, as in the First Advent.

Besides, the redemption of man's sin is possible only through man's life on earth (cf. Part I, Ch. I, Sec. VI, 3[2]). In order to fulfill the purpose of redemption, Jesus had come as a man. However, since the salvation through Jesus' cross is only spiritual, the original sin still remains inherent in our physical body. Therefore, Christ must come again in order to complete the physical salvation. Accordingly, the Lord will come in the flesh as in Jesus' coming because he would not be able to attain this purpose if he would come again in a spiritual body alone. We have previously clarified, in many ways, that the Lord should come at the Second Advent in the flesh, as in Jesus' coming, and not in a spiritual body.

If the Lord would come again in a spiritual body, it would be illogical that the spiritual body, which can be seen only by spiritual eyes, transcendent of time and space, should come on the clouds, which is a kind of material. Moreover, if the Second Advent will surely be realized not in a spiritual body but in the flesh, where has the Lord been staying in the air as a physical body, and how can he come on the clouds? About this question, one may ask what miracle would be impossible for God, almighty and omnipresent, to perform. However, God cannot ignore the laws which He has set up. Consequently, God need not and cannot work His providence in such a non-principled way that Christ, coming again in flesh the same as ours, should come on the clouds, after having waited in the air among some worlds other than the earth. Based on the proof that we have hitherto dealt with, we can admit with no doubt that the Lord's Second Advent will be realized by his birth in the flesh on earth.

3. WHAT DOES THE BIBLICAL PASSAGE SAYING CHRIST WILL COME ON THE CLOUDS SIGNIFY?

If the Second Advent of the Lord is to be realized by a birth on the earth, we must know the significance of the Biblical passage saying that he will come on the clouds. To know this, we must first understand the meaning of the word "clouds." We read in Revelation 1:7:

> Behold, he is coming with the clouds, and every eye will see him, every one who pierced him; and all tribes of the earth will wail on account of him. Even so, Amen.

From this we know that all men will surely see Christ coming again. Meanwhile, at the time when Stephen was martyred, only the saints whose spiritual eyes were open could see Jesus sitting at the right hand of God (Acts 7:55). Consequently, if Jesus, who is in the spirit world, should come in a spiritual body as he now is, he will be seen only by those whose spiritual eyes are open; so it would never be that every eye will see Christ coming again. Therefore, we can understand that it is because he will come in the flesh that the Bible says every eye will see the Lord at his coming. The Lord, in the flesh, cannot come on the clouds, so the "clouds" are surely symbolic.

The same Biblical passage goes on to say that every one who pierced him will also see him. Those who pierced Jesus were the Roman soldiers of his days. However, those Roman soldiers, of course, cannot see the Lord coming again. It is because, if the Roman soldiers are to be able to see the Lord coming again on the earth, they must be resurrected, but it says in Revelation 20:5 that those who will be resurrected at the time of the Lord's Second Advent are only those who will participate in the first resurrection, and the rest of the dead would not come to life until the thousand years (the millennium) are ended. Therefore, we must interpret "those who pierced" as a parable, regarding it to be the appellation for those who, having believed Christ will come again on the clouds, will disregard and persecute him when he comes again most unexpectedly through a physical birth on the earth. If "those who pierced" should be interpreted as a parable in this way, there would be no reason why we cannot interpret the word "clouds" in the same passage, also, as a parable.

What, then, is the word "clouds" likened to? "Clouds" would denote that which is vaporized (purified) from the dirty water on the earth. Water symbolizes the fallen man (Rev. 17:15). Then we may understand that the clouds would signify the devout saints, whose minds are always in heaven and not on earth, completely reborn from the fallen race of men. Again, "cloud" is often used, either in the Bible or in the classics, as a word representing a crowd (Heb. 12:1). We may see that the word is also used in that way, even today, in the languages of both East and West. The pillar of clouds by day which led the Israelites in Moses' course represented Jesus, who was to come later as the leader of the same nation; the pillar of fire by night represented the Holy Spirit, who, as the object of Jesus, was to lead the Israelites by the fire of inspiration. From the a-bove, we know that Christ's coming on the clouds means that he will appear as the leader of the Christians, the Second Israel, amidst a group of reborn saints. As we have previously studied in detail, when Jesus answered the Pharisees' question as to where the Lord would come again (Luke 17:37) by saying that where the body is, there the eagles will be gathered to-gether, he meant that the Lord would come to the place where the devout saints would be gathered together, which signifies the same thing as the coming on the clouds.

If we should thus interpret the cloud as a parable, we may as well think that the Lord came on the clouds at the time of the First Advent. This is because Jesus, though he was in fact born on the earth, was surely one who came from heaven, seen from his significance and value, just as the Bible says, "The first man [Adam] was from the earth, a man of dust; the second man [Jesus] is from heaven," (I Cor. 15:47); "No one has ascended into heaven but he who descended from heaven, the Son of man." (John 3:13) This is the reason why it was believed that the Lord would come on the clouds, even at the first coming (Dan. 7:13).

4. WHY DID JESUS SAY THAT THE LORD WOULD COME ON THE CLOUDS?

There are two reasons why Jesus foretold that the Lord would come on the clouds. First, it was to prevent the delusions of antichrists. If it had been clarified that Christ would come on earth in the flesh, the confusion caused by the delusions of many antichrists could not have been prevented by any means. Since Jesus appeared as the Messiah from a low and humble position of life, any humble man who had attained a certain spiritual standard could arise, calling himself the Lord of the Second Advent, thus dazzling the whole world into a great delusion. But fortunately, this kind of confusion has been avoided because all the believers, knowing that Christ would come on the clouds, have looked up into heaven. However, since the time is now full, God will surely tell us, straightforwardly, that Christ will be born again on the earth.

Second, it was to encourage those saints who were walking the difficult path of faith at that time. There are numerous other examples in which Jesus said things in such a way that they sounded illogical in order to encourage the saints to fulfill God's will as rapidly as possible. To draw examples, Jesus, in order to make his disciples believe that the Second Coming would be fulfilled right away, said, ". . . for truly, I say to you, you will not have gone through all the towns of Israel, before the Son of man comes." (Matt. 10:23) Again, when Jesus had told Peter of his approaching martyrdom, he asked Jesus what would become of the disciple John; then Jesus replied, "If it is my will that he remain until I come, what is that to you?" (John 21:18-22) According to this word of Jesus, some of his disciples were looking forward to the Second Advent, which they thought might take place during John's lifetime. On another occasion, Jesus said, "Truly, I say to you, there are some standing here who will not taste death before they see the

Son of man coming in his Kingdom," (Matt. 16:28) which made his disciples think that they could possibly see the Lord coming again in their lifetime.

In this way, Jesus spoke as if the Lord were coming very soon; this encouraged his disciples so much that even under the oppression of the Roman Empire and the persecution by Judaism, they were all filled with the Holy Spirit (Acts 2:1-4), and then they could found the early Christian Church, all from an ardent hope for the Second Advent, which they thought was imminent. It was also to stimulate and encourage the saints who were under severe tribulations that he told them he would come on the clouds from heaven in the power and glory of God with the trumpet call of the archangel, and fulfill all things like a flash of lightning.

SECTION III
Where Will Christ Come Again?

If Christ is to be born as a man in flesh on this earth, and not to come again in a spiritual body, he will surely be born in a certain nation of God's elect in some place of God's predestination.

Where, then, would the place of predestination be, and which nation would be God's elect?

1. WOULD CHRIST COME AGAIN AMONG THE JEWISH PEOPLE?

Some Christians believe that Christ will come again among the Jewish people, based on the following Biblical records: at the time of the Second Advent, the number of the sealed would be a hundred and forty-four thousand out of every tribe of the sons of Israel (Rev. 7:4); Jesus said to his disciples, ". . . truly, I say to you, you will not have gone through all the towns of Israel before the Son of man comes." (Matt. 10:23) Jesus said to those listening to him, "Truly I say to you, there are some standing here who will not taste death before they see the Son of man coming in his Kingdom." (Matt. 16:28) However, in order to know the truth of the matter, Christians must know the fundamental providence of God.

On another occasion (Matt. 21:33-43), Jesus clearly indicated, in his parable of the vineyard, that the Lord would not come again to the nation that would persecute and kill him, but take the Kingdom of God (the heritage) from them and give it to the nation producing the fruits of it (at the time of the Second Advent). In this parable, Jesus meant God, by the owner of the vineyard; God's heritage, by the vineyard; the chosen nation of Israel in charge of God's heritage, by the tenants; His prophets, by the servants; the Lord, by the owner's son; and a certain other nation which will be able to fulfill God's will in receiving and serving the Lord of the Second Advent, by another nation producing the fruits.

Why, then, did Jesus say that the Lord was going to come again to the sons of Israel? In order to elucidate this question, let us first study what the word "Israel" really means.

Israel is a name meaning "he prevailed," which Jacob received from the angel of the Lord after he had prevailed in wrestling with the angel at the ford of Jabbok, which he did in order to establish Abel's position for the substantial offering (Gen. 32:28). Jacob, by succeeding in the substantial offering after thus establishing Abel's position, could lay the family-level foundation for the Messiah. Therefore, his offspring who succeeded this will on that foundation are called "Israel." God's elect, "Israel," thus means the people of God who have triumphed in faith, and does not necessarily mean the lineal descendants of Jacob.

This is why John the Baptist said to the Jews, "Do not presume to say to yourselves, 'We have Abraham as our father'; for I tell you, God is able from these stones to raise up children to Abraham." (Matt. 3:9) Paul said, "For he is not a real Jew who is one outwardly, nor is true circumcision something external and physical. He is a Jew who is one inwardly and real circumcision is a matter of the heart, spiritual and not literal." (Rom. 2:28-29) Again, he testified, saying, "not all who are descended from Israel belong to Israel." (Rom. 9:6) These were Paul's words to reproach the Jews who were proud of being the chosen nation just because they were lineal descendants of Abraham, even though they did not live in accordance with the will of God.

Therefore, it can be said that Jacob's descendants had been the chosen people of Israel at the time of their departure from Egypt, but they were no longer "Israel" when they rebelled against God in the wilderness. Therefore, God abandoned all of them to perish in the wilderness, and led into Canaan only their descendants who followed Moses, as the real Israel. Of the descendants who went into the land of Canaan, those of the Northern Kingdom, which consisted of the ten tribes that rebelled against God, perished because it was no longer the chosen nation of Israel; only the Southern Kingdom of Judah, which consisted of the two tribes which followed God's will, could, as the true chosen people of Israel, receive Jesus. Nevertheless, these Jewish people, too, completely lost their qualification as the chosen people when they crucified Jesus.

Who, then, would be the chosen people of Israel after Jesus' death on the cross? They are the devout Christians who, taking up the faith of Abraham, have succeeded to the mission which his lineal descendants have failed to carry out. Therefore, the Bible clarified that the center of God's providence of restoration has been shifted from the Israelites to the Gentiles (Acts 13:46), by saying, "Through their [the Jews] trespass, salvation has come to the Gentiles, so as to make Israel jealous." (Rom. 11:11) Therefore, we may understand that the chosen people of Israel, who are to establish the foundation for the Messiah of the Second Advent, are not the lineal descendants of Abraham, but the devout Christians who have taken up the faith of Abraham.

2. CHRIST WILL COME AGAIN TO AN EASTERN NATION

As Jesus said in Matthew 21:33 in a parable, the Jewish people, by delivering Jesus to the cross, fell to the position of the tenants who killed the son of the vineyard owner. Which nation, then, shall be the one that will succeed to God's heritage, taken away from the Jewish people, and produce the fruits of it? The Bible teaches us that the nation is in the East.

We read in the Bible (Rev. 5:1) that in the right hand of God there was a scroll, written within and on the back, sealed with seven seals, ". . . and no one in heaven or on earth or under the earth was able to open the scroll or look into it," and John, seeing it, wept profusely. Then, the Lamb went and took the scroll from the right hand of Him who was seated on the throne (Rev. 5:7) and opened each of the seven seals (Rev. 6:1).

We read the record of the Lamb having opened the sixth seal (Rev. 6:12) and, as an intermediate scene before the opening of the last seal, there is the record in Revelation 7. The Bible goes on to say in Revelation 7:2-4 that another angel ascended from the rising of the sun with the seal of the living God and sealed the chosen servants of God on their foreheads, and the number of those sealed was one hundred and forty-four thousand. It is again written that there stood the Lamb, the Lord, and with him one hundred and forty-four thousand who had been sealed (Rev. 14:1).

From these Biblical verses, we may know that Christ will be born in a country in the East—that is, from the rising of the sun—and place a seal on the foreheads of the hundred and forty-four thousand, the first chosen among the people of the land, with his name and his Father's name (Rev. 14:1). Therefore, we see that the nation which would take over God's heritage and produce the fruits for the Second Advent of the Lord is in the East. Then, which of the many nations of the East will be the very nation?

3. THAT NATION OF THE EAST IS KOREA

Now we know, as previously elucidated, that Christ would not come again among the lineal descendants of Abraham, but to the nation that would take their heritage and produce the fruits of it; that the nation which would produce the fruits should be one of the Eastern nations. From ancient times, by the "Eastern nations," we refer to Korea, Japan, and China. Meanwhile, Japan, among the three, is the nation that has worshipped Amaterasuomikami generation after generation; moreover, she entered the period of the Second Advent as a totalitarian nation, and as will be discussed later, she is the nation which persecuted the Christianity of Korea. China, being a communist nation, is on the Satanic side, together with Japan.

Therefore, the nation of the East where Christ will come again would be none other than Korea. Now, let us prove, from several viewpoints based on the Principle, that Korea should be the nation that can receive the Lord of the Second Advent. The nation where the Messiah will come must meet the following conditions.

(1) This Nation Must Lay the Nationwide Foundation for the Restoration by Indemnity

In order for Korea to become the nation that can receive the Messiah, she must lay the nationwide 40-day foundation for the separation from Satan for the cosmic restoration of Canaan.

What, then, are the grounds for the Korean people to lay this foundation? If the Lord should come again, in Korea, the Korean people will become the "Third Israel," God's elect. Abraham's lineal descendants, who had been persecuted in Egypt while serving God's will in the Old Testament Age, were the "First Israel," while the Christians, who, branded as heretics by the First Israel, having taken over the providence of restoration while serving the resurrected Jesus, were the Second Israel. Meanwhile, we have already learned through previous statements that the Lord will be branded as a heretic, even by the Christians, the "Second Israel"; just as it is prophesied in Luke 17:25 that the Lord must first suffer many things even at his Second Advent, as in Noah's days. If so, God will have to abandon the Christians when they persecute the Lord of the Second Advent, just as He abandoned the Jewish people who refused Jesus (Matt. 7:23). Then, the Korean people, who are to accomplish the third providence of God by serving the Lord of the Second Advent, will become the Third Israel, the chosen nation.

The First Israel suffered the 400-year slavery in Egypt, which was the Satanic world at that time, in order to establish the 40-day foundation for the separation from Satan to start the course of the nationwide restoration of Canaan. Likewise, the Second Israel also struggled and overcame the 400-year persecution by the Roman Empire, which was the Satanic world at that time, in order to establish the 40-day foundation for the separation from Satan to start the course of the worldwide restoration of Canaan. Naturally, the Korean people, being the Third Israel, must suffer slavery for a certain length of time corresponding to the number "40" under a nation of the Satanic side in order to establish the 40-day foundation for the separation from Satan to start the course of the cosmic restoration of Canaan. This was actually the 40-year period in which Korea suffered persecution as a vassal state of the Japanese Empire.

Under what circumstances did the Korean people come to suffer the 40-year slavery under the Japanese Empire? Japan's imperialistic and aggressive control of Korea was extended according to the "Eul-sa Treaty of Protection," which was a treaty committing Korea's entire diplomatic rights to the care of the Foreign Affairs Ministry of the Japanese Empire, and which was concluded in 1905 between Hiro-humi Ito of Japan and Wan Yong Lee of Korea, a pro-Japanese Minister of Education at that time. Japan, in fact, deprived Korea of rights in all fields, such as politics, diplomacy and economics, by interfering with the entire domestic administration, through the governor and secretaries whom the Japanese placed in every district. This was the "Eul-sa Treaty of Protection."

Japan, after her annexation of Korea by force in 1910, completely deprived the Korean people of their freedom, imprisoning or slaughtering numerous patriots, and worst of all, invading the royal palace and even killing the Queen. During the Korean Independence Movement on the first of March, 1919, Japanese killed countless good citizens of Korea. Moreover, at the time of the great Kanto Earthquake of Japan in 1923, the Japanese people, by fabricating groundless rumors, massacred innumerable innocent Koreans living in Tokyo. Meanwhile, countless Koreans, who could not bear the Japanese tyranny, had to immigrate into the vast Manchurian wilderness in search of freedom, leaving the fertile soil of their fatherland in the hands of the Japanese. There, they struggled for the liberation of their fatherland, undergoing unspeakable hardships and privations. Japanese soldiers, searching village by village for patriotic Koreans, detained sometimes whole villages, including the aged and young, in one building and massacred them by setting the building on fire. Japan continued such tyranny until the day of the fall of the empire. Koreans who died either at the time of the Sam-il Independence Movement or in the wilderness of Manchuria were mostly Christians. Further, towards the end of the Imperial Government, Japanese forced Korean Christians to worship at Shinto shrines and imprisoned or slaughtered countless Christians who objected to it. Besides, the oppressive policy of Japanese Imperialism toward Korean Christianity shortly before her August 15 liberation was atrocious. However, with the admission of defeat in World War II by the Japanese Emperor Hirohito, the Korean people were finally liberated from bondage.

In this manner, the Korean nation, during the 40 years after the "Eul-sa Treaty of Protection" in 1905 until their liberation in 1945, went through persecution, not less severe than that which the "First Israel" and the "Second Israel" suffered respectively in Egypt and in the Roman Empire. Since the Independence Movement arose chiefly among the Christians at home and abroad, it was mostly the Christians who suffered the persecution.

(2) This Nation Must Be God's Front Line and Satan's Front Line

Since God in the beginning blessed Adam to have dominion over the whole creation, He had to allow Satan to realize, ahead of Him, the non-principled world in the pattern of the blessings. Meanwhile, God has been restoring this world to the Heavenly side. Therefore, at the consummation of human history, as previously stated, this world is necessarily split into two worlds:

one of democracy and the other of communism. Since the Lord is coming in order to restore the fallen world to the original world of creation, it is evident that God should work His providence to restore the communist world to the Heavenly side, centering on the country where the Lord of the Second Advent is coming. Therefore, Korea, where the Lord will come, should become the front line of God's immense love and, at the same time, that of Satan's growing hatred; in other words, where the two powers of democracy and communism should conflict with each other. The 38th parallel of Korea was formed according to this providence of restoration.

That which lies on the line of rivalry between God and Satan, for the condition as to which is right, is the offering of sacrifice. Since the Korean people are the offering of sacrifice as a nation placed on that line for the universal restoration, God has to cut this nationwide sacrifice in two, just as He had Abraham cut his offerings. This is why Korea is cut in two by the 38th parallel separating her into two nations—one of Cain-type and the other of Abel-type.

Naturally, this 38th parallel is the very front line for both democracy and communism, and, at the same time, the front line for both God and Satan. Therefore, the war which broke out on June 25, 1950 across the 38th parallel of Korea, was not merely a conflict between fellow countrymen caused by the severance of the land, but the confrontation between the two worlds of democracy and communism, and, further, the confrontation between God and Satan. Since this agitation assumed a worldwide nature for the purpose of the providence of restoration, the mobilization of many U.N. member-nations in the Korean War helped them to unconsciously participate in God's providence by working for the liberation of the fatherland.

At the moment of the fall of the first human ancestors, the Heavenly side and the Satanic side were split apart at this one point. Therefore, life and death, good and evil, love and hatred, joy and sorrow also were split apart at this one point and have been in conflict for the long period of history ever since. The conflicting pairs were respectively divided into the two worlds of democracy and communism. These, again, came to conflict on the worldwide level, centering on Korea. Therefore, Korea has confronted a great chaos with religions and ideologies, politics and economics conflicting here; all of these gradually influence the whole world. This is because these kinds of phenomena, rising first in the spirit world, are to develop substantially centering on Korea, the center of the providence of restoration, and to further expand to become worldwide. However, we must know that the coming of such chaos is the sign of the coming of the world of a new order, just as it was written, ". . . as soon as its branch becomes tender and puts forth its leaves, you know that summer is near." (Matt. 24:32)

When the Pharisees asked Jesus about the place of the Second Advent, Jesus answered by saying, "Where the body is, there the eagles will be gathered together." (Luke 17:37) Eternal life and eternal death are to confront each other in Korea, which is both God's front line and Satan's front line. Therefore, Satan, symbolized by the eagles, is supposed to gather here in search of the people of death, while the Lord is also coming to this land in search of the people of life.

(3) This Nation Must Be the Object of God's Heart

In order to become the object of God's heart, we must first walk the path of blood, sweat and tears. By being under Satan's domination, man came to stand in opposition to God. Therefore, God, with a parental heart, full of sorrow over the loss of His children, has wandered in the sinful world to save the children of corruption. In order to save mankind, who had rebelled against Him, God had His loving children sacrificed by

Satan, finally suffering the sorrow of having to give His son, Jesus, to the cross. Therefore, since the fall of man up to the present day, God has grieved day after day, while any individual, home or nation which has struggled against the Satanic world for the will of God, has not been able to avoid the way of blood, sweat and tears.

How can we expect to be comfortable and complacent as children walking the path of filial piety and loyalty as the object of the parental heart in such grief? The nation that can receive the Messiah must walk the way of blood, sweat and tears, because its people must become children of filial piety by standing as the object of God's sorrowful heart. Since the First Israel walked the path of tribulation, the Second Israel did the same. The Korean people also, as the Third Israel, must necessarily walk the same path. The historical course of untold misery, which the Korean people have gone through, was the necessary way for them to walk as the people of God's elect. As a result, the path of affliction has led the Korean people to a great blessedness.

Next, the nation to be the object of God's heart must necessarily be a people good in God's sight. The Korean nation is a people of homogeneous lineage, having a long history of more than 4000 years. Even during the dynasties of Kokuryo and Silla, when the national power was in the prime state, Korea only repelled aggressive foreign powers and never once invaded other countries. Considering that Satan's first nature is his aggressive arrogance, it is evident, seen merely from this aspect, that the Korean people are on the Heavenly side. God's strategy has been that of winning victory from the position of being attacked. Therefore, even though countless prophets and good men have been sacrificed in the course of history, and God allowed His son, Jesus, to be crucified, the result has always been a victory for God. Both in the first and second World Wars, the Satanic side was always the first to attack, but both times the victory was won by the Heavenly side. In like manner, the Korean people have been invaded by innumerable nations in the course of history. Nevertheless, this was only to win the final victory as the nation on the Heavenly side.

The Korean people are, by nature, endowed with a religious gift. Their religious nature has always tried to pursue, apart from reality, that which is more than reality. Therefore, the Korean nation, which is endowed with a strong God-revering thought, from very ancient times when her cultural standard was low, until the present, has never valued any religion which pursues everyday happiness by worthlessly deifying natural objects. The Korean people, as a whole, have a national character which highly values loyalty, filial piety and virtue. It is a tendency, coming from the very undercurrent of her national character of valuing loyalty, filial piety and virtue, that this nation, as a whole, loves such noble stories as "Chun Hyung" and "Shim Chung."

(4) This Nation Must Have Prophetical Testimonies Among the People

Concerning the prophetical testimony revealed to the Korean nation, first, we learn that this nation has a Messianic idea according to the revelation given to its people. The First Israel believed, from the testimonies of its prophets (Mal. 4:2-5, Is. 60:1-22), that the Messiah would come in the future as its King, and, establishing the Kingdom, would save the people. The Second Israel went through the difficult path of faith in the hope that the Messiah would come again.

Likewise, the Korean nation, as the Third Israel, has believed since the 500-year reign of the Yi Dynasty the prophecy that the King of Righteousness would appear in that land, and, establishing the Millennium, would come to receive tributes from all the countries of the world. This faith has encouraged the people to undergo the bitter course of history, waiting for the time to come. This was truly the Messianic idea of the Korean people which they believed according to "Chung Gam Nok," a book of prophecy. Since it includes the prophecy that a new king would appear in Korea, the rulers have outlawed this ideology. Moreover, the rulers during the Japanese regime suppressed the idea by burning the books in order to annihilate this ideology. After Christianity was introduced, this idea was trodden down as a superstition. Nevertheless, this Messianic expectation, which is deeply rooted in the Korean soul, has continuously been handed down until the present time. Interpreted correctly, the King of Righteousness—Chung-Do Ryung (the person coming with God's right words)—whom the Korean people have so long waited for, is a Korean-style name for the Lord of the Second Advent. God revealed through Chung Gam Nok, before the introduction of Christianity in Korea, that the Messiah would come again, at a later time, in Korea. Today, many scholars have come to ascertain that most of the prophecies written in this book coincide with those in the Bible.

Secondly, the reality is that the believers of every religion within this nation are receiving revelations that the founder of their own religion will come again in Korea. As we have stated in detail in Part I, Chapter III, it is true that, seen from the history of development of the cultural spheres, all religions are being united into one religion; namely, Christianity. Christianity, in the Last Days, is the final religion which can fulfill the purpose of the innumerable other religions which have appeared until now. Consequently, Christ, who is coming again as the center of Christianity, is supposed to accomplish, wholly, the purpose of all religions, which the respective founders intended to realize during their lives on the earth. Therefore, the Lord of the Second Advent, seen from the viewpoint of his mission, represents the second coming of the founder of every religion (cf. Part I, Ch. V, Sec. II, 4). Naturally, the founders of many religions, who the respective followers think will come again in Korea to fulfill their expectations, according to what they received by revelations, will not return as different individuals, but, in fact, will return through one great personage, the Lord of the Second Advent. Each religious body has received revelations different from others concerning the Second Coming of the Lord. Buddhism is saying that Miruk-Bul(Buddha) is coming, while Confucianism says Jin-In (True Man), Chun-Doism says Choi Su Un (its founder), and the Chung-Gam-Nok group says Chung-Do Ryung (Man with True Words) will come.

Third, we can denote the fact that many spiritual signs regarding the Lord coming again in Korea are appearing like mushrooms after a rain. God's word of promise that He will pour down His Spirit upon all flesh (Acts 2:17) is being realized among the Korean people today. Therefore, countless men of religion are receiving very clear revelations concerning the Lord's Second Coming in Korea in many different ways, by contacting many spirit men of various levels: from the realm of miscellaneous spirits to the realm of the paradise level spirits. Nevertheless, the leaders of the present Christian world, due to their spiritual ignorance, are still unresponsive, and have refused to pay heed to such things. This is similar to what happened in Jesus' day, when the chief priests and rabbis, who should have been the first to know of the coming of the Messiah, were entirely unaware of the fact due to their spiritual ignorance, while, on the other hand, the astrologers and shepherds knew of the message through revelations.

Jesus said, "I thank thee, Father, Lord of heaven and earth, that thou hast hidden these things from the wise and understanding, and revealed them to babes." (Matt. 11:25) By this, Jesus lamented over the spiritual ignorance of the leaders of

Judaism at that time, and, at the same time, he thanked God for His pouring down grace, by revealing heavenly things to the believers of that time, who were innocent like babes, though not learned.

(5) All Aspects of Culture and Civilization Must Bear Fruit in This Nation

As already mentioned (cf. Part I, Ch. III, Sec. V, 1), only with the unification of religion and science, or spiritual civilization and material civilization, which have been developed to overcome man's two aspects of ignorance, could the fundamental problems of man be totally solved and the ideal world of God's creation naturally be realized. The world which the Lord should realize at the Second Coming must be one where science has developed to the utmost degree so that all cultures which have developed on the vertical course of history in the providence of restoration can be restored at once horizontally, in the society centering on the Lord of the Second Advent, thus realizing the cultural society of the highest degree. Therefore, all religion and science—and accordingly, the two aspects of culture, spiritual and material—must be absorbed and harmonized under one truth centering on Korea, bearing fruit which belongs to the ideal world of God's desire.

First, all the aspects of civilization concerning development on the land must also bear fruit in Korea. Accordingly, the Continental-culture of the ancient age, born in Egypt, was shifted to be the Peninsular-culture of Greece, Rome, and Iberia. This Peninsular-culture was again shifted to be the Island-culture of England. Then the Island-culture became the Continental-culture of America, and returned to the Island-culture of Japan. Now, this cycle of the pilgrimage of culture must be completed and finalized as the Peninsular-culture in the land of Korea, where Christ should come again.

Second, the aspect of civilization concerning rivers and seas must bear fruit as the Ocean-culture of the Pacific where Korea is located. The River-culture, which first developed on the Rivers Nile, Tigris and Euphrates, was shifted to be Mediterranean-culture centering around Greece, Rome, Spain and Portugal; then, this Mediterranean-culture was again shifted to be the Atlantic-culture centering on England and America; this culture will finally bear fruit as the Pacific-culture, where America, Japan and Korea are equally situated on the coastal line.

Third, the aspect of civilization which concerns the climate must also bear fruit in Korea. From the standpoint of climate, the action and multiplication of all living things begin in spring, flourish in summer, bear fruit in autumn, and, after the harvest, are stored away during the winter. The cycle of spring, summer, autumn and winter is not repeated solely by the year. Examining the unit of a day, we find that morning corresponds to spring, noontime to summer, evening to autumn, and night to the winter. Again, the childhood, youth, manhood, and old age of a man's life also follows this pattern; and all human history, too, unfolds like this. This is because God created the world by the principle of climatic change.

God created Adam and Eve in the spring-season. Accordingly, the civilization of mankind was supposed to start as the temperate-zone civilization of Eden, be shifted to the tropic-zone civilization as of the summer season, and, after shifting itself to the cool-zone civilization of the autumn season, it was finally to return to the frigid-zone civilization of the winter season. But, due to the fall, man fell to the status of a savage. Without being able to produce the temperate-zone civilization, he came to live a primitive life in the tropic-zone. Thus, he produced the tropic-zone civilization on the ancient continent of Egypt. This civilization, shifting from the Continent to the

Peninsular (Greece, Rome, and Iberia) and the Island (England), produced the cool-zone civilization. Transferred back to the Continent (Russia), it came to produce the frigid-zone civilization. Now is the time when the temperate-zone civilization of the New Eden should be produced in the Peninsular-culture. This must necessarily be realized in Korea, where all aspects of civilization must bear fruit.

SECTION IV
Jesus' Day and Today from the Standpoint of Time-Identity

The period of the First Advent and that of the Second Advent are the periods of providential time-identity. Therefore, all the situations developing centering on the Christianity of today are similar to those which developed centering on the Judaism of Jesus' day.

To take examples: first, there is the point that today's Christianity, like Judaism, is attached to the authority and rites of the church, while the inner contents are corrupt. The leading class of people, the chief priests and rabbis of Jesus' day, enslaved by the conventional principles of the Mosaic law, were all corrupt in their spiritual lives. Therefore, the more conscientious the people were in their faith, the more they desired to relieve their spiritual thirst by following Jesus, who was at that time branded as a heretic. In like manner, the leading class of today's Christianity, including the priests and ministers, is captive to the traditional church rites and authority and is becoming spiritually darker every day. Therefore, it is the actual situation today that devout Christians are wandering in the spiritual mountains and plains in search of new leaders and true ways to experience the inner light of faith, apart from external circumstances.

Next, as previously discussed in detail, Christians of today will be the first to persecute the Messiah at the time of the Second Advent, as did the followers of Judaism at the First Advent. Jesus, who came to fulfill the Old Testament words according to the prophets, and on that foundation to establish a new age, did not merely repeat the Old Testament words, but had to necessarily give new words for the new age. The chief priests and rabbis, who criticized Jesus' words and conduct, according to the limits of what was allowed by the Old Testament words, ended by delivering Jesus to the cross because of their mistaken standard of judgment.

Likewise, the purpose of Christ's Second Coming is to establish the new heaven and new earth (Rev. 21:1-4), on the foundation of the spiritual salvation belonging to the New Testament Age, laid by the Christians. Therefore, at the time of the Second Advent, the Lord will surely not simply repeat the New Testament words, given 2000 years ago, but will give the new words necessary to establish the new heaven and earth. However, the Christians of today, who are captives to scriptural words, will surely criticize the words and conduct of the Lord of the Second Advent, according to the limits of what the New Testament words literally state. So, it is only too clear that they can be expected to persecute him and brand him a heretic. This is the very reason Jesus said that, at the Second Coming, the Lord would first suffer many things (Luke 17:25).

On the other hand, the same manner of things will happen, just as at the time of Jesus, in our reception of the revelations concerning the Second Advent, or the words the Lord will give us at the Second Advent. At the time of Jesus' coming, God did not give the message of the Messiah's arrival to the chief priests and rabbis, but to the gentile astrologers and innocent shepherds. This is like the case of the father who, due to the ignorance of his own child, has to confide in his step-child.

God may not reveal the message of the Second Advent to the Christians of today, who are blindly keeping the conventional attitude of faith, but rather to the laymen, to the heathens who are thought of as gentiles, or to men without any religious faith, but who are very conscientious. Those who accepted the Gospel of Jesus were not the leading class of Judaism, who called themselves God's elect, but people of lower classes, and gentiles. Similarly, at the Second Advent, the laymen or the non-Christians may be the first to accept the Lord's words, rather than the leading class of Christianity, who consider themselves the "chosen people." That is why Jesus in lamentation said that those who would enjoy the marriage feast which he would prepare may not be those invited, but those called in at random from the street (Matt. 22:8-10).

Next, at the time of the Second Advent, as at the time of Jesus, there will be many believers who will be going to Hell in place of Heaven, for which they headed at the start. The chief priests and rabbis, who had the mission of leading the people of God's elect, should have been the first to know of the Messiah's arrival and should have taken the initiative in leading the chosen people before him. In order to make them fulfill this mission, Jesus visited the temple first and taught them the Gospel. Due to their disregard for his teaching, he was forced to wander about the seashore of Galilee, making the fishermen his disciples and dealing mainly with the people of a lower standard, such as sinners, tax-collectors, and harlots. Finally, the chief priests and rabbis delivered Jesus to the crucifixion. Then, they continued, believing that they had done a righteous thing by punishing the traitor of God, to devote their loyalty to the sacred office, to recite scriptural passages, to contribute tithes and to offer sacrifices for the rest of their lives. They never imagined themselves headed for the place they went after their physical death, which was, most unexpectedly, Hell. Unfortunately, they deviated into Hell through the path which they believed would lead them to the Kingdom of Heaven.

When we truly understand the fact that these are the phenomena that could happen in the very same manner in the Last Days, each and every one of us should contemplate the matter most seriously. Innumerable Christians of today are dashing on the way which they think will lead them to the Kingdom of Heaven. Nevertheless, this very road is apt to lead them into Hell. Therefore, Jesus once said that the Lord would be compelled in the Last Days to reproach many saints who had faith strong enough to cast out demons and do almighty works in his name, by saying, "I never knew you, depart from me, you evildoers." (Matt. 7:23) To reflect on the matter with a deep understanding, no one else is placed in a more dangerous position then the saints living in such a transitional period of history as today. If they, like the Jewish leaders of Jesus' day, should take the wrong direction in their faith, everything will end in naught, no matter how devout their life in faith may have been. That is why Daniel said, ". . . those who are wise shall understand." (Dan. 12:10)

SECTION V
The Cause of the Confusion of Language and the Necessity for its Unification

If man had perfected himself without the fall and had realized the world of one great family resembling a human body with God as the head and all men as the members, there would have been no reason for so many languages to have come about on the earth. Those who speak different languages cannot communicate with each other. The confusion of human language came about because men's vertical relationship with

God was cut off due to the fall. Since this caused the severance of their horizontal relationship with one another, all men have long been separated and have formed many nations according to different geographical circumstances. On the other hand, there is a scriptural record concerning the confusion of language which suddenly came about among Noah's descendants, who had all been speaking the same language in the beginning. The following are the particulars of the story.

The Canaanites, descendants of Noah's second son Ham, who had sinned before God, once began to build a high tower of Babel, exalting the will of Satan. Meanwhile, the descendants of Shem and Japheth, who had been on the side of God, came to cooperate with the construction. Therefore, God confused their language in order to prevent them from helping the work of Satan, by making it impossible for them to communicate with one another (Gen. 11:7).

Nothing could be more miserable than the fact that we, as the same offspring from the same parents, having the common feelings of joy and anger, cannot share them with one another because of the difference in the languages which express them. Therefore, in order that the ideal world of one great family, under the Lord of the Second Advent as the True Parent, might be realized, all the languages must necessarily be unified. Since the language was confused due to the tower of Babel exalting the will of Satan, the languages of all nations must now be unified, according to the principle of restoration by indemnity, centering on the Heavenly tower, and exalt the will of God. In this way, the whole of mankind will become one people speaking one language, thus establishing one world of one culture.

NOTES

NOTES